Ecology
of African Pastoralist Societies

D1565832

Ecology
of African Pastoralist Societies

Katherine Homewood

Professor of Anthropology
University College, London

with a chapter by Dr Sara Randall
Anthropology, University College, London

JAMES CURREY
OXFORD

OHIO UNIVERSITY PRESS
ATHENS

UNISA PRESS
PRETORIA

James Currey Ltd
73 Botley Road
Oxford
OX2 0BS
www.jamescurrey.co.uk

Ohio University Press
19 Circle Drive
The Ridges
Athens OH 45701-2979
www.ohio.edu/oupress

Unisa Press
PO Box 392
Unisa
Muckleneuk 0003
www.unisa.ac.za/press

British Library Cataloguing in Publication Data
Homewood, Katherine
    Ecology of African pastoralist societies
    1. Pastoralist systems - Africa 2. Range ecology – Africa
    3. Livestock - Ecology - Africa 4. Herders - Africa -
    Social conditions 5. Human ecology – Africa
    I. Title
    636.2'0845'096

ISBN 978-0-85255-990-1 (James Currey paper)
ISBN 978-0-85255-991-8 (James Currey cloth)
ISBN 978-1-86888-531-2 (Unisa paper)

Library of Congress Cataloging-in-Publication Data
available on request

ISBN-10: 0-8214-1840-8 (Ohio University Press cloth)
ISBN-13: 978-0-8214-1840-6 (Ohio University Press cloth)
ISBN-10: 0-8214-1841-6 (Ohio University Press paper)
ISBN-13: 978-0-8214-1841-3 (Ohio University Press paper)

Typeset in 10.6/11.6 pt Bembo by Long House Publishing Services
Printed and bound in Malaysia

Contents

List of Photographs, Figures, Tables & Boxes   x
Acknowledgement   xii
Photographs & Map of African Pastoralist Societies   between pp. 4 and 5

1

Introduction to the Ecology of African Pastoralists   1
    Background   1
    Theories of African pastoralist ecology   3
    Book structure & sequence   7

2

Origins & Spread of African Pastoralism   10
    Origins   10
        Tracing pastoralism in prehistory   10
        Emergence of pastoralism in African prehistory   12
        Spread of pastoralism through Africa   16
    Emergence of present-day African pastoralist societies   20
        Fulani in West Africa   20
        Tuareg   25
        Emergence of pastoralism in North East Africa: Arab and Beja   29
        Horn of Africa: the Somalis   31
        Nilotic pastoralists of the Sudd   34
        Emergence of pastoralism in East Africa: Maasai and Turkana   36
        People of the Great Lakes: Tuutsi and Hutu   40
        Emergence of pastoralism in Southern Africa   43
            Tswana   44
            Pastoralist history in South Africa: Xhosa and Zulu   46
        South West Africa: Damara, Herero and San   47

3

Pastoralist Environments, Constraints & Strategies   50
    Biophysical environments   50
        Arid and semi-arid climates   52
            Rainfall and seasonality   52
            Aridity, unpredictability and productive potential   53
            Drought   56
        Soils   58
        Fire   59

Organizing the diversity of vegetation types   59
Topography, geology and drainage lines   61
Disease constraints   61
Ecological models & pastoralist ecosystem dynamics   63
Equilibrium theory and the disequilibrium debate   65
Summary on equilibrium/disequilibrium   69
Social & political environments   72
Tenure and access   72
Conflict, raiding, war and displacement   74
Political use of environmental narratives   79
Pastoralism and conservation   80
Pastoral land use & production strategies   82
Land use and livestock management: mobility and
transhumance   82
Production strategies   86
'Pure' pastoralism and milk-based pastoralism   86
Exchange pastoralism   87
Agropastoralism   87
Pastoralism and trade   90
Subsistence versus commercial pastoralism   91
Hired herders and absentee stockowners   92
Pastoralism as a component of land use and economy   93

4

Contemporary Pastoralist Systems   94
Saharo-Sahelian pastoralism   94
Central Sahelian systems: Tuareg & Fulani   99
Wet savannas: Fulani of the Adamawa plateau & Central
African forest-savanna mosaic   103
Pastoralists in wetlands I: Fulani in the Inland Delta of the
Niger   107
Pastoralists of North East Africa & the Horn: 111
The Atmaan Beja   112
Somali pastoralism   114
Pastoralists in wetlands II: peoples of the Sudd   120
East African pastoralists   124
Maasai   124
Turkana   126
Oromo-speaking peoples of Southern Ethiopia:
Borana and Arssi   128
Southern Africa   130

5

Pastoral Livelihoods & Economy   132
  Analysis of pastoralist economies   133
    Modelling pastoral economic decisions   134
      Empirical approaches: statistical modelling   135
      *Theory-driven modelling: Cost/benefit, optimality and stochastic
        dynamic models*   136
      Systems and stimulations   137
  Labour   138
    Labour needs, strategies and returns   138
    Stratified societies and socio-economic class   140
    Gender   141
    Age   143
    Factors affecting division of labour: summary   144
  Land   145
    Ecological influences   145
    Historical changes in land tenure and access   148
  Livestock   153
    Livestock as capital and commodity   153
    Livestock ownership: concepts and mechanisms   154
  Sustainable livelihoods framework   156

6

Biology of the Herds   158
  Herd composition   158
    Species   159
    Breeds   160
    Age/sex composition   161
  Biology of livestock production   162
    Pastoral products   162
    Variation in herd performance   162
    Management of herd reproduction   164
    Impacts of drought and disease on herd biology and performance 165
  Livestock diseases   167
    Trypanosomiasis   167
    East Coast fever   169
    Rinderpest   171
    Contagious Bovine Pleuro-Pneumonia   171
    *Epidemiological implications of conflicting
      knowledge systems*   172
    Policy implications   174

7

Pastoral Food Systems, Diets & Nutrition   177
    Pastoral diets   179
      Methods and methodological problems   179
      Pastoralist diets   180
      Protein and energy in pastoral diets: calorific and monetary
        trade-offs   182
        Seasonal variation   184
          Unimodal vs bimodal rainfall climates   184
          Complementary food sources and energy adequacy   184
          Seasonal stresses: workload, disease challenge and
            energy balance   185
    Growth patterns & anthropometric status   185
      Growth trajectories: height for age, weight for height   185
      Growth outcomes: pastoralists vs cultivators   186
      Intra-household, socioeconomic and caste variation   188
    Livestock per person ratios in evaluating food security   189
    Food crises & famine   192
    Nutrition & health in pastoralist groups   193
      Nutrition and infection   193
      Lactose intolerance   194
      High animal-fat diets and CHD   195
    Change in pastoralist food systems   195
      Shifting trade-offs in pastoralist food production,
        consumption, sale and exchange   195
      Pastoral food systems and development   197

8

African Pastoralist Demography   199
    SARA RANDALL
    Data quality   200
    A pastoralist demographic regime?   202
      Livestock demography   202
      Labour requirements   202
      Environmental stress   203
      Isolation and marginalisation   203
    Fertility   205
      Seasonal stress   206
      Sexually transmitted diseases and infertility   207
      Sexual networking and infertility   207
      HIV and AIDS   210
      Marriage   211
    Mortality   215
      Adult mortality   218

Migration & movement   220
   Transhumance   221
   Sedentarisation   222
   Migration   223
Is there a pastoralist demography?   225

9

Diversification, Development & Change in Pastoralist Systems   227
Pastoralist production, privatisation & commercialisation   228
   Spontaneous commercialisation in pastoralist systems 229
      Milk selling and dairying   229
      Commercialisation of animal sales   231
   Case studies of commercialisation   232
      North Africa: Libya   232
      West Africa: Fulani in Nigeria and Niger 232
      The Horn: Somalia   234
      East Africa: Maasai and Samburu in Kenya 235
      Southern Africa: Botswana   236
      Conclusions on commercialisation of pastoral livestock production 237
Diversification   238
   Trajectories and dimensions of diversification   238
Corollaries of diversification & development   244
   Intensification and sedentarisation   244
Gender issues   245
      Women's activities and workloads   245
      Access to and control over land, livestock and natural resources 247
      Milk management   248
   Education, development and diversification   248
Conclusion: The futures of African pastoralism   250

Bibliography   253
Index   287

List of Photographs, Figures, Tables & Boxes

Map African pastoralist societies (see colour section between pp. 4 and 5)

Photographs in colour section

1   Hodda: Kel Interberemt Tuareg, Mali, 1982
2   Hodda walking through dry season camp, River Niger, Mali, 1982
3   Newly married Tuareg woman in her wedding tent, Mali, 1982
4   Bella and Tuareg women dressed up for Eid, Mali, 1982
5   Fulbe (Fulani or Peul) Gaobe on transhumance in Oudalan,
    northern Burkina Faso, dry season, 1998/1999
6   Fulani Gaobe women making mat, Burkina Faso, 1996
7   Pokot pastoro-foragers, Lake Baringo, Kenya 1983. Pokot people are,
    like the Maasai, linguistically part of the eastern Nilotic group.
    They speak a Kalenjin language, but outwardly show many cultural
    similarities to the Karamojong
8   Il Chamus Maasai in *ambatch* reed boat, bringing a bull to the main
    shore of Lake Baringo having led it swimming from an island where
    the herd has been grazing, Lake Baringo, Kenya, 1983
9   Oromo elder, Tana River, Kenya, 1974
10 Maasai secondary school student herding during school holidays, Longido,
    Tanzania, 2007
11 Nuer child with goats and cattle in late dry season, Ayod, Sudan, 1976
12 Damara goat kraal, Namibia, 1998

Figures

2.1	African pastoralist environments: biophysical features	17
2.2	Sahara-Sahelian pastoralism around the Inland Delta of the Niger	21
2.3	Historical trade routes managed by the Tuareg	26
3.1	Rainfall variability as a function of aridity	53
3.2	Variation in plant production with rainfall	55
3,3	Rainfall deviation from the long-term mean in Africa, 1900–2000	57
3.4	Logistical curve of population growth showing operation of density-dependent factors	65
3.5	Hypothetical (and contested) sequence of overstocking, overgrazing and environmental degradation, as postulated by equilibrium thinking	67
8.1	Reported levels of proportions of children surviving in different pastoralist populations	219
8.2	Indirect estimates of Tamasheq childhood mortality, 1965–2000	219

Tables

2.1	Arab and Arabicised agro/pastoralists of NE Africa	30
3.1	Comparative scheme of eco-climatic classifications	54
3.2	Determinants of arid and semi-arid savanna vegetation types	60

3.3	Ecological, production and tenure correlates of equilibrium and disequilibrium model	71
3.4	Scales of conflict affecting pastoralist groups	77
3.5	Association between pastoralism and mobility	89
6.1	Indicative production characteristics of livestock species	159
6.2	Age/sex structure of agropastoral and pastoral cattle herds	162
6.3	Major infectious diseases of sub-Saharan livestock	166
6.4	Trypanosomiasis control methods and their applicability	169
7.1	Percent dietary calories derived from different diet items	181
7.2	Nutritional and calorific values of pastoral foods	183
7.3	Percentage of each age/sex class in different weight-for-height categories	187
7.4	Dietary composition and energy intake for wealthy and poor Maasai	189
7.5	Alternative systems for summing livestock holdings across species	190
7.6	Systems for summing households as consumer or reference adult units	190
7.7	Livestock per person ratios for East African pastoralists	191
8.1	Fertility estimates for pastoralist populations	204
8.2	Percentages of women reporting no live births (primary sterility)	209
8.3	Measures of polygamy and attitudes to divorce	213
8.4	Age at first marriage	214
8.5	Probability of dying before age 5	217
8.6	Estimates of adult mortality: e_{20}	220
8.7	Estimates of maternal mortality using sisterhood	221
8.8	Animal ownership and animal husbandry after sedentarisation (% of households, 2001)	222
9.1	Outline of diversification of pastoral livelihoods	239

Boxes

7.1	Economic values of milk for consumption, exchange or investment in the herd	196
9.1	Poverty and pastoralist diversification: examples from Northern Kenya	243

Acknowledgement

With thanks to the members of the UCL Human Ecology Research Group for the many discussions which have over the years shaped the material and ideas in this book.

1

Introduction
to the Ecology of African Pastoralists

Background

The defining characteristic of pastoralist peoples is their association with domestic grazing animals. Popular conceptions of pastoralism have often focused on 'pure' pastoralists living a nomadic or transhumant existence and subsisting entirely on the produce of their herds. It has become increasingly clear that these are the exception rather than the rule. Even where such 'pure' pastoralist people can be found, they often intergrade seamlessly with other economic occupations, either as individuals or as groups. Some definitions of pastoralism focus on the economic occupation, others on the cultural importance of livestock, but, however defined, pastoralist groups, households and individuals are continuously shifting into and out of livestock-based livelihoods according to the vagaries of climate, disease, political and economic opportunity and constraint. They include people who rely on livestock for their subsistence, stockowners, hired herders and livestock traders; agropastoralists for whom livestock are a vital component of livelihoods, resource use, production system and long-term investment strategy; and people who have few if any animals, but for whom livestock represent a cultural identity and a medium of social exchange, of defining and maintaining relations, a currency and language. This underlies a further definition of a pastoralist as one for whom pastoralism is an ideal, even if not a reality (Hodgson, 2001). While defining pastoralism and pastoralists, it is important to bear in mind the wide range of livestock-related activities these embrace, and the strong continuities they maintain with other rural and urban livelihoods, and with wider trajectories of development and change throughout rural Africa. This discussion of the complexities of defining pastoral societies leaves concepts and categories deliberately somewhat fluid. The fluidity makes it possible to stress the strong continuities with other societies and production systems, while setting clear boundaries for the scope of

1

the book. It would constrain rather than add to understanding or to the analysis of these societies to tighten the definition any further.

Livestock ownership and holdings wax and wane with local and regional environmental conditions, climate, forage availability, disease, political security and alternative economic opportunities, making it impossible to give an estimate of the numbers of African pastoralists that is both precise and meaningful. In the early 1980s, Sandford (1983) put the numbers of people primarily dependent on livestock for their subsistence at around 30 million. Similar estimates are used today (Fratkin, 2001). According to where the lines are drawn, including agropastoralists with considerable but less central dependence on livestock would enormously increase this number. However defined, Africa has many millions of people who rely on livestock, embracing an enormous variety of different ethnic, ecological and economic groups.

African pastoralist groups have generally been mobile peoples, commonly exploiting lands that are marginal for agriculture, often operating outside formal administrative networks and maintaining few records. All the same, they make up a major sector of Africa's food production systems: milk and meat from domestic livestock have been estimated to account for over 25% of tropical Africa's food production, measured in grain equivalents, and excluding South Africa (Jahnke, 1982). Although an increasing proportion of smallholders manage improved breeds in higher-potential areas, the overwhelming majority of livestock production still comes from pastoralist and agropastoral herds, indigenous breeds managed under extensive conditions on unimproved rangeland. Pastoralist livelihoods and production mesh closely with local, regional and international economies: they have a major input and influence on the ecology both of farming systems and of areas often incorrectly seen as unmanaged and unproductive wilderness.

Stereotyped views of the ecological impacts and social structures are still common, but over the last few decades in-depth studies increasingly challenge these conventional wisdoms, and at the same time reveal strong continuities underlying the great diversity of pastoral systems. Pastoralist land use and livestock management, pastoralist economies and subsistence, and the human biology of pastoralist groups – nutrition, disease and demographic characteristics – are all beginning to be better understood as the patchwork of individual studies has grown. At the same time, understanding is growing of the political, social and economic issues affecting pastoralists, particularly concerning tenure, access to or exclusion from the resources necessary for livelihoods, from economic wealth and political power, and the conflicts that may result. Pastoralists operate within a wide range of ecological conditions, but under rather similar constraints, leading to common experiences and common lessons to be learnt throughout African rangelands. In particular, many pastoralist groups are centred on arid and semi-arid lands over which they move to find forage and water for their herds and to avoid disease challenge brought by seasonal vector population increases. Mobility has implications for ecology, politics and administration. The usually peripheral, often cross-border position of pastoralist groups with respect to modern African states means involvement in unofficial cross-border livestock smuggling, raiding and outright warfare.

Despite recurring themes, individual studies tend to be taken in their regional contexts, and there has been rather little cross-fertilisation between East, West, North (mostly Francophone) and South African studies.

Given the extreme environmental, epidemiological, demographic, economic and socio-political problems faced by the majority of pastoralist groups, there is a need for an integrating review for academics, professionals and others. The present book aims to bring together and integrate in a single volume material on the ecology of pastoralist groups from East Africa and the Horn, Southern Africa, the Sahel and West Africa. The book portrays the diversity of pastoralist systems and the ways in which they interact with other forms of land use, while analysing common characteristics and issues across the broad range of pastoralist societies, and their linkages, interactions and continuities with less livestock-centred systems.

Theories of African pastoralist ecology

While this book is primarily concerned with reviewing and integrating the wealth of empirical, ecological studies of pastoralist systems which have appeared over the last few decades, and deliberately emphasises these empirical foundations, there is also a unifying body of theory which both supports and emerges from this compilation of grassroots research. The book's synthesis of the ecology of pastoralist societies draws on three main areas of theoretical debate. Taken together, these form a framework within which the great diversity of pastoralist ecologies, and their trajectories of change, can be understood. These three theoretical areas comprise, firstly, the ecological dynamics of tropical arid and semi-arid ecosystems, and the associated rationales and patterns of pastoralist use of these rangelands, particularly mobility in response to environmental fluctuations. This area in turn both draws on and influences theories relating the social, political and economic dimensions of resource tenure and management and the way systems of access and control interact with social and spatial structures in the ecology of pastoralist groups. This second area of theory focuses on the nature and implications, both positive and negative, of the flexibility and fuzzy boundaries (social and spatial) which pastoralists have customarily used to structure entitlements and manage access to key resources. Finally, current changes in land tenure make it necessary to draw on, develop and re-shape theories of development, livelihoods, and diversification in pastoralist systems, coming back full circle to the trajectories and implications of change for the ecology of pastoral systems in general and land use in particular. The framework built on these three areas of ecosystem dynamics, land tenure and diversification theory helps to organise, understand and predict continuities across pastoral societies in the broadest sense. This encompasses the broad context of individuals, households and groups moving between livelihoods which, on the one hand, are centrally dependent on livestock production, and, on the other, those which are at first sight remote from pastoral landscapes, but which form part of the wider network of opportunities and strategies pursued by pastoral people.

In addition to the central theoretical framework built on these three areas, the book also draws on ideas from the social anthropology of pastoralist groups, touching on kinship, hierarchies of power, identity, ethnicity, cultural ideals and discourse, insofar as these shape the ecology (particularly the political ecology) of pastoralist societies. It also draws on evolutionary ecology and anthropology to the extent that the understanding of social and economic behaviour of pastoralist societies, once dominated by structural-functionalist approaches, is now seen overwhelmingly in terms of flexible and adaptive individual decision-making. Although such decisions may be primarily governed by economic or reproductive (and at some level evolutionary) rationalities, these are strongly contingent on sociocultural circumstances which produce a wealth of complex trade-offs and situation-specific strategies in response to shifting opportunities and constraints. Ecological, economic and evolutionary modelling is only beginning to make a useful contribution to organising that diversity. While based on ethnographies, borrowing from the rich theoretical literature of social anthropology, and structuring economic understanding at least in part on models which broadly relate to evolutionary ecology, this book focuses on the applied ecology of resource use, the associated environmental impacts and the direct livelihood implications of land use and land-use change.

Theories of ecosystem dynamics have had such a major impact on policies affecting pastoralist land-use management that it is important to introduce them here, though a full exposition is given later (Chapter 3). The present section sets out a brief overview of the debate over disequilibrium dynamics and its significance for pastoralist management. Briefly, ecological models developed in relatively stable and predictable western temperate ecosystems centre on density-dependent processes of population regulation, which operate to return the system to a predictable equilibrium point, characterised by a climax vegetation state (and associated with specific sizes of different plant and animal populations). Major fluctuations, such as a disproportionate though temporary increase of any one of those populations (for example through an artificially high concentration of livestock), are seen as potentially overshooting carrying capacity and consequently damaging resources to the point of causing permanent irreversible degradation of productive capacity and/or biodiversity (Homewood, 2004). This deeply held model has both consciously and unconsciously influenced Western observers' understanding of tropical arid and semi-arid landscapes, leading to potential misinterpretation of rapidly and markedly fluctuating vegetation states, ground cover, and associated aggregation or dispersal of grazing and browsing animals including livestock. On the basis of equilibrium models, the changes witnessed in these systems have commonly been taken as evidence of environmental degradation. However, working from long-term empirical evidence, development workers and rangeland ecologists increasingly suggest that tropical arid and semi-arid lands may not be governed by density-dependent processes to the same extent as more predictable, temperate grazing lands, and may not be well characterised by a single-climax successional state. Instead, tropical arid and semi-arid lands may often be driven by the interplay of strongly fluctuating and randomly interacting biophysical factors of rainfall, drought, fire, and epidemic disease,

1 Hodda: Kel
Interberemt Tuareg,
Mali, 1982
(© *Sara Randall*)

2 Hodda walking
through dry season
camp, River Niger,
Mali, 1982
(© *Sara Randall*)

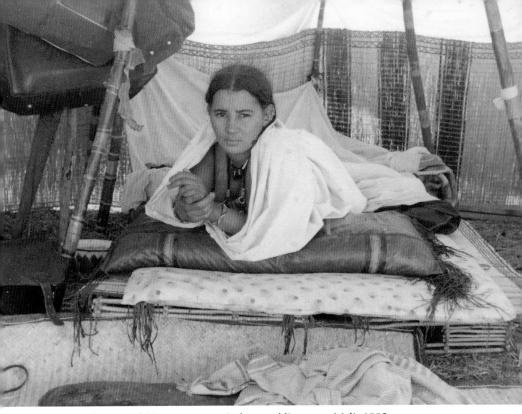

3 Newly married Tuareg woman in her wedding tent, Mali, 1982
(© *Sara Randall*)

4 Bella and Tuareg women dressed up for Eid, Mali, 1982 (© *Sara Randall*)

5 Fulbe (Fulani or Peul) Gaobe on transhumance in Oudalan, northern Burkina Faso, dry season, 1998/1999. While the men move the cattle, the women (who own the tents) take care of moving the household belongings. These women were obviously happy to be going on transhumance with their menfolk, and were looking forward to having plenty of milk (© *Solveig Buhl*)

6 Fulani Gaobe women making mat, Burkina Faso, 1996 (© *Sara Randall*)

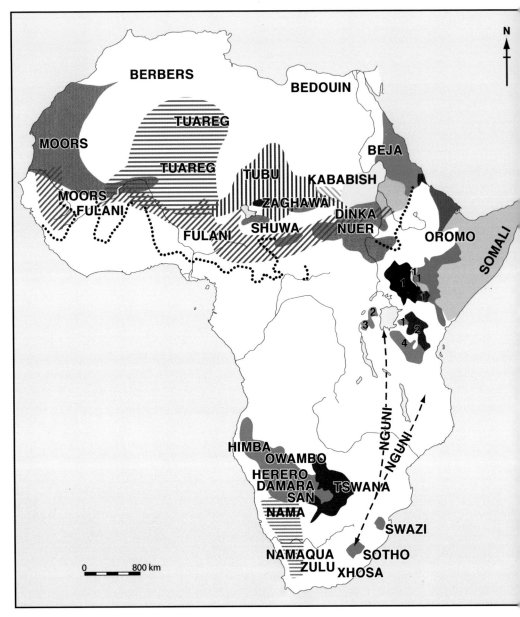

N

BERBERS

BEDOUIN

MOORS

TUAREG

TUAREG

BEJA

MOORS
FULANI

TUBU

KABABISH

ZAGHAWA

FULANI

SHUWA

DINKA
NUER

OROMO

SOMALI

2
3

1 1
1
1
1

1
2
4

HIMBA
OWAMBO
HERERO
DAMARA
SAN

TSWANA

NGUNI
NGUNI

NAMA

SWAZI

NAMAQUA
ZULU

SOTHO
XHOSA

0   800 km

adapted from Jahnke (19
Boutrais (19

African pastoralist societies (see Chapter 2 for historical detail of linguistic affiliations)

AFROASIATIC GROUP

Semitic

Moors

Baggara

Jamaala

Sudanese 'Arabs'

Other Semitic

NILO-SAHARAN GROUP

Saharan

Nubian

Midob

Beir

Didinga

West Nilotic

East Nilotic

Karimojong Cluster   1 - Turkana

Maasai Cluster   1 - Samburu
2 - Maasai

South Nilotic

Berber

Tuareg (Tamacheq)

North Cushitic

Beja

East Cushitic

'Afar

Oromo   1 - Gabra

Somali

Other East   1 - Dassenetch
Cushitic

CONGO-KORDOFANIAN GROUP

West Atlantic

•••••• Southern limit of Fulani

Fulani

Benue - Congo (Bantu)

1 - Kuria   3 - Tusi
2 - Hima   4 - Sukuma

Tswana

KHOESĀN GROUP

Namaqua
Nama   } Khoekhoegowab
Damara
Sān

7 Pokot pastoro-foragers, Lake Baringo, Kenya, 1983. Pokot people are, like the Maasai, linguistically part of the eastern Nilotic group. They speak a Kalenjin language, but outwardly show many cultural similarities to the Karamojong
(© *Katherine Homewood*)

8 Il Chamus Maasai in *ambatch* reed boat, bringing a bull to the main shore of Lake Baringo having led it swimming from an island where the herd has been grazing, Lake Baringo, Kenya, 1983 (© *Katherine Homewood*)

9 Oromo elder, Tana River,
Kenya, 1974
(© *Katherine Homewood*)

10 Maasai secondary school
student herding during school
holidays, Longido, Tanzania,
2007
(© *Sara Randall*)

11 Nuer child with goats and cattle in late dry season, Ayod, Sudan, 1976
(© *Douglas H. Johnson*)

12 Damara goat kraal, Namibia, 1998
(© *Sian Sullivan*)

with the whole system shifting chaotically between multiple alternative stable states. Change is a salient characteristic of these systems, and should not immediately be equated with degradation. Conservative management, commonly advocated by outside observers in an attempt to stabilise chaotically fluctuating environments and production systems, needs to be reassessed in terms of the costs of lost production and its potentially adverse impacts on the biodiversity of otherwise dynamic systems (ibid.).

The practical corollary of these large and unpredictable variations in tropical arid and semi-arid environments, is that most sub-Saharan pastoralist groups associated with such environments have evolved resource-use systems based at least in part on mobility and common property resource management (Niamir-Fuller, 1999a). In order to ensure access to key resources of water, pasture and minerals, to avoid environments seasonally associated with disease vectors, to evade specific raiding and security problems, and to access markets, different pastoralist groups have perennially sought access to and control of extended rangelands encompassing all the major resources they need, whatever the vagaries of their biophysical and politico-economic environments. Although there are instances of individualised private tenure, access has generally been contingent on membership of, or client relations with, the wider social group. That group commonly monitors, polices and enforces rules of access, often through a warrior age-set or caste responsible to a council of elders or to a high-ranking leader from a noble social stratum. Territorial defence has often focused on key point-centred resources (water points, swamp or highland drought-refuge pasture). Social and spatial boundaries defining access to these resources have been both flexible and fuzzy, with some level of ranked access to the social group of users always possible through managing social relations, and spatial boundaries around point-centred key resources expanding and contracting according to circumstances, rather than defence of rigid perimeter boundaries (Turner, 1999a).

The customarily communal nature of pastoral rangelands has given rise to several areas of influential theoretical debate. Hardin's 1968 'Tragedy of the Commons' postulated that, with livestock owned individually and rangeland held in common, the incentive for individual profit inevitably drives overstocking and environmental degradation at the expense of the group. Fifty years of national and international policy and development interventions have been based on this thinking, although it rapidly became apparent that Hardin's formulation confused the very real implications of open access and scramble competition with the actual situation in most sub-Saharan African pastoral systems involving highly effective (albeit communally managed) regulation of common property resources. Jointly with the equilibrium thinking outlined earlier, the Tragedy of the Commons has underpinned powerful national and international policy pressure to privatise rangelands (Toulmin and Quan, 2000), with drastic implications for individual, household and group access to the basic means of pastoral production and associated livelihoods. This drive for privatisation has interacted with twentieth-century colonial and post-independence trajectories of boundary formation, which have themselves left most pastoral populations marginalised on the geographical and political periphery of

African nation states, fragmented between adjacent and often hostile nations, under intense pressure to sedentarise, and often drawn into violent and destructive geopolitical confrontations (Galaty and Bonte, 1991).

Even where pastoral groups have been relatively unaffected by such conflicts, they have tended to be poorly served by emerging infrastructures of transport and communications, health and education, poorly represented in national political fora, and ill-placed to compete successfully for private title to their customary rangelands, whether as individuals or as cooperatively functioning groups. A whole body of theory has grown up around the way fluctuating biophysical, socio-political and economic environments have shaped the evolution of flexible systems of land and resource tenure in Africa (Berry, 1993). The need to maintain that flexibility commands proportionally great investment of people's time and resources (Guyer, 1997). Though flexibility has been a source of resilience in the face of environmental problems, it has also become a major weakness (Peters, 2004). Elites and outside entrepreneurs have been well placed to exploit the opportunities and ambiguities to take control of land, water and other natural resources key to the pastoral system, and to exclude pastoralist groups less able to manoeuvre through the complex and multi-layered legalities and national-level as well as local political deals. This has left pastoralists immensely vulnerable to land loss, eviction and exclusion from their customary ranges in favour of private and corporate ownership of land, dominated by elites and outsiders including expatriate entrepreneurs, and state gazettement of protected areas. Detailed analyses have been made for specific regional and national cases (e.g. Galaty, 1999; Shivji, 1998; Igoe and Brockington, 1999). The impacts on mobility and access to key resources are not only drastic, but are seen by many as likely to put an end to pastoralism and pastoral societies altogether. More immediately, there are devastating implications for individual entitlements and sustainable livelihoods, and for spiralling trajectories of poverty, particularly among the most marginalised ethnic groups (such as the Kalahari San – Hitchcock, 1996) and sections of society (women – Talle, 1988).

Overall, the trajectories of development and change in pastoralist land use and livelihoods can be understood in terms of theories dealing with the classic dimensions of local knowledge and experimentation producing robust indigenous solutions to managing persistent problems; of response to the opportunities provided by sporadic, genuinely useful technical innovations; and of political economy which puts the wealthy and powerful in a position to benefit from these innovations, at the expense of the poorest (Ellis, 2000). Increasingly, however, these trajectories of development and change are constrained by the dwindling opportunities for pastoralist groups to pursue livestock-based activities. The classic categorisation of means of production (land, labour and capital, or livestock in the case of pastoralist groups) can be extended to consider the 'pentagon' of social, natural, human, financial and physical assets as the defining dimensions of any livelihood (Carney and Farrington, 1998). With privatisation of the range, exclusion from key resources of pasture, water and minerals, and loss of access to seasonally shifting disease-free areas, people's ability to manage livestock successfully is eroded. Pastoral livelihoods disintegrate further with the conflicts and violence that commonly erupt around contested access, whether over pastoral resources (as recently in Somalia, and currently in Darfur) or over internationally valued oil and other mineral deposits (as in southern Sudan – Johnson, 2003). As land and livestock become harder to access and manage, less of the sustenance of formerly pastoral individuals, households and groups comes from livestock-based activities. Diversification comes about in many cases as a forced response to the dwindling opportunities for pastoral livelihoods, and for the very large numbers of evicted, displaced and refugee former pastoralists (*Economist*, 2001) there is little likelihood of re-entering the pastoral production system.

The broader theories of diversification of rural livelihoods in sub-Saharan Africa (Bryceson, 1999; Bryceson and Jamal, 1997) apply to pastoralists (Homewood et al., forthcoming). Over time, people's economic activities and spatial locations change, as do their aspirations and cultural ideals. As well as those driven by necessity, relatively well-off pastoral households may also diversify away from livestock-based activities, as a mechanism for managing risk. They may develop other rural activities (farming; wildlife enterprises; trade and transport) and also establish rural-urban links, with town-based branches of the family exploiting complementary opportunities. Urban jobs may buffer the biophysical shocks impacting on rural production, and offer opportunities for access to education and health care, while the rural base continues to produce food and sometimes saleable surplus which acts as a buffer against economic downturns and job losses (as occurred with structural adjustment – Bryceson and Jamal, 1997). For the very well-off, diversification is also key, with some level of engagement with pastoral production (usually as absentee herdowners) remaining as part of a broad portfolio of investments. These individuals and households are in a position to network with national elites and take advantage of the opportunities that emerge with new technical, political and economic developments. Pastoral groups have always combined livestock-based activities with other means of generating income or sustenance, and individuals and families have always moved into and out of pastoral production. The current rate and scale of diversification of pastoral livelihoods, and the changing aspirations and cultural identities which accompany diversification (Heffernan et al., 2001) underline the complexity of defining and conceptualising pastoralist societies.

Book structure & sequence

Following this chapter, the book begins with a review of the origins and history of African pastoralist groups. It traces the origins (indigenous or otherwise) of the domesticated species on which pastoral production systems depend, and their spread through sub-Saharan Africa over the last several millennia. Chapter 2 goes on to outline the emergence of pastoralist groups in different sub-Saharan regions, sketching the historical, social, political and economic interactions that have shaped their present-day manifestations as Fulani, Tuareg, and Arabicised pastoralists of North East Africa; Cushitic peoples of the Horn, Nilotic pastoralists of the Sudd; East African Maasai, and Turkana; current and former cattle-keeping groups of south-eastern Africa (Tswana) and South Africa (Zulu, Xhosa); and Khoi-speaking pastoralists of south-west Africa.

Chapter 3 outlines the biophysical and sociopolitical environments within which pastoralists operate. In particular, the chapter introduces the central ecological theories of ecosystem dynamics, the challenges to those theories, and the resulting debates over management that have dominated pastoral systems over the last two decades. It looks not only at the biophysical but also at the socio-political environment, with its corresponding unpredictability and variation, including resource competition and conflict and their escalation into violence. It outlines analytical approaches to pastoralist land-use and livestock-management strategies, focusing on mobility and transhumance, and categorises the different types of pastoral production system. The central equation sees pastoral produce as commonly commanding favourable calorific and monetary terms of trade against cultivated produce, but as limited by dry-season and drought constraints on production, making it necessary to combine pastoral production with other activities, whether foraging, farming, fishing, or trade. Chapter 4 describes the ecology of the main contemporary pastoralist systems around Africa, drawing on past and recent ethnographies, developing an understanding of the range and diversity of pastoral ecologies as a basis for the cross-cutting themes developed in subsequent chapters.

In Chapter 5, the economics of pastoralist production and pastoral systems are explored. Starting with a consideration of the analytical possibilities offered by modelling individual decision-making (contrasted with classic structural/functional approaches), the chapter goes on to consider the limits to the applicability of ecological, economic and evolutionary models in highly mobile pastoral systems, where household composition may change rapidly and where household members continuously shift between multiple alternative activities and spatial locations. Land, labour and livestock are each examined in turn with respect to patterns of access and control, introducing theories of land tenure in pastoral systems, of their interrelation with ecosystem dynamics and land-use patterns, and of the current rapid shift from common property resources to private ownership. The biology of the herd is set out in Chapter 6 with a review of both empirical and modelling approaches to the analysis of herd management in terms of species, breed and age/sex composition. The chapter also includes an overview of the epidemiology of livestock diseases, and of the contrasting pastoralist and Western perceptions of disease and its management, issues central to a number of aspects of pastoralist ecology and economy.

Chapter 7 reviews pastoralist food systems, diet and nutrition, critically exploring ideas of a characteristic pastoral diet and seeking generalisable patterns of dietary intake in terms of protein and energy, and of the associated patterns of growth and anthropometric status. The chapter looks at the shifting use of pastoral produce as food, as investment in the herd or as commodities for trade, and at the social implications of these shifts, as well as at famine in pastoral systems. Chapter 8 draws on national census and other large datasets to examine the common assumption that there is a characteristic pastoral demography, with a particular emphasis on issues of data quality. Studies of pastoralist demography (fertility, marriage patterns, mortality, migration patterns, demographic patterns of disease and disease-related infertility) are analysed in relation to ecological, cultural, and economic differences between populations. Chapter 9 concentrates on the issues of diversification, development and change in pastoralist groups. Continent-wide impacts of changing patterns of land tenure and resource use and their implications for pastoralist ecology are examined. Trajectories of economic development, particularly commercialisation and its implications for the security of subsistence livelihoods, are reviewed in the context of the extreme environmental variability of African pastoralist systems and the changing scope for mobility in response. The actual experience of development interventions and of their supposed beneficiaries is examined, and a brief conclusion draws together the possible futures of pastoralism and pastoralist societies in Africa.

2

Origins & Spread
of African Pastoralism

Before the invention during the last 10-15,000 years of food-producing economies based on domesticated plants and animals, people around the globe lived by collecting food as gatherers, hunters and fishers. Conventional wisdom held that domesticated livestock (alongside cereals, pottery, weaving and metalworking) were Middle Eastern innovations which spread through Africa, bringing about a gradual transformation of formerly stone-tool-using gatherer-hunter economies (see, for example, Bokonyi, 1976). However, the early independent, indigenous origins of distinctively African livestock and crops, pottery, weaving and metalworking techniques have now been firmly established (Ehret, 1998, 2002; Mabogunje and Richards, 1985; Hall, 1990), alongside their progressive incorporation of imported innovations. This chapter looks first at the types of evidence available to reconstruct the origins of the different African domesticate and pastoral systems. It then outlines the origins and emergence of African pastoralist peoples up to the present day.

Origins

Tracing pastoralism in prehistory: evaluating the evidence

Types of evidence from which pastoral origins can be traced range from classical archaeological work on faunal remains and artefacts, through comparative linguistics and ethnography, to recent developments in genetics. The remains of domesticated animals offer some of the clearest archaeological evidence of a potential pastoralist presence (Robertshaw and Collett, 1983a, b). Species undergoing domestication commonly show an initial decrease in size, a shift in proportions of limb length to overall body size and in skull shape and dentition, as well as changes in less well-preserved characteristics of coat colour and hair type. The age/sex composition of faunal remains may indicate a selectively culled and therefore managed population rather than a natural death assemblage. Reconstructed ecological environments with which remains are associated may suggest that species were not in their natural habitat (MacDonald, 2000; Holmes, 1993; Gautier, 1987; Zeder and Hesse, 2000; Zeder et al., 2006). However, these criteria are often ambiguous. It can be hard to distinguish between wild and domesticated members of the same genus where the wild ancestors are or were present in the same area (Davis, 1987; Gautier, 1987; Zeder et al., 2006). Size reduction may indicate the restricted diet of early captive pre-domesticated animals, or artificial selection for smaller more manageable animals, but it could also be due to the context of climatic change within which early domestication took place (Davis, 1987). It can also be difficult to distinguish between bones of different genera (for example, metapodials of sheep and goats), or different species within the same genus. Sexually dimorphic remains of a single species may be misinterpreted as evidence of size changes associated with domestication (e.g. cattle in Catal-Höyük – Russell et al., 2005).

Alongside faunal remains, a wealth of rock art records the emergence and changing forms of pastoralism (eg. Sahara: Lhote, 1966; Camps, 1982; Dupuy, 1992; Muzzolini, 1991; Marshall, 2000; Smith, 2000). Along with such artefacts as Egyptian wall paintings and Zimbabwean figurines, these representations may give evidence of chronology, the varieties present, husbandry practices, the cultural importance of livestock and the changing organisation of herding societies as well as people's ethnic affiliations. Other forms of rock art are seen not as literal representations, but rather as symbolising trance experiences, religious beliefs, social organisation and tensions inherent in the society (Lewis-Williams, 1981). The emergence of pastoralism among former foragers in South West Africa is recorded not by the depiction of domesticates in rock art, but by the changing social relations apparent in art and artefacts (Kinahan, 1991, though Smith, 2000 advises caution).

Traces of the technology associated with animal husbandry, such as leather, wooden or pottery milking and storage containers, calf ropes and other cords, corrals associated with dung which can be dated, all indicate pastoralist presence (Kinahan, 1991; Hall, 1990; Beach, 1994). Distinctive pottery styles known to be associated with pastoralist economies at other sites may indicate pastoralism even in the absence of other evidence. In some cases, the location of sites in areas unsuitable for agriculture is used as evidence for specialised pastoralism (Marshall, 1994). Similarly the location of faunal remains in environments reconstructed as unsuitable for the wild species is taken as evidence of domestication and pastoralism (Wendorf et al., 1984, 1987; Wendorf and Schild, 1998; Gautier, 1987; Zeder et al., 2006). Pastoralism is, and has always been, most commonly carried out alongside one or more other equally important occupations: pastorofishing around Lake Turkana (Marshall, 1994) and further west in the Holocene Sahara (Gowlett, 1988); pastoro-foraging in the Sahara (Gautier, 1987) and Southern and Southwest Africa (Kinahan, 1991; Wilmsen, 1989); agropastoralism in the south-east of Southern

Africa (Hall, 1990; Beach, 1994); camel pastoralism married with trading economies in the West African Sahara (Bernus, 1981). In East Africa, there has been a particular interest in distinguishing the emergence of specialised pastoralism from the more generalised use of domestic livestock in a mixed economy, agropastoral or otherwise. Here the presence of small querns has been taken as associated with limited use of grains, evidence of an emphasis on pastoralism (Robertshaw and Collett, 1983a; Marshall, 1994). By contrast, sites with evidence only of pastoralist activities may have been bound up with a broader set of subsistence activities at spatially separate, economically linked locations (cf. Kinahan, 1991).

Alongside these archaeological approaches, genetics and linguistics are revolutionising our understanding of the history of domestication. Over the last few years it has become possible to analyse the degree of divergence between individuals and populations through Y-chromosome and mitochondrial (mt)DNA. mtDNA (inherited exclusively from the mother) is effectively isolated within the mitochondria from processes of recombination which otherwise shuffle and reassort maternal and paternal chromosomal DNA. Because of its shape and structure, the Y chromosome (which determines male sex) cannot pair fully with its partner X chromosome and it is also largely prevented from recombination. This means that direct maternal and paternal lineages can be traced with unprecedented accuracy and time depths, allowing a rather different understanding of the origins and trajectories of domestication for different species (Zeder et al., 2006). However, the overarching framework and synthesis over the last decade has built on seminal work in comparative linguistics and ethnography to make the prehistory of Africa become visible in new ways (Vansina, 1990; Ehret, 1998). This work has driven innovative (often provocative) analyses and integration of archaeological and other data as to the peoples and processes involved in the origins and spread of domesticates through the African continent from around 10,000 years ago up to recent times (Ehret, 2002; Schoenbrun, 1998).

Emergence of pastoralism in African prehistory

Between 18000 and 13500BP, Africa experienced an arid period, with forests receding, and wooded savannas and more arid zones spreading. Comparative linguistics and ethnography suggest that four major groupings inhabiting Africa during this period each contributed in major ways to present-day African pastoralist societies (Ehret, 2002).

The Afroasiatic or Afrasan people occupied the area from the Nubian Nile to the Red Sea Hills and north Ethiopian Highlands. Archaeology shows that they specialised in the collection of wild sedge or grass roots and grains, which they threshed, winnowed and roasted or ground on stones to prepare flour. Comparative ethnography and linguistics suggest that they practised male (and later female) circumcision, and had patrilineal clans with hereditary ritual or religious leaders (who were not politically powerful chiefs). They worshipped ethnically restricted deities (in one descendant group, this clan deity became the Jehovah of the Old Testament). They used stringed instruments (not drums) to make music, and had characteristic housing styles. Over the ensuing millennia, the Afroasiatic grouping became ancestors to the Cushites of North East Africa, proto-Berber peoples who spread across North Africa and proto-Chadic groups (who spread south through the west-central Sahara).

Niger-Congo peoples centred in West Africa had specialised hunting stone toolkits, carved bone, ivory and wooden fish hooks, used wild yams and had a specialised knowledge of plant-derived poisons. They had a clan-based, matrilineal social organisation with hereditary clan chiefs, and developed distinctive drum-based music and dancing. Their beliefs centred around a Creator divinity, individual spirits of place, and ancestor veneration. They gave rise to the Bantu languages and cultures which spread throughout sub-Saharan Africa, developing highly successful mixed farming and agro-pastoralist economies, and playing a major part in the origins of present-day pastoralist societies.

Ancestral Khoisan-speaking gathering and hunting peoples are associated with the East African microlithic Wilton arrowhead tradition, the use of bow and arrow and poisons, and digging sticks for gathering tubers and rhizomes. This tradition traces back to 22000BP in present-day Zambia and by 16000BP stretched from the Zambezi to the Ethiopian highlands. They used stringed instruments, not drums, and their rock art shows a long tradition of shamanic beliefs and trance-dancing. Widely assimilated or displaced as food-producing economies spread, Khoisan peoples and languages nonetheless left important loanwords that have become central to South Cushitic languages. Throughout Eastern and Southern Africa, Khoisan-speakers adopted livestock rearing alongside gathering and hunting, evolving pastoro-forager economies *in situ* (Kinahan, 1991; Wilmsen, 1989, 1991).

Between 11000BP and 8000BP the Middle Nile was inhabited by Nilo-Saharans, to the south and west of the Afrasan, and separated from them by the increasingly dry and inhospitable Sahara. Their technology and root words suggest that they hunted plains game with spears (and, much later, bow and arrow). They may have believed in animating forces representing spiritual power or danger. They gave rise to the Sudanic civilisations.

The influence of these four groupings on present-day patterns of food production and technology in general, and the spread of pastoralism in particular, can be traced back through the common roots of words used across a wide range of present-day African languages. Their separate and distinct social, political and ritual organisations, and cultural (including musical) traditions, have handed down beliefs, practices and structures shaping those of present-day peoples. Other ancestral African peoples and traditions have left few identifiable traces in present-day African societies. From around 12000BP, perhaps driven by changing climatic and environmental conditions, people in North East Africa, South-west Asia and the southern part of East Asia all independently invented the domestication of animals and plants for food.[1] In each case, the process seems first to have centred around the domestication of

---

[1] The domestication of dogs is thought to date back to at least 14000BP, unrelated to food production.

a focal animal species, with local pre-agricultural traditions of wild plant management later refined into production of domesticated plants. Over the next few thousand years another 7-10 independent centres of domestication arose worldwide, including several more in Africa. The present discussion focuses on the origins of the livestock species which underpin present-day African pastoralist societies.

African ecoclimatic zones and conditions of 12000-11000BP resembled those of the present day. Between 11000BP and 9000BP climates were warm and wet, Lake Chad reached its maximum extent, and perennial watercourses flowed from the Central Saharan Tibesti and Hoggar massifs. During this period, Khoisan-speaker traditions were found throughout the eastern and south-eastern wooded savannas. The Afrasans were associated with Mediterranean climate regions throughout Northern Africa and the Red Sea Hills. Sudanic-speaking Nilo-Saharans spread north as savanna vegetation expanded northward into the Sahara. Coming into interaction with the Afrasan peoples, they adopted the use of wild grains, and transposed the techniques of wild sedge and grass collection and preparation to new species of wild cereals including *fonio*, and wild forms of sorghum and pearl millet. The moist warm period also meant a southward extension of Mediterranean climates, habitats and faunas including *Bos primigenius africanus,* the wild ancestor of African (and European) indigenous cattle domesticates, and present in North Africa into historical times. The Saharo-Sahelians of the Middle Nile are thought to have domesticated cattle first. They left domesticated cattle remains dating to 9400-9200BP, alongside evidence of North Sudanic wild grain use (Nabta Playa – Wendorf et al., 1984, 1987; Wendorf and Schild, 1998, 2001; and Bir Kiseiba: Egypt – Gautier 1986, 1987; Marshall, 1994; MacDonald, 2000; Blench and MacDonald, 2000). These pre-date the first food-producing economies of the more northerly Nile Valley and Delta (Holmes, 1993; Stanley and Warne, 1993), and the first domestic cattle in South-west Asia, by a thousand years or more (cf. Russell et al., 2005). Nilo-Saharan invention of ceramics (before any middle Eastern or European pottery) underpinned their development of cooked porridges and gruels (in contrast to the Afrasan baked breads).

North Sudanian culture and demography were gradually transformed by their cattle keeping. Between 10000BP and 9000BP these Sudanic people began cultivating sorghum and millet derived from their wild grains, and later gourds and cotton as well, developing spinning and weaving. At the same time, another tradition was associated with rivers and lakes throughout the southern Sahara during the climatic optimum 11000BP-9000BP. Aquatic peoples combined fishing with harpoons and other gear with hunting, from Lake Turkana in the north of present-day Kenya, through the Hoggar Mountains of the Central Sahara, to the bend of the Niger River, using pottery closely related to that of the Sudanic peoples. As the climate and the Sahara became drier after 9000BP, freshwater resources dwindled. In the Middle Nile, the North Sudanians' domestication of cattle and dryland grain crops allowed them to specialise in dryland environments away from freshwater habitats. Their merging of Aquatic and Sudanic 'agripastoral' traditions (Ehret, 2002), not only around the Middle Nile but probably also the inland bend of the Niger and Lake Chad at its greatest extent, gave rise by 8000BP to the distinctive, long-lived Sudanic tradition, village-based (rather than in scattered homesteads), fishing, keeping cattle and cultivating grain. These peoples had a characteristic house type, monotheistic beliefs, practised lower incisor removal on adolescents (but not circumcision), and used sideblown animal horn trumpets.

During the period 11000-7500BP, indigenous domestications also emerged among the Afroasiatic-speaking peoples of the Horn and the North Sahara. Linguistic evidence suggests that well before they domesticated cattle these peoples had diverged into southern and northern branches. The southern branch became cultural ancestors to the Cushitic speakers of the southern Red Sea Hills and northern Ethiopian Highlands. The northern branch diverged further into two broad groups. One spread north out of Africa, across the Sinai peninsula into present-day Palestine and Syria, where their cultural descendants became the Semites. They became managers of populations of wild sheep and goats in the Zagros Mountains (Zeder and Hesse, 2000) and, around 11000BP, the first known domesticators of sheep and goats, which spread back into North-east Africa from their Southwestern Asian origin.[2] By 9000BP sheep and goats appear in Capsian[3] tradition sites, among the early Cushites of the Red Sea Hills; and, after 9000BP, in Sudanic sites. The linguistic evidence shows that Eastern Saharo-Sahelian peoples acquired goats (and sheep) from the Cushites, while Saharo-Sahelian peoples who had already spread westward to the central Sahara acquired sheep (and goats) from the Capsian descendants of the Afrasans as they extended west across the Mediterranean steppe of the north Sahara. They gave rise in due course to both the proto-Chadic domesticators of cattle, and proto-Berber peoples. Their various languages retained traces of an ancestral word for a protected or domesticated animal, attached to different species in each group (Cushites: cattle; ancient Egypt: pigs; Semitic languages: sheep and goats; Chadic peoples: cattle (Ehret, 2002)). By 9000BP, domesticated cattle were being reared across the North Sahara and throughout the Red Sea Hills. Donkeys, domesticated in the Red Sea Hills, spread from Africa to South-west Asia before 6000BP.

Proto-Cushites of 9000BP were thus herders of sheep and goats as well as cattle. They worshipped a single sky god through clan ritual experts. Their present-day cultural heirs in the Red Sea Hills region are the Beja; other Cushitic groups spread throughout the Horn of Africa. Far to the west, proto-Chadic keepers of cattle, sheep and goats spread through the central Sahara and, from 8500BP to 7500BP, south of the Lake Chad Basin. Their interaction

---

[2] Other than cattle and donkeys, modern African pastoralist livestock species are generally accepted as having been introduced. The species directly ancestral to present-day domestic sheep, goats, horses and camels had no wild populations naturally present on the African continent when domestication took place, though there have been suggestions of an early indigenous domestication of Barbary sheep in North Africa and the Central Sahara, later replaced by wool-bearing sheep from the Middle East (Muzzolini, 1991; Holmes, 1993; MacDonald, 2000).
[3] The Capsian tradition was a megalithic culture leaving dolmens and other remains throughout North Africa; Berbers were associated with such sites in the last millennium BC (Camps 1982; Ehret 2002).

with and assimilation of Sudanic farmers gave rise to a culture centred on Sudanic crop and livestock technologies, alongside Chadic language, social and political systems.

Meanwhile, other domestication traditions came into being which would in due course influence the ecology of present-day pastoralist groups. Between 8000BP and 9000BP another Afroasiatic language group far south in the Ethiopian highlands domesticated *enset,* a relative of the banana, whose stem and shoot are eaten (not the fruit). By 8000-7000BP it had become the dietary staple. By 6000BP a new indigenous Cushitic cropping system had emerged, based on the indigenous domesticates *tef* and finger millet. As they spread south they assimilated many former Omotic peoples, and a new agricultural tradition, based on livestock rearing and cultivation of *enset* alongside Cushitic grain crops, came to dominate the southwestern Ethiopian highlands.

Far to the west, in the wetter woodlands fringing the rainforest, Niger-Congo peoples developed the West African planting tradition, based on yam cultivation alongside fishing and the domestication of oil palm and other tree crops, and of guinea fowl. They adopted Sudanic pottery and, between 8000BP and 7000BP, goats. Their adoption of cattle was probably limited by tsetse vectors of trypanosomiasis, widespread in these wetter woodland environments. They gave rise to the Benue-Kwa, cultural ancestors of Bantu and others.

Spread of pastoralism through Africa

Across North Africa, the descendants of the Capsians (and ancestors of the Berbers) practised a Mediterranean form of agropastoralism by 7000-6000BP, based on cattle, sheep and goats alongside cultivation of the Middle Eastern wheat and barley domesticates. There are domesticated cattle remains dating to or before 7000BP in the central Sahara near Tibesti and the Hoggar (see Fig. 2.1; MacDonald, 2000). From 7000BP on, pastoralism based on domesticated cattle, sheep and goats spread south leaving vivid portrayals in rock art through the Central and Southern Sahara (Lhote, 1966; Smith 1992a). Animal sculptures on decorated stone pestles, grindstones and axes may belong to the same tradition, linking plains sites with rock art in the mountain massifs as poles of transhumance cycles (Camps, 1982). Other artifacts include waisted stones thought to have been used for tethering cattle (MacDonald, 2000). The first traces of domesticated cattle begin to appear south of the Sahara around 6000 years ago (MacDonald, 2000; Marshall, 2000, 1994; Grigson, 1991). People with domesticated animals moved gradually south and west through a time of growing desiccation in the Sahara, leaving the oases populated, and shifting the range of their cattle herds towards the regions of present-day Niger, Senegal, Chad and Sudan. The Niger floodplain stretched to the Tichit escarpment up till 5000BP (MacDonald, 1994; McIntosh and McIntosh, 1988; Marshall, 1994). From 5000BP to 4000BP, conditions began to become too dry for cattle in the Sahara (though hippopotamus persisted in Ténéré until 3000BP).

Between 8000BP and 7000BP, the eastern Sahelians spread southward across what is present-day central Sudan, reaching the northern fringes of East

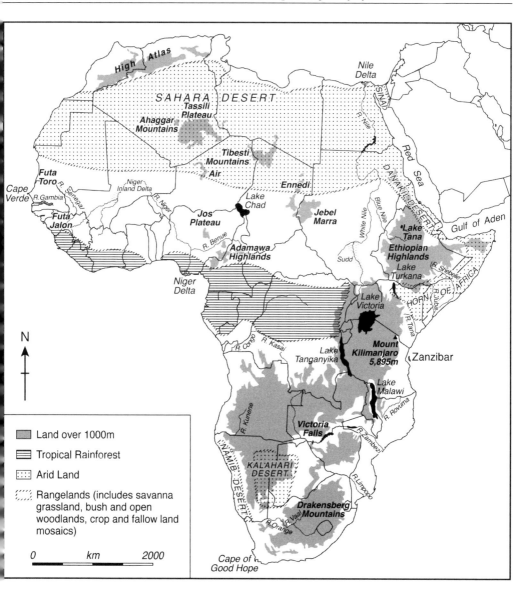

Figure 2.1 African pastoralist environments: biophysical features
Source: After Kwamena-Poh et al. (1982)

Africa by 6000–5000BP. As they spread they assimilated many formerly Aquatic peoples. Within this mix, the Sudanic cultural legacy is visible in Nilotic groups, characterised by scattered homesteads and an absence of kings and chiefs. There are continuities between the Aquatic custom of living in centralised villages with sacral kings, pre-dynastic early large Sudanic kingdoms and later Ancient Egypt's divine kingships (Ehret, 2002). As they spread south the eastern Sahelians also left some Aquatic groups relatively unaffected, including those isolated from contact by the wetlands of the present-day Sudd (the Bahr el Ghazal flood basin), and by the surrounding tsetse belts. These people remained primarily fishers, adopting livestock and grain cultivation more gradually between 7000BP and 5500BP. Their languages all share the same root word for harpoon, a tool of central importance. The Western Nilotic Dinka and Nuer of the Sudd are their cultural heirs.

Between 7500BP and 5500BP these various food-producing peoples domesticated new species of plant and animal to add to their different agricultural and pastoral traditions, acquired other domesticates from the peoples with whom they interacted, and derived an increasing proportion of their diets from domesticated plants and animals; their populations grew and intensified as a result (Ehret, 2002). However, food-collecting traditions still dominated Africa around the Equator and further south. The archaeological evidence suggests that, during the ensuing millennia, first sheep and goats and later cattle spread into East Africa and then, after a second hiatus, from east into south-eastern and southern Africa. It has been suggested that this southward spread was delayed by disease challenge (see Chapter 6). The bands of woodland and wooded grassland inhabited by disease vectors would have presented serious disease challenges from tsetse-borne trypanosomiasis and tickborne diseases like East Coast Fever (ECF), as well as other wildlife-borne diseases like Malignant Catarrhal Fever (MCF), blocking the movement of livestock species in general and of cattle in particular (Gifford-Gonzalez, 2000). The colonising herders would have been as unfamiliar with these diseases as their herds were immunologically inexperienced and lacking in evolutionarily selected resistance. Although indigenous knowledge developed to allow effective avoidance or management of these disease challenges (Chapter 6), and in due course cattle spread in the wake of more resilient species of domesticate, the necessary knowledge may have taken a considerable time to emerge (Gifford-Gonzalez, 2000). As climatic conditions deteriorated from around 4500BP and these habitats became more arid, vector population distributions would have shrunk along with the wetter wooded and woody grassland vegetation providing their preferred environment. Trial and error, and the accumulating indigenous technical knowledge of these new and changing environments, may have equipped herding peoples to navigate through potential disease hazards with increasing skill and success.

Between 7000BP and 6000BP the Southern Cushites moved south from the Ethiopian Highlands into the dry lowlands east of Lake Turkana in present-day Kenya. They brought their sheep, goats, cattle and donkeys with them, but with the shift in habitat they took up cultivation of the Sudanic sorghum and other crops in place of their own, retaining finger millet cultivation where conditions allowed. Their interaction with new peoples (whether East Sahelian, Aquatic round Lake Turkana, or Khoisan-speakers) led to changes in their subsistence economy, but they retained distinctive Afroasiatic house building, religion, and circumcision practices. Between 5500BP and 3000BP they spread through present-day Kenya and into north central Tanzania. Also from around 5500BP, several different peoples of the Sudanic tradition spread into the lands between the western and eastern Rifts. East Central Sudanian peoples from the Bahr el Gazal flood basin of the Upper Nile moved southward along the western Rift. Their mixed economy originated in the Aquatic fishing, gathering and hunting tradition, but they had already adopted cultivating and herding, and as they moved into the diverse montane, forest, lake and savanna habitats of the western Rift, and encountered Bantu and other new peoples, they experimented with new types of food production. East Sahelian speakers moved south with their cattle, goats, sheep and sorghum through what is now South Sudan and northern Uganda, reaching southwest Uganda by 3000BP. Between 2000BP and 1000BP a group of Nilotic speakers, also of the East Sahelian grouping and originating from north of the Sudd, spread into what is now central and eastern Uganda.

The Sahara had presented little in the way of a barrier to interaction and diffusion for the previous few thousand years. However, as the climate grew drier from 4500BP, the Sahara became a 1500km-wide belt of extreme aridity, constraining the movement of people, livestock, and their diseases. When that disease barrier was breached by rinderpest in the nineteenth century, the immunological inexperience of people and livestock proved catastrophic to the sub-Saharan region and especially to pastoral societies (Ford, 1971; Kjekshus, 1977).

Meanwhile, the West African Planting tradition peoples developed their distinctive yam-based cultivation systems and populated the forests and wooded savannas of west and central Africa (Vansina, 1990; Ehret, 2002). Between 4000BP and 3000BP a group near the confluence of the Congo and Kwa rivers spread across the rainforest belt at its narrowest point. They gave rise to two parallel expansions of particular importance to the emergence of pastoral and agro-pastoral societies. Firstly, ancestral savanna Bantu cultures spread eastward through the moist woodland savannas south of the rainforest, reaching the western Rift by 3000BP. Secondly the Ubangian peoples (derived from Niger-Congo speakers of Adamawa in Cameroon) expanded across the savanna north of the rainforest.

The final domesticates to be added to African pastoralism were camels, which rapidly became of enormous importance to Saharan groups. Camels are thought to have been introduced into the Horn of Africa in 4500-3500BP on established trade routes across the Red Sea direct from Southern Arabia, and possibly along the coast from Egypt. They spread from the eastern desert to the Sudan, and west along the mountain massif stepping-stones of the South Saharan highlands: Ennedi, Tibesti, Tassili, Ahaggar, Adrar n'Iforas (see Fig. 2.1), perhaps as early as ca. 3500-2500BP (Mason, 1984), and at any rate by the first centuries of the Christian era (Levtzion, 1985; Camps, 1982). Pack camels virtually replaced wheeled transport with carts or mules from Morocco throughout the Maghreb AD300-600 as the Romans retreated. With the Arab and Islamic conquest of Egypt in the seventh century and the Hillalian invasions of the eleventh century, camels became established throughout North Africa. Camels are still spreading through arid parts of East Africa, Namibia and other desert areas.

The preceding sections have traced cultural, economic and linguistic traditions of ancestral peoples. However, cultural continuities should not be taken to imply any rigid correlation of physical origins among the diversity of present-day pastoralist peoples. The spread of archaeologically, linguistically or ethnographically recognisable forms should not be taken to imply physical expansion or displacement so much as cultural shift alongside limited migration or population movement. Present-day pastoralist peoples are the products of highly dynamic, complex, fluid, shifting networks of different influences and interactions, producing continuously evolving identities, in which cultural, economic and linguistic strands can be teased apart in separate ways. There are no simple unbroken chains of physical ancestry, nor simple correlations of economic and ethnic antecedents. The names given to present-day groupings of pastoral peoples may convey a misleading sense of distinct, separate categories. They are a shorthand embodying change through time as communities interact with, incorporate or drift apart from particular cultural, linguistic, economic and/or physical influences (Waller and Sobania, 1994; Spear and Waller, 1993; Kinahan, 1991; Wilmsen, 1989; Spear, 1997; see below). The twenty-first-century identities of those peoples known as Fulani, Maasai or San are current and transient manifestations of a diverse and continuously changing reality. The physical, cultural and economic roots of present-day communities are bound up and closely shared with those of surrounding, superficially distinct peoples. Their current identities have emerged recently, constructed as much for political ends whether of the people themselves or of other communities around them, as by any basis in physical, cultural or economic ancestry (eg. Fukui and Markakis, 1994).

Emergence of present-day African pastoralist societies

Fulani in West Africa

Prehistoric Saharan rock art in Tassili depicts calf ropes, cattle lines, and internal arrangements of huts, which all have their parallels in contemporary Fulani (Peul) culture (Smith, 1992a). The weapons depicted there look like spears or long-hafted, long-bladed axes of characteristic Peul shape. The metal blades still found today resemble blades from around 2800BP in Aïr (Niger) and from Mauritanian metal-working sites. The markings on the faces of the people represented in Tassili rock art, the style of representation of men, women and animals, cattle horn shapes, coat patterns, ornaments and earmarkings, all have parallels in ethnographic descriptions of various Peul groups. Despite these striking similarities and the potential continuities they imply, it is important to bear in mind the diverse roots of present-day Fulani. Fulani speak a Niger-

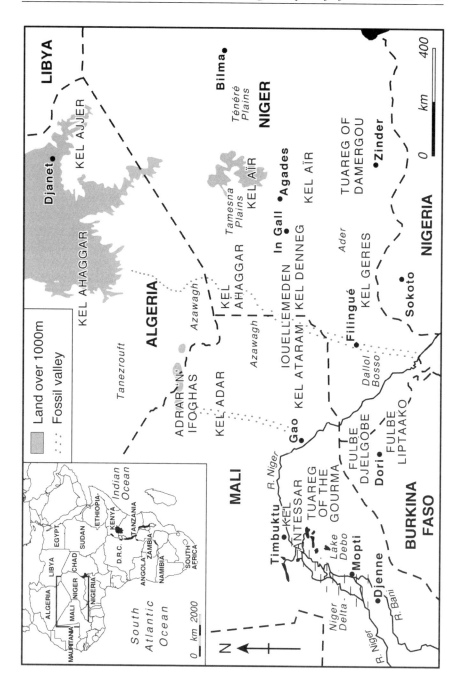

Figure 2.2 Sahara-Sahelian pastoralism around the Inland Delta of the Niger
Source: After Bernus (1990)

Congo language, whose area of origin seems to have been in or around the Senegal Valley, with variants being spoken by the Toucouleur, the Serere and the Wolof (Horton in Ajayi and Crowder, 1985).

As well as this linguistic ancestry, Fulani show strong influences from far south-western outlier Berber peoples, in terms of their pastoral livestock and technologies, as well as elements of physical ancestry. Despite myths of an eastern origin (common among Islamicised peoples), Fulani are thought to have emerged around 1000BP along the southwestern fringes of the Sahara as cattle pastoralists. They spread eastward between the twelfth and nineteenth centuries, coming to occupy areas throughout the West African savanna, wherever pasture and water resources, relative absence of cattle disease, and relative political freedom made cattle pastoralism a successful option. Post-fourteenth century Arab authors called the western Sudan 'Takrur', and distinguished the sedentary (Toucouleur) and nomadic (Fulani) peoples. Over the last 500 years different Fulani populations have spread from Senegal in the west through to Chad, and from Mali and Niger in the north through Central African Republic south to the borders of the Congo and through Cameroon, Nigeria, Ivory Coast and Bénin to the southern coast of West Africa. Throughout this range, they live alongside other linguistic groups with other economic specialisations. In some of these areas the history of Fulani pastoralists is better known and has had a major regional impact: the cases of the Inland Delta of the Niger, and of the Adamawa highlands on the border of Cameroon and Nigeria, are outlined here (Colour map and Figs 2.1 and 2.2).

The complex interrelations between Fulani pastoralism and the other economic specialisations of the inland delta of the Niger can be traced back into prehistory. Bozo, Dogon, Nono, Somono, Bambara, Songhai, Marka ('men of Mali') and many others, including Hausa and Mossi urban traders, now make up the complex ethnic, linguistic and economic mix of the Delta. All of these groups individually are now outnumbered by Fulani, who in the 1980s were estimated to make up one-third of the population (Gallais, 1984). The Bozo fishing people are generally acknowledged as the first inhabitants of the region, their ritual cultivation of the wild *Digitaria* grass *fonio* harking back to fisher-forager origins (ibid.), while the Nono are associated with the practice of indigenous (flooding) rice cultivation dating back to at least 3500BP. During the ninth-eleventh centuries AD the Empire of Ghana emerged 300km to the west, influencing the growth of the Delta economy. With the rise of the Empire of Mali in the thirteenth century (cf. Ehret, 2002:324), the Niger River became one leg of the triangle of commerce in salt from the Sahara, slaves from the south and gold from the west. When Mali later fell to the Songhai, the trade networks linking the south through the Sahelian centres and the Saharan routes to the Maghreb shifted eastward with the main Songhai concentrations downstream of Lake Debo (Fig 2.2). Diallo Fulani arrived from Futa Toro in the west (Fig 2.1) in the fourteenth century, towards the end of the Empire of Mali. As the first pastoralists in the Delta, they continued to filter in during Songhai rule. They progressively occupied the western part of the Delta, displacing or assimilating earlier inhabitants. At the beginning of the fifteenth century the state of Macina (Maasina) began to emerge, as Fulani subjects of the Malian (and Tuareg) empires settled to exploit the opportunities for trade. Towards the end of the sixteenth century the Portuguese maritime trade began to undercut traffic through the interior. Moroccan invaders from the Maghreb overran the Songhai in 1591, and by the mid-seventeenth century the Songhai empire had disintegrated. Waves of immigrant Fulani followed the Diallo and progressively came to occupy the whole of the western part of the Delta (Gallais, 1984). Downstream of the Delta, the Tuareg Empire flourished from the end of the seventeenth to the mid-eighteenth century; upstream the Bambara state of Segu expanded in the eighteenth century, leaving the Delta a political void (Fig. 2.3).

In the nineteenth century Uthman dan Fodio, a Fulani Islamic scholar, rose against the Hausa state of Gobir. Together with his followers, he conquered the whole Hausa empire and adjacent lands, and established the Sokoto Caliphate, extending at its zenith as far east as Adamawa and south almost to Ibadan (Adamu, 1986). His example inspired other Islamic revolts. The Fulani leader Ahmad Lobbo broke away from the Bambara state of Segu and set up an Islamic state in Macina, based on the Dina code in the western Delta (1812-62). The Dina was established by the conquering Fulani as a theocratic natural resource management system (Adamu, 1986; Gallais, 1984; Moorehead, 1991; Legrosse, 1999; Vedeld, 2003; see also Chapter 4). Under the Dina all Delta inhabitants had to settle in a permanent base, or forfeit their land-use rights. Rimaibe (slave) villages were established to cultivate for the ruling Fulani. The Dina established a detailed record of resource use, listing fish dams, transhumance routes, village grazing grounds and markets within the Delta. It codified the use of natural resources 'along the lines of ethno-professional specialisations' (Vedeld, 2003). Fishing resources were left under the management of other ethnic groups such as the Bozo and the Somono, but integrated into the new overall framework of governance, and placed under the control of 'masters of the water', who regulated spatial and temporal access, and to whom a proportion of the catch was due. The Emir dismantled traditional Fulani political structures, deposing traditional leaders (*ardo*) and establishing Islamic religious leaders in their place as *dioro*, masters of grazing resources. The Dina established the rank order of movement for the aggregate herds (Chapter 4), their transhumance routes, stopover and crossing points, and inheritance rules for cattle, property and official positions.

Resistance to the tremendous changes brought about by the Emir and his successors over three decades crystallised into an opposition which joined with Toucouleur invaders from the west. In the 1850s and 1860s the western Delta was taken over by the Toucouleur Empire, which incorporated the two big Bambara states of Segu and Kaarta and stretched from Futa Jalon to Timbuktu (Kwamena-Poh et al., 1982). The savage wars that ensued depopulated the inner Delta, concentrated people into large villages, and liberated the Rimaibe who had been settled by the Fulani as cultivating slave settlements. By the 1890s, the Delta had become a fringe of the Toucouleur Empire, with the laws of the Dina retained and enforced by people hostile to the formerly dominant Fulani. During the 1890s the French established control over the Delta along with much of the rest of West Africa. From its 1000-year role as the political and commercial backbone of West Africa, the inland Delta of the Niger dwindled to the status of a backwater.

The Adamawa Plateau highlands of Nigeria and Cameroon (Fig 2.1) were overrun by the nineteenth century Fulani *jihad* and became part of the Sokoto Caliphate. The original farming inhabitants – Gbaya, Niamniam, Boum and other cultivating groups – were subjugated to a regime that favoured livestock herding over farming in terms of land management and rights. The conquering Fulbe established lamidates (centralised political hierarchies around leaders known as *laamido*), and developed a semi-sedentary lifestyle managing their herds and overseeing the farming villages which supplied their grain. In their wake came the Bororo Fulani, taking advantage of the pastoralist hegemony on the plateau to rear their cattle, exchange pastoral produce for grain and on occasion supply skilled herding labour to the ever more sedentary Fulbe. The Bororo were not integrated into the Fulbe lamidates; they negotiated grazing and water rights within individual lamidates in return for tax, and moved on if demands become exorbitant. A settled and socially stratified Fulani society emerged in these relatively short-lived Fulani states, alongside more mobile pastoralist Fulani communities. In Sokoto, Uthman dan Fodio's lieutenants became emirs and developed a political hierarchy, with continuing implications for contemporary politics in the region.

The Fulbe of Adamawa established pastoral primacy: herds could graze as they wished; farmers had to seek permission to cultivate, and had to alter their practices to accommodate the herds' priority requirements. Millet (which stands and ripens into the dry season when fodder is short and herds may ravage fields) gave way to maize, with its shorter wet-season growing cycle. In the face of the dry-season needs and depredations of Fulbe herds, intercropping and green manuring were mostly abandoned, and manure used for fertiliser. The interdependence between Fulbe and farmers shifted from a master-servant to a more contractual and commercial relationship during colonial and post-Independence eras. Livestock ownership was originally the prerogative of the Fulani, but peasant farmers of the plateau have increasingly acquired livestock as an integral part of their farming system.

Today the Fulani comprise more than 5 million people 'scattered through the length and breadth of the West African savanna' (see colour map, Boutrais, 1994c). They live in many different countries and environments, moving among and settling alongside other groups and pursuing a wide range of lifestyles, mostly associated with livestock. Contemporary Fulani, although identified by their common language, have thus come to comprise a broad array of economies, sub-ethnic groups and social forms, from primarily agricultural or agropastoral Fulani of the Senegal Valley, to the mobile pastoral Wodaabe subclan of the Mbororo Fulani (e.g. Bocquené, 2002), to more settled, centralised, socially and politically differentiated Fulani livestock trading communities in Nigeria. Contrary to the image of arid land pastoralists, some Fulani are relatively sedentary livestock producers on the high-potential Adamawa and Mambila Plateaus. Fulani extend through the humid countries of Bénin to the south and of Central African Republic in the south-east to the fringes of the Congo, adapting their livestock production and trading to prevailing conditions (Boutrais, 1978, 1986, 1988, 1994a; *Cahiers d'Etudes Africaines*, 1994; Burnham, 1999; Azarya et al., 1999; also Chapter 4).

Tuareg

Over 3000 years ago, Berber groups with a tradition of rearing small stock spread south through the increasingly arid Sahara. Rock art shows that earlier groups used horse-drawn chariots, probably with metal wheel rims, light one-man structures used by nobles or chiefs for hunting or warfare, not trade or other transport. The Garamantes emerged around 3500BP, retaining their own nomadic pastoralist lifestyle centred on horses and wool-bearing sheep while dominating other Saharan peoples up to the Roman period around 2500BP. By now the Sahara had become so dry that, apart from the narrow coastal strip, it formed a barrier to political unity and caused a shift in pastoralist ecology. Representations of horses are replaced by camels in rock art. Contemporary sources record the spread of camel-borne nomads through south-east Roman Africa and a Berber ruling class established south of the Sahara by the fifth century AD (Dupuy, 1991; Ehret, 2002:226). From the seventh century on, Arab invaders from the Middle East swept through North Africa, meeting and eventually overcoming Berber resistance, driving ripples of North African camel-borne Berber groups south and west away from the invading Arabs. Ibn Hawqual, Al Yaq'ubi and Ibn Khaldun all mention the presence of Berbers south of the Sahara in 500-1000AD.

The Saharan and Maghrebian Berbers of the early Arab period formed a loose but culturally coherent federation of Sanhaja from North Africa to sub-Saharan Africa (Levtzion, 1985). Camels allowed the North African nomads to penetrate further into the Sahara, settle or control the oases, reach the southern fringes of the desert and ultimately establish the Saharan trade that earlier light horse-drawn chariots could not sustain. By 700AD West African gold from the Empire of Ghana and other Sudanese states was being ferried across the desert by camel. The Saharan groups retained close links with the Maghrebian Berbers throughout the ninth-eleventh centuries, with the trade for gold, ivory, slaves, ostrich feathers and Saharan salt from sub-Saharan Africa forming the basis of constant communication with North Africa (McDougall, 1998). The towns that developed along the southern fringe of the desert became major ports of call and their rulers, as well as the traders, became Islamicised, while the common people tended to retain their earlier beliefs.

In the eleventh century, Hillalian Arabs swept across North Africa from the east. In the western Sahara a group of Berber Sanhaja nomads, the Almoravid *jihad*, conquered present-day Morocco, Algeria and much of Spain. The Almoravids overran the Empire of Ghana in 1076AD, as well as other Sudanese states. Over-extended, they soon lost control of the Saharan-Sudanese zone. By 1150AD the Almoravids were replaced in Morocco, Algeria, Tunisia, Tripolitania and much of Spain by the Almohads, who themselves fragmented in the thirteenth century into a scatter of small states. These political upheavals did not stop the steady growth of the broader decentralised economy operated by the Berber nomads.

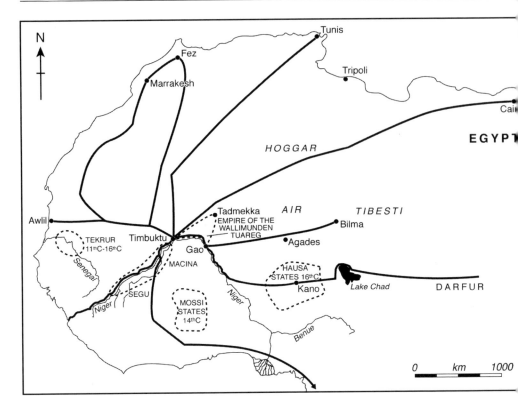

Figure 2.3 Historical trade routes managed by the Tuareg
Source: Simplified from Kwamena-Poh et al. (1982)

> No power was able to dominate the whole of North-West Africa for long, and in the mountains of the interior and the desert oases, Berber tribes were beyond the reach of centralised rule. (Kwamena-Poh et al., 1982)

From oral history and other records, present-day Tuareg groups begin to appear around 1000AD. The Igdalen and Iberkoreyen Tuareg were the first wave of Tuareg Berbers to reach the Aïr (Figs 2.1, 2.3; Bernus, 1984). The Igdalen have remained based there to the present day; others spread south. During the eleventh century, the impact of the Beni Hillal and Beni Sulayn Arabs in Tripolitania and the Fezzan brought the Isandelen ancestors of the present-day Itesen and Lisawan to the Aïr. Bernus traces further waves of Tuareg immigration through the ensuing centuries, with the Aïr acting as channel and filter for groups from Tripolitania, the Ahaggar and Adrar n'Iforas. The Hoggars of the Aïr, together with other groups from the Ahaggar, arrived as recently as the nineteenth-twentieth centuries (Fig. 2.2).

Timbuktu (Fig 2.2, 2.3) started as a Tuareg wet-season camp, and by the tenth century was well established as a Sahelian trading centre and centre of Islamic learning. By the mid-thirteenth century, the Tuareg lost control of Timbuktu to the growing Empire of Mali, but in the fifteenth century they repossessed the city. Timbuktu continued to grow as a centre of Islamic learning, and became the southwestern tip of a loose empire controlled by the Wallimunden Tuareg in the seventeenth-ninteenth centuries. Meanwhile, the Macina area became settled by Fulani as part, first, of the Malian empire, later of the Segu and eventually as the Fulani Macina state. Over the whole period from the first few centuries AD to 1500AD, political power in West Africa progressively shifted from Southern Sudanese states like the Empire of Ghana to the northern savanna with the growth of the trans-Saharan trade (Last, 1985). Islamic conquests throughout the Mediterranean opened new markets in North Africa and beyond. Different, rival trade networks arose (Fig 2.3), crossing the Sahara in the far west to Morocco; from Timbuktu north to Tunis, Tripoli and Egypt in the north-east; from Hausaland and Kanem-Borno north through the Aïr and the Hoggar or through Bilma to Tunisia and Tripoli, or west to Darfur and on northward to Egypt. The trade had major impacts on the political, economic, and social affairs of the West African kingdoms and beyond. Its effects on the price of gold throughout the Islamic world seem also to have impinged on the trade of the south-east African states of Mapungubwe and Great Zimbabwe (see below and Hall, 1990).

The Tuareg established an infrastructure of brokers, landlords, traders and craftsmen to supply accommodation, banking, brokerage, storage and other services to the trans-Saharan trade (Bernus, 1981; Lovejoy and Baier, 1975). To the Tuareg the Sahara was not so much a barrier to trade as a network of established routes through which they controlled long-distance relations and guaranteed relatively safe passage between the Mediterranean and the Sudan (Bernus, 1981). At the heart of this Tuareg trading network was the Sultanate of the Aïr, set up in 1405 and installed at Agades in the mid-fifteenth century. This sedentary chiefdom was established to regulate the smooth operation of trade and caravans, and to arbitrate among potentially warring nomadic Tuareg tribes. In marked contrast to Tuareg practice, the Sultan was polygamous, taking a wife from each of the five great noble Tuareg groups. Legitimate offspring were debarred from succeeding to the Sultanate. Only illegitimate sons, generally fathered on concubines of slave origin, could inherit. The rules of succession and marriage thus determined that the Sultan remained linked to all five main noble Tuareg groups, while no group could exercise undue influence. The Sultanate did not compete with the nomadic pastoralist Tuareg groups, but rather facilitated their economic enterprises. The trading network regulated by the Sultan of Aïr was extensive. For example, the Tuareg eventually gained control of the Bilma oasis in the late eighteenth century. Although they did not settle the oasis, they controlled the Bilma caravans which operated three times a year with up to 20,000 camels each. The intriguing political system of the Sultanate functioned successfully for around 450 years, until the French took control in the early twentieth century.

As the various Tuareg groups spread through the Sahara and its southern fringes, they developed different economies complementing their pastoralist activities, controlling millet farming in the Damergou, ravine farming of vegetables in the Aïr massif and cultivation of dates in oases (Bernus, 1981). Depending on their origins and fortunes, different groups and different social strata within groups concentrated on trade, on pastoralist activities, on religious specialisation, on war, or on farming. Throughout their range Tuareg peoples operated alongside other groups, becoming part of an ethnic mosaic whose composition shifted with period and region. On the southern margins of their range the Tuareg incorporated other sub-Saharan African groups, and elsewhere they intergraded to various extents with Arabic-speaking peoples. They established a highly stratified society, with noble, vassal, freedman, slave, religious, craftsman and other castes of varying importance in different Tuareg populations. Half-caste Tuareg formed their own groups in a system that generally maintained physical separation of black slave and Berber noble, despite their close interdependence within camp and household. In many cases dependants were established to farm or herd Tuareg holdings while nobles were engaged in other areas.

The Tuareg established no nation or country, but the economic, military and political power of their loose federation controlled the workings of the Saharan trade and influenced the affairs of well-nigh half the continent, until the French established control over much of West Africa and the Sahel as well as the Maghreb to the North. In 1893 the French took Timbuktu. The different Tuareg groups were unable to work together either to oppose or to negotiate with the French. Some remained neutral, some allied themselves with the French, some fought the invaders. The most violent conflicts were in the settled areas, like the Damergou, while the nomads of the arid zones were less affected. By 1906 the French had overcome Tuareg opposition in the southern Sahara, and had deposed and replaced the Sultan of Agades. In 1913 they commandeered the Bilma salt caravans, and many camels died under their management. In 1914 the Tuareg revolted, in response to the call for a *jihad* from the Senusi of Tripolitania. A Maghrebian leader kept up a Tuareg guerrilla war until 1920, but again the lack of Tuareg unity doomed it to failure. The French operated through a small number of relatively amenable leaders, taxing the Tuareg direct, bypassing (and destroying) the traditional structures whereby the *amenokal* or drum group leader received tribute from vassals and freedmen and distributed animals and booty according to need and merit. The French freed Tuareg dependants and in the settled areas gave them their former masters' holdings and herds, outlawing customary Tuareg claims on livestock or grain. The Tuareg were hard hit by the heavy French requisitioning of camels for military and trade purposes. Losing the caravans destroyed the basis of Tuareg trade and subsistence. Monetarisation of a formerly exchange economy exacerbated their problems.

By the 1950s the camel caravans had to some extent recovered. Despite competition from motor transport, caravans of 25–28,000 camels still operated in the 1950s and 1970s (Bernus, 1981). The Bilma caravans traded three times a year, the biggest being the autumn caravan which included all the camels being taken for the *cure salée*. In 1950 the caravan carried 300 tons of millet, with butter, sugar, tea, cloth, manufactured goods, fodder, fuel and dried vegetables from different Tuareg economies, millet from the Damergou, and vegetables from the Kel Owey, exchanged in Bilma for 2000 tons of desert salt and 400 tons of dates (Fig. 2.2).

In each of the several nations where the Tuareg are based, including Niger, Mali, Algeria and Libya, national Independence exacerbated their political weakness and ultimately their economic and cultural decline (Galaty and Bonte, 1991). By the end of the twentieth century, three decades of climatic downturn in the Sahara and Sahel had hit their pastoralist economy hard, and conflicts and civil wars affecting the nations central to their range dispossessed and dispersed many Tuareg as destitute refugees in Senegal and elsewhere (Chapters 4 and 9).

Emergence of pastoralism in North-east Africa: Arab and Beja

This section takes the picture of emerging pastoralism in the Nile delta, valley and adjacent lands up to the present-day radiation of Arab, Berber and Cushitic-speaking groups across Egypt and the Sudan, and their interlinkages with pastoralism in the Maghreb, the Horn, southern Sudan and sub-Saharan regions. There are obvious continuities between Afrasan agropastoralist traditions, with their small stock, wheat and barley, and the agropastoralists represented in Pharaonic and Old Testament records. North-east African pastoralism took on some of its present-day form first with the introduction of camels around the time of Christ, and then with the Arab invasion and expansion from 700AD. The Arab period brought with it a new language, religion and technology, including water management techniques that revolutionised cultivation possibilities (Beaumont et al., 1989). The Islamic religion incorporated North and North-east African Arab and Arabicised pastoralists within a shared frame of reference.

The colonial era emphasised a further layer of structure and differentiation. Tribes were seen as separate, discrete groups, and the practice of indirect rule selected, operated through and reinforced 'traditional chiefs'. The ethnic constructs this elicited were as much a response to indirect rule as an expression of indigenous and customary structures (Asad, 1970; Kurita, 1994; Ahmad in Toulmin and Quan, 2000). In Sudan, the British registered tribes (*gaabila*), each associated with a recognised homeland (*Dar*). The *Dar* centred on a dry-season refuge with communal and reserved grazing areas containing permanent water sources, linked by established migratory routes to wet-season grazing (*Kharif*), with leadership of sections and subsections following a recognisable lineage-related pattern. Present-day Arabicised pastoralists of Egypt, Sudan and Chad recognise ethnic divisions but also the strong continuities between those superficially separate affiliations. Table 2.1 lists Arab groups as primarily keepers of cattle (*ab Baggara*), camels (*ab Abbala* or *Jamaala*), or agro-pastoralist (*Adnaan* or *Hasawna*). Cattle-keepers commonly operate cooperative settlement, migration and herd management in groups of 15-20 households for security and economies of scale in labour; camel-keepers operate in groups of 5-10 households (Bonfiglioli, 1992).

Table 2.1 Arab and Arabicised agro/pastoralists of NE Africa

Group	ab Baggara	ab Abbala	Adnaan/ Hasawna
1° Occupation	Cattle	Camels	Settled agropastoral
	Rzeigat	Zeyyadiya	Shaigiya
	Habbaniya	Mohamid	Bedariya
	Beni Halba	Mahria	Johama'a
	Beni Khozzam	Nawaiba	Shukriya
	Messeriya Humr	Beni Hussein	Ja'aliya
	Misseriya Zurg	Hamar	
	Walad Himed	Kawahla	
	Ta'asha	Kababish	
	Rufa al Hoy	Shanabla	
		Beni Jarran	
		'Amaliya	

Source: After Bonfiglioli (1992)

Alongside Arab groups the pastoral peoples of North and North-east Africa and the Horn include Cushitic-speaking peoples like the Somalis and the Beja; speakers of Saharan languages like the Zaghawa, Bideiyat and Teda; and Nubian-speaking people (like the Meidob). To the south they abut on the Nilotic peoples of southern Sudan, northern Uganda, and Kenya. Throughout North-east Africa, pastoralist groups interdigitate with primarily cultivating groups to whom livestock are also important (Hawazma and Kawahla Arabs with Fur and Nuba–Manger, 1988; Tubiana and Tubiana, 1977; De Waal, 1989a; Hadendowa with West African Hausa immigrants – Morton, 1993; Kawahla and Hamar with Berti – Holy, 1974). The long history of interaction of these many groups encompasses, on the one hand, established relations of trade and exchange and, on the other, periodic violent and predatory raiding and/or slaving. In what is now the Sudan, there is a centuries-old history of raiding of the black agropastoral populations of the periphery by the agents of the central state, from the days of Turco-Egyptian rule through to the present-day state-armed and -backed Arab militias (Johnson, 2003; de Waal, 2004). This book does not deal with the complexities of history and politics of these more or less arabicised and Islamicised pastoralists of North-east Africa contesting key pastoral and other natural resources through the ages, trading, and operating on the broader political and economic scale in the rise and fall of different states (but see Salih, 1990; Keen, 1995; Johnson; 2003; de Waal, 1997, 2004). Rather, this section uses Beja groups as an illustration of the ecology of pastoralism as it evolved in the region.

Present-day Beja peoples speak a common (Cushitic) language, but neither see themselves as an ethnic category nor indeed call themselves Beja. They are made up of separate groups, each tracing separate genealogies back to an idealised Arab descent. They see themselves as primarily Arab, with strongly positive feelings for Arabic language, education and Islam (Morton, 1993). The camel pastoralism and associated farming systems of the Beja have been described in historical and ecological context (Morton, 1990; Hjort and Dahl, 1991), as has their ongoing diversification across urban-rural divides (Morton, 1993; Pantuliano, 2002). Language, material artefacts and some Beja social institutions are similar to those of Somali and Afar camel-herding Cushitic-speakers of Ethiopia and the Horn, though Hjort and Dahl (1991) suggest that they diverged long before acquiring camels and developing their caravanning and camel-based pastoralism. The introduction of their characteristic *durra* sorghum cereal dates back around 2000 years, although sorghum is an African indigenous domesticate and wild sorghum seeds are known to have been gathered and possibly managed in a pre-agricultural system 8000 years BP at Bir Kiseiba (Wendorf et al., 1992).

What is now Beja country, between the Nile and the Red Sea, has periodically over the last millennia been an important trade route between the Middle and Far East, and the Egyptian, Greek, Roman, Persian, Arab, Turkish and Christian empires of the Mediterranean and Western Europe. From the time of the Ptolemies on, the Red Sea ports traded in ivory, slaves, war elephants, tortoise shell, and later gum arabic and wild senna. Following their acquisition of camels, pre-Beja peoples are recorded as beginning to raid Roman and Nubian settlements from the third and fourth centuries on. In the ensuing centuries they became guides, camel breeders, traders and caravanners as well as raiders. The Beja were drawn into a wider political arena and Arabicised over a thousand years of contact. The importance of Beja camel caravan routes, and Beja supplies to the Red Sea ports, waxed and waned depending on the relative security and commercial prospects of the Silk route of Inner Asia, the Spice route along the Arabian Peninsula and the Red Sea shipping routes, as well as routes along the Nile itself. There has thus been a fluctuating but long-term tradition of inland camel caravan transport as well as involvement with both international trade and local commerce in livestock and pastoral produce, services and labour to the Red Sea ports. The traders settled in the urban areas became Islamicised Hadariba Beja shipowners and merchants, while the rural Beja herd-owning Bedawiet communities supplied transport camels, pastoral produce including animals for slaughter, and labour. There was, and is, considerable movement between rural herding communities and the labour gangs working the docks as well as the urban settlers running urban dairying and livestock trading concerns. Morton (1993) makes a broad division into three economic groupings: Bisharin (livestock traders: *bishar* is Arabic for trade), Atmaan Beja (labour migrants) and Hadendowa, many of whom are settled cultivators – cf. Ausenda, 1987) as well as urban Beja. Morton (1993) documents the many factors contributing to the decline of Hadendowa rangelands and pastoral economy. These include pressure from other Beja groups, the changing regional and national economy, Sudanese agricultural development, and macroeconomic changes (cf. Chapter 9).

Horn of Africa: the Somalis

This picture of Somali history in regional ecological and economic context is based on Lewis (1961, 2001), Cassanelli (1982), Farah (1997), Hogg (1997a),

Prior (1994), and Little (1994); the development of Somali commerce and economy over the last centuries until the recent turmoil is drawn from Swift (1977), Behnke (1983), Doornbos (1993), and Little (2003).

Somali people have linguistic, physical and ecological affinities with other South-east Cushitic-speaking groups like the Afar, Oromo and Beja. The Somali language is closest to Rendille and to the language of Boni gatherer-hunters of north-east Kenya (Helander, 1999). Somalis divide linguistically into two often mutually unintelligible main dialects, indicating divergence ca. 2000BP, and therefore Somali-speakers' presence in the Horn at or before this date (Cassanelli, 1982). The Somalis, however, commonly claim a noble Arab descent dating back around a thousand years, and subscribe to a genealogy that unites all Somali clans and lineages into six main patrilineal clan-families: the Dir, Isaq, Darod, Hawiya, Digil and Rahanweyn (Farah, 1997). Of these, the first four have long been primarily pastoralist, and some, like the Darod, are dispersed throughout the Horn. The Rahanweyn and the Digil, by contrast, have long been more settled agropastoralist clan-families, largely in the relatively productive cultivable lands between the Jubba and Shabeelle rivers (Chapter 4).

First-century AD Greek sources mention trading settlements along the Somali coast, known for their incense, aromatic woods, ivory, ostrich feathers and hides. These were exchanged for imported rice, dates and sugar. The rhythm of the trading settlements was dictated by the pastoralist seasonal cycle. During the long hard dry season, coastal settlements would double or treble in size and trade would blossom. Herding families sloughed off their dependants to leave as few mouths to feed as possible, and those temporary migrants, elders, women and children, young men supernumerary to the necessary herding labour force, would converge on the towns where they could call on kinship ties, trade gathered and hunted products, or find temporary employment. Over time these towns attracted Arab and other merchants and developed a stratified urban culture with sultans, elders, traders, artisans and slaves. Sultans ruled through controlling key resources by force of arms – wells, trade routes, market towns. Influential individuals from pastoralist families might settle in the coastal towns and intermarry with the merchant families. These alliances formed the basis of a network of political, economic and commercial links that extended from the camel herds – the capital resources of a kinship group – through into the urban hierarchy and back. Itinerant holy men laid the foundations of the distinctive Somali form of Islam, centred on local saints and sheikhs, which became one of the strong unifying features of Somali identity.

The coastal trading towns never established any great control over the interior. Leadership normally derived from personal courage, political skill and wealth, and was not usually inherited. A few leaders founded politico-religious dynasties, such as the unusually cohesive and long-lasting Ajuraan federation of Hawiya clans. They established administrative control and exacted tribute from the upper Shebeelle to the coast as far south as the Jubba River (Cassanelli, 1982) for several generations until the seventeenth century. They were the exception rather than the rule. Somalia developed neither a complex state nor a strong external livestock trade. A brief flowering of radical Islamic reform in the nineteenth century led to religious settlements being established around Bardheere. A *jihad* erupted from this area in 1819, peaking in 1840, but its apparent success united opposition from traditional Somali forms of Islam (built on veneration of and mediation through saints), and it collapsed in 1843.

Somalia's trade in ivory, resins and other gathered and hunted products never came to match the scale of other parts of the Zanzibar trade network. Although camel caravans are documented, they were minor – 15-20 camels at most in any one caravan (cf. Tuareg caravans – Lovejoy and Baier, 1975; Bernus, 1981). It was not until the late nineteenth or early twentieth centuries that a wide range of byproducts of subsistence pastoralism – milk, ghee, meat, hides – were exported. Chapter 4 gives an account of Somali pastoral resources and of their patterns of use under changing social and economic conditions. Chapter 10 outlines in more detail the initial rise and subsequent fluctuations of the Somali livestock trade. Both are vulnerable to drought and disease undermining production, and civil disruption impacting on labour (through loss or diversion of manpower), on livestock (through predatory raiding) and on markets (by disrupting the links between hinterland, urban centres and coastal ports).

The colonial period partitioned the Somali peoples among five nations: imperial Ethiopia, French-speaking Djibouti, Italian Somaliland, British Somaliland and British-controlled Kenya. Problems inevitably arose as local groups maintained customary but now cross-border movements for livestock migrations, trade, kin and other relations. Conflict escalated as post-Independence Somalia fought neighbouring states to bring the divided Somali peoples together under a single Somali nation. Ever-present local rivalries were increasingly enlisted into wider-scale and ultimately geopolitical confrontations. The peripheralisation and marginalisation of Somali pastoralists within each of these neighbouring states (and even within their own – Doornbos, 1993), together with defiance of imposed restrictions on movement and trade, exacerbated an already established pattern of resolving intergroup competition and conflict through force of arms rather than negotiation.

Under Siad Barre's presidency the ruling Marehan clan extended their control over the lucrative coastal trading ports. Further inland they established extensive private holdings in formerly communal rangelands, often by coopting aid resources intended for more general water development (Little, 2003: 40-41). Rural people were increasingly excluded by the emerging urban stratified society, relegated to its lowest ranks, and at the same time progressively squeezed out of livestock production. The once strong links between rural and urban people and economies were disrupted, culminating in today's isolation of wartorn, dangerous, violence-ridden urban centres from their hinterlands.

Throughout the Horn, states armed individual groups to fight, sometimes as allies of the government (e.g. Ethiopia armed the Boran to repulse Somalis – Hogg, 1997a), sometimes simply to divide and rule. Violence spiralled with the influx of modern weapons. At the time of writing, Somalia and Somali pastoralism have been torn apart by decades of international and civil war. These have culminated in the collapse not only of Somali state and civil society (de Waal, 1997; Chabal and Daloz, 1999; Lewis, 2001), with Somaliland and Puntland seceding as self-declared independent areas (Little, 2003), but also of wider Somali social and economic relations throughout the Horn of Africa. A later chapter outlines the patterns of conflict and war in the Horn, and their correlates of disrupted production systems, livelihoods and national economies, displaced peoples, refugees, relief and the devastation of violence and loss (Chapter 4). Despite Somalia's collapse, the informal pastoral economy is resilient. A study of Somali traders and middlemen working the north Kenya markets suggests that, where the collapse of the Somali state and the isolation of the coastal towns has undermined the formerly lucrative Gulf export trade in livestock, the presence both of informal financial institutions and also of the north Kenya markets has provided effective alternative channels. However, civil society, with security for small producers and local urban markets, has largely collapsed, with armed violence, disruption, uncertain and irregular supplies and pricing in the capital Mogadishu and important centres like Kismayo as well as throughout the hinterland. In particular, the many pastoralist women who lived by supplying milk to urban markets, have seen their established livelihoods dwindle and disappear (Little, 1994, 2003: 60-61).

Nilotic pastoralists of the Sudd

> The emergence of the ancestral Nilotes from the larger Eastern Sudanic family, centred around the confluence of the Blue and White Niles, may have begun some 5-4000 years ago at a time when there was a substantial southward movement of the cattle-keeping complex into the southern Sahara, the Sahel and the southern Sudan....The gradual drop in the level of the Nile... and the southward retreat of the vegetation belt at this time were probably factors in the adoption of herding by the Nilotes and their movement south... (Howell et al.,1988: 212)

With Lake Turkana draining into the Nile system ca. 7000BP and again ca. 3500BP, conditions in much of central-southern Sudan are thought to have been too wet for Nilotic herders to exploit until after 3000BP, when the Sudanic ancestors of the present-day Western and River-Lake Nilotes spread into the new pastures left by the most recent major fall in lake and river levels around the present-day Sudd. Howell et al. (1988) suggest that cattle-keeping Nilotes probably occupied the western edge of the Bahr el Jabal floodplains by the middle of the first millennium AD. The Dinka and Nuer diverged from the Shilluk and other Lwo-speaking peoples, and the Sudd was progressively colonised through periods of low rainfall, river and flood levels such as the seventeenth-fifteenth centuries AD, along with continued movements that led to the southward migration of the Western Nilotes and eventually the spread of the Lwo in East Africa. The shift and growth of population, largely by assimilation and incorporation rather than by outright replacement, has meant a considerable degree of shared physical and cultural ancestry among the peoples of the Sudd.

Twentieth-century Western perceptions of the peoples of the southern Sudan have been fixed in ethnographic space and time by Evans-Pritchard's classic 1940 work on the Nuer. This picture was to a large extent the product of the ecological and historical context at the time of his original study. In Southern Sudan as elsewhere, colonial indirect rule brought into being and/or crystallised ethnic and regional divisions. These were at best poor representations of the fluid and dynamic long-term processes of, and shifting relations between, peoples currently differentiated as Dinka, Shilluk, Anuak and Nuer, and more broadly as Nilotic pastoralist versus Arab (Kurita, 1994; Johnson, 2003). More recent anthropological and historical work focuses on the longer-term perspective, and differentiated experiences, of continuously changing ecological, social and political relations in response to factors both internal and external to the area (Johnson, 1982, 1988, 1991, 2003; Hutchinson, 1996; Kurimoto and Simonse, 1998; Markakis, 1993). Recent studies unpick the balance of forces which have driven the working and reworking of ethnicities and associated economic, cultural, social and political relations among the Nilotic peoples of this region, and in some cases pulled them back together (Kurimoto and Simonse, 1998; Markakis, 1993).

One of these many continuities is created by the generation and ageset systems widespread among Nilotic pastoralists (Kurimoto and Simonse, 1998). Nilotic ageset systems channel and spur conflict and confrontation, both within groups (as growing youths try to wrest power from older men) and between them (as those same youths prove themselves ritually, and acquire material wealth as the practical basis of power, by raiding rival neighbouring groups). Ageset systems at the same time embody institutions for conflict moderation and reconciliation, through the influence of elders. The shared terminology and synchrony of agesets across a region can provide a basis for common ground among neighbouring groups shifting between peaceful exchange, competition and conflict over contested resources. Ageset systems may have often in the past mediated an 'essentially balanced condition of "reciprocal raiding"' between rival local groups, involving neither heavy casualties nor total decisive victories, but keeping in view the possibility of negotiated solutions (Lamphear, 1994, 1998). Agesets offered the possibility of merging discrete units into wider regional political and often military associations. Alongside geopolitical tensions, increasing availability of modern weapons, and the emergence of individual military leaders, agesets laid the basis for an escalation to all-out modern warfare.

Sudan achieved Independence in the 1960s and since the 1980s has been locked into civil war, often seen as conflict between Arab Islamic North and black Christian South. Such simple dualisms do little justice to the complex roots of civil war in the Sudan (which can be traced back to long-established patterns of raiding and slaving on the periphery of the state in the early nineteenth century and before), nor to the nuances of interaction within and between different factions in the northern Sudanese government, among the Southern fighters, and among international groups with vested interests in Sudan's natural resources (Johnson, 2003). Conflict between the Ngok Dinka and Humr Baggara Arabs has involved the disenfranchisement of black southerners, and confiscation and armed robbery of their livestock, crops and material goods (Salih, 1993; Keen, 1995). Black agropastoralists have suffered enslavement and genocide, through violence and famine created by hostile neighbouring groups and militias armed and supported by the Sudanese national government (a situation now being re-enacted in Darfur). Rebel armies emerged among the peoples of the Sudd, as progressively more Dinka, Nuer, Pari, Huduk and other southern peoples were dispossessed, dispersed and destroyed. Despite internal dissension fuelled by the divisive tactics of the Sudanese government, and by donor governments' manipulation of rebel leadership changes (Johnson, 2003), the Sudanese People's Liberation Army (SPLA) emerged as the dominant southern force. Originally strongly identified with the Dinka, it has grown by merger and assimilation (e.g. Pari – Kurimoto, 1994), both fed and manipulated by Western support.

Despite the devastation, with mass displacements of people and profound disruption of production and economy, these Nilotic groups still see themselves largely as pastoralist and agropastoralist peoples. Nuer refugees, scattered north to Khartoum or driven from their former grazing, farming and fishing areas, nonetheless continue to express their aspirations and carry out their social transactions through livestock. Where possible, those livestock are known animals whose individual stories embody a whole history of alliances, marriages, friendships and settlements. Where necessary, social transactions take place through purchased animals – 'cattle of money'. Where not even that possibility remains, they are expressed and made valid through cash, termed 'money cattle' (Hutchinson, 1992, 1996).

Emergence of pastoralism in East Africa: Maasai and Turkana

The present section summarises the current state of knowledge on the emergence of pastoralism in East Africa (Robertshaw, 1990; Robertshaw and Marshall, 1990; Marshall, 1989, 1990, 1994, 2000). Here, all four ancestral strands of Sudanic, Afrasan (Cushitic), Niger-Congo (Bantu), and Khoisan traditions have come together in societies that range from the specialised pastoralism of the Maasai and Turkana, to the distinctive mixed farming and herding of the Great Lakes. Once the barrier presented by disease vector habitats was breached (Chapter 6; Gifford-Gonzalez, 2000), domestic stock spread into East Africa from the north, appearing in the archaeological record near Lake Turkana around 4000BP, with sheep and goats possibly as early as 5000BP in otherwise gatherer-hunter sites. The earliest sites represent a mixed economy, with herding alongside hunting and fishing (Lake Turkana GaJi sites – Marshall, 1990; Marshall et al., 1984), and in other cases farming sorghum and millet (Robertshaw and Collett, 1983a and b). The sequence of dates suggests a continuing southward spread of domestic stock down the Rift Valley and its associated highland areas. The people who pastured their sheep, goats and humpless long-horned cattle around Lake Turkana 4000 years ago, and fished and hunted there, included both Sudanic and Cushitic-speaking elements, and met and mixed there with Khoisan-speaking gatherers and hunters. The newcomers, with their food-producing economies, are thought to have spread by interaction and assimilation as much as by conquest and replacement. Some see south Cushitic speakers as dominating the Rift Valley grasslands and South-Central Kenya by 3000BP (Phillipson, 1985; Spear, 1993a). Meanwhile, Nilotes from a probable area of origin between Lake Turkana and the Ethiopian Highlands are thought to have differentiated into the River-Lake, Plains and Highlands linguistic subgroups between 4000BP and 2000BP. Southern (Highland) Nilotic-speakers farming sorghum and millet, herding and hunting spread southward west of the Rift Valley by 3000BP (Spear, 1993a:9)

Current thinking in East African archaeology sees specialised pastoralism arising as the product of emerging exchange relations between progressively more specialised farmers, pastoralists and hunters, against a background of common and easy movement between these groups (Marshall, 1990). The Pastoral Neolithic and Elmenteitan traditions both show specialised dependence on pastoralism by 3000BP, but display consistent differences in their material culture, with some sites suggesting the retention of a gatherer-hunter specialisation, or perhaps simply the traces of people who had lost their livestock. The Pastoral Neolithic sites lack signs of cultivation or of cultivated grains. Where querns indicate some use of cereals, their small size suggests that only small quantities were used. There is no indication of wild cereal use. Marshall (1989, 1990, 1994) developed this into a picture of specialised East African pastoralism, less dependent on cereals than most other forms of African pastoralism. Between 3000BP and 1500BP 'cultivation was certainly not a large-scale activity on any site yet found, and there is no evidence that wild plant foods were an important food source' (Marshall, 1994:33). Sites like Ngamuriak (ca.2000BP – Marshall, 1990) and Sambo Ngigi indicate that between 3000BP and 2000BP strongly specialised pastoralism emerged alongside high levels of exchange and intercommunication with equally specialised farming and hunting groups. At Ngamuriak, faunal remains indicate large cattle herds together with sheep and goats. Simple, lightly built huts, dung layers, an absence of plant remains and grindstones, and site location relative to water, grazing and gradient all resemble present-day specialised herding economies of pastoral Maasai, Samburu, and Borana (Marshall, 1990).

Sites with traces of domestic stock but no recovered grains, grinding equipment or wild faunal remains do not necessarily indicate 'pure' pastoralism. In South-west Africa, Kinahan (1991) has interpreted such sites in the context of neighbouring sites to suggest communities operating a network of herding, gathering and hunting activities, with each subsistence activity centred on a different set of resources and therefore spatially (and/or temporally) separated without being a separate community. Nonetheless, in East Africa the presence of present-day 'pure' pastoralists, their relation to specialised farming and hunting communities, the location and nature of archaeological sites and the materials they contain have been convincingly used to interpret sites like Ngamuriak as belonging to specialised pastoralist communities. The bimodal climate allows year-round milk production, as cattle have a greater chance of regaining condition, conceiving and calving each year than is the case in West Africa, and the calving period is staggered, spreading milk availability (Marshall, 1990, 1994). Pastoralists came to dominate the Rift Valley by 2000BP, stretching from the Indian Ocean to Lake Victoria and from the Kenya Highlands to central Tanzania (Marshall, 1994, 2000; Robertshaw, 1990; Phillipson, 1985). During the first millennium AD, Highland Nilotic speakers spreading through the Rift Valley absorbed the South Cushitic speakers that had preceded them, and established communities largely ancestral to the present-day Kalenjin-speaking Kipsigis, Nandi, Pokot, Sebei, Marakwet, Tugen and Datoga.

During this same period of the first millennium AD, the Plains Nilotes were differentiating into the linguistic ancestors of Maa- and of Karimojong-Teso speakers. At the same time, Eastern Cushitic-speakers, also combining herding with farming and hunting, spread into East Africa from Ethiopia (Spear, 1993a). Bantu-speaking peoples were also expanding into East Africa from the West and South-west, bringing with them new cultural values and subsistence practices centred on root crops and iron tools. By 1000AD most or all of the pastoral groups in East Africa had adopted iron implements (Sutton, 1993). From around 1000BP, Plains Nilotes linguistically ancestral to the present-day Maasai and other Maa-speaking groups spread southwards through Kenya, and between the sixteenth and nineteenth centuries came to dominate the Rift Valley from North Kenya to central Tanzania as far south as Dodoma. The history of interaction, assimilation, extinction and replacement among these various peoples in East Africa from 500BP to the present has become better known through the work of historians such as Waller (1979, 1985, 1988, 1990, 1993), and Lamphear (1992, 1993, 1994, 1998).

Present-day groups like the Maasai have emerged not by immigration as a ready-formed ethnic and economic entity, but by the blending of mingled and interacting strands, some already resident, others more recently arrived. Sirikwa communities came to occupy a geographical and ecological niche between 800BP and 400BP that anticipated the pastoral Maasai specialisation. They also contributed to Maasai physical ancestry and economic base when the invading Plains Nilotes established control over parts of the Sirikwa range in the eighteenth century. The bulk of the remaining Sirikwa communities gave rise to the Kalenjin-speaking peoples of the Western Highlands, but others were assimilated into Bantu groups and made a clear contribution to the language and social forms of agropastoral peoples like the Kurya (Sutton, 1993:46-7). Different groups currently recognised as discrete East African tribes – Maasai (Spear and Waller, 1993), Samburu, Turkana (Lamphear, 1993), and Rendille – cannot be traced back in time as separate and distinct entities. They are current manifestations of continuously evolving identities, with different subgroups and different combinations of cultural, linguistic and economic traits diverging and others merging, adopted, abandoned and reshaped for social, political and economic reasons.

The recent history of the Maasai has been described and analysed in detail (e.g. Anderson, 2002; Spear and Waller, 1993; Hodgson, 1999a and b, 2001); as has that of the Turkana (Lamphear, 1993, 1994, 1998). Both groups grew by the assimilation of recruits from a wide variety of neighbouring peoples, as did the Zulu and Xhosa in Southern Africa. In all these cases ageset systems provided both a spur and a framework for such integration to take place (Kurimoto and Simonse, 1998). The nineteenth century was a time of pastoralist military and political dominance across East African rangelands, as well as of internecine warfare between pastoralist groups contesting control of key pastoral resources. This changed at the end of the century with the devastation brought by rinderpest and the ensuing resurgence of trypano-somiasis (Ford, 1971; Waller, 1988, 1990) exacerbated by colonial military and economic interventions. The Turkana were caught between British and Ethiopian Empires, the Maasai between British and Germans. Overall, the advent of the twentieth century brought administrations that progressively drew up boundaries – national, regional and tribal, as well as demarcated areas reserved for wildlife and other state concerns – and put considerable effort into enforcing these on what had been highly mobile peoples and fluidly shifting ethnic and economic groupings (Homewood, 1995; Sobania, 1991), favouring some and undermining others (Anderson, 2002). The effect was to force people into defining themselves in new ways that carried major implications for their access to or exclusion from particular resources (Waller, 1988; Anderson, 2002). The present-day mosaic of sharply defined tribal groups and areas, which appears in such striking contrast to the far-flung scatter of Fulani or Tuareg peoples across the nations of West Africa, was called into being more as a result of colonial perceptions of East Africa's divided peoples, than as an accurate portrayal of long established boundaries. Superficially distinct ethnic groups are in large part a product of the colonial era, which tended to create separate identities and attempted to fix separate areas for their use (Kurita, 1994). The great variety of these pastoralist and agropastoralist groups is in part the product of a process of differentiation of which some branching tips have become extinct. Others emerge as new and distinct groups from ethnic and linguistic interactions between other peoples, such as the Ariaal from the Maa-speaking, cattle-keeping Samburu and the Cushitic-speaking, camel-keeping Rendille (Fratkin, 1991).

The more peripheral to the nation state, the more divided and fragmented between adjacent nations, the more marginalised the group subsequently became. Interactions with the colonial administration branded the Turkana as rebellious and violent, while the much smaller Jie group were armed by the government as allies in pacification raids against other pastoralists and profited from colonial delineation of formerly contested territory in their name (Kurimoto and Simonse, 1998). Similar contrasts influenced the historical trajectories of the different Maa-speaking groups (Anderson, 2002). All East African pastoralist groups lost access to major rangeland resources as land was taken for colonial settlers and wildlife conservation (Anderson, 2002; Rutten, 1992; Homewood, 1995; Igoe and Brockington, 1999; Shivji, 1998; Homewood et al., 2004). Pastoralist land use and livestock production were attacked as being environmentally unsound and unproductive. Pastoralist peoples, mobile and difficult to tax or service, with less ready access to schooling and ultimately jobs, gained little real political voice in much of colonial and postcolonial East Africa (but see Galaty, 1993; Galaty and Ole Munei, 1999; also Markakis, 1999), a situation widespread today (Homewood et al., 2001; Igoe and Brockington, 1999; Chapters 5 and 9).

As the twenty-first century begins, Maasai and Turkana, among other East African pastoralists, and in common with rural livelihoods across Africa, continue their age-old pattern of dynamic shifts into and out of pastoralism, with progressive diversification of livelihoods into farming, wildlife tourism and other non-farm enterprises (Chapter 9; Thompson and Homewood, 2002; Homewood et al., forthcoming). Alongside this, a silent and accelerating process sees the poor and very poor becoming not merely stockless but landless, rural squatters, drifting into urban slums or relief camps (van den Boogard, 2002; Brockington, 2002 and 2001a). Nonetheless, livestock remain central to Maasai and Turkana social and linguistic idioms (*Ewoloto* – Potkanski, 1999; Turkana – Broch-Due, 1999) and, where people have the choice, to their economic strategies (Homewood et al., forthcoming, Thompson and Homewood, 2002). Despite enduring similarities, contrasts are developing between Maasai under different national political and economic systems. Those occupying land now subdivided into privately held plots (as on Kenya's former Group Ranches – Rutten, 1992) have very different options from those on land belonging to the state or to the wider 'village' association (as is the case in Tanzania). Elsewhere in East Africa, groups like the Kuria retain the raiding ethos of an earlier age alongside their agropastoralist economy (Fleischer, 1999).

People of the Great Lakes: Tuutsi and Hutu

Between the first millennium BC and the first millennium AD, as specialised pastoralism was becoming established in other parts of East Africa, a particular conjunction of farming and herding traditions came together in the fertile region between the western shores of Lake Victoria and the Lakes of the western Rift. It gave rise to powerful, politically sophisticated states, and contributed to the present-day relations between peoples now labelled Twa, Hima, Tuutsi and Hutu (Ehret, 1998; Schoenbrun, 1998).

The Great Lakes region sits at the juncture of present-day south-west Uganda, north-west Tanzania, eastern Rwanda and eastern Burundi. It comprises the lands between Lake Victoria to the east, Lake Kivu to the west, the Victoria Nile to the north, and the Malagarasi River and Lake Tanganyika to the south and south-west. This region encompasses a tremendous diversity of landforms and ecoclimatic conditions, from afroalpine zones through montane and lowland forest to dry savanna grasslands, to well watered, fertile lakeshore, swamp and riverine lands. Pollen studies suggest that before the first millennium BC much of this region was forested. Archaeological as well as linguistic work suggests that there was a wide, sparse scatter of small settlements of Khoisan-speaking gathering, hunting and fishing peoples. The first food producers settled in the western parts of the Great Lakes region over 3000 years ago, and included different food-producing traditions seeking correspondingly different combinations of rainfall, soils and vegetation.

Bantu cultivators of root crops, fishers, and early users of iron technology moved into the Great Lakes region from the west. Nilotic and South Cushitic speakers from the north and north-east brought different forms of livestock-keeping and millet and sorghum cultivation. From 3000BP, the Bantu used their iron implements to clear farmland from forest, and to till the heavy soils of the bottomlands. Ironworkers contributed to forest clearance through charcoal-based smelting. Livestock-keepers spread, as farmers cleared not only the woody vegetation and tall grasses of lakeshore and riverbank, but also, with them, the vectors of lethal livestock diseases. Areas of 'wilderness' woodland, often left on poorer soils with limited water, retained vector populations and created the conditions for controlled exposure of stock to disease challenge and building and maintaining immunity (Chapters 3 and 6).

What are taken as separate ethnic groups in the present day do not represent any simple lines of descent from any of these past individual traditions. Great Lakes Bantu had integrated secondary cattle products (milk and blood) into their food systems by 500BC. By 1000AD their expansion had largely assimilated Cushitic, Sahelian and Sudanic societies, and Bantu languages came to dominate the Great Lakes area, retaining many loan words from the other linguistic traditions. During the period 300-800AD, characteristic features of more recent Great Lakes peoples were already forming, with densely settled lakeshore and riverine societies using root crops and fish, interlinked with more mobile pastoral societies. Contrary to widespread myths of origin, which cast Hima and Tuutsi as pastoralist incomers arriving from the north-east since the fifteenth century, linguistics and comparative ethnography suggest that they are not different ethnicities but rather new specialisations or castes within the overall regional synthesis of fishing, root cropping, and goat, cattle and cereal production. These seemingly distinct peoples, each with characteristic food-producing systems, all speak the same languages, share the same clan systems and derive from a complex but strongly local process of synthesis and evolution.

From 800AD on, there was a progressive specialisation as livestock-keeping, cereal-cultivating societies expanded from lakeshore, riverine and montane areas into the drier central savannas. According to the Nile river-level records, the region experienced very dry periods between 950 and 1100AD and again between 1200 and 1450AD. During these periods livestock-keeping expanded in the central Great Lakes savannas, strongly tied into the political spheres of new large settlements that appeared in these savanna zones. The proliferation of local terminology for cattle colours and horn shapes and specifically for Ankole cattle between 1000 and 1500AD bears out this explosion of pastoralism. From an early date, cattle provided both a high-yielding form of production which allowed accumulation, and the basis of stock friendship networks. They also provided a form of moveable wealth, allowing patron/client relations to be established through cattle gifts. In due course these strong social relations, and the strong inequalities they signified, could be extended over far greater areas than could land-based systems.

Clientage based on gifts of cattle developed in the fourteenth and fifteenth centuries and formed the basis for the emergence of Great Lakes states and kingships. As these expanded, they increasingly competed for productive lands, both with 'firstcomer' peoples already using those lands, and in due course with each other, spurring the emergence of military structures to expand and defend their territories. Great Lakes social organisation, institutions and political systems of kingship and nobility emerged on the basis of ownership, control and deployment of cattle. Powerful healers and mediums also emerged, as the moral economy of gift-giving and the hierarchical relations this established triggered counterbalancing ideas of the moral and spiritual position of firstcomers to the land. Firstcomers were incorporated into the political system either as titled owners of the land, as holders of ritual and spiritual roles, or in some cases (as in the emergent Tuutsi-led Rwandan state from the fifteenth century on), as acknowledged, but dispossessed, firstcomer Twa. Parallel analyses trace the evolution of gender relations in Great Lakes states, as increasingly patriarchal control of cattle (and of women's sexuality) led women to develop alternative pathways of power and control through their sons and as spirit mediums.

In the Rwanda, Burundi, Nkore and Bunyoro kingships, not all royal clans are pastoralist, nor are all pastoralists royal, but all royal groups display pastoral symbols (Bonte, 1991). Thus 'pastoralist identity and material culture were grafted onto the deep roots of chiefship and royalty' (Schoenbrun, 1998: 232). As these hierarchies emerged, social relations shifted. Where any one individual would earlier have farmed, herded and hunted, after the fifteenth century we see the appearance of 'what are today the hierarchical ethnic categories named *batúá, bahutu* and *batuutsi*...to the east and north, *baírù* is used instead of *bahutu* for "farmer", and *bahima* instead of *batuutsi* for "herder"' (Schoenbrun, 1998: 155-6). Great Lakes pastoralism is not so much a distinct ethnic or cultural tradition, as one facet of a wider mixed farming regional economy, in the context of a politically highly stratified society where the ruling elites adopted or emphasised pastoral symbols as an expression of their status. European travellers in the mid to late nineteenth century (Speke, Grant and Stuhlmann) gave accounts of this mixed farming and of the huge herds of longhorn humpless Ankole cattle belonging to various kings.

In the 1890s, the region was devastated and herds destroyed by rinderpest (Chapters 3 and 6). Raiding and counter-raiding intensified as Hima and Tuutsi sought to rebuild their cattle holdings, and the farmers suffered. Cattle plague and famine left human and livestock populations open to new epidemics, bringing depopulation and collapse of the complex symbioses between herder and farmer, and also of 'ecological control' (Ford, 1971; Kjekshus, 1977). Without intensive grazing, burning, clearing and cultivation, woody vegetation spread back across much of the area and, with it, trypanosomiasis vectors. There were repeated epidemics of trypanosomiasis in the Great Lakes region in the first half of the twentieth century, driving herders to move away with their animals, disrupting the ecological controls of burning, grazing, manuring and waterhole maintenance, and the centuries-old social and political dominance of Hima and Tuutsi. Long-established social inequalities and emergent ethnic identities were accentuated by colonial administrations: for example, in Rwanda the Belgian administration turned a Tuutsi majority elite into a solely Tuutsi elite. Rwanda and Burundi emerged at Independence as Hutu majority and Tuutsi minority-led states respectively. Since Independence repeated violent and at times genocidal conflict has erupted between what are now seen as distinct ethnic identities of Hutu and Tuutsi, with Twa repeatedly drawn into the violence.

The diverse and productive Great Lakes mixed farming systems persist, overlaid by forced migration, refugee populations and international interventions, in a region shattered by recent genocide. Small numbers of Hima graze their Ankole cattle in Lake Mburo National Park, Uganda, relics of the Great Lakes pastoralist tradition (Hulme and Infield, 2001).

Emergence of pastoralism in Southern Africa

Our understanding of the emergence and spread of pastoralism and agro-pastoralism in southern Africa, of the interactions of these economies with gathering, hunting and trading, and of the foundations for recent and present-day ethnic and economic patterns of livestock-keeping in southern Africa, builds on anthropological perspectives on the relations of production, as well as archaeological evidence for means of production, together with ethnographic and linguistic evidence (Lewis Williams, 1981; Kinahan, 1991; Hall, 1990; Wilmsen, 1989; but see Smith, 2000: 233). Early sites suggest there were pastoralists in widely separate areas of southern Africa by 2000BP (Smith, 2000: 225-6). These include Mirabib in Namibia (sheep and pottery from the fourth century – Kinahan, 1991) and Lotshitshi on the edge of the Okavango in Botswana (cattle remains from before 300AD). Much of the pastoral vocabulary used by southern African Bantu groups is derived via Khoekhoe languages, and Wilmsen sees these early pastoralists as closely related to the ancestors of modern Khoisan-speaking peoples (Wilmsen, 1989). The following account puts together an overview based on material for east and south-eastern (Hall, 1990), central (Wilmsen, 1989), southern (Smith, 2000; Jacobs, 2003), west and south-western parts of southern Africa (Kinahan, 1991).

Disease vectors and their habitats are again likely to have stalled the spread of livestock, especially cattle, from East into South-east and southern Africa (Gifford-Gonzalez, 2000). In the Eastern half of southern Africa, agropastoralist communities appeared in the first centuries of the first millennium AD. By the second half of the first millennium archaeological sites reveal patterns of social differentiation associated with state formation. These sites show not only a broad economic reliance on domestic stock as well as grain, but also established trade. From the modest beginnings of the Toutswe ceramic tradition (ca. 700AD) they go on to yield precious objects of glass, metal, and cloth originally brought from the East coast, where Muslim traders exchanged goods from all around the Indian Ocean for ivory and gold. Some sites of the interior show internal differentiation of types, styles and sizes of buildings, best interpreted in terms of differentiation between high and low status, rich and poor, secular and sacred, noble and commoner. Satellite towns show less differentiation, with fewer and less exclusive trade goods, and themselves are surrounded by satellite settlements of small, informal, perhaps temporary cattle camps and farms. They are interpreted as bound together in a two-way flow of tribute (cattle, labour, grain, locally produced salt or gold) passing to the centre of power, and prestige goods being distributed back to local chiefs in return. Centres of power could only maintain their position and the lifestyle of their ruling elite with a continued supply of exclusive prestige items, obtained by trading surplus extracted from rural subjects. Sites like Mapungubwe and Toutswemogala emerged in the tenth-eleventh centuries and lasted around 400 years, with the trading network on which Mapungubwe depended being captured by Great Zimbabwe between the eleventh and sixteenth centuries (Hall, 1990; Beach, 1994). These differentiated societies declined and disappeared by 1300AD, due to environmental, economic, and/or sociopolitical reasons.

Further west, such as in the eastern Botswana site of Matlapaneng, there is little evidence of far-flung trade. In these areas, Khoisan-speaking foragers and pastoroforagers seem to have been absorbed into the hierarchical organisation developed by Bantu-speaking cultures. Tswana placenames acknowledge prior land ownership by herding Khoisan. The smaller, relatively transient, and informal cattle camps, with their remains of game and stone tools alongside domestic stock, suggest the economically subordinate position of pastoroforagers within the centralised structure of these agropastoralist and trading societies, without implying any correlation of physical ancestry and economic role (Wilmsen, 1989).

Socially differentiated states such as Mapungubwe, Great Zimbabwe and later Mutapa rose initially on the basis of cattle production within a successful agropastoralist production system which allowed accumulation of surplus, and later on the control of trade by emerging elites in exotic and prestige gold, ivory and other goods as well as cattle. The evolution of various forms of military organisation made it possible for elites to enforce social and economic control. While prestige goods obtained through trade were a vital part of maintaining the structure of these societies, livestock were the basic currency of social transactions. In particular, cattle became central to the everyday network of alliances that underpinned social, political and economic life for the commoner as well as the noble in Bantu-speaking societies such as the Shona and Tswana groups, including, for example, the most basic and universal transaction of wives for cattle (Kuper, 1982). The Bantu-speaking pastoralist and agropastoralist societies that came to dominate east and south-eastern parts of southern Africa by the nineteenth century all emerged from variants of this same pattern of social, political and economic structures. The next section describes the emergence of the pastoralism-based Tswana polities that came to form the core of present-day Botswana, though these are no longer primarily pastoralist societies (Wilmsen, 1989). Subsequent sections briefly outline the emergence of pastoralist, agropastoralist and expansionist Xhosa and Zulu military states of Southern Africa as well as the pastoroforagers of South-west Africa.

Tswana. By the mid-eighteenth century small Tswana-speaking groups of 100 or so families, herders of goats and/or cattle, established themselves on the margins of the Kalahari. The Zulu *mfecane* of the 1820s set off ripples of conquered and displaced groups who in turn raided and displaced further communities as far as west of Lake Ngami in present-day Botswana. Here Tswana and Herero groups fought for grazing rights, and Ndebele raided Kalahari and Okavango peoples for over fifty years in the mid-nineteenth century. South of the Kalahari, Tswana-speaking groups grew by incorporating refugees from the *mfecane* and from Boer raids. In the first half of the nineteenth century various Tswana groups developed the *kgamelo* (milk jug) system. This used a highly stratified class ranking, political structure and the *mafisa* system of clientage through cattle loans to contain and manage a rapid population increase (Hitchcock, 1990). In the 1830s these groups comprised a few hundred people each, but by the 1860s they had grown to tens of thousands, moving rapidly from a peripheral position to complete dominance. In the process cattle and other tribute (ivory and other valuable trade products of hunting and gathering) were expropriated from the San and Bakgalagadi peoples of the Okavango and Kalahari. The dispossessed mostly became landless serfs, although occasional individuals were incorporated into the middle ranks of the Tswana social order. Other groups, like the Pedi, were brought under the control of Tswana-speaking groups without being reduced to the status of serfs, and between 1850 and 1900 the different Tswana-speaking groups consolidated as a loose federation of states.

Botswana has developed a highly successful commercial and export-oriented economy which looks superficially less like indigenous pastoralism than Western commercial ranching, with fenced private grazing and watering points, and intensive veterinary and marketing systems. Within this national structure large commercial ranching concerns operate alongside small herdowners (Behnke, 1985). Less well-off livestock owners employ Khoi-speaking (San or Bakgalagadi) herders, while they themselves pursue the more lucrative option of labour migration to South Africa, resulting in a spatially and socially very stratified system. Much land is privately owned by the elite, tracing their privileged position directly back to the nineteenth-century social order. Less well-off Tswana keep their animals on communal land, which is also used by large operators during good grazing conditions. In the dry season, the large operators can retreat to privately owned ranches and maintain their livestock's condition. At the lowest level, silent but institutionalised discrimination ensures that most San/ Bakgalagadi have neither land rights nor rights to animals (Hitchcock, 1996), despite strong evidence that these groups, often stereotyped as archetypal hunter-gatherers, had been established pastoralists (Wilmsen, 1989; Hitchcock, 1990).

The Ngamiland San had been pastoroforagers, herding livestock and hunting for ivory and other specialist products, with thriving trade networks lasting into the nineteenth century, when they came under increasingly extractive demands. Their herds were expropriated, the ivory was hunted out, the feather trade collapsed (see below). By the 1890s the basis of the Kalahari economy had collapsed. From the 1890s it re-emerged as a cattle economy, under the spur of the *kgamelo* restructuring of grazing systems by successive Tswana leaders. Dispossessed San-speakers became a secondary labour pool, forced into competition for menial herding work. Those who failed to take such work were driven deep into the most inaccessible and marginal parts of the Kalahari as marginal gatherer-hunters (whence the current government is now forcibly evicting them in the name of conservation). By the 1930s most San-speakers were below the poverty level of the Tswana rural poor, and San-speakers who built up livestock holdings had them confiscated (Hitchcock, 1996).

Pastoralist history in South Africa: Xhosa and Zulu. The Xhosa and Zulu federations emerged in the wake of penetration of the interior by Portuguese adventurers. Portuguese settlers had a particularly marked impact in disrupting prior patterns of control, both political and economic, and in making widespread the practice of slavery as a basis of local economic and military strength as well as of trade to overseas plantations (Hall, 1990). Some societies like the Mutapa were able to recover from the initial Portuguese impact: others like the Tonga were driven into a marginal, defensive and ultimately untenable lifestyle. Loose networks of relatively small chiefdoms were taken over by Portuguese, or alternatively came progressively under the sway of lineages commanding special wealth and power by virtue of position, trade relations, and access to foreign mercenaries and weapons, sometimes against pressure from Portuguese-led private slave-recruit armies.

Both the Xhosa and the Zulu groups grew mainly by incorporating other groups, including Khoikhoi pastoralists. These groups represent a mixture of physical ancestries, and their cultural identities reflect that mingling. The Xhosa emerged as the amaTshawe followers of the seventeenth-century leader Tshawe, and accepted into their society any who followed this leadership. Their loose federation of chiefdoms moulded effective armies from military agesets. They maintained their agropastoral economic base alongside relatively long-lived trading relations with settlers across the East Cape frontier. In the nineteenth century, however, increasing pressure from the expanding white economy and state control made the Xhosa vulnerable to pressures from within. Peires (1989) has described how the emergence of local prophets led to a mass sacrifice of Xhosa livestock in expectation of spiritual and economic salvation. In the present day, livestock retain strong social as well as economic significance in a group whose economy has centred for some time on migrant labour, remittances and pensions (Ainslie, 2005).

By contrast, the Zulu kings emerged from a similar loose federation of relatively small chiefdoms through adroit political manoeuvring and military innovation, building large armies organised from slave recruits and ageset regiments. The disruption of Zulu trade by conflicts between the French and the Portuguese in the late eighteenth century set off a military and political expansion by Shaka, overrunning neighbouring chiefdoms and beyond. The Zulu armies enlisted men from conquered communities, and took the women as wives. The weakness of the Zulu expansion lay in their tendency to fragment. Mzilikazi broke away, leading two Zulu regiments north into Zimbabwe, where they settled in around 1840 and grew by raiding to form the founders of the present-day Ndebele peoples. Ripples from the *mfecane* reached as far north as Tanzania, where the present-day Ngoni people trace a Zulu descent. From the middle of the nineteenth century on, as thousands of Voortrekker families moved inland, conflicts intensified in a way that the Zulu were ill-prepared to combat. Settler commandos with firearms raided settlements, took cattle, and captured people. The dependence of the pioneers on Zulu labour, and the high rate of deaths and desertions, perpetuated the process. In the 1860s the discovery of major gold and diamond deposits brought a rapid change, with swift industrialisation and spectacular growth of the white economy at the expense of underdevelopment of the black populations. Despite all the ensuing transformations, the cattle economy continues up to the present day. MacKinnon (1999) traces its persistence and even growth in the face of state constraints on Zulu food and cash-crop production. She documents the continued cultural importance of cattle as social and legal currency, and their role in a migrant-labour remittance economy, under segregation. She also documents the role of state and capital in driving economic differentiation with cattle through the high bridewealth set by patriarchs, chiefs and royals in collaboration with white business associates.

South-west Africa: Damara, Herero and San

Botswana sites west of the Okavango suggest earlier pastoralist occupation, and a pattern rather different from that of East and South-east southern Africa (Wilmsen, 1989). There seems to have been a southward drift of Bantu-speakers into the northern fringes of arid southern Africa, but whereas in the East and South-east strongly differentiated societies emerge over the second half of the first millennium AD, in the West there is no evidence of centralisation or of economic or social dominance by Bantu-speaking peoples until the mid-nineteenth century. Rather, there is evidence of a Khoisan-speaking agropastoralist economy with some relations to small-stock holding, iron-working Bantu horticulturalists. Linguistics and archaeology, backed up by palynological studies of climatic and vegetation changes (Maley, 2001) suggest that proto-Herero-speaking Bantu people moved south through savanna corridors which opened up at the time of maximum forest retreat in 2500BP. They entered the arid western part of southern Africa around 2000BP, and acquired both domestic animals and the vocabulary of pastoralism from the Khoisan-speaking pastoralists there (Wilmsen, 1989; Maley, 2001; Smith, 2000). Rather than local gathering and hunting peoples being replaced by the arrival of a new ethnic group of pastoralists (such as Herero), the Hungarob site in Namibia may demonstrate a single technological tradition changing slowly over 4000 years by *in situ* innovation, not through ethnic succession but as a result of the progressive acquisition of livestock (Kinahan, 1991). This took place around 1500BP or earlier, and came eventually to transform social relations into a more socially differentiated, less egalitarian pastoralist community by the start of the present millennium (Kinahan, 1991). Despite the transformation of social relations brought about by accumulation of livestock within pastoroforager communities, and despite some evidence of coast-to-coast trade (e.g. of shell ornaments found far inland in Western Botswana), and local exchange of resources (e.g. fish), there is no sign of the centralised hierarchies which emerged in the East on the basis of trade (Wilmsen, 1989; Kinahan, 1991).

The Kalahari was the watershed of the Eastern and Western areas of influence. Cattle, small stock, millet and sorghum were used alongside gathered products in Nqoma and Tsodilo, on the fringes of the Okavango. Artefacts and ornaments demonstrate trade with the East coast by the ninth century, probably in exchange for gathered wild resources of gums, pigments, ivory, ostrich feathers, aromatic woods and dyes (Wilmsen, 1989). The people of Nqoma-Tsodilo and elsewhere in the Kalahari may have traded independently to begin with. However, some contemporary sites, like Matlapaneng, appear already tied into eastern hierarchical structures. From the eleventh century, trade from these sites seems to have been captured by the emerging states of Mapungubwe and later Great Zimbabwe and Khami. Thus Western Kalahari salt, ivory and cattle, and later ostrich feathers, came to feed into the Eastern hierarchies, and the interior became a subsidiary partner and producer rather than receiver of wealth. These items formed the basis of a trade network which became established between the eleventh and nineteenth centuries. In the nineteenth century Western 'explorers' and missionaries followed alternative routes connecting Lake Ngami with the Cape and the East coast.

The first direct trade between Europeans and Khoi-speaking pastoralists on the South-west coast in present-day Namibia began from the eighteenth century on (Kinahan, 1991). The growth of European trading points on the Atlantic coast rapidly depleted Khoisan pastoralist herds in exchange for goods contributing little or nothing to the basis of production. European incursions led to trading being replaced by raiding. As in North East Africa and the Horn, where modern weapons enter the scene, a long history of balanced reciprocal raiding and trading is radically changed. Khoi-speaking Nama people from the Cape (Oorlams) were equipped with guns, horses and oxwagons from their long contact with Cape settlers. In the nineteenth century, they began to raid cattle from the people of the hinterland, preying on other less well-equipped Nama communities, as well as on Damara, Herero and San pastoralists. The people furthest from the trade routes were the last to acquire guns and horses. These Khoisan-speaking 'Bushmen', Bakgalagadi and Herero people, were at a disadvantage, lacking weapons and losing control of outlets for their products and sources of supplies.

The colonial period brought devastating conflict and repression. The Herero (and Herero-speaking Ovambanderu) lost much of their land and were left hemmed in by Ovambo, Oorlams and Tswana groups in Ngamiland. In the mid-1890s, the German military government of South-west Africa set out to destroy the Herero leadership in northern Namibia and break their economy. 12,000 head of cattle were confiscated in 1896-7. With further losses to the great rinderpest epidemic, itinerant traders confiscated remaining cattle in payment of debts. By the turn of the century the Herero had few cattle left and were on the way to becoming the wage-labour force desired by the colonial economies. In 1904 the Germans launched a war of extermination, killing Herero, San, Damara and eventually Nama, irrespective of involvement. Intra-group conflicts were fiercely exacerbated by this attack. Most Herero fled to Ngamiland in Botswana, where after decades of apparent demographic stagnation they have re-established both herds and human populations, secured a strong position in the Botswana economy, and developed a strongly distinctive culture (Pennington and Harpending, 1997). Throughout the twentieth century, much Namibian rangeland was allocated to settlers from South Africa. In the present day, Damara agro-pastoroforagers continue to rely on natural resources both as gathered wild produce and to pasture their livestock, and interact in complex ways with the new independent state of Namibia promoting 'community-based' wildlife tourist enterprises (Sullivan, 1996a, 2001).

3

Pastoralist Environments, Constraints & Strategies

This chapter looks at four main issues. Firstly it explores the main character-istics of the biophysical environments used by pastoralist systems. It then goes on to review equilibrium thinking and the disequilibrium debate, which structure competing models of the dynamics of pastoralist systems, and alternative implications for their resilience. Thirdly, it reviews the main social and political dimensions interacting with biophysical factors to shape present-day pastoralist resource use and livestock management, including the ways environmental discourse has formed part of state interventions seeking to re-shape pastoralist systems and societies. Finally, it looks at mobility and trans-humance as core pastoralist strategies in dealing with shifting biophysical and social environments, and sets out a broad economic typology of pastoralist systems.

Biophysical environments

Pastoralist communities arguably show a close correlation with certain types of biophysical environment and come under more direct constraints as a result of their environments than do many other societies. Environment does not determine culture, but features of the environment – climate, topography, soils, drainage, vegetation, fauna and disease organisms – all set up constraints and opportunities that pastoralist societies have found ways to overcome and exploit. The livestock central to their strategies are directly affected by the biophysical environment, and these effects resonate through the social, economic and political systems for which livestock constitute an enduring idiom.

The great majority of Africa's pastoralist peoples inhabit arid and semi-arid areas (see map in colour section). It is by no means a perfect correlation, but it is still a meaningful one, with major practical implications. The association is produced partly by ecological factors. Arid and semi-arid areas have unpredictable rainfall and rain-fed crops risk failure. In these areas livestock become of enormous importance to subsistence, because they can be moved about to exploit natural vegetation growth wherever rain has fallen, and can turn sparse, patchy and transient primary production into milk and meat for human food. The very arid areas of the Sahara, the Sudan, Egypt and the Horn as well as Namibia are all home to pastoralist groups, however thinly scattered.

The main forest belt of Cameroon, Central African Republic, Congo, and DRC, as well as the miombo (*Brachystegia* species) and mopane (*Colophospermum* species) woodlands of East and South-East Africa, have comparatively fewer pastoralist communities. Humid areas with forest or dense woodland allow the tsetse vector of trypanosomiasis to breed, and few livestock are sufficiently resistant to withstand heavy tsetse challenge without intensive protection. Such areas are avoided, other than for seasonal use of their fringes during periods of reduced disease risk. Some pastoralist communities inhabit humid areas of moist forest or forest-grassland mosaic, where the risk of trypanosomiasis and other vector-borne diseases is dealt with using effective prophylactic drugs and insecticides (Boutrais, 1988) or because the area is high and the climate sufficiently cool to limit disease vectors (like the Adamawa Plateau used by WoDaaBe Fulani in Cameroon – Boutrais, 1986). However, cool moist tropical montane environments are also among the most productive areas for farming. Where pastoralist communities have become politically marginalised they have tended to lose control of high-potential areas of this type, as happened in Kenya in the early twentieth century (Anderson, 2002; Spear and Waller, 1993). In other cases such high-potential patches are settled and farmed by people with strong links to pastoralism. Wa'Arusha of Northern Tanzania farm well-watered mountain slopes, not so much as a coping strategy adopted by impoverished pastoralists, but as a deliberate move to exploit the benefits of farming and of trade while retaining cultural and economic links with pastoral Maasai (Spear and Waller, 1993; Spear, 1997). Social, political and historical as well as ecological factors underpin links between pastoralism and arid/semi-arid areas.

Jahnke (1982) defined 'Tropical Africa' as Africa south of the Sahara, excluding South Africa. Based on FAO estimates, he classified 37% of this land area as arid, with an estimated 30% of all tropical livestock units (TLUs); 18% is semi-arid, and carried 27% of TLUs. So, taken together, arid and semi-arid zones accounted for an estimated 55% of that land area but carried more than 50% of cattle and more than 60% of sheep and goats. The population density of these areas has grown rapidly over the last decades (Raynault, 1997) as have the numbers of livestock and the area of land under cultivation (Bourn and Wint, 1994; Bourn et al., 2001). There are major problems in measuring production in pastoral zones (see below, and Chapter 6), but FAO estimates suggest that over 40% of milk produced in 'Tropical Africa' is produced in the arid zone alone, and over 50% of meat in arid and semi-arid zones. These are by definition the areas of least productive potential, suggesting a striking association of livestock production with arid and semi-arid areas. Most of these livestock are associated with local production systems rather than Western-style ranching concerns (Galaty and Johnson, 1990b; see also Jahnke, 1982; Raikes, 1985; Sandford, 1983).

Arid and semi-arid climates

Rainfall and seasonality. As far as most arid and semi-arid land production systems are concerned, rainfall is the main limiting climatic factor. Rainfall is of primary importance for pastoralists because of the new plant growth it supports and also the temporary availability of surface water it creates. Tropical African environments tend to have a 'summer' rainfall regime largely associated with the Inter-Tropical Convergence Zone (ITCZ). This is a low pressure zone produced by the heating effect of the overhead sun, which causes warm air to rise and the trade winds to be drawn in from north and south. Where those winds travel across relatively warm bodies of water they pick up moisture. When the air meets in the ITCZ, it is warmed and rises; as it does so, it cools again and the moisture falls as rain. The sun is directly overhead at the Equator twice a year, at the Equinoxes. The ITCZ follows the overhead sun with a lag of a few weeks, and the Equinoxes are followed by rainy periods on the Equator. Equatorial rangeland areas like South and Central Kenya thus have a bimodal pattern with two rainy seasons a year. The further from the Equator, the shorter the gap between the periods when the sun is overhead, and the two wet seasons gradually merge into a single short rains at the Tropics of Cancer and Capricorn. The ITCZ thus to a great extent regulates the seasonal pattern of rainfall in different rangeland areas, whether it is bimodal or unimodal, and also how wet or conversely arid an area will be.

The ITCZ dictates the arid and strongly seasonal climate of the Sahel, with a single brief summer rainy season and a long (9-month or more) dry season, as it does the relatively more favourable bimodal rains regime of Maasailand. Africa's most arid deserts, the Sahara and the Namib deserts, lie along the northern and southern Tropics, at the extreme ends of the ITCZ's range of influence. In many pastoralist systems, cycles of movement have long operated on the basis of exploiting this latitudinal variation in rainfall. For example, Kel Denneg Tuareg customarily moved between wet-season pastures in the arid, mineral-rich, brief-flushing pastures of the Sahara, and dry-season ranges in the south, where their stock grazed crop residues and the wetter, coarser, less nutritive pastures in the farming zone (Bernus, 1981).

The impact of the ITCZ is modified in a number of ways by broader atmospheric circulation patterns and by local conditions. The northern part of the Horn is partly affected by the Mediterranean climate system which it borders. East Africa as a whole is drier than would be expected from its equatorial position, because the strong heating effect of the Himalayan land mass captures for the Indian monsoon system moisture-laden winds that would otherwise bring rain to East Africa. Also, winds from the north-east crossing the arid lands of the Horn and the Arabian peninsula bring little or no rain. Local topography also modifies the general pattern established by the ITCZ. For example, the East African mountains trap orographic rainfall from the

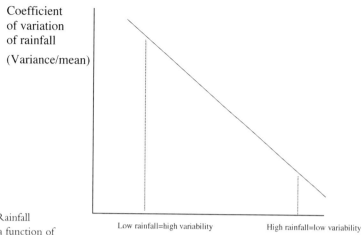

Coefficient
of variation
of rainfall
(Variance/mean)

Low rainfall=high variability

High rainfall=low variability

Mean annual rainfall

Figure 3.1 Rainfall
variability as a function of
aridity

prevailing winds, leaving dry rainshadow areas (e.g. eastern Serengeti, Mkomazi, Rift Valley). Lake Victoria creates its own weather patterns: warm moist air rises from the Lake, cools as it moves away, and falls as rain on surrounding uplands (Jackson, 1977:30). Similar effects prevail around much smaller bodies of water (e.g. Lake Baringo (Sutherland et al., 1991). These local and regional effects mean that areas such as Turkana in North Kenya, where one would expect a bimodal rainfall pattern, may show a single rainy season associated with one of the periods of overhead sun. Finally, global climatic changes affect the ITCZ. With shifts in global temperatures, and changes in the extent of the ice cap and thus in the contrast between Northern and Southern hemisphere temperatures, the ITCZ has in the past lain far from its present position. Its movement north during the Holocene made the Sahara and Central and Eastern Sudan a relatively moist and favourable environment for human settlement around 8000BP (Nicholson and Flohn, 1980; Prentice and Jolly, 2000). Its return to its present-day position brought aridity to the Sahara and Western Desert of Egypt (Sincell, 1999), a bimodal climate to East Africa, and perhaps set off the development of specialised East African pastoralism (Marshall, 1990, 1994, 2000).

Aridity, unpredictability and productive potential. The lower the mean annual rainfall, the greater the variability and unpredictability of that rainfall in space and time (see Fig 3.1; Le Houérou, 1989: 46). Thus the more arid the area, the less predictable the timing and location of rain. Tropical rain in such areas falls along storm tracks perhaps 10km broad, and sites 20km apart may show no correlation in their day-to-day rainfall totals. There can also be considerable variation between years as to the onset and timing of rainfall through the year.

The main determinant of forage growth in arid and semi-arid environments is simply plant-available moisture, but this is not easy to measure direct. Water

Table 3.1 Comparative scheme of eco-climatic classifications

Annual rainfall (mm)	West Africa		Combined classification			East Africa
	Aubréville, 1949	Keay, 1959	West/East equivalence	Jahnke, 1982	Growing days	Pratt and Gwynne, 1977
100	Saharian	Desert			0- < 90	Desert
200				Arid		Very arid
300	Saharo-Sahelian	Sahel				
400						Arid
500						
600						
700	Sahelo-Sudanian	Sudan				Semi-arid
800						
900				Semi-arid	90-<180	
1000						
1100	Sudano-Guinean	Northern Guinea				Dry sub-humid to semi arid
1200						
1300		Southern Guinea				
1400				Sub-humid	180-<270	
1500	Guinean-forest					
1600		Derived savanna				Humid to dry sub-humid
1700						
1800		Rainforest				

Source: After Jahnke (1982:17)

availability is not defined only in terms of rainfall totals. As well as total amount, distribution, run-off, run-on and evaporation day by day and month by month are all important components of plant-available moisture. Temperature is primarily important in that it creates the conditions for evaporation, whether direct or via plants as evapotranspiration. Various indices of climatic aridity attempt to combine rainfall totals, distribution, temperature and/or evaporation to give some meaningful index of conditions relevant to plants and animals. All illustrate the same continuum from arid to humid, but tend to divide the range up in slightly different ways.

Table 3.1, simplified from Jahnke, 1982, gives a basis for comparison between the different schemes that occur in the literature. Perhaps the most useful scale with respect to any production system is the system of 'growing days' – the number of days on which there is sufficient moisture available to support plant growth (<90 growing days = arid, 90-180 growing days = semi-arid). Data are more commonly available to explore the relationship between rainfall and primary production for individual African rangeland systems (e.g. Serengeti – McNaughton, 1985; Braun, 1971, 1973; Sinclair, 1975; Sinclair and Arcese, 1995; East and Southern African grasslands – Deshmukh, 1984). Different regressions apply for rangeland systems in different regions of Africa (Le Houérou and Hoste, 1977; Le Houérou, 1989; Hoffmann, 1999; see cross-continental syntheses in e.g. Frost et al., 1986). Up to around 1000mm annual

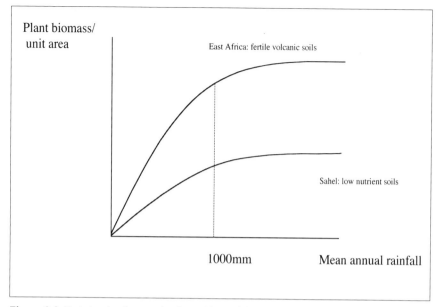

Figure 3.2 Variation in plant production with rainfall

rainfall, there is a linear increase in plant biomass production with increasing rainfall, with the slope of the relationship largely determined by soil nutrient availability (Fig 3.2 and below).

Net primary production is usually approximated by measuring peak biomass, which is affected by grazing regime, and the general dynamics of plant growth, death and removal (Deshmukh, 1984). Broadly speaking, each additional mm of rain produces an increase of 2kg/ha of dry matter in the Sahelian and Sudanian zones and 4kg/ha in the Mediterranean Basin (Le Houérou and Hoste, 1977). Le Houérou and Hoste take consumable dry matter as being half of this total above ground production – i.e. 1kg consumable dry matter per hectare for every additional mm rainfall in the Sahelo-Soudanian zone, and 2kg/ha/mm for the Mediterranean Basin. For East African sites, which are typically of high nutrient availability, the relation between rainfall and *peak* above ground biomass production is close to that found by Le Houérou and Hoste for the Mediterranean Basin (ca. 8kg.ha^{-1} for every mm rainfall above 20mm – Deshmukh, 1984). Above around 1000mm rainfall, further increase in precipitation does not bring increased production. Also, rainfall is not the only factor determining plant-available moisture. Temperature and albedo[1] affect evaporation, and cool high zones have relatively greater plant-available moisture for the same rainfall.

---

[1] The albedo is a measure of the extent to which solar radiation is reflected off the earth's surface. Normally it is high for bare surfaces and low for thick vegetation such as forest canopy.

Drought. The onset of drought does not correspond to any simple numerical threshold level of rainfall deficit. Drought can only be seen in terms of the ability of a given society to deal with variability, with low rainfall, and with prolonged runs of low rainfall years. It is very often not the intensity of drought that matters, in terms of the actual level of rainfall experienced. More important is whether the timing of any rain that does fall is such as to allow grass and crop growth. Once germinating, the plant must grow. If the rains begin and then fail at the critical stage, the seedling dies. It is not the absolute deficit of rain in a single year, but rather whether there is a run of successive years with poor rainfall, that will determine whether a community experiences major drought hardship. Communities living in arid and semi-arid lands all have the ability to cope with low rainfall years, but when these are prolonged over several years, coping mechanisms become stretched (Rasmusson, 1987).

Current analyses have collated data for from across the continent for the last century and more (Hulme et al., 2001; Desanker and Magadza, 2001, Nicholson, 2002). The climates of different African regions are influenced in a variety of ways by the temperature anomalies of the southern oceans. In particular, El Niño effects are associated with drought in the Sahel, and temperature anomalies of the Indian Ocean with heavy rainfall in East Africa. Apart from regions near the equator, much of Africa experienced high rainfall in the 1950s (Fig 3.3). This was reversed in the 1960s, with equatorial Africa having a decade of high rainfall, high lake levels, and high primary production, while other areas experienced a deficit (Desanker and Magadza, 2001). The 1970s, 1980s and 1990s have shown one or two high rainfall years, but overall there has been a progressive decline, particularly in the Sahel (Fig 3.3; Rasmusson, 1987; Pearce, 1991; Hulme, 1992; Desanker and Magadza, 2001; Hulme et al., 2001; Nicholson et al., 2000; Nicholson, 2002). Mean rainfall is estimated to have decreased by 20–49% across the Sahel between the periods 1931–60 and 1968–97, and generally by 5–10% across the rest of the continent (Desanker and Magadza, 2001), though southern Africa as a whole (Nicholson, 2002; Hoffmann, 1999) and localised areas of East Africa show little in the way of an overall downward trend (Baringo – Sutherland et al., 1991; Machakos – Tiffen et al., 1994; Mkomazi – Brockington and Homewood, 2001).

Declining rainfall totals across the Sahel and to a lesser extent other parts of Africa may also to a limited extent be affected by local land-use patterns (e.g. Charney et al., 1975; Sinclair and Fryxell, 1988; Nicholson, 2002). Where land cover is reduced by deforestation and heavy grazing this affects albedo and consequently evaporation, and may set off a vicious circle of declining rainfall totals, deteriorating vegetation cover, and further decline in rainfall. Current modelling work explores the possible scale and impact of such feedback effects between vegetation cover and Sahelian rainfall (Sincell, 1999 citing Claussen; IPCC, 2001; Reynolds and Stafford Smith, 2002). They are clearly secondary to the overwhelming importance of the El Niño/Southern Oscillation phenomenon, alongside other ocean surface temperature anomalies, in determining sub-Saharan extreme climatic events. When the southern oceans are relatively cooler, the Sahel has wetter years, and in warmer years (El Niño

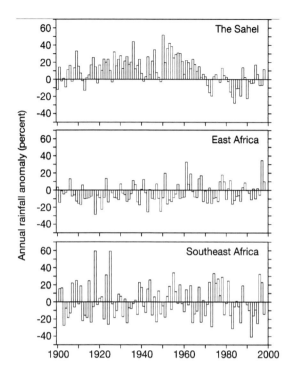

Figure 3.3 Rainfall deviation from the long-term mean in Africa, 1900–2000

Source: After Desanker and Magadza 2001: 495

Southern Oscillation or ENSO events) the Sahel is drier. By contrast, rainfall in East Africa shows the converse relation to El Niño, and is strongly influenced by the Indian Ocean temperature anomalies. Temperature changes interact with shifting rainfall patterns. Temperatures across Africa have risen by around 0.7 degrees C during the twentieth century. The warming is greatest across the interior of the Sahel and central southern Africa. Climate change in sub-Saharan Africa is increasingly understood as a symptom of global climatic processes largely or completely outside the control of African peoples (Gowlett, 1988; Nicholson and Entekhabi, 1986; Pearce, 1991; Nicholson et al., 1998, 2000; Nicholson, 2002; Desanker and Magadza, 2001).

The implications for pastoralist systems of dominant theoretical models for understanding changing climates are explored in a subsequent section. One practical outcome of the climate fluctuations is that farmers, in continuously experimenting and adapting (Richards, 1985), have responded to runs of good rainfall years by expanding the area of high-value moisture-dependent crops. Under these conditions farming populations have become established in marginal areas in runs of good years. When conditions deteriorate again, pastoralists seeking dry-season refuge, grazing and water in more humid areas with better soil/water relations are thrown into conflict with farmers who have converted these resources to cultivation. Impoverished herders are driven to settle and farm in the very areas that cultivators are abandoning, and drought coping mechanisms become seriously stretched for farmers and herders alike.

Soils

Some African rangelands have soils of naturally high mineral fertility. Such areas include those associated with volcanic rocks, such as many parts of the Great Rift Valley, riverine sediments in floodplains (Adams, 1992), and certain clays weathered *in situ* in montane environments. In these areas, exceptional types and levels of primary productivity are possible. Mineral content, protein content, digestibility, crude fibre content and other measures of forage quality all improve with high nutrient soils, and this is reflected in livestock performance (Chapter 6).

However, the great majority of African soils – around 95% of the continental soil mantle – are infertile lateritic soils. They have been weathered from ancient, much leached, infertile rocks with low mineral nutrient content (D'Hoore, 1964). Under arid and semi-arid rangeland conditions, these soils carry a low vegetation cover and have a low organic content. Together, these factors result in poor physical structure, high erosion and run-off rates and frequent waterlogging which dissolves and draws up oxides of iron and aluminium, which in turn precipitate to form a hardpan difficult for root penetration. Nutrients are a limiting factor of importance equal to or even greater than water in arid and semi-arid Africa, particularly in many Sahelian zones (Breman and De Wit, 1983; Reij et al., 1996). The lack of nitrogen and phosphorus makes for poor plant growth and a low nutritive value of forage, and much of indigenous African agropastoral land-use practice revolves around soil-fertility management, with livestock playing a significant role in the process (Scoones and Toulmin, 1999; Hilhorst and Muchena, 2000; Ramisch, 1999; Mortimore, 1998, 2005; Osbahr and Allan, 2003).

Research on the impacts of selection, nutrient stripping and nutrient concentration by wild herbivores helps to understand the ecological impacts of domestic livestock (McNaughton, 1988, 1990; see also Tolsma et al., 1987; Stelfox, 1986). Recently, detailed studies on long-established transhumance routes of Fulani pastoralists have shown the long-term implications of nutrient redistribution by cattle (Turner, 1998a, b). Pastoralist grazing, browsing, lopping, manuring, burning and trampling all redistribute nutrients, with far-reaching effects on structure and patterning in soils, vegetation type and species composition (Belsky, 1987; Stelfox, 1986; Sullivan, 1999b). Extensive mobility allowing pasture selection is or has until recently been central to livestock practice in most pastoralist systems, alongside pasture modification by grazing and burning. Transhumant pastoralist range-use strategies commonly trade quality of forage against quantity, compensating for nutritionally below-maintenance dry-season forage with high-quality nutrient intake in the wet season. Within these broad strategies, relatively mobile pastoralists like the Maasai create high-quality calf pastures near settlements through selective grazing and nutrient concentration (Stelfox, 1986). Their active production is recognised, and such calf pastures have been used as a strategy to establish claim to a particular area prior to securing private ownership (Grandin, 1986). In some systems, the high concentrations of nutrients that accumulate in the livestock enclosures are periodically removed and used to manure fields; in others, these sites are cultivated once the settlement is moved and rebuilt elsewhere. The cattle enclosure 'scars' are visible on the landscape for decades as hotspots of fertile growth (Homewood, 1992b).

Fire

Fires remove dead matter, return nutrients to the soil as mineral ash, open gaps in vegetation cover and free up space, resulting in a flush of new growth. The passage of fire removes the dormant stages of disease organisms and their vectors. Pastoralists in African rangelands and elsewhere use fire to improve range conditions for grazers. Historically, fire is likely to have been a major tool in the expansion of livestock production through habitats initially impassable due to disease vectors (Gifford-Gonzalez, 2000). Fire impacts depend on the temperature at which the fire burns, which in turn depends on the amount of dry matter available and the ambient temperature, relative humidity and wind speed. Fires set early in the dry season (when relative humidity is high, most ground cover still green, and dry standing biomass limited) are relatively cool. They will burn dry matter and may scorch seedlings but are unlikely to kill saplings or trees. By contrast, fires burning through an area for the first time late in the dry season meet a large biomass of dry matter, high environmental temperatures and low relative humidity. Under these conditions, particularly with a strong wind fanning the flames, they may reach temperatures of 700-800°C, consuming green growing as well as dead dry matter, setting tree canopies alight, destroying woody vegetation, subsoil fauna and flora, and causing lasting damage, especially to forest edges.

Concern over the impacts of hot fires, and a poor grasp of indigenous knowledge, led many colonial and post-independence administrations to ban burning by pastoralist groups. Paradoxically, excluding the controlled early burns means that more dry matter builds up, setting up conditions for devastating wildfires at a later stage. The positive impacts of controlled use of fire are now progressively better understood (Whelan, 1995; Laris, 2002, 2003) and its role in modifying and enhancing vegetation types, and forestalling damaging wildfire as well as controlling disease vectors (Sutherst, 1987; Whelan, 1995; Laris, 2002), is slowly coming to be accepted by official authorities. Nonetheless, the use of fire to manage grazing is still a contentious issue in many systems throughout Africa (Laris, 2003).

Organising the diversity of vegetation types

Bell (1982) produced a simple two-way classification of soil and water conditions that neatly organises and explains a great deal of the variation between rangeland vegetation types in different parts of Africa (Table 3.2). This classification uses the extremes of the continua of soil mineral and water availability to clarify the way rangeland vegetation is largely determined by the interaction of soil and water relations. In areas with high water availability and high nutrient content in the soils, there is potentially tall forest growth. The history of land use, fire regime and grazing/browsing pressures as well as of

Table 3.2 Determinants of arid and semi-arid savanna vegetation types

Soil mineral Nutrients	Water availability High	Low
High	Forest/grassland mosaic High plant + animal biomass *Adamawa Plateau* *E. Africa Rift*	Short grass; Seasonal pulse of high-quality growth Temporary high plant + animal biomass *Serengeti; Saharan pastures of the* cure salée
Low	Tall grass/woodland High grass/Low animal biomass Fire climax *Miombo* and *mopane* *Sudano-guinean savannas of the CAR*	Sparse grassland, Limited production. Quality declines as rainfall increases Low animal biomass Annual/perennial balance shifts+grazing *West African Sahel*

After Bell (1982)

large mammal damage dictates the balance between forest and grassland in these high-potential areas (Laws, 1970; Pellew, 1983; Dublin, 1991, 1995).

Where there are high soil nutrients but low rainfall, production is water-limited. In such areas, there is a pulse of high quality primary production during the wet season, wherever moisture is enough to support plant growth. Such areas are typically exploited seasonally by wet-season dispersal of trans-humant pastoralists and/or by in-migration of wildlife herds (Serengeti/Ngorongoro – Homewood and Rodgers, 1991; Mkomazi – Brockington, 2002; Simanjiro Plains – Kahurananga, 1981; Igoe and Brockington, 1999). Grazing stimulates rapid plant growth so long as there is moisture available to maintain that growth. Where arid climate limits the options and topography concentrates sparse run-off, and where mineral nutrients are particularly highly sought, such areas may see a wet-season concentration of pastoralist herds that are more widely dispersed at other times (Hungarob Ravine pastoralists in the Namib Desert – Kinahan, 1991; *cure salée* aggregations of Tuareg from widely distant regions – Bernus, 1981).

High water availability, combined with poor soil minerals, results in a rank growth of tall-stemmed grasses with a high fibre content, low nutritive value and low palatability. Although the early growth stages of these grasses may be good forage, they rapidly reach the stage of such low digestibility that they are of little use to herbivorous mammals. The tall stands of grass that develop are easily set on fire, and areas with this type of soil/water conditions tend to develop a fire climax vegetation with fire-tolerant or -dependent species (perennial grasses: *Themeda triandra*, *Hyparrhenia* spp.; trees: *Brachystegia* and *Pterocarpus* spp in Tanzanian woodlands; *Colophospermum mopane* further south). Similar environments characterise the guinean and sudanian zones of the West African Sahel. Finally, where both water availability and soil nutrients are poor, grass growth can be of high nutritive value, but of limited quantity. As plant-available moisture increases in such areas, grass growth is increasingly affected by low mineral nutrient availability, and forage quality declines as quantity increases, as in the West African Sahel.

Although each of the cells in Table 3.2 is illustrated with a particular example, the ranges used by pastoralist communities tend to have a mixture or mosaic of more than one of these types of soil, water and vegetation conditions. In areas with diverse topography and geological make-up, the skill and knowledge of the herders exploit the opportunities and avoid the constraints of each component of their environmental mosaic (Coppock et al., 1986 – Turkana; Homewood and Lewis, 1987 – Baringo; Bernus, 1981 – Tuaregs of Niger; Legrosse, 1999 – Fulani, Inland Delta of the Niger).

Topography, geology and drainage lines: wetlands in drylands

Arid-land communities also manage microenvironments for water harvesting and for maximum effect in its use (Ludwig, 1987; Beaumont et al., 1989). Topography, geology and drainage lines can create pockets of water availability in otherwise arid areas (Scoones, 1993) and most pastoralist systems hinge on access to such key resources as regular dry-season and drought refuges (Homewood, 1994). On a larger scale, whole arid-land ecosystems revolve round the wet-season dispersal/dry–season concentration cycle of movements of wildlife, domestic stock and people (Amboseli – Western, 1975; Sudd – Howell et al., 1988; Johnson, 1991; Baringo – Homewood, 1994; Inland Delta of the Niger – Gallais, 1984; Moorehead, 1991; Legrosse, 1999). Such trans-humant cycles may operate on the basis of topographic diversity, with dry-season concentration round groundwater (swamps and rivers – ranging from the large scale such as the Inland Delta of the Niger, or the Sudd, to the small scale such as the swamps of the Amboseli system of Kenya Maasailand) or high, cool montane areas with year-round green growth (e.g. Maasai in Ngorongoro), rather than using latitudinal variation (see section below on transhumance). Sometimes conditions dictate the converse, with wet-season concentration/dry-season dispersal (as for Hungarob in Namibia – Kinahan, 1991). Dry-season and drought access to wetland, swamp and riverine resources on the one hand, or alternatively highland refuges on the other, is of central importance to pastoralist systems (Chapter 4). Loss of access to these areas can mean collapse of the pastoral system (e.g. Homewood, 1993; Woodhouse et al., 2001).

Disease constraints

Disease constraints have played a major part in shaping the pattern and tempo of the spread of livestock-keeping economies through sub-Saharan Africa over the last 5000 years or more (Chapter 2). They continue to be of major importance to pastoralist systems (Chapter 4), and contrasting approaches to disease management have major implications for epidemiology (Chapter 6). Tsetse-borne trypanosomiasis is endemic across 10 million km^2 of Africa and affects all livestock species (Bourn et al., 2000). Mild infections reduce an animal's productivity, or mean poor survival of young; more serious infections kill outright, or through increased vulnerability to drought, poor nutrition and intercurrent disease (ibid.). Trypanosomiasis is associated with wooded grassland and forest areas, by definition the areas of higher rainfall and/or groundwater that are of importance to livestock in dry-season or drought periods. The vectors are slow-breeding and their developmental cycle is strongly affected by temperature, so at higher altitudes trypanosomiasis ceases to be a problem. Different species and breeds of livestock show differing degrees of susceptibility to challenge, related to their histories of exposure to disease challenge that have resulted in generations of natural selection for resistance to particular pathogens (Chapter 6). The epidemiology of trypanosomiasis and the fluctuating patterns of susceptibility are also influenced by different populations' and cohorts' immunological experience of tsetse challenge (Ford, 1971). Recent analyses suggest a significant and steady increase of people, areas farmed and numbers of livestock across the Sahel over the last decades, both a cause and a result of trypanosomiasis decline (Bourn and Wint, 1994). Intensive use of prophylactic drugs in high-potential areas (Boutrais, 1988) means that pastoralism may operate in high-risk zones, with constant medication and care of individual animals.

Other endemic diseases of livestock also limit production, excluding livestock from some areas on a seasonal or permanent basis and reducing their productivity and viability in others. East Coast Fever (ECF) and other tick-borne diseases (Chapter 6) are major agents of mortality associated with specific vegetation types (e.g. long grass) and with wildlife as alternative hosts and reservoirs of infection (e.g. Norval et al., 1992). Particular vegetation types may be avoided seasonally (e.g. Maasai – Potkanski, 1994), or modified by burning or heavy grazing to minimise disease risk by controlling vector populations (Sukuma – Birley, 1982). Colonial settlers excluded herds and banned burning, and epidemic outbreaks of what was probably formerly a low-level endemic disease ensued (Giblin, 1990, 1993; Waller and Homewood, 1996). In Central African Republic, Mbororo and Fulbe herders spend much of their time on disease control, de-ticking animals by hand. In Kenya, intensive dipping triggered a cycle of acaricide resistance among the vectors and disease resurgence among the livestock (Norval et al., 1992). Early warning systems based on remotely sensed environmental factors affecting vector populations (Rogers et al., 1996, 2000) have had limited practical impact as yet, but simple vaccines can be highly effective (Chapter 6; Home-wood et al., 2006).

Customary livestock management limits exposure to many potential disease challenges other than tsetse and ECF. Maasai herders avoid areas where wildebeest have been calving until the placentas have been dispersed. Their understanding of Malignant Catarrhal Fever (MCF) is that it is transmitted by contact with wildebeest placentas. The Western understanding of the disease is that it is a respiratory infection endemic in the wildebeest population and commonly contracted by wildebeest newborn calves, which it affects only mildly. It is lethal to cattle. Avoidance of pastures where there are wildebeest placentas is a sure operational criterion for avoiding infection (Rossiter et al., 1983). Knowledge and understanding of disease patterns associated with particular environments are important in pastoralist decisions over where, when and how to move herds, and over range management by burning and herd mobility. Such knowledge is likely to have taken a considerable time to evolve. The archaeological evidence for a phased spread of cattle (but not small stock) through eastern and southern Africa may reflect the relative susceptibility of cattle to vector-borne diseases such as trypanosomiasis and East Coast Fever. Early herders needed time to develop indigenous knowledge to overcome these disease challenges (Gifford-Gonzalez, 2000).

Ecological models & pastoralist ecosystem dynamics

Since the early decades of the last century, many professional ecologists and successive administrations have tended to view pastoralist land use and livestock management as environmentally problematic. Pastoralists have often been seen as accumulating animals and overstocking the range, overgrazing, and bringing about the progressive degradation of arid and semi-arid rangelands in Africa. Increased grazing pressure was held to affect the species composition and vegetation cover of the rangelands, leading to a loss of palatable species and an increase in bare ground (Brown, 1971; Lamprey, 1983; Le Houérou, 1989). Bare ground was seen as exacerbating erosion and leading ultimately to a long-term decline in both primary and secondary production. Overstocking and overgrazing were assumed either to be inherent in the pastoralist system of communal land tenure and private livestock ownership (Hardin, 1968) or to be knock-on effects of alienation of land (Hjort, 1982), decay of social order (Little, 1985), and of impacts of water development on rates of sedentarisation (Sinclair and Fryxell, 1985). A variant of overgrazing theory sees albedo effects of overgrazing as leading to reduced rainfall, drought and famine (Charney et al., 1975; Sinclair and Fryxell, 1985; Claussen in Sincell, 1999).

Degradation has been defined in different ways. Some emphasise the biophysical, for example:

> reduction or loss, in arid, semi-arid and dry sub-humid areas, of the biological or economic productivity and complexity of rainfed cropland, irrigated cropland, or range, pasture, forest and woodlands resulting from land uses or from a process or combination of processes, including processes arising from human activities and habitation patterns such as:
> i. Soil erosion caused by wind and/or water;
> ii. Deterioration of the physical, chemical and biological or economic properties of soil; and
> iii. Long-term loss of natural vegetation. (Hoffmann et al., 1999)

Other definitions emphasise social and economic criteria. Thus, for an area where high livestock densities may be associated with changes in biophysical measures, observers focusing on biodiversity might perceive degradation, while a socioeconomic focus would take sustained high production as evidence that degradation could not have occurred to any significant degree (Abel and Blaikie, 1990; Scoones, 1993).

Some rangeland ecologists have at times called for drastic measures (destocking, relocation, population limitation – for example, Brown, 1971; Sinclair and Fryxell, 1985) to combat perceived pastoralist-induced degradation. In some cases extreme measures have been imposed, and there are many cases of eviction (with or without resettlement and compensation) on the grounds of potential or alleged actual overgrazing and degradation. In apartheid South Africa, 'Betterment Schemes' were imposed in a misguided attempt to combat degradation in the communal areas (where 75% of the country's population lived on 13% of the land – Turner and Ntshona, 1999; Beinart, 1984, 1994). In Sahelian, East and South-East Africa, decades of livestock and range development interventions sought to tackle perceived or real rangeland degradation by changing systems of land tenure and livestock management thought to be responsible. The consensus is that the hundreds of millions of dollars poured into livestock development schemes based on these assumptions failed to achieve much positive change.

Michael Horowitz (1979) and Stephen Sandford (1983) first drew attention to the lack of empirical evidence and the contradictory assumptions underlying the 'Mainstream view' of rangeland degradation under pastoralist use. The criticisms of this conventional wisdom included:

– the lack of evidence for long-term degradation in many arid and semi-arid areas, where, during an average study, year-to-year variation is often greater than any long-term trends;

– the extent to which the concept of carrying capacity can be meaningful in a system where rainfall, hence primary production, hence forage availability are very variable, and the main limiting factors are water and grazing;

– the validity of data purporting to show a steady increase in numbers of livestock, and of the assumptions that pastoralists maximise herds for cultural rather than economically and ecologically rational reasons;

– the extent to which it is biologically possible that, in areas where there genuinely has been an increase in animal numbers, such a trend could be maintained if the environment were truly undergoing degradation;

– the extent to which genuine increase in numbers and genuine decline in production result from improvident increase, or compression of people and animals as a result of dispossession;

– the extent to which assessment of productivity takes into account the management goals of the system. Commercially-oriented producers specialising in high quality beef for urban and/or export markets have different production goals from pastoralist and agropastoralist producers more concerned with daily supply of milk and of draft labour for farming, on the one hand, and a relatively secure wealth store and investment, on the other. To the extent that the concept of carrying capacity is useful in very variable systems, these differences in production goals would imply different 'economic' and 'ecological' carrying capacities for different management goals.

Those criticisms triggered a paradigm shift over the last 2–3 decades in the understanding of the ecological dynamics of arid and semi-arid rangelands in general, and more particularly the dynamics of pastoralist ecology across African rangelands. In particular, assumptions that the natural state of rangelands was to progress towards a climax successional state, and then to fluctuate around an equilibrium characterised by an identifiable carrying capacity, have been challenged (Behnke et al., 1993; Vetter, 2005). Through the 1980s and

1990s studies proliferated reassessing the conventional understanding of individual pastoralist ecosystems, from the viewpoints both of the biophysical evidence and the biological functioning of rangeland systems (e.g. Ellis and Swift, 1988; Homewood and Rodgers, 1987, 1991; Homewood, 1994; Scoones, 1995; Nicholson et al., 1998) and of the historical and social context of colonial and post-Independence narratives of degradation in Africa (Anderson, 1984; Bell, 1987; Swift, 1996; Leach and Mearns, 1996). At the same time, Noy-Meir's and Caughley's work changed broader ecological views over arid and semi-arid land systems worldwide (Noy-Meir, 1982; MacNab, 1985; Caughley et al., 1987). These separate influences have culminated in current debates over the relative importance of equilibrium versus disequilibrium processes in driving arid and semi-arid rangeland dynamics. This is not only a theoretical debate. The ways we understand the population and ecosystem processes we observe, and the very different interpretations offered by equilibrium as opposed to disequilibrium thinking, entail radically different implications for the management of pastoralist and other systems (Behnke et al., 1993; Vetter, 2005).

Equilibrium theory and the disequilibrium debate

The debate hinges on the way populations grow, on the factors which limit that growth, and on the resulting stability, resilience, persistence or conversely degradation of the communities and ecosystems affected by those changing populations. Broadly speaking, equilibrium theory sees a growing population as being limited primarily by density-dependent factors (Fig 3.4). Equilibrium theory suggests that, in a population at low density in a favourable environment, individuals can easily find food and shelter. They grow rapidly, mature early, reproduce successfully and show low rates of mortality, for example from infectious diseases which are not easily transmitted at low population densities. This corresponds to point A in Fig 3.4.

However, as a population grows, it becomes increasingly hard for individuals to find food, shelter and suitable breeding sites, and transmission of diseases becomes increasingly problematic. As a result, individuals progressively grow

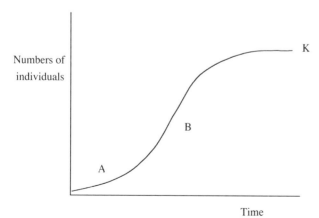

Figure 3.4 Logistical curve of population growth showing the operation of density-dependent factors

more slowly, reach sexual maturity later, and have fewer offspring, themselves less likely to survive to sexual maturity or to reproduce successfully. Overall, fertility declines, and mortality rises. As a result population growth rate begins to slow (point B, Fig 3.4) and in due course numbers plateau at K, the carrying capacity. This represents a maximum number of individuals in the population, given the resources available for them to exploit.

Equilibrium thinking makes statements about community and ecosystem processes as well as individual populations. In particular, equilibrium thinking sees ecosystems as progressing through a linear sequence or 'succession' of vegetation stages from colonisation of bare landscapes through to the development of a 'climax' vegetation type for local conditions of climate and soils. Species with colonising life-history strategies with rapid and prolific reproduction, rapid maturation with little investment in individual offspring, and excellent dispersal abilities thrive in the early stages of succession. By contrast, slow-maturing, slow-reproducing specialists with limited dispersal abilities, locked into intricate symbiotic interrelations with other species, are well adapted to later stages of succession. This Clementsian theory of succession and its relevance to equilibrium theory is reviewed in more detail elsewhere (Behnke et al., 1993). According to this thinking, species populations which overshoot carrying capacity disrupt climax communities and push the ecosystem back to a lower successional stage, which may be less productive or diverse. This happens where species newly introduced to a favourable environment and released from natural enemies undergo a population eruption, or where species populations are held excessively high (as may be the case in some South African communal lands: see below). Equilibrium thinking suggests that such temporarily very high densities can entail permanent or long-term damage to the productive capacity of the environment, perhaps through destruction of particular food species or through erosion and loss of topsoil. A population crash may ensue, and if and when the population eventually stabilises this will be at a new, lower value of K: the destructive impact on resources effectively resets carrying capacity at a lower level. Equilibrium thinking carries the expectation of environmental degradation wherever density-dependent limitation does not operate effectively. As well as chronically heavily stocked and grazed South African communal lands (see below), the drought phases of boom-and-bust vegetation production and livestock numbers in other arid and semi-arid African rangelands have tended to be interpreted in this light (e.g. Lamprey, 1983; Fig 3.5).

Other work links this hypothetical sequence of overgrazing and degradation to a postulated positive feedback or vicious cycle, whereby overgrazing and increasing bare ground could drive climatic deterioration through albedo effects (Charney et al., 1975; Sinclair and Fryxell, 1985; Claussen in Sincell, 1999). The implication is that local land use could drive regional climate downturn: overgrazing by pastoralist herds might, for example, be causing Sahelian droughts. Current reviews see this effect as vastly outweighed by the impact of global atmospheric processes on African regional climates (Nicholson, 2002; Desanker and Magadza, 2001). Sahelian droughts and other extreme climatic events of tropical arid and semi-arid Africa correlate closely

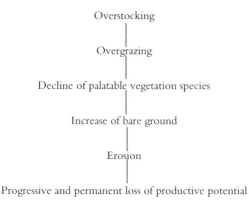

Overstocking

|

Overgrazing

|

Decline of palatable vegetation species

|

Increase of bare ground

|

Erosion

|

Progressive and permanent loss of productive potential

Figure 3.5 Hypothetical (and contested) sequence of overstocking, overgrazing and environmental degradation, as postulated by equilibrium thinking. Source: After Lamprey (1983)

with surface temperature anomalies of the southern Oceans (Pearce, 1991; Nicholson and Entekhabi, 1986; Nicholson et al., 1998; Desanker and Magadza, 2001; Nicholson, 2002). These two models have very different implications: rather than causing their own climatic problems through overstocking and overgrazing, Sahelian pastoralist livestock and livelihoods are jeopardised by global climatic and atmospheric processes, driven by populations and processes remote from Africa.

Disequilibrium thinking questions the application to tropical arid and semi-arid ecosystems of equilibrium thinking in general, and, in particular, concepts of carrying capacity and linear succession to climax. It emphasises that populations are not necessarily primarily limited by density-dependent effects, nor do they necessarily function within linear ecological sequences of successional stages. Physical factors in the environment – extreme climatic events, fires, floods, volcanic eruptions – all have effects which commonly operate quite independently of the size and density of the population affected. The scale of the mortality inflicted by these extreme events is not related to nor determined by the characteristics of the population. It is generally agreed among biologists that even a small and intermittently acting density-dependent influence exerts some regulatory effect on a population over time, but that density-independent factors can cause potentially massive fluctuations. The disequilibrium debate then revolves around the following:

- the extent to which an ecosystem is driven by density-dependent or density-independent processes;
- whether any massive fluctuations that are observed do cause significant (measurable, permanent, irreversible) degradation, and
- whether the vegetation states observed represent degraded stages relative to the climax state of a linear succession, or represent neither degradation nor damage but multiple alternative states in a situation where biophysical variability does not allow for any one linear succession to climax.

Disequilibrium thinking suggests that models and frameworks derived from the ecology of relatively more predictable temperate ecosystems may constrain understanding of very variable and unpredictable tropical arid and semi-arid ecosystems. While more temperate or humid ecosystems may be characterised predominantly by equilibrium processes, arid and semi-arid tropical systems may be characterised more by extreme variability in rainfall (and hence in plant production and animal biomass) as well as by chaotically interacting random events of fire, flood, drought and epidemic. Rather than a smooth population response to changing availability of food or transmission of disease, tropical arid and semi-arid systems may show boom-and-bust fluctuations with rapid build-up, great mobility and catastrophic die-offs of both wild and domestic herbivores. Rather than progressing along a smooth successional sequence to a climax state, vegetation formations may show chaotic shifts between multiple alternative relatively stable states, depending on past trajectories and current interplay of rainfall, fire, epidemic disease, herbivore densities and impacts, and on recruitment, regeneration, maturation and decline of woody species.

Carrying capacity implies some steady state to which a population will tend. This concept (and by extension the concept of overshooting carrying capacity) is thought to have limited validity where massive intra- and interannual variation in rainfall (Fig 3.1) and hence forage production (Fig 3.2) mean that forage resources available for animals are extremely patchy and unpredictable in space and time. Across much of arid and semi-arid Africa, wild and domestic herds move over considerable distances to optimise use of pasture and other resources. In these ecosystems some areas are denuded of ground cover in the dry season. These landscapes have often been seen as degraded, deteriorating environments resulting from improvident pastoralist herd accumulation and overgrazing. In a significant number of cases, though potentially heavily grazed and, in the dry season, temporarily unproductive, they have now been shown to return rapidly to peak production with the next rains, with no long-term decline of production. Some recent and current studies suggest that the vegetation states observed in many savannas are better understood not as degradation, but as the product of chaotic shifts between multiple alternative stable states, driven primarily by an interplay of biophysical factors beyond pastoralists' control (Dublin, 1991, 1995; Ellis and Swift, 1988; Homewood, 1994; Sullivan, 1999; Homewood et al., 2001; Laris, 2002, 2003).

Some cases may be best understood as fluctuating across the grey zone between primarily equilibrium and primarily disequilibrium systems (Scoones, 1993, Coppock, 1993). Others may be artificially driven towards quasi-equilibrium processes by severe constraints on mobility, intense economic pressures to increase livestock numbers, and regular recourse to supplements and inputs to buffer the shortages that result. In the communal lands of South Africa, a high proportion of the population occupies a small proportion of the nation's surface area in some of the less agro-ecologically favourable zones, and the particular conditions of the South African migrant labour and remittance economy mean that homelands residents still need to invest in livestock as one strand of livelihoods and wealth store (MacKinnon, 1999; Ainslie, 2005). This may in some places have led to such high stocking rates that the conventional wisdom can offer some explanatory power. Hoffmann (pers. comm.) suggests that some heavily stocked and grazed South African communal lands are unlikely at any point in the last 10,000 years to have displayed the extremes of (lack of) plant cover, species composition, edible biomass, surface run-off, sediment loss, soil organic matter content or pH currently measured in these ecosystems, were it not for the particular social and historical land-use context now creating those conditions. It is possible that extremely high densities, severe constraints on mobility, use of inputs and intense incentives to invest in more livestock, may all conspire to override density-independent processes and shift the communal land systems towards more equilibrium dynamics, by artificially forcing them up against a quasi-Malthusian ceiling, despite their semi-arid and primarily disequilibrium nature. However, it is debatable whether meaningful definitions of degradation would be consistent with the sustained production these areas maintain. More generally, South African systems are rather different in eco-climatic, politico-demographic and socio-economic terms from the rangelands throughout most of the Sahel, the Horn, East and South-East Africa. Their agro-pastoralist systems have been so altered over centuries as to represent an extreme case.

The debate between supporters of equilibrium and disequilibrium models is rooted in theoretical disagreements, but also in different researchers' empirical experience. It carries a sharp political edge because of its extreme applied importance in determining policies which risk victimising local users, on the one hand, or endangering environmental values, on the other. Some ecologists support a conventional view of carrying capacity, overstocking, and environmental degradation in rangelands (Illius and O'Connor, 1999; Cowling, 2000).[2] Others, often with primarily South African experience, point to literature on the impacts which high densities of animals confined to small areas for long periods can have on semi-arid environments (Hoffmann et al., 2003). By contrast, a vast majority of development workers and researchers in East and West African arid and semi-arid lands, where pastoralists are relatively mobile and livestock still constitute a central dimension of the household economy, find the disequilibrium framework more consistent with empirical experience (Sullivan and Rohde, 2002; IIED drylands and pastoral land-tenure series; Francophone ecologists working in Sahelian rangelands, e.g. Boutrais (1994b), and many East African ecologists – Ellis and Swift, 1988; Behnke et al., 1993; Homewood, 1994; Homewood et al., 2001).

Summary on equilibrium/disequilibrium. The fluctuations in ground cover, species composition and production in savanna may or may not show a progressive downward trend. Where they do, that trend may or may not be primarily associated with local land use rather than, for example, global climatic change. Sandford (1982) predicted considerable variation between and within systems

---

[2] They argue that as density dependence occurs in key resource areas (which is almost by definition the case) it follows that disequilibrium perspectives should be rejected for the wider ecosystem. However, disequilibrium thinking argues that key resource dynamics and disequilibrium dynamics operate in parallel at different temporal and spatial scales. Several authors therefore see this challenge to disequilibrium thinking as of doubtful validity (e.g. papers in Behnke et al., 1993; Sullivan and Rohde, 2002).

on the basis not just of aridity but also of local ecological factors such as soils and topography, on the one hand, and local political and socio-economic factors, on the other. Detailed work shows that individual cases of grazing and/or browsing impacts are complex and differentiated (Turner, 1998a, b, 1999b; Sullivan, 1999b). They neither simply refute nor fully bear out one or other view of rangeland processes. The two opposed models may be extremes along a continuum, rather than mutually exclusive. The more arid and unpredictable the ecosystem, the more closely it may correspond to a 'dis-equilibrium' system; Ellis (1995) suggests that disequilibrium dynamics dominate wherever mean annual rainfall shows a coefficient of variation greater than 30%. However, the 'new' view may have explanatory power even in relatively less arid systems (e.g. Stott, 1997 – tropical woodland and forests), while equilibrium thinking may have some heuristic value in highly constrained cases in arid rangelands.

Disequilibrium thinking builds on empirical evidence that the more arid the system, and the more variable the rainfall in space and time, the more variable plant production will be and the greater the potential fluctuations in animal numbers, whether domestic or wild. Savannas under these conditions may not operate as equilibrium systems which progress naturally along a sequence of successional vegetation stages towards a single climax, but which are easily pushed to a state of ecological collapse by the impact of outside influences of grazing pressure or fire. Arid and semi-arid rangelands may instead move continuously between multiple, alternative, relatively stable states, largely driven by disequilibrium, non-density-dependent, abiotic influences. In this view, grazing pressure and fire contribute to the observed state at any one time but are unlikely to be driving any long-term or irreversible trend, and are only two of many influences, the most powerful of which are probably non-anthropogenic factors. At the other end of the eco-climatic spectrum equilibrium systems are more predictable, and land use can be adjusted to make the most of predictable and density-dependent relations between rainfall and primary and secondary productivity. This expanded view of rangeland ecology has fundamental policy implications for sub-Saharan Africa.

Different situations may correspond to different positions along a con-tinuum between equilibrium and disequilibrium, and individual systems may move to and fro along that continuum. Also, both models may contribute to complementary insights where either alone could constrain understanding. In a parallel debate, economists and biologists have read the evidence over the determinants and environmental implications of climate change in completely different ways. Economists are interested in the major fluctuations that dominate the system and that call for immediate and major practical inter-ventions. Biologists, by contrast, have focused on the relatively small but steady creep of long-term directional change. These different perspectives led to major rifts in the IPCC (Parmesan and Yohe, 2003). Although both approaches look at the same data, each focuses on a different aspect of change and emerges with a different understanding of the important features of the system. Each is correct in its own terms, but neither is complete without the other.

Table 3.3 Ecological, production and tenure correlates of equilibrium and disequilibrium models

	Equilibrium	Disequilibrium
Ecology - plant production	–Relatively stable climate –Primary production is relatively stable and predictable year to year	–Climate varies unpredictably –Primary production varies unpredictably (tightly linked to rainfall)
Ecology - animal production	–Livestock population is density-dependent –Change in stocking density produces predictable qualitative and quantitative change in vegetation	–Livestock population is density independent –Livestock population tracks unpredictable forage production
Herd management and land tenure	- Carrying capacity can be predicted (whether ecological or economic – MacNab, 1985) - Stocking density can be tailored to carrying capacity –Private tenure of land, water	- Carrying capacity calculations not useful guide to forage availability at any given place/ time - Opportunistic and mobile grazing practices more appropriate –Common property resource management systems with fuzzy social and spatial boundaries allow flexible use of range resources

Source: After Oba et al. (2000: 37)

Given the political ecology of environmental degradation discourses, and the uses to which they are put, we need to test case-specific allegations of environmental degradation through poor land-use practice. Where there is good evidence that a system is largely operating on disequilibrium lines, livestock keepers may do better to track current range conditions, wherever possible managing major physical agents such as fire (for example, by early burning to avoid wildfires), and keeping options open for rapid redeployment as conditions change (McCabe, 2004). Rather than the conservative stocking rates/destocking of pastoralist systems so commonly advocated, and the exclusion of fire or other disrupting factors, optimal management of disequilibrium systems may mean restocking to accelerate recovery after catastrophic die-offs and to keep grazing and browsing pressures at a level which avoids excessive spread of woody species, limiting potential eruption of disease vectors (Ford, 1971; Kjekshus, 1977; Birley, 1982; Giblin, 1990; Homewood, 1994). Heavy grazing may foster bush encroachment where grazing removes grass cover, reduces fire incidence and allows woody vegetation to grow up to dominate the system, but it is also possible for 'undergrazing' to drive reversion from grassland to less productive bush and thicket.

Vetter's (2005) clear, concise and balanced synthesis finds ways to incorporate strongly polarised views within a common framework. At the same time, political ecology analyses show that the scientific debate is readily distorted by vested interests (see section below on environmental narratives), and that entrenched official positions founded on equilibrium models have often resulted in sustained negative pressures on land use and livelihoods. In the interests of social justice, sustainable local livelihoods and good environmental practice, disequilibrium thinking should be borne in mind in assessing degradation claims in arid and semi-arid land pastoralist systems.

Social & political environments

This book focuses on the ecology of pastoralist societies, but strategies of resource use, mobility and livestock management are as much a response to social and political dimensions as to biophysical factors. The brief histories of the emergence of pastoralism and of present-day pastoralist groups given in Chapter 2 sketch some of the ways those social, political and historical dimensions come into play. This section draws together the main features. Among pastoralists as in other groups, competition for resources is managed through social institutions governing tenure and access (Niamir Fuller, 1999a; Turner, 1999b; Toulmin and Quan, 2000). However, there may be cases where competition is intensified by the often extreme and relatively unpredictable variations in abundance and distribution of key grazing and water resources (Cassanelli, 1982 – Somalia). Besides competition over grazing and water, livestock are commonly raided (Turkana – Hendrickson et al., 1998; McCabe, 2004). If social institutions are unable to manage the tensions, violent conflicts may erupt; where one or both sides have modern weapons, those confrontations become massacres, with state (in)action tipping or even guiding the balance (Keen, 1995; Johnson, 2003; de Waal, 2004).

Tenure and access

Current systems of tenure and access, and their trajectories of change, are outlined briefly here (and in more detail in Chapters 5 and 9). Different pastoralist groups show a great variety of indigenous systems of tenure and access (Potkanski, 1994; Thébaud, 1995a; Lane, 1996a, 1998; Mortimore, 1998; Adams et al., 2001). Indigenous African pastoralist tenure systems for grazing land, water or other natural resources, have generally worked as common property resource management systems regulated by different user groups. Continual open-ended negotiation has often allowed flexible use, with continuously re-evaluated access to point-centred key resources (Turner, 1999b). The boundaries around those key resources have commonly been fuzzy in terms of the spatial extent of biophysical resources they encompass, and in terms of the social composition and membership of the user group. Rights depend on birth, kinship, investment of labour and social contracts. Overlapping groups of users and customary channels of negotiation have allowed adaptive flexibility in response to seasonal, annual and long-term changes (Turner, 1999b; Niamir-Fuller, 1999a).

Colonial administrations tended to interpret absence of clear, cut-and-dried individual property rights as absence of legal framework, rather than as a manifestation of alternative systems evolved in the context of an unpredictable and variable environment. These administrations imposed their own legal frameworks, derived directly from the property law of European colonising nations. Specific areas were designated as homelands for specific ethnic groups. Leaving aside here the colonial creation of 'traditional' groups and chiefly hierarchies, colonial legal frameworks tended to take previously communally-owned land to Crown or state, opening the way for European and other settlers' purchase of land and acquisition of legal title. In some parts this led to massively inequitable land distribution (Toulmin and Quan, 2000). Overall, especially post-Independence, it replaced functioning common property resource management with effectively open access systems which the state, having extinguished customary systems of regulation, was unable to control. Customary systems often continue to operate alongside formal national legal frameworks.

Post-Independence administrations were mostly influenced by economic theories developed in other contexts. These led either to privatisation of land (on the basis of economic theories postulating that private tenure was essential to investment, and to economically and environmentally sustainable development, e.g. Hardin, 1968) or to state ownership, on the basis of socialist ideology. Over the past decade, this state land has increasingly been made available for private purchase. Both paths have been open to manipulation by elites, who have in many cases used their privileged access to money, information and power, and the complexities of new national land law and its foreign language expression, to secure large areas for personal gain. Poor people have typically been unable to purchase title; holders of secondary rights have become increasingly vulnerable (particularly women, whom the colonial system generally excluded from land ownership – e.g. Hodgson, 2000a). The upshot is that now, at the outset of the twenty-first century, there are throughout sub-Saharan Africa plural legal systems which provide alternative authorities and channels for negotiating access and securing tenure. In the conflicts that result, the well-placed benefit at the expense of the more vulnerable (McAuslan, 2000; Chapter 9).

Throughout sub-Saharan Africa, pastoralist peoples and pastoralism as a land-use system are frequently marginalised in the process (Lane, 1998; IIED, pastoral land tenure programme). Settled peoples have an advantage in claiming tenure over mobile groups, and are better represented both in official administrations and in processes of consultation. Pastoralists in arid and semi-arid lands are among the most mobile of African peoples. They are often sporadic or seasonal rather than continuous users of most resources. Both their social groups and their spatial movements are of necessity flexible and fluid. There are relatively few contemporary systems established under pastoralist hegemony, and those are mostly in decline (Inland Delta of the Niger – Gallais, 1984; Legrosse, 1999; Adamawa – Boutrais, 1994; Ahmad in Toulmin and Quan, 2000). Across Africa, pastoralism is being progressively squeezed out of an intensified agricultural landscape (Bourn and Wint, 1994; Maina, cited in Toulmin and Quan, 2000) in an opposition of the mobile and the settled, the desert and the sown, recognised since the fourteenth-century writings of Ibn Khaldun. The crucial determinant of pastoralist ecology is the extent to which pastoral peoples can maintain flexible access to seasonal resources, and mobility to exploit them (Niamir-Fuller, 1999a; Turner, 1999a; Behnke, 1993). Where access and mobility are extremely constrained (e.g. communal areas of South Africa), the ecological rationale for pastoralism may become increasingly stretched (Baker and Hoffman, 2006; Chapters 5 and 9).

Conflict, raiding, war and displacement

Ownership of the key pastoral production resources of water, fertile land and livestock has continually been contested by different ethnic and occupational groups throughout sub-Saharan rangelands. The social organisation of many pastoralist groups has developed in the context of engaging in and managing negotiation and conflict over biophysical resources (Kurimoto and Simonse, 1998). Ageset or generation systems (where these exist), the ritual proving of manhood through combat and livestock raiding, the practised cooperative manoeuvres of herding, cutting out and splitting up, the physical skills and fitness involved in ranging over wide tracts of difficult country, and the fighting ethos, all lend themselves to coordinated military organisation (e.g. Lamphear, 1998). At the same time, the systems of negotiation between councils of elders, and the common cultural features allowing synchrony and assimilation between agesets of rival groups, provide pathways to reconciliation and resumption of normal conditions of trade and exchange in the aftermath of violent conflict. Through a combination of military organisation, innovative leadership, and processes of inclusion and assimilation, some groups have achieved spectacular expansions in the past, generally 'as much the spread of a culturo-linguistic system as a direct armed invasion' (Lamphear, 1994, 1998 – Turkana; Waller, 1985 – Maasai; Hall, 1990 – Zulu).

Livestock raiding is a time-honoured pathway for young men to establish themselves as herdowners and household heads. Captured livestock may form the basis of marriage and bridewealth payments; their redistribution buys social and political influence, and the power to orchestrate further raiding. This custom continues for many pastoralist groups within the framework of contemporary civil society (Heald, 1999; Fleischer, 1999; Hendrickson et al., 1998; McCabe, 2004). Local-level 'redistributive' raiding between relatively evenly matched groups can have major impacts on household livelihoods and economies, but the internal social networks of pastoralist societies help to buffer individual impacts. Where one group is armed with modern weapons and the other not, impacts have been far more serious, with long-term implications for survival. The real devastation comes when 'redistributive' raiding on the local scale is replaced by 'predatory' raiding operating an effectively commercial scale of violent livestock theft, as has been described for Turkana areas of northern Kenya:

'Predatory' forms of raiding have overwhelmed [the] social framework through their sheer intensity and scale ... the growing involvement of actors from outside the pastoral system ... has significantly undermined pastoral livelihoods and the socio-economic integrity of the pastoral system as a whole.... Predatory raiding is driven by a criminal logic contrasting sharply with former notions of balance and reciprocity. Predatory raids are largely initiated by people outside [the pastoral area] including armed military or bandit groups ... as well as 'economic entrepreneurs'. The motives are commercial: to procure cattle in vast quantities whether to feed warring armies or to sell on the market for profit... (Hendrickson et al., 1998: 191)

This form of predatory raiding has a long history in the Sudan (Johnson, 2003) and in Southern Africa (Wilmsen, 1989, 1991) where it effectively destroyed former pastoralist systems. Raiding can thus be an important constraint, with potentially critical impacts on local pastoral economies (Kurimoto and Simonse, 1998; McCabe, 2004; Hendrickson et al., 1998) merging into wider regional and international rivalries and conflicts (Mirzeler and Young, 2000; Hussein, 1998, Johnson, 2003). It is a major driver of famine and food insecurity in many contemporary pastoral systems in sub-Saharan Africa (Keen, 1995; Johnson, 2003, 2004; Hendrickson et al., 1998).

Apart from livestock raiding, there is ever-present competition with more settled farming people over key grazing and water resources, leading to recurrent conflict which is expressed through continual jockeying for rights of access, tenure and use, and may escalate into violence and war. There are no data adequate to demonstrate any trends of increasing frequency, intensity or scale of violent conflict over key natural resources (as opposed to conflicts of interest and non-violent forms of competition) between pastoralists and settled farming populations (Hussein, 1998). Herder-farmer relations continue to shift between cooperation, competition and conflict as they have for millennia. However, over the last century the nature and impacts of conflict have changed. In particular, the introduction of modern weaponry has changed the stakes. Acquisition of modern weapons can give the definitive advantage to one group (e.g. Oorlams over other Khoi pastoralists – Wilmsen, 1989; contemporary northern Uganda – Mirzeler and Young, 2000; McCabe, 2004 – impacts of differential arming/disarming of neighbouring groups in and among the Turkana). Over the past decade, state-armed Arab militias have repeatedly mounted ethnic cleansing or even genocidal attacks against effectively unarmed neighbouring, black agropastoralist groups in Western and South Sudan (Johnson, 2003, 2004; Keen, 1995; de Waal, 2004). Where there was formerly at least the theoretical possibility of balanced and reciprocal raiding between groups, total victory or at least heavy casualties have become new possibilities (Turton, 1996).

In many cases, particularly in Southern Sudan and the Horn of Africa, a lethal synergy has developed between local rivalries and geopolitical conflicts or international oil interests, that has meant decades of devastation (Johnson, 2003; Allen, 1996; Fukui and Markakis, 1994; Markakis, 1993; Hogg, 1997a). At the international level, the beginning of the twenty-first century sees major wars in many parts of Africa, most in the less densely settled border areas which are also commonly pastoralist areas (Galaty and Bonte, 1991). Pastoralist groups have been disproportionately drawn into such conflicts, in part because of the colonial legacy of boundaries which left many pastoralist groups fragmented between mutually hostile neighbouring nations[3] (Markakis, 1993; Galaty and Bonte, 1991). Commonly marginalised (even where they form the ethnic majority – Doornbos, 1993), and cast as subversive minorities within whichever nation they find themselves, pastoralist groups have, under different circumstances, ended up being co-opted by the state, and armed as militias fighting against dissident (or simply unwanted) groups, enlisted against their cross-border kin, or in other cases drawn into civil war against their own national governments.

Even where no war is evident, tensions over access to land and the concomitant intensifying competition for key resources, whether through population growth or the political economy of distribution, have meant that even apparently stable nation-states harbour considerable tensions and conflict issues around pastoralists, expressed through silent discrimination and silent violence (Hitchcock, 1996; Homewood et al., 2004).[4] Not only are basic services such as health, education and infrastructure often below-average, but the actual physical security and human rights of mobile pastoralist groups may be threatened, creating tensions around the most fundamental expectations citizens have of their governments. State agencies in conjunction with powerful outsiders (whether entrepreneurs or conservationists) commonly use modern weapons to coerce, evict and exclude pastoralists from their customary rangelands (Lane, 1996, 1998; Peluso, 1998; Brockington, 2002; Shivji and Kapinga, 1998). For example, Kenya and Tanzania have been stable since Independence, a stability that has been attributed to different groups' relative equality of access to economic benefits and/or political power (Klugman et al., 1999). Tanzania is seen as having shared power among a very wide range of ethnic groups, none of which dominates numerically, politically or economically, and also as having maintained relatively small differentials between the richest and the poorest, leading to an inherent stability (ibid.). However, the rapid, extensive alienation of pastoralist land for commercial farming, protected areas and private enterprise throughout Tanzania (particularly Maa-speaking areas – Shivji, 1998; Lane, 1996, 1998; Igoe and Brockington, 1999; Igoe, 2002, Chatty and Colchester; 2002; Homewood et al., 2004) has meant tens of thousands of displaced people and rising tensions over resource access, with an increasing incidence of violent confrontation[4] (Shivji and Kapinga, 1998: 43). By contrast, in Kenya, the transition to multiparty politics saw 'ethnic clashes' in the 1990s which centred in pastoralist and agropastoralist areas of the Rift Valley. The conflict killed hundreds (some estimate thousands) of Kikuyu and Kipsigis, and displaced tens of thousands more (some estimate hundreds of thousands – Klopp, 2001, 2002). These 'ethnic clashes' are generally thought to have been driven by extremely wealthy

---

[3] Tuareg: Algeria, Chad, Niger, Mali, Senegal; Maasai: Kenya, Tanzania; Boran: Kenya, Ethiopia; Somali: British Somaliland, Italian Somaliland, Ethiopia, Kenya, Djibouti; Beja: Eritrea, Sudan

[4] See e.g. http://www.ippmedia.com/ipp/guardian/2006/08/08/71991.html and 71990.html. For current 'anti-livestock policies' in Tanzania, invoking degradation narratives with this environmental discourse, see http://www.thisday.co.tz/News/1565.html. For policy framework enshrining these narratives, see URT (1997).

people central to Moi's regime, determined not to cede political power, and able to exploit existing concerns over land allocation among their potential followers, particularly Maasai (Galaty and Ole Munei, 1999; Galaty, 1999).

Four common dimensions thus come together to trigger and fuel conflict in a wide range of different sub-Saharan pastoral systems (Stewart, 2002):

(i) Ethnic differences aligning with and emphasising cultural identities and economic divides. The complex, constructed and shifting nature of ethnic identities heightens rather than negates their role in conflict.

(ii) Economic differences (either where very poor people feel they have nothing to lose by violence against the better-off, or where extremely wealthy people seek to defend their monopoly of resources against the demands of others).

(iii) Environmental factors (either where extremely rich resources are seen as there for the taking by *force majeure*, or where environmental deterioration means increasing need and contestation).

(iv) Failure of the social contract (particularly where the state condones or pursues abuses of people's constitutional and/or human rights).

A separate typology of natural resource conflicts (Hussein, 1998) gives cross-cutting dimensions of scale (Table 3.4). Individual violent disputes and local-scale raids, however lethal, are probably often overlooked in the national and international media. State violence may often be presented (and internationally perceived) as enforcement against poachers, trespassers or other outlaws, but may in fact represent eviction and forced displacement that destroys livelihoods on potentially enormous scales (Lane, 1996; Peluso, 1993; Brockington, 2002) or may operate more subtly through differential arming and disarming of neighbouring groups whose relative abilities to defend themselves against violent attack are then drastically changed (McCabe, 2004; Keen, 1995). Finally, political violence has been the most drastic and destructive form of conflict, affecting many pastoralist populations in the present day (Johnson, 2003, 2004; de Waal, 2004).

Table 3.4 Scales of conflict affecting pastoralist groups

Conflict Type	Definition
Individual violent disputes	Violence between individuals at local level Theft/livestock raiding Murder
State violence	State action supporting politically dominant resource users against others Mass eviction
Political violence	Military violence to subjugate populations and control resources War between armies within or between states Raiding livestock and/or slaves Destruction of villages

This section does not attempt a full analysis of conflict and war affecting pastoralist societies, but rather emphasises the ways conflict and war interact with pastoralist ecology. Briefly, violent conflict disrupts patterns of resource use (Bonfiglioli/NOPA, 1992; McCabe, 2004). Transhumant systems and migratory routes are suspended or lost. Whole areas of key seasonal grazing are vacated for security reasons or necessarily ceded to stronger groups. Modern weapons tip the scales in long-established patterns of reciprocal raiding or political conflict, meaning disastrous losses of livestock, territory and lives for the less well-armed (Bonfiglioli/NOPA, 1992; McCabe, 2004; Johnson, 2003, 2004).

Whether through continuous low-key contestation or outright war, conflict means displacement that is more or less forced. Pastoralists made destitute by conflict are drawn to relief camps where they can find food, water and shelter, and which become shanty towns. This includes internally displaced people silently or forcibly evicted from their grazing lands by conservation initiatives (Igoe and Brockington, 1999; Brockington, 2002; Brockington and Homewood, 1999; Chatty and Colchester, 2002) and development projects (Lane, 1998) or violence (McCabe, 2004; James, 1996; Johnson, 2003; Hutchinson, 1996; Dietz, 1996; Klopp, 2001), as well as those who are forced to cross international borders and become refugees (Markakis, 1993; Bonfiglioli/NOPA, 1992), dependent on relief (de Waal, 1997). Definitions are complex and numbers hard to estimate. Bonfiglioli (1992) quotes UNHCR estimates that, of 44.8 million refugees in Africa in 1989, over half were in the Horn of Africa (Ethiopia, Somalia, Djibouti and their neighbour states), many of them destitute pastoralists. Most Saharo-Sahelian nations have seen wars across or within their borders that have driven pastoralists to become refugees (Algeria, Niger, Mali, Chad, Sudan, Uganda, and others). Worldwide, there are thought to have been around 12-14 million cross-border refugees in 1999. Many of these are in Africa, the site of most armed conflicts within and between nations (UNHCR, cited in *The Economist*, 2001). Over and above cross-border refugees, there are thought to be around 12 million internally displaced people in Africa alone, in circumstances as bad as or worse than refugees. Around half or more of the refugees and displaced people in Africa are pastoralists, and of the total African refugee population, around half are in the Horn of Africa. Sudan has over 4 million displaced people, not counting cross-border refugees, and there are 500,000 displaced people in Ethiopia and Eritrea (*Economist*, 2001; see also Bonfiglioli/NOPA, 1992; de Waal, 2004).

Mobility may be a positive choice for many pastoralists (Turton, 1996), but forced displacement, concentration in relief camps, and forcible repatriation are not (Allen, 1996; Hutchinson, 1996; Bassi, 1997). As far as Southern Ethiopia is concerned:

> ... since the late 70s the region has been awash with modern automatic rifles and ammunition, thousands of people have been almost continuously displaced and separated from their means of livelihood... (Getachew, 1996)

Such forced movements or forced settlement create and fuel further competition over resources and further conflicts (e.g. Boran returnees in Moyale,

Ethiopia – Bassi, 1997). International political conflicts are then played out through local inter-ethnic competition.

Some observers see global geopolitics as sweeping pastoralism aside (Markakis, 1993), but for others, these events are old ethnic rivalries over pasture and water being played out through a new idiom of confrontation: 'International aid means new resources to be manipulated by local groups in the interests of old political and economic cleavages' (Bassi, 1997). Relief systems can play into the hands of those rivalries (Somalia and Ruanda – de Waal, 1997; see also Little, 2003). In Kenya, manipulation of drought relief has operated as a form of silent state violence against famine-stricken Oromo, Somali and Boran pastoralists in north-east Kenya, while favouring the central, urban electorate (Hendrickson et al., 1998).

For the purposes of this volume it is important to emphasise that, alongside the biophysical factors driving pastoralist mobility and resource use decisions, there are always powerful and frequently overwhelming social and political forces affecting those decisions. Pastoralist use of natural resources is not a simple response to biophysical conditions.

Political use of environmental narratives

Debates over ecosystem dynamics in general, and degradation in particular, are made more complex by having major political and philosophical as well as scientific dimensions. As well as empirical evidence and theoretical work focusing on the biological ecology of these systems, analyses of the environmental discourse and the political-ecology dimensions underpinning the debate are now beginning to emerge (Swift, 1996; Sullivan and Rohde, 2002). In the case of the disequilibrium debate in African rangelands, and more generally debates over resource use, powerful groups commonly invoke ecological theories such as equilibrium theory to support suggestions that local land use drives environmental degradation, and to justify attempts at intervention and control (as predicted by political ecology – Stott and Sullivan, 2000; Sullivan and Rohde, 2002; see Anderson, 2002 – Baringo forests; Brock-ington, 2003, 2006 – Tanzania). There is not the scope in this book to review the multiple and nuanced voices that historians have traced within what are too easily portrayed as monolithic state policies (Beinart and MacGregor, 2003; Anderson, 2002; Moore and Vaughan, 1994). Despite those diverse influences and internal debates, dominant colonial and postcolonial state narratives have tended to portray local users as likely to degrade environments and natural resources through poor management and unsustainable use, whether in dryland farming (Mortimore, 1998), forestry (Sunseri, 2005) or rangelands (Lamprey, 1983; Swift, 1996; Anderson, 2002), whether or not the biophysical evidence supports such degradation, or any causal attribution to local users.

There are compelling if not always consciously recognised reasons for established administrative and scientific authorities to downplay local expertise in resource management. The use of equilibrium theory environmental dis-course for political-ecological purposes is clear from the persistent reiteration of sometimes demonstrably false assumptions in the policy and practice of many sub-Saharan governments. These commonly allege environmental degradation by, and poor productivity in, mobile pastoralist systems, even where the weight of biophysical evidence contradicts official views. Biophysical characteristics of the environment are commonly invoked to support measures which are primarily political attempts to control people and resources. During the colonial and post-Independence periods, pastoralist societies across Africa have experienced numerous state interventions, generally couched in the language of environmental conservation, rehabilitation and sustainable management of fragile and threatened habitats or production systems. Such interventions include sedentarisation, tenure change or eviction, particularly through privatisation of formerly common property rangelands, or gazetting of protected areas within rangelands (Igoe and Brockington, 1999); restrictions on stocking rates and exclusion of pastoralist stock from areas designated for rehabilitation through soil conservation and water harvesting initiatives (e.g. Baringo – Anderson, 2002); forced stock culling (see Jacobs, 2003 for a powerful account of the Bophuthatswana donkey cull). The environmental discourse, which may or may not draw on sound biophysical evidence and analysis, has been widely invoked to underpin such actions since colonial times (Brown, 1971) up to the present day (United Republic of Tanzania, 1997; Brockington, 2003, 2006).

One well-researched example concerns the Tanzanian government's policy towards livestock production, which emphasises the goal of replacing extensive pastoralism with more intensive and sedentarised production, partly on environmental grounds (United Republic of Tanzania, 1997) and which takes a hardline approach to evicting pastoralists from areas of conservation interest (Igoe and Brockington, 1999). This is despite a decade of attempts by concerned environmental scientists to raise awareness of the positive ecological and economic contributions of extensive pastoralism in this semi-arid region (IIED drylands series; IIED pastoral land tenure series; Tanzania Natural Resources Forum, 2006; Homewood et al., 2001), and the major constraints on any widespread intensification and associated use of more input-dependent breeds (Homewood et al., 2006; Homewood et al., forthcoming). In present-day Tanzanian law, village lands are nominally owned by the village and managed by the village government (Village Land Act, 1998), though there is considerable pressure to maintain and extend state control through the (supposedly community-based and -oriented) mechanism of Wildlife Management Areas (WMAs). However, pastoral lands are defined under general land law as empty and therefore open to reallocation by the state (Land Act, 1998; Williams et al., forthcoming) paving the way for numerous pastoral evictions (Brockington, 2002). This is an example of a much wider phenomenon of displacement for conservation (Brockington et al., 2006) or for large-scale cultivation whether state-owned (Lane, 1996a, b, 1998 – Barabaig evictions) or private (Igoe and Brockington, 1999).

Pastoralism and conservation

The particular interplay of pastoralism and wildlife conservation has been explored in detail elsewhere (Homewood and Rodgers, 1987, 1991; Brockington 2002,

2004; Brockington and Homewood, 1996, 1999, 2001; Homewood and Thompson, in press; Homewood et al., forthcoming). Extensive pastoralism has co-existed alongside wildlife populations for centuries, and many rangeland habitats in part created by pastoralists have maintained significant levels of plant as well as animal biodiversity. During the twentieth century, the 'fortress conservation' model, based on exclusion of consumptive use, dominated colonial and later post-Independence administrative conservation policies. This model had emerged from a particular conjunction of social and historical dimensions peculiar to the West (nineteenth century industrialisation; Victorian era natural history and millenarian concerns; the rise of ecology as a science and a profession on the back of industries exploiting renewable natural resources including wildlife – Lowe, 1983). On the basis of this imported model, protected areas were established across the colonised world. Local resource use by former residents or by reserve-adjacent dwellers was criminalised, and access to protected areas and in particular to wildlife became the preserve of the social and scientific elite (Mackenzie, 1987). The Western 'wilderness' idyll came to underpin a widely held policy goal of restoring landscapes and ecosystems to some imagined 'pristine' state untouched by humans (Neumann, 1996, 1998). Protected areas have been gazetted throughout African savanna rangelands, particularly in East and South-east Africa, where productive grasslands and a mosaic of habitat diversity sustain a spectacularly large mammal wildlife. Pastoralists have consequently lost access to very significant proportions of the grazing and water resources they formerly used. These measures generate large numbers of displaced people, with no access to areas formerly central to their production and livelihoods (Chatty and Colchester, 2002; the many other cases include the Afar in Awash National Park – Farah, 1997; Allen, 1996; Parakuyo in Mkomazi – Brockington, 2002; West et al., 2006).

From the 1980s on, conservation thinking began to re-orientate around 'conservation with development' (CWD) models that are more inclusive of local users and residents. This shift emerged from a combination of three new developments: a growing awareness of the impacts of conservation on the human rights of local people, particularly the poor; concerns that with structural adjustment programmes ('rolling back the state') protected areas would only survive through enlisting the support of reserve-adjacent dwellers and a dawning awareness that, given the right conditions, local institutions and systems can be very effective in managing for ecological sustainability. This new CWD paradigm emerged alongside 'green development' economics in the prevailing neo-liberal environment (Pearce and Moran, 1994; Castree, 2003; Homewood and Thompson, in press). CWD and green development thinking both see sustainable use of natural resources as generating revenue to underpin community development. Pastoralist areas, such as the East African rangelands, which support spectacular wildlife and an established tourist industry, seem to offer ideal conditions and 'community-based conservation' initiatives have proliferated.

However, the practical experience of such projects has been mixed. There are commonly issues over defining the community of users: who is, or is not included. There are problems over levels of participation: devolution of control has been far less than is generally claimed, and in many cases community participation has been passive, if not actually coerced. Community-based conservation seems often more rhetoric than reality, with conservation goals being imposed rather than emerging as local priorities, and costs outweighing benefits for most local people. Indigenous knowledge has rarely been incorporated in appropriate ways (e.g. Goldman, 2003). Devolution of decision-making and other powers is minimal, community-level governance has been weak and in some cases blatantly corrupt (Blaikie, 2006; Menzies, 2004). Tenure rights are pivotal, and where pastoralists have clear title to land (as in the case of the privatised rangelands around the Maasai Mara in Kenya) then individual landowners can make lucrative deals. Where land is still largely controlled by the state, government agencies have been reluctant to cede the right to manage revenue (Homewood et al., 2005). Either way, there seems commonly to have been a concentration of benefits in progressively fewer hands as a result of community conservation initiatives (Homewood et al., 2005; Homewood et al., forthcoming). The associated restrictions mean that access to natural resources becomes harder for the poorest whose livelihoods most rely on using, processing and selling them.

Pastoral land-use & production strategies

This section looks at general principles of mobility and transhumance in response to unpredictably fluctuating environments, and develops a broad working classification of types of pastoralist systems, building on the cases presented in earlier chapters and developing a framework within which to place the many variants of pastoral production. Popular conceptions of pastoralism picture a nomadic lifestyle, whereas there is a range of conditions of mobility, with most pastoralists and agropastoralists having a semi-sedentary lifestyle. Again, popular conceptions of pastoralists evoke Maasai herders or Tuareg men of the desert, living on a milk and meat diet and scorning farmers, their work and their crops. In fact, only a small number of African pastoralist groups derive most of their food and the products they use directly from their herds. The framework developed here rests on both ecological and economic criteria. Ecological criteria of degrees of mobility and their relation to pastoral/agropastoral lifestyles are examined alongside more economic concepts of pure, milk-based, exchange-based pastoralism and agropastoralism, as well as of subsistence versus various degrees of commercialisation.

Land use and livestock management: mobility and transhumance

All pastoralist systems juggle the same basic production constraints of forage, water, minerals and disease, in a wider context of alternative possible economic activities, changing markets, and shifting security. Many African pastoralists are operating in arid or semi-arid environments, dominated by variability and unpredictability of both rainfall and primary production through seasonal and interannual fluctuations. Most pastoralist strategies involve movement and patch use, though lifestyles range from very mobile to relatively sedentary (Niamir-Fuller, 1999a; Turner, 1999a; Baker and Hoffman, 2006). Transhumance can be defined as the seasonal movement of livestock herds between spatially distant sites so as to make best use of pasture, water and mineral resources; to minimise exposure to disease and risk of crop damage; and/or to take advantage of other temporary opportunities (markets, social gatherings, etc.) dictated by seasonally changing conditions. The overwhelming universal ecological rationality of transhumance is suggested by the many different livestock production systems which use this practice, including most sub-Saharan pastoralist groups, Mediterranean pastoralist systems (including those of southern Europe, the Near East, and the Maghreb), European mountain transhumance systems (e.g. Swiss Alps, Pyrenees), Middle East (Kirghiz, Turkmen and Afghan), Central Asian (Mongolian cattle, small stock, horse and camel pastoralism), Siberian (from reindeer through to cattle, small stock) and New World transhumant systems (Andean camelid pastoralists). Australian pastoralist systems use comparable mobility, though many herd movements are managed by road train.

In areas where the spatio-temporal pattern of key resources is predictable, transhumance involves regular movements between wet and dry season in tropical and subtropical regions, or winter and summer pastures in more temperate and boreal zones. In increasingly arid and unpredictable systems, movements may be more frequent and less predictable in terms of precise locations, according to patchy rainfall and forage conditions. Transhumance may then involve movement between a fixed home base and a wider range of possible locations, depending on the conditions in any given year (e.g. Turkana – McCabe, 2004). Movement may be made more complex and frequent by major security problems, with raiding and violent conflict making certain areas too hazardous to use. Depending on the livestock species involved and on the local conditions, transhumance may entail cumulative annual displacement of anything from a few kilometres (typical of Maasai who may move 20-50km between wet and dry season sites), to hundreds (some Fulani pastoralists, including many using the Inland Delta of the Niger) or even thousands of kilometres (Saharan Tuareg camel pastoralists – Le Houérou, 1989). From the grand transhumant cycles of the Wodaabe Fulani and of some Tuareg camel herders, to the micro-movements of the most sedentary agropastoralists, Sahelian strategies tend to integrate livestock feeding on crop stubble in the dry season, manuring of fields, and keeping of livestock away from the maturing crops during the wet season, with optimising access to essential minerals and nutrients, and minimising exposure to disease. Movements may be altitudinal, where local topography provides the necessary contrast in patterns of resource availability (e.g. Maasai of Ngorongoro, moving between plains and highland), or catenary, where the local topography creates relatively subtle differences between floodplain and higher surrounding land (e.g. Dinka and Nuer in South Sudan). In other cases transhumance may be more a latitudinal system (some Fulani groups move between Sahelian, Sudanian and Guinean zones of the West African rangelands).

Transhumant movements may be undertaken for one or more of a whole range of possible reasons, and it can be difficult to tease out their relative importance. A number of studies have shown the significantly better health and production of transhumant animals compared with those in sedentary herds, and the central driving factor has commonly been the need to manage herd condition through making best use of forage, water and mineral availability. Pastoralists use mobility to optimise quality and quantity of forage (which varies with growth stage, mineral and nutrient content, and availability of crop residues). Wetlands represent key dry-season resources within arid lands (Scoones, 1991; Woodhouse et al., 2000), as do highland refuges. Different livestock species may follow different transhumant patterns according to their specific requirements (e.g. camels, cattle, sheep, goats – Coppock et al., 1986, 1988; McCabe, 2004). Elsewhere, grazing successions allow temporal sequences of different livestock (and wildlife species) to exploit an area as it passes through changing states (e.g. Sudd – Howell et al., 1988; Homewood and Rodgers, 1991:199). These states can be managed by controlling times of passage (e.g. Gallais, 1984; Legrosse, 1999 – Inland Delta of the Niger) and/or sequence of species (Sutherst, 1987) or herds (Legrosse, 1999; Turner, 1999b) or by manipulating grazing (Birley, 1982) and burning (Sutherst, 1987; Laris, 2002, 2003). Seasonal use of salt licks is important in rangelands that are nutrient-poor, or where minerals act as purgatives for herds debilitated by internal parasites (Baxter, 1991).

It is also important to minimise exposure to disease, and many pastoralist transhumance systems have developed to make the best of seasonal patterns of vector population increase and decline, and to balance disease opportunities and constraints with those of seasonal forage availability and of varying forage quality. Cattle transhumance is often timed to leave high-risk parts of the range as the rains come and vector populations increase (Boutrais, 1983), moving into drier rangelands where vector-borne disease is of little if any importance, to exploit the temporary flush of annual grasses in the wet season. As the rains come to an end and seasonal pastures are used up, the herds commonly return to wetter areas with more woody vegetation, and with better dry-season forage availability from perennial pastures and crop residues. These areas have potentially high populations of insect vectors of disease, and a higher incidence of disease transmission overall, but with the onset of the dry season vector populations decline and the risk is relatively lower during this time. Animals in good condition can withstand a degree of tsetse challenge, and a low level of exposure stimulates a degree of immunity. Similar considerations, trading disease risk against forage availability and quality, drive seasonal transhumance on a more local scale in many other systems, such as the Il Chamus in Baringo (Homewood, 1994), and Maasai in Ngorongoro (Potkanski, 1994).

Besides forage, water, minerals and disease, a number of other considerations enter into the decision to undertake transhumance. Many Fulani families in northern Burkina Faso saw as central the need to minimise crop damage by keeping herds away from growing crops until these have been fully harvested; other more mobile Fulani groups moved nearer to markets to earn a cash income through seasonal sales of pastoral produce (Hampshire, 1998; Buhl,

1999). Others use transhumance to facilitate participation in social gatherings (Bernus, 1981). In some densely populated communal lands of South Africa, movements are largely dictated by labour and other economic and logistic constraints, and respond in only very limited ways to changing water and grazing conditions (Baker and Hoffmann, 2006).

There is also considerable variation as to who may be involved. At one end of the scale, a household may simply send their cattle with a transhumant herder while staying put themselves, as has commonly been the case in the past for West African Sahelian and Sudanian agropastoral groups. Where a household has labour to spare, one or more young adult males may take the family herd(s) on transhumance. However, depending on household demography and the broader network of livelihood strategies, sending one or more adult men on transhumance can have major implications for a family's management of farming labour, and for the overall household economy. Among households concentrating more strongly on pastoralism, the whole family may move with the animals, except perhaps those who are too elderly, too young or too unwell to move. Finally, some pastoralist groups travel everywhere with the herds, irrespective of people's age and health. Families may join together to travel and camp (Turkana – McCabe, 2004); seasonally, large groups of families may congregate (as do Tuareg at the *cure salée* – Bernus, 1981).

Transhumant systems depend on access to key resources of grazing, water and minerals at any given season, and on rights of through passage between those sites. This raises questions of tenure and access. Most transhumant systems have been based primarily on common property resource management systems. These centre on control by the group of key water, pasture, mineral and other resources, and on negotiation of access to others as the need arises. Control of key resources gives access to surrounding areas, but often the exact radius controlled and used varies with conditions.

Turner (1999) emphasises that Saharo-Sahelian transhumant land tenure has commonly been defined by point-centred, key limiting resources around which the radius of control fluctuates according to conditions, rather than territorial definition by perimeter boundaries. Access operates through order of priority and precedence, not total exclusion. Permission to use grazing depends on graded access, contingent on grass condition, not on fixed spatial boundaries. Access may be negotiated through token gifts, labour provision, trade, relations of intermarriage, fostering and adoption, or payment in cash or in kind. Customary institutions managing transhumance are inherently flexible with fuzzy social and spatial boundaries, unlike 'modern' Westernised tenure systems based on imported European legal codes. Through colonial and post-Independence periods land has been progressively alienated to settlers and state enterprises. The spread of privatisation means that transhumant pastoralists are increasingly excluded from seasonally key resources by perimeter boundary fences. Through-routes are disrupted and pastoralists are losing user rights as the spread of crop cultivation takes precedence over pastoralism across most African rangelands. New common property management institutions specifically set up to govern such resources are vulnerable to being monopolised by leaders or gatekeepers operating in their own interests rather than those of the wider group (Legrosse, 1999). Many see this loss of freedom to move as the greatest threat to pastoralism (Niamir-Fuller, 1999). Developing innovative policy and institutions to support flexible movement and access presents a major challenge (Scoones, 1995).

Production strategies

'Pure' pastoralism and milk-based pastoralism. The Ngisonyoka Turkana derive more than 80% of their dietary energy from pastoral products, though other sections of the Turkana have a far lower average dependence on pastoral foods (Galvin, 1985; Coughenour et al., 1985; Little et al., 1992; Little and Leslie, 1999). In a number of groups (Ngisonyoka Turkana, some pastoral Maasai, and some Fulani communities), there may be seasonally total reliance on pastoral products. In other groups, there may be a cultural ideal that prescribes a total or near-complete pastoral diet for specific social age and sex classes, such as Maasai warrior agesets and Tuareg noble women (though few would meet the ideal). However, the ecology and economics of pastoral production make this the exception rather than the rule (see below and in Chapters 5 and 7). Those groups popularly seen as 'pure' pastoralists are more likely to practise milk-based pastoralism.

Milk is virtually a complete food, and in theory pastoral products could provide an adequate protein, calorie and even vitamin intake, but in practice milk production is highly seasonal. It is dictated by calving or kid production and by duration of lactation. These in turn depend on species and age/sex composition of the herd, forage availability, watering pattern and travel regime of the herds, and are therefore highly variable from season to season, year to year, and affected not just by local conditions but by the availability of labour to make the best of these conditions. Dahl and Hjort (1976), among others, have attempted to work out the theoretical herd sizes required to support a pastoralist family on pastoral products alone, given seasonal and interannual variability. In practice this is an exercise of academic interest only. The numbers of animals necessary would be too great to be managed by the size of family they could reliably support through the dry season. The simple outcome is that all herding peoples have recourse to other items of diet which they must obtain by gathering/hunting (such as the Ngisonyoka Turkana – Coughenour et al., 1985; the Kalahari BaSarwa or San pastoroforagers of the nineteenth century – Wilmsen, 1989; and the impoverished Tuareg of the present day – Randall, 1988); as pastorofishers – (Turkana, Il Chamus); farming (Tuareg of the Damergou and Kel Owey of the Aïr – Bernus, 1981; Il Chamus – Anderson, 1988; Djafun Fulani – Boutrais, 1986; Benefice et al., 1984); by exchange or sale (Fulani – Hopen, 1958; Boutrais, 1978); by fully fledged commerce (Tuareg – Bernus, 1981; Fulani – Dupire, 1962a; Kerven, 1992) or through the many possible forms of small-scale diversification (Little et al., 2001) including, for example, artisanal mining for gold (Hampshire, 1998) or gemstones (Sachedina, forthcoming). The pastoral systems discussed in this book all display some combination of these methods of food acquisition, production or income generation.

Exchange pastoralism. The economics of pastoral food production and exchange are such that milk, milk products and meat all command generally favourable terms of trade relative to cultivated cereals and root crops (Chapters 5 and 9; Swift, 1986; Zaal and Dietz, 1999). Pastoral products are seen as high-quality foods by most farming and urban populations. Both the calorific and the monetary terms of trade are such that the pastoral producer can generally obtain by barter or purchase an amount of grain which more than covers food needs, in exchange for an amount of pastoral produce which could not meet those needs. In extensive systems, where livestock convert extensive rangeland forage to milk and meat, terms of trade remain favourable so long as the means of production are not seriously impacted by drought or disease. As livestock production gets progressively more intensive, and as the cost of inputs like fodder, veterinary care, construction materials and water increase, so the terms of trade may be less favourable. Given that the basic terms-of-trade equation is commonly strongly in favour of pastoral produce, it is not surprising to find that many pastoral systems operate on the basis of sale or exchange to get cereal or other crop produce for supplementing the diet, and that with rapid urbanisation these markets are growing (Tiffen, 2006). In addition to the sale and exchange of milk or meat, some pastoral systems derive income in cash or in kind from the sale or barter of hides (McPeak and Little, 2006), of dung and/or animal labour (Toulmin, 1983a). The Uda'en, a Fulani clan of Niger and Nigeria, herd sheep and goats and sell the skins. In the pre-colonial period, there was a significant trade across the Sahara in these skins, which constituted an important source of 'Morocco' leather.

Agropastoralism. The term agropastoralism encompasses a wide range of systems found throughout Africa, including any system which combines livestock keeping and farming. The term therefore includes not only those societies which centre culturally and economically on livestock, but also those many societies, widespread and largely dominant in rural sub-Saharan Africa, which centre primarily on cultivation but which make extensive use of livestock as a wealth store, as a source of draft power and of manure (Toulmin, 1992), and as an important element of social contracts (Kuper, 1982). These societies may primarily emphasise the tools and products of cultivation – granaries, bananas, yams, cassava, the hoe – while readily investing in small and large stock as part of their integrated mixed farming systems. The integration of farming and herding has proved to be an immensely successful, lasting production system, with different variants having emerged across the continent from different combinations and permutations of the ancestral food-producing traditions outlined in Chapter 2, along with more recently developed, adopted and evolving domesticates and technologies. Cultivation-centred agropastoralism accounts both numerically and in terms of areal extent for most rural peoples across the Sudanian zone of west and central Africa, and across southern and eastern Africa (Tanzania, Zambia and Zimbabwe, in particular), as well as more southerly areas (e.g. Lesotho) and suitable parts of north-eastern Africa (Ethiopian highlands, Nuba mountains). Agropastoralist peoples who combine farming and mobile (rather than zero-grazed) livestock include the mixed farming groups of the Great Lakes, most of the southern African peoples touched upon in this book (Chapters 2 and 4), and many north-east, east and south-east African examples mentioned only in passing (Zaghawa, Karimojong, Kuria, Sukuma, Gogo, Nyamwezi, etc.).

These highly successful and widespread societies centre on integrating farming and stock-keeping and fall largely outside the scope of this book, which is concerned with more specialised forms of livestock keeping, with a strong cultural and economic focus on livestock. It is not possible here to do justice to the diversity and scale of agropastoralist systems across Africa. Their historical evolution and present-day forms have been documented in many other studies (see Ehret, 1998, 2002 for an historical account; Scoones and Wolmer, 2002; Tiffen, 2006 for current trajectories; present-day case studies include Bambara – Toulmin, 1992; Hausa – Mortimore, 1989; Kofyar – Stone, 1996; Tugen – Dietz, 1987; Meru – Spear, 1997; Pare – Kimambo, 1969; Kiwasila, forthcoming; Gogo – Williams, 2006; Shona – Wilson, 1990; communal homelands of South Africa – Jacobs, 2003). The present book is limited to an overview of the interaction between agropastoralism and more specialised livestock-keeping systems. This is not to treat cultivation-centred agropastoralist societies as a remainder category. The book emphasises continuities between pastoral and agropastoral systems, their complementarities and conflicts (e.g. Fulani agropastoral societies – Chapters 2 and 4; pastoral diets – Chapter 7; trajectories of diversification and development – Chapter 9).

There are many ways to integrate farming with herding, both spatially and socially. Contrary to the received wisdom, there is no simple evolutionary progression towards greater integration (see Scoones and Wolmer, 2002 for cases in Ethiopia, Mali and Zimbabwe). Widespread agropastoralist cultivation of rainfed crops in drylands systems may extend into cultivation of more agroecologically favourable areas, with irrigated crops in river and groundwater areas, and high-density, intensive montane systems where more favourable soil and water conditions allow a wide range of crops (cf. Spear, 1993b). A broad band of cattle/small stock/millet agropastoralist systems stretches from the west coast across the Sahel to the Nile and into the Horn, grading into cattle/maize where less arid conditions permit (e.g. throughout the Sudanian/Guinean zone south of the Sahel). Similar cattle/small stock/millet/maize systems are found throughout East and South-east Africa. Local variants focus on cultivation of *tef* grain and *enset* staples in Ethiopian agropastoral systems, and cassava (drier) and banana (wetter) staple cultivation alongside livestock in East and South-east Africa. Fricke's classic 1979 analysis of cattle-keeping systems in Nigeria suggested that progressively more sedentary lifestyles correlate with progressively greater involvement with cultivation and decreasing dependence on livestock.

As this suggests, farming and herding complement but may also conflict or compete with one another (McCown et al., 1979). Cultivation benefits from associated herding through the provision of manure and draught or traction power, and the wealth store role of livestock. Many African systems have inherently poor soil fertility. This is a particular problem with Sahelian soils, or wherever it is not possible to fallow sufficiently frequently. Under these

Table 3.5 Association between pastoralism and mobility

Livestock	Cultivation system	Mobility	Example
Nomadic	–	Unconstrained by cultivation	Wodaabe
Semi-nomadic	Limited	Limited constraints on mobility	
Semi-sedentary	Greater dependence	Fixed homestead + seasonal transhumance	Maasai
Sedentary zero-grazing stock Stock in enclosure	Intensive cultivation system – terraced, manured, permanent fields	Fixed homestead year-round	Kofyar/ Chagga montagnards

After Fricke (1979)

circumstances the use of manure can raise yields by an order of magnitude. Bambara farmers in Mali have long invested in wells to attract Fulani herds during the post-harvest dry season (Toulmin, 1992) and are increasingly investing in their own animals. Stubble-grazing cattle manure and trample the village fields, and improve the yields of short-cycle millet (Ramisch, 1999). Bambara farmers also maintain lower-yielding bush fields, more often moved, but not manured. As well as enhancing soil fertility and crop yield, oxen are used throughout the Sahelian zone as draught animals. An ox-plough can treble the area cultivated. Arid-area farms cannot generally be tilled before the first rains have softened the soil. Ox-ploughing is particularly important where it is vital to plough and sow as soon as the first rains start so as not to waste any time in the short growing season. As well as ploughing, oxen can be used to draw cartloads of crops to market for sale where the only alternative may be to headload them.

Finally, livestock play an essential role as a wealth store. With a good harvest, purchase of livestock is a better way to invest the profits than either banking money or storing grain. Banks are few and far between in rural arid and semi-arid rangeland areas of Africa, and in any case local currencies are subject to rapid inflation and sudden devaluations. Some agropastoralists have highly developed grain-store systems, but even the best of these suffer losses of the order of 30% to invertebrate and vertebrate pests. At the same time, profits invested in livestock yield a good rate of return in the form of herd increase. In their turn, livestock derive certain benefits from being integrated into a mixed farming system. In particular, they can graze on crop residues and stubble at the same time as they trample their own manure in to fertilise the field. In some systems crop residues make up over 90% of cattle intake in the dry season.

However, livestock inputs do not all help crop farming, and cultivation also imposes certain constraints on livestock. In the most arid systems, manuring is more likely to 'burn' the crop than to enhance the yield (Buhl, 1999). Elsewhere, manure is thought to introduce noxious weeds and farmers prefer not to use it (Kiwasila, forthcoming). Where population densities grow and where cultivators settle around permanent water, access to dry-season water and grazing becomes difficult both for transhumant livestock temporarily in the area, and for resident agropastoral livestock which must be kept from damaging crops, water channels or other structures associated with water points and irrigation. Labour bottlenecks mean that people are needed in the fields at the time when livestock should be moved to wet-season pastures to minimise infection and maximise nutritional benefits. This problem is resolved in a number of ways. Agropastoralists may accept a lower level of production (Chapter 6) or may use fencing, fodder supplements and veterinary inputs to overcome the disadvantages of keeping livestock resident. In some cases agropastoralists entrust their animals to transhumant herders (as the Bambara did with the Fulani before the 1980s droughts, though the practice is less common now). In many cases division of labour is achieved by splitting the household. Some societies have been split by caste into mobile herders and settled farmers (as for the hierarchical societies of the Tuareg and Fulani, with pastoralist nobles taking the crops of their cultivating slaves). In higher population-density systems there may be strictly defined division of land use by zoning. Elsewhere, fields are fenced and stock roam free.

In some sites with special ecoclimatic attributes, particularly montane areas, high-density systems have evolved (e.g. the Kofyar of Nigeria). In some cases long-established practices of zero-grazing stall-fed cattle (Meru, Chagga, Kikuyu, Pare) merge into recently intensified high-potential systems. Intensified systems in high-potential montane areas, as well as in peri-urban locations, are most likely to adopt new high yield breeds for dairying, and to have access to the technologies necessary for making the most of their productive capabilities.

Transhumant pastoralists with a largely milk- or exchange-based system tend to develop herd structures that differ from those associated with mixed farming and settled agropastoralism. In mixed farming systems, a supply of milk is less important than a supply of large animals strong enough to draw plough or cart, and the sex ratios reflect this (Chapter 6). The management of the animals changes radically. Animals associated with settled agropastoralists may have higher exposure to disease and poorer nutrition than transhumant animals (Table 1 in Scoones, 1991). Oxen require extra inputs while they are working, but the forage resources available to them year-round are poor. However, the relatively more sedentary nature of agropastoral systems makes them in principle more accessible to extension services presenting opportunities for higher-yielding breeds, alongside veterinary support.

Pastoralism and trade. Several major pastoralist groups have historically combined livestock-centred production and culture with long-distance trade, dealing not only in pastoral produce and crops, but also in high-value commodities carried overland by pack animal. Tuareg groups developed a continent-wide trading network channelling salt, ivory, gold and slaves as well as other commodities, underpinning a coast-to-coast commerce that linked West and North Africa, and charted the Sahara as navigable routes rather than an impassable barrier (Chapter 2; Lovejoy and Baier, 1975). In the same way the Beja of the Red Sea developed and maintained trade routes which waxed and waned with the Silk Road and the spice trade (Chapter 2). While the continental importance of these trading systems has fluctuated with competition from shipping and more recently motor and air transport, there have been continuities. Much local trade still relies on pack and draught animals, and long-distance trading skills have in some cases transposed into new contexts (Somalis are prominent in overland heavy lorry transport throughout East and Central Africa; Beja dockworker groups, which evolved along lineage-based *dia*-paying group lines, re-emerge among immigrant and refugee communities in Europe).

Subsistence versus commercial pastoralism. There is no clear boundary between subsistence and commercial pastoralism. Up to the 1980s there was a tendency to confuse 'commercial' with Western-style ranching operations and 'subsistence' with indigenous African systems running on apparently customary lines. As the history of the Tuareg empire makes clear, African stockmen may be producing and trading on an international scale from operations which appear 'traditional', 'subsistence' transhumant systems. This confusion in terminology masks the socio-economic and operational continua between subsistence (<25% of gross returns from sale or exchange), partly commercialised systems (25-50% of gross returns from sale or exchange) and commercial systems (> 50% of gross returns from sale or exchange – Swift, 1986). Within the broad array of Fulani societies, for example, it is easy to identify systems spanning this whole range. Hopen (1958) described small family systems in Gwandu where in the 1950s the man herded the cattle and milked them, and his wife sold the milk and purchased grain for food. These typify the subsistence/exchange pastoralism end of the scale in present-day Burkina Faso, with the relatively impoverished Peul mostly subsisting as cultivating agropastoralists in the aftermath of the late-twentieth-century droughts. Among the wealthiest herdowners, women were secluded, selling no milk despite having a surplus. In the same way, among the strictly orthodox Islam Fulbe of the Adamawa Plateau, the increasing importance placed on female seclusion has encouraged herdowners to go over to live animal and/or meat sales. This means that milk production is converted into calf growth and survival, producing more animals for offtake, while women are shielded from a public role selling milk. The established Fulani commercial operators in Nigeria run a major beef trade on an international scale (Chapter 9) from indigenous operations which on the face of it appear to be 'traditional', 'subsistence' transhumant systems (Kerven, 1992).

   The full range of systems often coexist side by side, as in Fulani societies and in Botswana and Kenya with small and large-scale operators (Behnke, 1983, 1985). It is not uncommon for primarily subsistence pastoralist communities to supply animals to commercial operations which then fatten and sell them on (Sandford, 1983). Although any one pastoralist household might sell only a few animals, and rarely at that, in aggregate the subsistence operation feeds the commercial. In some cases there have been major transitions to countries becoming dominated by commercialised systems, where formerly much of the land was occupied by small-scale, family 'subsistence' systems. Behnke's (1983) analysis of processes in Libya, Somalia and Botswana suggests that systems at the subsistence end of the scale show a low livestock: person ratio; labour-intensive herding and husbandry; efficient extraction of a wide range of products – milk, meat, hides, dung, labour (even marginal products are extracted, as the opportunity costs of people's labour are low); a very large number of people supported or employed at a relatively low material standard of living, but with a relatively good security of livelihoods and entitlements; communal tenure of land and water resources; social redistribution of livestock and access rights as well as labour; and low investment capital other than land/labour/animals.

These characteristics contrast with those of commercial livestock production systems where there are a large number of livestock per person; low labour inputs; private land tenure; a focus on a single product or a narrow range of products; private investment (even if this is low per unit animal or area, commercial enterprises tend to be large concerns and therefore involve large sums overall); high rates of return per individual (even if returns are low per animal or per unit area, the concerns are so large and the returns are distributed among so few people that the profits to shareholders can be great). Development experience from the 1960s on suggests that it is not possible to force an easy transition to a more commercial system, as has often been tried (Sandford, 1983; Behnke, 1983; Chapter 9). Market conditions, patterns of control over basic productive resources, market security, and alternative possibilities for those outmigrants dispossessed by commercialisation all play their part in cases of spontaneous transition. Where commercialisation of livestock production has come about with no safeguards many pastoralists are dispossessed. A large underclass of hired herders emerges, serving absentee stockowners, and swells the numbers of the destitute – whether poor urban migrants or displaced people squatting in or drifting through increasingly privatised rural landscapes.

Hired herders and absentee stockowners. Throughout pastoral areas there is a widely-recognised increase in absentee stockowners and hired herders. All pastoral systems seem to have the possibility of labour for hire, but many historically had payment systems that allowed the hired man to re-establish himself in the pastoralist enterpise. The trend now, especially after several decades of spreading commercialisation, changing land tenure, and climatic downturn, is that herders are taken on for such poor pay that they are unable to re-establish themselves. This is a result both of their inability to build up their own herd, and of the increasing difficulty of ensuring access to the necessary grazing and water resources. This compounds the problem that former systems of loan and redistribution tend to crumble when set against greater market possibilities (White, 1986 – Fulani; Little, 1985 – Baringo Il Chamus). Many systems show a progressive dispossession of the subsistence herder while allowing the opportunist investor to profit, if s/he can establish exclusive access to land or livestock. Where such investors are outsiders, as is often the case, they can gain access by approaching destitute ex-herdowners who retain customary rights of access within communal grazing areas

(Homewood, 1994). Outsiders can then place their stock with such destitute pastoralists for a small fee. The more destitute the herders looking for such opportunities, the lower the fee and the more remote the chances of herders re-entering the pastoral economy as owners in their own right. This widespread practice puts increasing pressure on the social institutions which nominally regulate it (Bourbouze, 1999; Williams, 2006). Climatic fluctuations driving livestock losses and impoverishment, and transfer of land from common property to private tenure, both act to increase the numbers of hired herders and absentee herdowners (Homewood, 1994).

Pastoralism as a component of land use and economy. The case studies presented in Chapters 2 and 4, and the framework presented above, make it clear that, just as there are many forms of pastoralism, there are also many ways in which pastoralist occupations and economies tie in to other patterns of land use and subsistence. Pastoralism is rather one facet of local, regional and international patterns of land use and economy. Pastoralist individuals, households and communities maintain links with and undergo transitions between herding and farming, hunting and gathering, trade and other pursuits. Pastoralism is in no sense an isolated activity. It is integrated in many ways and on many levels with ranching, caravanning, wildlife enterprises; farming; trade and seasonal labour migration. Any understanding of pastoralist systems and strategies must be based on an understanding of the ways in which individuals and households operate a network of activities spanning several or all of these possibilities, and their ecological and economic interactions. As a prelude to these analyses, the next chapter presents case studies describing the ecological and environmental variety of a number of pastoralist systems.

4

Contemporary Pastoralist Systems

This chapter sketches examples of the main pastoralist ecosystems in different parts of Africa, in each case outlining the main features of the natural environment and their exploitation by recent and contemporary pastoralist groups. The chapter acts as background for the analyses and syntheses of material on pastoralist economy, herd biology, pastoral food systems, demography, and processes of development and change that follow in the rest of the book.

Different authors use the terms Saharan, Sahelian, Sudanian and Guinean to mean rather different things (Table 3.1: see also Le Houérou, 1989; Raynault, 1997). These latitudinal bands or zones of climate and vegetation dictate grazing, water and disease conditions for livestock and people throughout West and West-Central Africa. They make up stages along a continuum from arid to humid rangelands, and from the ephemeral, patchy growth of annual grasses in the arid areas to the fire climax, wooded, perennial grasslands, dominated by disease vectors, in the humid zone. By definition these zones abut and overlap. Where the following sections indicate rainfall, vegetation type and species composition in particular pastoralist systems, these are given as examples rather than as any exclusive definition of the type. Saharan Tuareg groups overlap with Fulani pastoralism in the northern and central Sahel. Fulani cattle-keeping systems extend across the full latitudinal span of the Sahel through the Sudanian into the Guinean zone described in the section below on wet savanna.

Saharo-Sahelian pastoralism: Tuareg

The Sahara runs East-West from the Atlantic coast to the Nile between latitudes 15-20°N and 25-30°N. It straddles the northern Tropic, receiving a mean annual rainfall of less than 150mm and in many parts less than 100mm or even 25mm. Several geographically and culturally distinct pastoralist peoples use this arid zone. Each crosscuts the Sahara in a sparse swathe stretching some 1500km north to south, linking into the Sahelian and/or the Mediterranean zones (colour map; Fig. 2.1). The Moors link the Maghreb to sub-Saharan Africa along the Atlantic coast and are separated from the Tuareg by a broad belt of dune desert. The Tuareg are centred on the Saharan massifs of Hoggar (Ahaggar) in Algeria and Aïr in Niger, and on the inland Delta of the Niger in Mali. They are separated from the Teda (Tubu) of Tibesti and Ennedi in Chad by the eastern Ténéré. The Teda are bounded to the north by the Libyan desert, and to the east abut on pastoral and other peoples of Darfur in the Sudan. Towards the wetter, southern, Sahelo-Sudanian zone, these groups spread out and intermingle with each other and with other groups of herders and farmers (such as the Fulani, Songhai, and Zarma peoples).

Rainfall is highly variable from year to year. The 350mm isohyet that marks the limit of rainfed cultivation shifts year by year, and the 150mm isohyet shows even more marked fluctuations (Nicholson et al., 1998; Nicholson, 2002). There has been a sharp downturn in the rainfall of most West African arid and semi-arid zones since the 1970s (Fig. 3.3). Potential pasture and water resources are widely spaced. Pastoral transhumant systems of the Saharo-Sahelian zone have by necessity been long-range and for many centuries have centred on camel pastoralism, with present-day northern Moors, Tuareg, Teda, Zaghawa and Kababish camel pastoralists commonly undertaking annual movements of 1000km or more.

The Saharan massifs with their water catchments have for thousands of years acted as stepping stones, staging posts, and crossroads in herd movements and trade networks. The range and variety of Saharo-Sahelian pastoralist ecosystems is illustrated by the Tuareg people of the 900,000 km² Aïr massif and its associated drainage basin in Niger (Figs 2.1, 2.2; Bernus, 1981). This area occupies the central southern Sahara, and is ringed by the outlying massifs of the Ahaggar and the Adrar'n'Ifoghas (Bernus, 1981, 1990). In the 1970s there were some 800,000 Tuareg people overall in Niger, Mali, Algeria and Burkina Faso, comprising hundreds of different subgroups. Of these the majority (estimated by Bernus as ca. 500,000 people in the late 1970s) occupied the western half of Niger, with the Aïr as focal point. The Aïr is a massif with a granite/gneiss plateau, bearing younger granite block-faulted mountains which are themselves capped with volcanic cones and flows. In the north of the Aïr, these peaks rise to 2000m. Immediately west of the Aïr lies the Talaq (clay plains) that merge into the Ténéré (desert plains) of Tamesna, an area rich in salt deposits and with high mineral content wells. Until recent decades the wet season brought a concentration of Tuareg, converging from the Ahaggar massif in Algeria to the north, from the Aïr to the east and from Sahelian zones to the south (Damergou and Ader), seeking Tamesna pastures and *cure salée*. Most of this Tuareg country is overlaid with windblown sand, and in the extreme north-west, dunes cover the plains.

The south and south-west flanks of the Aïr massif are carved into valleys and dry braided riverbeds, which converge with drainage lines from the Ahaggar and Adrar'n'Ifoghas massifs to form the great Azawagh fossil valley system linking the Sahara to the Niger river valley. The Azawagh runs southwest to the Niger border, through sandstone plains and fossil dune fields fixed by sparse vegetation. The Azawagh then turns south in Mali to become the Dallol Bosso around Filingué. All these fossil valleys run ultimately to the Niger River. The Gourma or right bank, inside the bend of the river, is a low-lying plain (3-500m asl) inhabited by the westernmost Tuareg of Niger, continuous with the Tuareg of Mali. East of the Aïr, Ténéré plains of Tafasaset grade into no man's land dividing Tuareg from Teda or Tubu territory.

The Tuareg described by Bernus (1981) depended on the relatively higher rainfall, rock pools and springs and run-off from the great Saharan massifs. Ground water seeps down and feeds a shallow water table in the dry riverbeds for some way out into the adjacent plains. There are *foggara* water collection and delivery systems further north in the Ahaggar mountains, but not in the Aïr. Where possible, Tuareg used surface and near-surface water, sometimes scraping shallow seepages or digging traditional wells up to 40m in depth. These wells, some dating back to pre-Tuareg, prehistoric times, had draft animals operating pulley and bucket systems. Far from the massif, rock strata hold water at a great depth (often high in sodium chloride, carbonate and/or sulphate). This water is sometimes tapped by modern cement-lined wells of 40-80m depth with boreholes and pumps. Further south and west, the Tuareg exploited the longer-lasting surface-water and more accessible ground-water resources of the central Sahel.

Saharan and Saharo-Sahelian vegetation zones shift with latitude, topography and altitude. The ecoclimatic zones of the Aïr become wetter from north to south, from east to west and from low to high altitude. North of the 150mm isohyet, rain brings a flush of *Aristida* annual grasses and *Cornulaca* herbs to the dunes, as well as sparse solitary tufts of the perennial *Panicum turgidum* and stands of wild sorghum. *Schouwia* ('*alwat'*) grows in special edaphic conditions found in parts of the Tamesna north of 17°N. The Saharan woody species *Tamarix* grows where conditions permit. South of the 150mm isohyet, brief, patchy dense growth of *Cenchrus bifloris* (Tamasheq – *cramcram*) becomes an important wild resource (Chapter 7). Moving south, barren sand, gravel and rock give way to shrubs and stunted trees along dry watercourses – first, *Acacia* species, and then a widening diversity (*Commiphora, Balanites, Salvadora, Boscia, Maerua, Calotropis* spp. and *Hyphaene* doum palms) and progressively taller growth. The shrubs and trees are an important source of fodder (Le Houérou, 1980). As number, diversity and size of plants increase, shrubs like *Ziziphus* and *Grewia* become common, and woody species are used for browse, fuel, fencing fields, livestock enclosures and utensils. Mediterranean species (*Olea, Rhus)* persist in the northernmost peaks of the Aïr at altitudes of over 1500m, with some of the olive trees over 3000 years old. South of the Tigidit scarp that marks the southern border of the Aïr massif, the dissected sandstone Tadarast plateau carries stands of *Commiphora africana* (*adaras*) from which the area derives its name. Still further south, beyond the 350mm isohyet, cultivated fields become increasingly common.

Bernus divided the Tuaregs of Niger into the nomads of the western flank of the Aïr and Ténéré plains of Tamesna; the Kel Owey and associated Kel Aïr groups of the Aïr massif; the Azawagh Tuareg (Kel Denneg and associated groups); the Tuareg of the southern border near Nigeria (Kel Gress of the Ader); and the Tuaregs of Western Niger (using, for example, the Gourma area within the bend of the Niger, Fig. 2.2). He saw each of these as made up of many subgroups varying in terms of geographical origin, physical ancestry, relative importance of various castes drawn from the highly stratified Tuareg society, and socio-economic specialisation at the time of his study (Bernus, 1981). Formerly highly distinct social strata, graded from noble to slave, changed with colonial impacts, with Independence and the post-Independence droughts, and most recently with the wars, forced displacement and refugee status that have overtaken many Tuareg. Many noble households hired labour or worked for themselves where once they depended on Bella.[1] Bernus' descriptions of Tuareg of the western Tamesna, of the Azawagh and the Aïr massif exemplify Saharo-Sahelian systems. Tuareg of the Gourma and the Ader are described later as examples of central Sahelian pastoralism.

Broadly speaking, the twentieth-century Tuareg of the Tamesna were specialised livestock herders who traded their pastoral produce for cereals, cloth and other goods. They participated to some extent in the caravan trade and concentrated on herding camels, though they had cattle and small stock too. They were drawn from a number of groups including the Kel Ahaggar whose base is in the Ahaggar massif of Algeria to the north, and Iullemedden Tuareg such as the Kel Denneg from the south. During the hot season of April-June the Tuareg gathered round the major permanent water sources, and the rhythm of pastoralist activity was dominated by the watering schedule. With the first rains between June and July, stock were moved to the Tegidda 'n-Tesemt salt springs to drink the strongly mineral waters and feed on the fresh growth: the high mineral intake *cure salée* is thought to purge the animals of their intestinal parasite load. At the same time, the Hoggars of the Aïr moved south at the start of the rains to meet the northbound ITCZ (Chapter 3). Tuareg from north and south converged on individual localities with high-potential seasonal forage and with major perennial water sources fed by the artesian water table. At the same time, the Tuareg collected grains from the dense stands of wild *Gramineae*. Different waves of Tuareg from different dry-season ranges arrived in sequence for their *cure salée*. As the southern Tuareg (Kel Gress and Iullemedden Kel Denneg) moved northward to take advantage of the *cure salée,* the Hoggars of the Aïr began to return further north still, keeping their herds ahead of the newcomers, while the Kel Ahaggar made use of forage on the plains south and west of Tegidda'n-Tesemt. With the onset of the dry season and cold weather, camels were moved to the *alwat* pastures of the north Tamesna. *Schouwia* plants continue to produce well into the dry season, forming a central wet-season forage resource with up to 2–4kg dry matter/ha/year. The camel camps were staging posts: exhausted camels from trading caravans were left to recover condition, and fresh animals taken.

---

[1] The Bella are descendants of former slaves (Fr. *captifs*) mostly raided from sub-Saharan black African farming communities. Tuareg society was (and in many places remains) strongly hierarchical: nobles raided and traded; vassals herded the livestock, slaves did household and farm work, blacksmiths managed metalwork, and with the adoption of Islam, a religious marabout class developed.

In the 1980s the Kel Owey and associated groups of the Aïr massif were specialised farmers and caravanners. They had permanent settlements where they grew irrigated cereals as well as vegetables and date palms along the narrow terraced banks of the watercourses of the Aïr. Wheat was grown for export, millet and maize for home consumption. The Kel Owey kept small and large stock, particularly camels, and ran a large part of the caravan trade. The caravan trade was crippled in the first decades of the twentieth century by conflict between the Tuareg and the French. By the 1950s and '60s, the Bilma salt caravan again numbered 20-30,000 camels three times a year. It carried 300 tons of millet in (together with hundreds of tons of butter, sugar, tea, cloth, dried vegetables, fodder, fuel and other goods) and brought out 2000 tons of salt and 400 tons of dates. In the 1970s Bernus (1981) estimated a similar scale of caravan trade, somewhat reduced by recent drought. More recently it was again disrupted by the recurrent civil unrest that has torn Niger, southern Algeria and Mali over the last decades. The need for cereals to be imported into the pastoral zone is largely undiminished, but the value of desert products has not kept pace with the relative desire for mass-produced items from industrialised countries. Lorry-borne manufactured products began to replace the caravan trade in salt and dates where tarmac routes allow, but from 1986 on there was a resurgence in camel transport (Bernus, 1990) which continues today (Pilkington, 2006).

The Azawagh, where the Kel Denneg were based, is a region of fossil dunes, with a sparse plant cover and fodder trees along riverbeds. During the wet season the Kel Denneg moved their cattle and small-stock herds north, making use of temporary surface water and of stands of wild *Gramineae* in their Saharan wet-season pastures. Between September and October they began to move their herds back to their Sahelian dry-season pastures, where fodder trees made year-round use possible. The *ineslemen* or religious caste of the Tuareg were the main cattle owners in the Azawagh. A few groups specialised in camel rearing, linked to caravanning, but this was rare among the Kel Denneg. Many of the Tuareg groups of this region formerly controlled slave communities of millet farmers further south in the Ader. Those farmers are now independent owners of the land they once cultivated as serfs, while the Azawagh Tuareg cultivated in an opportunistic way at the time of Bernus' study, sowing small fields and leaving them to be harvested on return from the *cure salée*. The major droughts of the 1970s and '80s, and widespread conflict, war and displacement during the 1990s have had drastic impacts on Tuareg societies (Randall, 1988, 2002, 2004; Bernus, 1990).

Saharo-Sahelian pastoralism is neither simply a matter of milk and meat production, nor is it self-sufficient, and it reached its peak in the context of major trans-Saharan trade. The cereals, cloth and other needs of the Saharan pastoralists can only be met by importing from, and thus by trading with, other areas. It revolves around camel husbandry, grading into cattle husbandry further south, but it comprises a mosaic of activities where rearing livestock for mobility, for trade, and for food operates alongside specialised farming, gathering and trading. Specialist groups have developed a major caravan trade and the exploitation of salt deposits alongside livestock rearing. Saharan pastoralism is particularly dependent on millet production in the rainfed Sahelian zone. For the Tuareg, progressively more distant markets offer increasingly higher livestock prices and cheaper millet. Periodically new markets develop – as with the export of animals direct to Libya in a thriving but still largely unofficial contemporary trade. However, Saharo-Sahelian pastoralists are often at the mercy of middlemen. The terms of trade for livestock against cereals are crucial, and are affected by crop-growing conditions in the south and by transport costs, as much as by conditions for livestock in the Sahara.

Central Sahelian systems: Tuareg & Fulani

In the central Sahel mean annual rainfall averages 200–600mm, with coefficients of variation ranging from 30 to 80%, a 3–4 month wet season, long runs of dry years and a major downturn since the 1970s. The water and grazing resources of these central Sahelian zones are still limited, if more reliable than the ephemeral pastures of the Saharo-Sahelian zone. Temporary wet-season surface water is found in dry riverbeds (*Dallol* in Fulfulde) and clay pans. The permanent rivers (Niger, Senegal, Chari, Nile) are fed by catchments outside the arid and semi-arid zone. There are also permanent groundwater ponds like the Mare D'Oursi in Northern Burkina Faso (Claude et al., 1991). The Tuareg and Fulani of western Niger and Mali make use of groundwater along the minor tributaries of the Niger river. With the northern limit of rainfed cultivation taken as the 300–350mm isohyet, the Central Sahelian zone is an area of competition and complementarity between farmer and herder, and many livestock-producing people in this zone are not merely dependent on exchange with cultivators, but raise their own crops as well as managing their herds.

In general, these pastoralists move to wet-season pastures that are typically relatively short-lived but of high nutritional value. In the dry-season ranges, less nutritious perennial grasses are supplemented by grazing crop stubble and by the many high-quality fodder trees and browse species, such as *Faidherbia albida* (Le Houérou, 1989). This annual transhumance also moves the herds from wetter areas as disease-vector populations begin to increase and the risk of infectious disease rises. The movements may be based on a latitudinal shift between wetter southern and more arid northern areas, on an altitudinal shift, or on more local catenary and topographic conditions. In the northern Sahel, medium-range cattle transhumance merges with long-range Saharo-Sahelian camel pastoralism. Groups like the southern Moors, the Illabaken Tuareg of central-north Niger, the Fulani of the Inland Delta of the Niger, the Wodaabe (Bororo) Fulani of Niger, Nigeria, and Cameroon and the Baggara Arabs of Darfur and Kordofan move their cattle on annual transhumant cycles of 150-300km each year. Further south, people practise shifting cultivation of millet on fallowed fields alongside livestock husbandry as short-range transhumant agropastoralists in a 20,000 km^2 zone, with livestock moved up to 50-100km annually to avoid crop damage (Le Houérou, 1989). This mixed cattle/millet farming system is intensifying in a broad band across the continent (Bourn and

Wint, 1994; Raynault, 1997), merging with sedentary agropastoral systems (Le Houérou, 1989; Mortimore, 1998).

The Tuareg and Fulani of the Gourma, the inner bend of the Niger in Mali, of Liptako in Niger, and Oudalan in Burkina Faso, herd mostly cattle, with small stock and a few camels, in a 50-200km cycle of herd movement. The sedentary agropastoralists of the Central Sahel, like the Bambara of Mali (Toulmin, 1992), use cattle and small stock as a wealth store, as draught labour and as a source of fertiliser in cultivation systems based on different varieties of millet. Their animals are sometimes taken on transhumance by Fulani herders, but more often are kept near the village. With the emphasis on ox-ploughing, their herd structure is half male, as opposed to the one-third male, two-thirds female ratio common in pastoralist and agropastoralist Fulani herds. Otherwise, the two systems have rather similar livestock production performances (de Leeuw and Wilson, 1987; Scoones, 1991).

The Tuareg of the arid zone extend south into these areas of rather more reliable grazing and water resources. Here they co-exist side by side with farming and herding populations whom they once dominated and with whom they are still interdependent. The co-existence can take many forms. Kel Gress (or Kel Geres) Tuareg of the Ader on the Nigerian frontier were stockmen with a strong hand in the politics of their region and a major role in the caravan trade. They operated a relay system with goods brought from the north by Kel Owey being redistributed by Kel Gress through a network of southern markets (Bernus, 1981). Kel Gress owned extensive farms but retained a primary interest in livestock and maintained a mobile lifestyle, camping in their own fields, grazing crop stubble and manuring the field for the next crop. At the southern end of their range, Kel Owey camels fed on the crop residues and coarse pastures of the Ader, while at the northern end of their range Kel Gress camels re-fed on the nutrient rich pastures of the Tamesna. Kel Gress used Saharo-Sahelian summer pastures to the east of the Kel Denneg, though they had to move their herds twice as far as did Tuareg of the Azawagh. The Iberogan of the Ader specialised in small-scale salt trade, exploiting salt deposits near Tegidda during the dry season, carrying the salt by donkey and moving their herds (mainly small stock) to a wet-season *cure salée* near In Gall, several hundred km from their dry-season pastures.

By contrast, the Tuareg of the Gourma are overwhelmingly 'Bella' in origin, drawn from a mixture of sub-Saharan peoples once dominated by Tuareg Berber nobles, and now united by common use of the Tamasheq language. The Gourma Tamasheq have a mixture of subsistence activities: they cultivate rainfed crops south of the 350mm isohyet alongside Zarma, Songhai and Fulani; they rear and trade livestock (but no longer participate in the wet-season movement to the *cure salée*); they hire their labour to the rice and other farmers of the Niger Delta for payment in cereals; they gather and eat wild grains, and sell firewood and other wild resources.

The Fulani of these Sahelian areas overlap and interdigitate with Tamasheq (Claude et al., 1991; Swift, 1984; de Bruijn and van Dijk, 1995; Hampshire, 1998; Buhl, 1999; Homewood, 1997). Livestock and crop production systems of Sahelian Fulani, and their interplay with other livelihood strategies, are described by Dupire, 1962a; Stenning, 1959; Swift, 1984; Grayzel, 1990; Claude et al., 1991; de Bruijn and van Dijk, 1994, 1995; Hampshire, 1998; Buhl, 1999. While the stereotype of Sahelian Fulani is of transhumant pastoralists, the recent literature tends to show many of these communities as caught in a vicious spiral of climatic downturn, impoverishment and environmental degradation, and as responding to these pressures by migrating and shifting from herding to cultivation. In the Sahelian zone, Fulani individuals and households are as likely to be moving into or out of pastoralism as to be established transhumant herders (Hampshire, 1998). The following section summarises the multifaceted pastoralism and dynamic resource-use strategies of Sahelian Fulani; later sections describe Fulani systems of the wet savannas further south, and of the wetlands of the Inland Delta of the Niger.

In a survey of over 8000 Fulani in the Sahel of Burkina Faso (Hampshire, 1998; Hampshire and Randall, 1999; Randall and Hampshire, 2004), all were engaged in herding animals, but this included herdowners, stockless people working for hire, international-level livestock traders gathering, moving and selling on large numbers of slaughter stock year-round, and agropastoralists or small-scale farmers using their dry-season slack period to raise a small income on purchase and resale of a few animals, by working local markets. A linked intensive study of 132 Burkina Fulani households showed that most owned fewer than ten cattle, while around a third had 10–100, and a few exceptionally rich households had 100–400 cattle, skewing the mean holdings upwards. Many Fulani households were managing other livestock in addition to the ones they actually owned, and were able to use the milk from the managed stock (Hampshire, 1998; Buhl, 1999). Around 1 in 5 individuals had been on transhumance in the preceding year, and one-third of households had at least one member on transhumance. Sahelian livestock productivity is generally low, but no lower than for livestock systems in comparable agro-ecological conditions with greater capital investment, while cattle taken on transhumance tend to produce better than do resident animals. Statistical analyses suggested that, in this particular study, production system and ethnicity were the main determinants of decisions to undertake transhumance, overriding environmental factors (cf. Little and Leslie, 1999; McCabe, 2004 – Turkana transhumance determined by range condition and security).

Alongside their livestock, the great majority of Burkina and Malian Fulani households farm cereals. Partly for ecoclimatic reasons, more northerly areas have a higher proportion of pastoralist Fulani households, compared with more agropastoralist and cultivating Fulani further south. However, production system also depends on sub-ethnic group within the Fulani, and on their historical trajectories (which have contributed to the present-day geographical distribution of primarily pastoralist as opposed to agropastoralist sub-ethnic groups). For example, Fulbe Djelgobe are more likely to be pastoralists, the Fulbe Gaobe and Fulbe Liptaako mostly agropastoralist, and Rimaibe primarily cultivators. Most agropastoralist Fulani in Burkina Faso integrated cropping with animal husbandry, using their millet stalk residues to feed livestock, and using or selling manure for fertilising household fields, but Djelgobe agropastoralists who mostly inhabit the more northerly zones, neither cut millet stalks for their cattle nor used the manure, which risks burning the crop in these more arid areas.

Crops were grown largely for home consumption. Pastoralist Djelgobe households might live off milk for a couple of months during the rains, but other families, based closer to markets, with greater reliance on cereals and access to relatively favourable terms of trade, might sell an animal to buy in grain. For Burkinabé Fulani in this study, cultivation was necessary to buffer demands on the herd and provide some level of food security, even though few if any households harvested enough to meet all their cereal needs. The 1994 devaluation of the CFA franc, together with the later ban on importation of subsidised EU beef, caused an effective doubling of livestock prices in northern Burkina, though these have since declined. More generally, crop/livestock terms of trade vary on a seasonal and annual basis according to supply and demand (Quarles van Ufford, 1999; Zaal, 1998).

Fulani livestock traders range from large-scale operators with considerable capital and international networks, to small-scale brokers with little or no capital trading on in-depth knowledge of local markets (Quarles van Ufford, 1999). The great majority of pastoralist and agropastoralist households surveyed in the late 1990s did not have the numbers, type or quality of livestock to take advantage of shifting markets. For the majority, livestock sales are a response to pressing household need, usually for grain to eat, not a response to external economic context. For this same majority, there is little question of selling grain to invest in livestock, because the grain harvested rarely meets household needs. Most Burkinabé Fulani supplemented their livestock and crop-based livelihoods with seasonal labour migration; contract herding; temporary labour migration to pan for gold; temporary migration with their animals to locations with better opportunities for selling milk and purchasing grain; local menial employment; gathering wild resources like *fonio* (*Panicum laetum*), *cramcram* (*Cenchrus bifloris*) and water lily (*Nymphaea lotus*) used for food; grass for mats; and *karité* (*Butyrospermum parkii*) for shea butter manufacture, consumption and sale. Rarely, Burkina Fulani engaged in artisanal work or market gardening (Hampshire, 1998). Livestock-based enterprises remain the cultural ideal even where everyday subsistence in reality is reduced to other endeavours. Many sorts of work are culturally unacceptable, and only Fulani who have moved far from their place of origin will engage in these (Bassett, 1994; Hampshire, 1998; Buhl, 1999; cf. Boutrais, 1994).

One in four Burkina Fulani households sent at least one person on seasonal labour migration. This varied according to household production system, with 1 in 3 cultivator and 1 in 5 agropastoralist but only 1 in 10 pastoralist households sending a labour migrant. It also varied with ethnic subgroup and village of origin. Environment is an important influence in a number of ways, but year-to-year fluctuations in yields had no obvious immediate effect on people's decisions as to whether or not to go on seasonal labour migration. Statistical modelling of patterns of seasonal labour migration emphasised the fact that culture and demographic factors, as well as environment and production system, were important determinants of who migrates.

In general, environment, economics and culture are all important determinants of livelihood strategies and production choices for the Sahelian Fulani, particularly whether to herd or to farm, and how to apportion labour. There is a clear environmental gradient, with cultivation becoming more likely the further south the location and the less arid the area, but this pattern is complicated by the way the gradient differs between ethnic subgroups. Ethnicity also influences production-system choices, and the ways in which mobility and pastoral lifestyle are integrated with tending crops. Transhumance may be driven by the need to find better forage and avoid livestock disease, by the lure of potential markets for pastoral and other produce, or by the primacy of cultivation and the need to avoid crop damage.

The pattern of shifting livelihoods and locations so common among Sahelian Fulani is partly but by no means always nor even commonly driven by impoverishment or environmental degradation. For those retaining a foothold in the Sahel, short-term migration by individuals or households may represent any one of a great variety of types of movement with different underlying reasons, and a decision to migrate can as readily be a response to opportunity as a measure driven by either economic or environmental necessity. Longer-term migration, for example by single men seeking work as herders in the expanding livestock economy of 1990s Côte d'Ivoire, is more likely to be driven by poverty and need (Bassett, 1994). The shame associated with ways of living not sanctioned by the powerful Fulani *pulaaku* social code is so great that people will move far from their natal family before taking such work.

Wet savannas: Fulani of the Adamawa Plateau & Central African forest-savanna mosaic

As the Sahelian zone grades into wetter Sudanian (4-600mm to 1000 mm per annum) and eventually Guinean (>1000mm) climates, pastoralist systems change their character (Blench, 1994). The strategies of pastoralism in the wetter savannas are illustrated by Fulani pastoralists of the higher altitude areas within the Sahelian zone, like those of the Mambila Plateau in Nigeria, the Adamawa Plateau (Cameroon – Fig. 2.1), as well as by the humid savannas of the highland Fouta Djallon (Guinea), and lower-lying Central African Republic (CAR). In all these areas, pastoralists tend to practise dry-season transhumance, occupying relatively permanent sites during the 6-9-month wet season and either shifting further south in the dry season, or entering the drawdown zone of areas flooded in the rains. Transhumance in the wetter savannas involves movements often of <100km, and rarely more than 200km, with many local small-scale movements as well as cross-border migrations between Nigeria, Cameroon, Chad and CAR. Throughout the wetter savannas, farmers' progressive shift to ox-plough cultivation, their use of livestock as a wealth store, and the extension of cash crops mean that pastures are dwindling. Wetlands that used to hold dry season grazing are progressively converted to cultivation, crop residues are less easily available for transhumant herds to use, and crops stand longer into the dry season, exacerbating conflicts between settled farmer and more mobile herder (Waters-Bayer and Bayer, 1994; Bassett, 1994; Blench, 1994; Niamir-Fuller, 1999). This competition between alternative land use and production systems reaches its peak in the wetlands of the major floodplain systems (see next section).

Boutrais' long-term work on the Fulani of the Adamawa Plateau has formed the backbone of a growing number of studies of pastoralist systems in subhumid and humid areas (Boutrais, 1978, 1983, 1986, 1988, 1994; Blench, 1994; Bassett, 1994; Waters-Bayer and Bayer, 1994; Bocquené, 2002). The Adamawa Plateau is a major highland formation continuous with the Mambila Plateau in Nigeria and stretching east and south-east across the centre of Cameroon to the Central African Republic border. Most of the plateau lies above 1000m, rising to over 2000m in the north-west, and falling away to the Tikar plain at 700m. The plateau has a rainfall of around 2000mm, permanent water, and a mosaic of soils including fertile areas derived from volcanic rocks. Montane grasslands at altitudes of over 1800m give way to *Hyparrhenia* pastures. Woody cover increases from 1500m down, and there are limited dry-season *Pennisetum* (Fulfulde: *sissongo*) and *Loudetia* swamp pastures along the waterlines. During the single 4-6-month dry season, strong winds dry the standing grass which ceases growth and rapidly loses nutritional value.

The Adamawa Bororo Fulani include different Fulfulde-speaking groups that arrived at various times from separate areas of origin and maintain some differences in types of cattle, in style of management, and in the extent to which they combine livestock-based enterprise with cropping, trade and religious work and engage in other, less customarily approved livelihoods (Boutrais, 1994a; Bocquené, 2002). Boutrais (1978, 1983, 1986, 1988) distinguishes the Djafun with their large red long-horned cattle (good milkers but relatively less drought- and trek-hardy), the more mobile and more purely pastoralist Akou from northern Nigeria, with smaller white zebu cattle (poor milkers, tolerant of drought and good walkers), and the Wodaabe, most purely pastoralist of all. Adamawa Fulbe favoured red-and-white cross-bred *gudaali* cattle. The Adamawa Bororo customarily operated in groups of 15-40 families, each under the leadership of small chiefs (*ardo*), commonly from the same lineage (*suuda*), in the Wodaabe but made up of co-migrating groups of different lineages in the Akou.

Boutrais' studies showed the different livestock-owning groups of Adamawa operating a range of livestock management systems, from the highly mobile to the virtually sedentary. Wodaabe, Akou and later Djafun left the plateau early in the dry season, moving their herds down the valleys that drain the plateau, trading the potentially increasing risk of tsetse and trypanosomiasis in the ever more wooded areas against the dry-season decline of vector populations and the lure of unused pastures. They returned in stages after the onset of the wet season, with the Wodaabe staying on transhumance longest of all. Bororo families commonly travelled together on transhumance. By contrast, the more settled Fulbe used hired herders, and preferred to keep their cattle relatively near their home village, so as to be able to oversee the herders as well as manage their political, religious, farming and commercial interests. Where animal densities were relatively low, transhumance was limited to local movements, exploiting crop residues and wetter grazing in local depressions on the plateau, and movements did not involve the herdowner or his family. The natron salt springs of the plateau *(lahore)* had originally been under the control of the lamidates (see also Chapter 2),[2] but tenurial changes on the plateau made their ownership and control ambiguous and at the time of the study they had fallen into disuse and been replaced by the use of imported salt. Among the Fulbe, only shepherds had a high milk diet. For reasons of religious orthodoxy and social prestige, Fulbe women do not market milk, and the Fulbe of Adamawa and other wet savannas have instead developed a livestock marketing trade to urban centres as far off as the capitals of the coastal West African states (Boutrais, 1994a; Blench, 1994). Finally, the peasant farmers kept their few animals around the village year-round, playing little part in the livestock trade.

Patterns of transhumance have changed with conditions of security, disease, land tenure and the centuries-long drift of Fulani groups east and south. During the nineteenth century rivalry and internecine strife between lamidates made raiding a major concern for anyone undertaking transhumant movements. At the end of the nineteenth century rinderpest decimated the herds and stopped transhumance. Trypanosomiasis epidemics between the 1920s and 1940s again interrupted herd movements. The colonial regime established relative security and a brief period of freedom from disease, and herds taking refuge on the Adamawa plateau rapidly recovered and multiplied. From the 1950s on, trypanosomiasis spread across the Adamawa plateau, precipitating major disease and vector-control programmes and ultimately leading to radical changes in land tenure. Trypanosomiasis epizootics in the Benue and Diamara lowlands spread up the wooded ravines which drain the plateau to those areas of the plateau where vegetation cover allowed the vectors to breed. Where cattle began to sicken and die, Bororo Fulani moved rapidly away. The more sedentary Fulbe were slower to go. Eventually the farmers, dependent on pastoralists for manure and for a market for their surplus grain, had to follow.

The French colonial administration, and later the post-Independence government, tried to persuade the plateau population to stay put, providing massive veterinary inputs of trypanocidal drugs and later instituting ultra-low volume (ULV) insecticide spraying campaigns and bush clearance. In large areas designated to be sprayed, whole populations were moved out while the residual insecticide took its year-long action. Costs spiralled as the trypanosomiasis belts shifted and spread. In the 1980s the government initially encouraged pastoralist resettlement in the vacated areas, but ran into tenurial difficulties because of the difference between the land-rights systems of the village-based Fulbe and farmers, and the more loosely defined access rights of the Bororo. Eventually customary land rights were abolished and the government began to privatise land tenure and develop state ranches. These programmes suffered all the familiar vicissitudes of comparable livestock development programmes elsewhere (Boutrais, 1983, 1994; Halderman, 1985; Wyckoff, 1985; Toulmin

---

[2] Lamidate : Fulbe principality (or *laamu*) headed by a *lamido*, a secular and religous ruler, in turn subject to an *emir* (commander or prince) who would himself be subject to the Caliph or Sultan heading the empire.

and Quan, 2000). Private land tenure has constrained the movement of Bororo herds and their access to water and other resources, and has changed the patterns of land use as well as the ability of different groups to maintain a foothold in the pastoralist system of the Adamawa plateau (Boutrais, 1994a).

In the wet savannas, dry-season transhumance pastures that Fulani opened up by fire and grazing have often, over the years, become their wet-season permanent pastures. From the 1920s on, there has been a steady drift of Fulani from Adamawa, Nigeria and Chad southwards into the wet savannas of the CAR, with annual rainfall of around 2000mm and a 9-month wet season. The Sudano-Guinean pastures are of relatively poor quality, and rapidly lose nutritive value in the dry season (Table 3.2). Where pastures have not been grazed during the wet season, the standing grasses are burned, stimulating a flush of high-quality new growth. Where pastures have been grazed during the wet season, there is no burn and a poor flush. Together with the paucity of good fodder trees, and in some cases an unfamiliarity or reluctance on the part of herders to make use of possible browse species, CAR Bororo have had either to transhume or at least to split their herds into a resident milk herd and a transhumant dry herd. The decision has depended on the interplay of many constraints including cultural preference, herd size, farming commitments and the knock-on effect of other transhumant herds passing through. In Boutrais' study, Chadian and Akou Bororo transhumed over distances of 500km a year into the wet CAR savannas and back to the north. Others, with few livestock and more farming or trade, had become semi-sedentary or settled outright in the wetter savannas. With 50-100 head, Wodaabe families worked together to grow crops and transhume together. With 100-300 head, part or all of the herd might be devolved to one or more sons to manage and take on transhumance, a system that was merging into pre-inheritance.

There is a trade-off between the year-round availability of green growth and the overall low nutritive value of these nutrient-limited fire climax savannas (where few browse species are known or exploited), and against high disease risk (with trypanosomiasis and tickborne disease challenge reducing productivity and making continual animal health care essential, with injections, dipping and tick removal). From being primarily concerned with finding pasture and water, herders become primarily responsible for disease control. In CAR, tick removal by hand could take up most of the labour of a herder and his wife and family (Boutrais, 1988), and knowledge of drug doses and injection technique became essential skills, while herds might often pasture untended. Expensive imported natron was needed to purge intestinal parasites and improve animal health and nutritional state.

Fulani pastoralists extend as far as the Congo River and graze their herds into the very edges of tropical rainforest. They are limited as much as by economic and political conditions as by ecology in these extremes of the wet savanna environment. The more sedentary Fulbe with their centralised political hierarchies have been adept in exploiting economic and political possibilities (cf. Burnham, 1975; Burnham and Last, 1994). Fulbe women do not market milk products. Instead, many Fulbe have specialised, for example in fattening rather than breeding stock, or in trading as merchants, transporters, middlemen and financiers. CAR Fulbe in many cases cornered political control of livestock communes set up during the 1960s, and of the livestock producers' associations into which these evolved in the 1980s. Fulbe and other leaders of these organisations have tended to claim private access to choice pastures, while in the dry season they continue to send their herds to graze the commons. The Fulbe have abandoned the traditional Fulani systems of pre-inheritance and the reciprocal, risk-reducing systems of stock loan and stock gift still practised in various forms by the Bororo groups.

By contrast, the mobile Bororo Fulani described by Boutrais had greater difficulty operating within the economic and political conditions of the CAR. Wodaabe, Akou, Djafun and Chadian Bororo women commonly marketed their milk products in exchange for cultivated foods. Elsewhere the calorific and monetary terms of trade normally favour or at least make viable the pastoral economy (Swift, 1986; Zaal and Dietz, 1999; Chapters 3 and 5). In CAR, Bororo were penetrating areas with manioc rather than cereal staples, where milk and milk products are little used or valued. In Bénin, the karité butter from the shea butter-nut tree is commonly preferred to dairy butter, and poor Fulani women gather, process and sell the plant product in lieu of their dairy trade (Schreckenberg, 1996). In CAR, Bororo women had to sell milk or butter primarily to Arab women traders selling on at a profit in big urban centres. Bororo women then bought manioc from Baya/Baka cultivators. Milk production is low at the best of times in the relatively low-nutrient, high-disease environment. Where the women could not make enough to buy food, the men had to sell stock. Where epidemics and quarantines blocked livestock movements and trade, CAR Bororo suffered serious food shortages. Impoverished, stockless Wodaabe became hired herders or settled and cultivated, as did the large polygamous Djafun families, wealthy in livestock but with many dependants to feed. Political hazards exacerbated Bororo problems. In the early 1980s many Bororo families were ruined when they crossed the Congo into Zaire, lured by an initial welcome, only to have their herds confiscated.

Pastoralists in wetlands I: Fulani in the Inland Delta of the Niger

In Mali, the Niger River follows a great loop that arches north into the Sahel before curving back to the Nigerian coast (Fig. 2.2). On the north-east leg of this loop, the Niger enters a stretch where the average gradient over 200km is 5cm/km. It is joined by other permanent rivers such as the Bani; together they break up into a number of major and innumerable minor channels fanning out across a broad floodplain. The Niger is fed by catchments in the humid zone 1000km to the west. When the catchment rains cause the river levels to rise, the Niger floods around 15,000km^2 of the 30,000km^2 plain. Because of the lag in movement of the mass of water, the flood begins upstream in October, arrives in December in mid-Delta, and reaches the downstream end of the Delta in February. The downstream areas stay flooded long after the upstream waters have drained away. The Inland Delta has a rhythm dictated by its own progression of flood and drawdown, onto which are superimposed the cycle of local rains and dry season, hot (daily temperatures rising to 45°C) and cold season (temperatures falling to 5–10°C). Rainfall varies from an average of around 5–600mm in the south-west to ca. 2–300 mm in the north east, with most rain falling in a single short season July–September. The floods rise from June to July, peak in September to December, falling January–February and with water levels at a minimum March–May. Gallais' classic work (1984) set out the complexities of land use in the inland delta of the Niger, with farmers, fishers and herders following the patterns of cultivable land, fish populations and grazing resources as their availability shifts through space and time. Continuous negotiation between customary and state rules complicates access (Hill, 1985; Moorehead, 1991; Legrosse, 1999; Turner, 1999b; Vedeld, 2003).

From a pastoralist viewpoint, the micro-topography of the Inland delta floodplain, and the spatial disposition of access points, are all-important. The *Echinochloa stagnata* pastures are the key grazing resource of the delta (Fulfulde: *bourgou*; French: *bourgoutières*). In the floods, the *Echinochloa*-dominated swamp grass species float upright putting out prolific shoots and leaves. During drawdown the unsupported stems lie flat, putting out new roots from every node and forming an abundance of medium quality, palatable forage. Grazing and burning stimulate regrowth. Barring one or two exceptional years, the extent of flooding has declined since the 1960s. It is recognised that over-grazing is not a hazard, given the continual recharge of soil fertility through silt deposition and the six-month resting period. However, the spread of rice cultivation means formerly key *Echinochloa* pastures are only accessible as post-harvest stubble or fallow, useful but not matching the dry-season green growth of the *bourgou*.

In the 1990s the Delta had 500,000 people, a million cattle, 2 million small stock, and produced 100,000 tons of fish each year (Moorehead, 1991). Here, unlike the Sudd, the demarcations between ethnic groups have long been rein-forced by sharp boundaries of economic specialisation. The Fulani made up around one-third of the Delta population, and then as now dominated livestock ownership and pastoralism in the area. Most were semi-settled, their cattle herds engaging in a long transhumance. For part of the year the Delta was and is used by more mobile Tuareg, Moors and peripheral nomadic Fulani, moving through the area as family groups with their mixed herds of camels, cattle, small stock and donkeys.

The legacy of the Dina (Chapter 2) has meant that pastoralist movements and lives were regulated with 'a complexity and precision exceptional for West Africa' (Gallais, 1984) The rules of access and order of precedence persist, though the loss of pastoralist political hegemony, and the encroachment of cultivation onto former grazing lands, are increasingly eroding the functioning of this sophisticated time-sharing system (Moorehead, 1991; Legrosse, 1999; Vedeld, 2003). In Gallais' account, the Fulani were primarily associated with the west bank. In contrast to Fulani practice outside the Delta, the herds were divided into three different management units. In upstream areas during the wet season and time of floods, most of the animals were sent on transhumance away from the Delta. A *dounti* herd (*ceetoji* – Legrosse, 1999) made up of a small number of milch cows was kept to feed the villages cut off by the floods, and might become trapped in a dwindling area. These animals were protected in straw shelters against biting flies and ticks, and stall-fed on grass cut from flooded pastures. As the floods receded and the village grazing grounds emerged, they were taken out to graze. They suffered serious disease challenge and parasite loads, and were not expected to survive to the next rains. Further downstream, the rains bring a flush to the village grazing grounds before the mid-Delta floods start to rise, and larger milk herds could be safely kept and then sent on transhumance in November. A core herd (*benti; benudi*, Legrosse, 1999) of cows in milk, calves and a very few bulls was kept as long as possible near the village, leaving late on transhumance, returning early, and travelling only a relatively short distance from the village. Twice a day the milk was carried back to the village overnight through the year if possible.

The main transhumant herds were made up of sterile and dry cows, heifers, bullocks, oxen, bulls and a few milk cows to feed the herders. Groups of cooperating herdowners pooled their cattle to make herds each of several hundred animals. These were pooled in turn to make a *garti* herd (Legrosse, 1999: *garci*) which might have thousands of cattle. During Gallais' study, the transhumant herds followed specified routes, organised as precisely as during the time of the Dina, though a greater number of individual itineraries were specified, rather than the single massive group transhumance originally established for reasons of security in the nineteenth century. The transhumant groups moved rapidly out of the Delta with the onset of rains and floods, moving up onto the drier terraces of the hinterland as surface pools filled, and with the flush of rainfed grasslands (*Aristida, Eragrostis, Pennisetum* and the wild gathered cereal *Cenchrus bifloris* or *cramcram*) and browse species (*Acacia, Balanites, Combretum*). Most herds left to the north-west of the Delta into Fulani country, with the banks of the Delta less densely settled than elsewhere. There were set crossing points, access times and meeting points for different groups. The massed herds then travelled laps of perhaps 15km each day, trying to avoid conflict with farmers sowing and weeding their fields. Herds starting from further north went due north into the Méma or into the 'Sahel' thornbush west of the delta. Once there, they camped near surface ponds while scouts sought patches of new flush after localised rainstorms. The herds moved a few km to pasture each day, returning at night. Transhumance was a testing time with predator attacks, thefts, animals straying, herders mistaking itineraries, a continual need to seek out pastures and to gather information at water points.

Towards the end of October, pastures of the Méma and 'Sahel' are fast running out, but herds returning to the Delta too early would be hemmed in by an enormous tailback of livestock. They might delay, only to face long marches at a fast pace, and risk losing exhausted animals. Gallais described the Diafaradjé return to the Delta, with daily marches of 30–40 km, little or no water or grazing left along the way, and tens of thousands of animals arriving on the banks of the Niger. Further north, groups coming from the Méma had a shorter distance to cover in easier laps, and were able to halt for longer to water and pasture their livestock. Legrosse (1999) describes the herds assembling at their specific intended crossing points, and the herders initiating negotiations for access. In Gallais' time the waiting zone was already much encroached upon by rice and millet fields spreading across transhumance routes and barring access to water points. The millet might be ready for harvest, but the rice was still standing, and conflicts would multiply between herder and farmer. There were tensions too between herder and government officials who chose this time to impose cumbersome procedures; between resident herdowner and those who are passing through, and between herdowner and herder in settling accounts. Through-passage and stopover both depend on negotiation with the masters of grazing land (*jowru*), each of whom controls tenure and access to his own area (*leydi*) and exacts payment in cash or in kind, while controlling the all-important order of precedence of individual resident or stranger herds within his *egguirgol* (aggregate herd) as it moves into and through the grazing areas. There is extensive negotiation between herdowners and *jowru* for inclusion and rank order of precedence within the *egguirgol,* and conflicts have grown more serious in the last decades (Landais, 1994; Legrosse, 1999). With the crossing into the Delta proper finally accomplished, there is a time of celebrations accompanying the triumphal return of the *egguirgol* to the senior village site for that group. Dues are paid to the *jowru*, and the *egguirgol* then splits into its component herds, which return to their own villages and their own celebrations.

Between November and January, the herds follow their traditional sequence of entry into the *bourgou* or flooding *Echinochloa* pastures. Different herding units attempt the crossings at different stages, the *garti* adult animals able to cross early while the waters are still relatively deep, and *benti* with their calves waiting to a later stage for conditions to be easier. Herds move by day and graze at night, or stop for a few days at a time, following the receding flood-waters, making use of the fresh pastures that emerge, leaving longer-exposed areas drying up fast. By February/March, the drawdown has exposed most of the Delta pastures. With good grass, abundant water and warmer nights, hundreds of thousands of cattle are dispersed through the Delta. In the down-stream areas, though, the cattle are still waiting to enter the Delta and the *bourgous* of Lake Debo. At the end of March, with the coming of the hot season, herders are free to leave their traditional grazing grounds and enter other pastures. Gallais describes the influx of foreign Fulani, Tuareg and Moors; nomadic families moving with a few score or hundred animals in mixed herds of camels, cattle, small stock and donkeys, a jumble of species strikingly different from (and looked down on by) the quasi-military progres-sion of the Delta Fulani cattle in their *egguirgol* groups of tens of thousands (Legrosse, 1999: 87).

Fires may be set in the higher grasslands (not in the *bourgou*), stimulating an immediate regrowth of a new, high-quality flush on these raised grasslands. The cattle's nutritional status, general health and milk production all improve. The month of March becomes a period of jockeying for position, so as to ensure access in April to the real *bourgou* zones at the major confluences in the Delta: Pondori near Djenna in the south, controlled by the Marka; Yongari on the right bank, and the biggest and most important *bourgou* area in the downstream Delta, where four Fulani groups control a total of 1500km^2, and

4–500,000 cattle can graze for 3-4 months. Though routes are determined by geomorphological features and flood levels, the *leydi* territories have undergone continuous change across the decades (Legrosse, 1999). The April–June stay in the *bourgou* proper is the best time of year for the Fulani. The *bourgoutières* are tremendously productive (*Echinochloa* and *Oryza* producing 7000–25000 kg dry matter/ha/year, compared with the rainfed pastures' 800–2500 kg DM/ha/yr – Penning de Vries and Djiteye, 1982). There is plenty of fresh milk, and milk is easily exchanged for fish and rice. This is a time of social gathering for the Fulani of the lower Delta, as well as a time when the semi-sedentarised can rediscover their pastoral roots. With the onset of the rains and the rising waters, the cycle begins again, interwoven with the farmers' and the fishers' own, different rhythms.

As for the wet savannas, wetland systems are the site of intense competition between farming and herding. In the Senegal River Valley, the Office du Niger area of the Inland Delta of the Niger in Mali, and in Sokoto, the conversion to wet rice cultivation of floodplain *bourgoutières* has meant the loss of dry-season grazing that supported millions of head of livestock. The fragile earthworks, dykes and canals increasingly preclude dry season livestock use of these areas (Landais, 1994; Legrosse, 1999: for a discussion of tenure and access see Chapter 9).

Pastoralists of North-East Africa & the Horn

The eastern end of the Sahel grades into the Nubian and Egyptian deserts, and the Eastern desert bordering on the Red Sea. Saharan and Sahelian climates and ecosystems persist to the very eastern seaboard of North-east Africa. The southern end of the Red Sea becomes the Bab al Mandab and turns into the Gulf of Aden along the northern coast of the Horn of Africa. Here the coastal plains, bounded by hills and mountains inland, demarcate a transition zone to a more Mediterranean style of climate. Instead of a summer rainfall regime dominated by the ITCZ, there is a shift to a winter rainfall regime. The eastern side of the coastal range has bimodal rainfall with climate and vegetation resembling East Africa (Le Houérou, 1989).

Throughout north-eastern Africa climates range from very low rainfall in the more northerly areas to progressively wetter in the south. Permanent rivers like the Nile and the Atbara, as well as smaller, seasonal or seep-away riverlines like the Gash and the Baraka, all depend on distant catchments outside the arid and semi-arid zone. These desert and semi-desert areas, with their riverine, groundwater, coastal and montane refuges, are inhabited by a great number of different Arabic- and Cushitic-speaking pastoralist and agropastoralist groups: the Beja of Sudan (Morton, 1993; Hjort and Dahl, 1991; Ausenda, 1987), camel-keeping Kababish (Asad, 1970) and cattle-keeping Baggara Arabs (Salih, 1990), Zaghawa and Kawahla (Tubiana and Tubiana, 1977; De Waal, 1989a). All these groups practise a mix of pastoralist, agropastoralist, farming, trading and wage labour activities whose precise balance depends on individual history and fortune as well as on patterns of colonial and post-Independence events in any given area. For example, Sudanese policies on land tenure, land use, and the extension of mechanised cash-crop cultivation have had a dramatic effect on the balance between farming and herding and on the patterns of movement open to pastoralists (Ahmed, 1988). River basin developments have destroyed crucial dry-season pastures (Adams, 1992; Beja – Hjort and Dahl, 1991; Morton, 1993). Security and political problems limit their essential mobility (e.g. Beni Amr – Hjort and Dahl, 1991). For many, the catastrophic droughts and epidemics of 1888-9 had already destroyed the basis of their pastoralist livelihoods (Sanasita – Hjort and Dahl, 1991; Pankhurst and Johnson, 1988; Ahmed, 1988); a century on, the 1984–6 droughts caused stock losses of 95% among Beja groups (Hjort and Dahl, 1991), Zaghawa and Fur (de Waal, 1989a).

Throughout North-east Africa, groups with pastoralist traditions inter-digitate with primarily cultivating groups who themselves have some stock (the Hawazma and Kawahla with the Fur and the Nuba (Manger, 1988; Tubiana and Tubiana, 1977; de Waal, 1989a); the Kawahla and Hamar with the Berti (Holy, 1988). Moving eastward into the Horn, Arabic-speaking pastoralist groups abut on and intermingle with the Cushitic-speaking Somali and Oromo peoples. These peoples have for centuries contested control of key pastoral, agropastoral and other natural resources, both among each other and also with successive colonial powers and state administrations. Over recent decades, political and economic actions by the state in countries like Sudan and Somalia have in some cases indirectly precipitated and in others actively encouraged predatory raiding, leading to the famines, civil disruption and massacres of Darfur, Southern Sudan and the Horn (cf. Chapter 3; Keen, 1995; Johnson, 2003, 2004; Lewis, 2001; Hendrickson et al., 1998), though their detailed analysis is beyond the scope of this book. This section briefly describes the types of pastoralist ecosystem and production system associated with the different Arabic- and Cushitic-speaking peoples of the Eastern Sahara, Sahel and North-east Africa. Highly mobile camel and small-stock pastoralism combined with *durra* sorghum farming in the more arid areas (e.g. Beja – Hjort and Dahl, 1991; Awlad Hamid of Darfur – Holter, 1988; camel pastoralists of northern Somalia) grade into more circumscribed cattle/small-stock trans-humance systems combined with cereal cropping (le Houérou, 1989), to the mixed agropastoralism of less arid Southern and Central Somalia (Baumann et al., 1993).

The Atmaan Beja

Hjort and Dahl (1991) describe the Atmaan Beja economy as a particular com-bination of camel rearing, caravanning and *durra* cultivation. Together with its long-established ramifications into farming, trade and urban wage-earning, and the gathering of wild resources whether for trade (gum arabic, senna) or for subsistence in time of drought (wild grains – Tubiana and Tubiana, 1977; de Waal, 1989) this pattern broadly illustrates the camel-based economies of other Arab or Arabicised pastoralist groups of North-east Africa. Dependence on grain farming, wild resource gathering or urban labour have probably always been part of a wide network of economic activities, of which pastoralism has always been only one facet (e.g. Kibreab, 1997).

The rural Beja inhabit sparsely wooded semi-desert areas with annual rainfall typically around 110mm, and with temporary rivers like the Gash and the Baraka that may flood once in 3-8 years, as well as smaller *khor* that carry water after rain. They operated in small family groups where 2-4 tents clustered in a small *khor*[3] would be spaced anywhere from a few hundred metres to several km from the next family group (Hjort and Dahl, 1991). *Diwab*[4] members were well known to each other and visited on a daily basis to exchange food and information. They were closely endogamous, with a strong cultural ideal of brother-sister solidarity, and neighbours were likely to be closely related. They used their *diwab* organisation of communal land tenure, and their common interests in camel herding, to maintain a common organisation of labour. This extends to the organisation of harbour labour work-gangs for young men migrating to earn in the urban areas (Chapter 9; Morton, 1993; Pantuliano, 2002). Access to cultivation plots depended on *diwab* membership, as did camel ownership, while other livestock were more easily transferable. The senior man of the *diwab* made all the decisions on livestock management even for animals that belonged to other individuals within the *diwab*.

For the Beja, territory was seen as the lands extending around core features of river valleys, mountains and passes (cf. Turner, 1999a: point-centred key resources). The Beja recognised particular tracts of land as belonging to specific local owners, although from the time of Independence the Sudanese government abolished customary rights and took these as state-owned grazing lands. Groundwater seeps through silt and rock fissures in the granite bedrock to provide permanent sources, sometimes at a considerable depth. Wells were owned by individual families, and immigrants might not open new wells without permission. Customary transhumance patterns moved between the seasonally flowing feeder *khor* and the permanent dry-season wells, with communities splitting into small groups to exploit the limited pastures of higher ground. Neighbours were usually allowed access on a reciprocal basis in return for a symbolic token of respect, and, when grazing and water were plentiful, access was easily negotiated by outsiders in return for a similar token gift. However, when resources were scarce, outsiders might be excluded. The rain each year determined the sorghum yield as well as the success of small-stock and camel reproduction. Sorghum or finger millet porridges were the dietary staple and where it was too dry to cultivate these cereals they were imported. Unusually for Arab- and Cushitic-speaking pastoralists, Beja men milked, as women were not allowed to milk any livestock (cf. Somali camel herders where women milk all livestock other than camels). Hjort and Dahl distinguished three types of Beja camel pastoralism, differing in ecosystem, patterns of resource use and types of camels and pastoral produce. These were *Aiririit* (Aulib Plateau), *Matiaat* (mountain and *khor*) and *Shallageea* (coastal) camel pastoralism. Both *Aiririit* and *Matiaat* are summer rainfall, summer

---

[3] Seasonal watercourse, generally dry.
[4] Extended family, clan, minimal lineage.

breeding, summer birth peak systems. The coastal *Shallageea* have winter rainfall, winter breeding and winter birth peak.

Aiririit: The Aulib Plateau, stretching west of the Red Sea Hills, has a Sahelian vegetation of *Acacia mellifera* and *tortilis* trees over *Indigofera spinosa* shrubs and tufts of *Panicum turgidum* grass, interspersed with ephemeral annual grasses. Primarily transport camels, *Aiririit* also produced a fair milk yield. In the Aulib, families with their camels and small stock each lived some 3–5km apart. Hjort and Dahl described two herding strategies. Households might stay on the plateau near their permanent home bases, travelling 5–6km/day or per week in different directions. Alternatively, they might move in cooperating groups of relatives, undertaking longer-distance treks to new pastures, with a series of short daily movements to pastures around each stopping point. The camels might go 2–3 days without water in the hot dry season and 5–8 days or even up to a month without drinking in the cool dry season. In the cool dry season the *aiririit* camels gave 6–10kg milk/day, though by the end of the dry season competition between people and calves became a problem. In years with good rains they grazed into the western flanks of the Red Sea hills and might move as far as the *Gunob* coastal strip to spend a couple of months feeding on the mineral-rich *Suaeda* salt bush, or undertake an easier transhumance on the Atbai north of the Red Sea Hills.

Matiaat: The slender fast *matiaat* camels have lower endurance and produce less milk, but are more easily managed than other types. They were reared in local transhumant systems, moving between *khor* and mountain. During the long dry season they wandered unherded up the *khor* to the higher ground, feeding almost exclusively on *Salvadora persica* browse, necessitating daily drinking from the permanent surface water of the mountains. They gave around 2kg milk a day. In the rains, hired herders took them to distant fresh grazing while the owners farmed. Goats gave 1–1.5kg milk/day, and their hair was woven into bedding mats and tent wall linings.

Shallageea: The *Shallageea* camels spent at least 6 months of the year on the coast, browsing on *Suaeda* salt bush, mangrove fruits and leaves, wading day and night into the sea until only their heads and humps were visible. The salty diet necessitated watering every 1–2 days. These camels were larger than the other two types, and while the *Suaeda* bushes were in fruit they could give 15-18kg milk/day or more, and could be milked every few hours. The households herding them were widely dispersed (1/km^2) and often divided the camels into milking and dry herds. When there was rain in the Aulib or Atbai, the Shallageea camels were moved to take advantage of this summer forage to supplement their winter wet-season coastal salt bush diet.

Somali pastoralism

The Somalis occupy a million km^2 of coastal plains, mountains and plateau hinterland of the Horn of Africa. Beyond the continually contested boundaries of Somalia itself,[5] Somali peoples have long inhabited the contiguous rangelands

---

[5] Now Somaliland and Puntland.

of Ethiopia, Kenya and Djibouti. In-depth studies of Somali pastoralism pre-date the violent turmoil of the last few decades (Lewis, 1961, 1988; Cassanelli, 1982). ....More recent studies (eg Baumann et al 1993, Prior 1994, Helander 1999, Little 2003) suggest that earlier observations on the basic pastoral resources and their patterns of use in Somali pastoralist ecology have broadly stood the test of time. However, the pastoral economy is in continual flux, changing in ways that ultimately impact on ecology. The twentieth century saw progressive privatisation of water and range resources, the development and collapse of a major live animal and meat export trade fuelled by demand from the Gulf States (Swift 1979, Behnke 1983, Prior 1994), the impacts of war (both civil and cross-border: de Waal 1997, Allen 1996, Hogg 1997, Lewis 2001, Little 2003), partial recovery and further collapse due to failure of certi-fication in the absence of a functioning State.

Between 1950 and 1970, Somali live animal exports rose dramatically with the growth of the Gulf State oil economies. The resulting social and economic changes that took place in Somalia have had fundamental implications for the structure of contemporary Somali pastoralism (in terms of who has retained involvement in pastoralism, and how), for the patterns of resource access and use which continue to underpin pastoral production, and ultimately for the viability of Somalia as a nation. Swift (1977) observed an overall shift from risk-avoiding species (camels and goats) to risk-prone but more highly priced cattle and sheep, despite little overt change in land use or livestock performance (in terms of livestock fertility, mortality, and pasture use). However, the Gulf livestock export trade drove rapid differentiation. Large producers were able to build wealth and then invest in private water development and fencing. This meant they gained *de facto* private dry season access to the grazing surrounding their water source, despite *de jure* communal tenure. The same wealthy indi-viduals were also able to invest in education for their kin, securing jobs, political influence, and administrative control. By contrast small producers were lured into production for the commercial market. This meant they had to restructure their own domestic production by decreasing their labour, shifting from labour-intensive husbandry and relative self-sufficiency, to low-labour, single-product concerns (Swift 1977, Behnke 1983). In drought, with serious fluctuations in terms of trade, small producers were less well able to survive than larger operators. Chapter 10 describes the changes in production system with progressive commercialisation, and the ways elite capture and pri-vatization of key resources affect customary networks of redistribution and risk management on the one hand and drive a hardening of once-fluid socioeco-nomic hierarchies, differentiation and dispossession on the other.

This process has been documented for different parts of Somalia with different pastoral ecologies. For example, water tanks supplied by lorry transport opened much of the northern *haud* plateau (see below) to permanent pasturing and private enclosure. In the Erigavo area of northern Somalia, wealthy and influential individuals were able to establish private ownership of large areas of rangeland and to stock coastal pastures with the large herds of animals awaiting export (Prior 1994). This set off a scramble for land claims in a very arid area, blocking the traditional migrations from the coastal *guban* up over the escarpment towards the plateau pastures of the hinterland, and pastoralists then found themselves having to spend long periods in the high mountains. The concentrations of animals that resulted built up unsustainable grazing pressure on the vegetation, and left the soil bare to be stripped from the steep gradients in uncontrollable erosion. The concentrations of livestock that resulted from this change of land tenure may have precipitated not only density-dependent mortality but also progressive and irreversible losses of productivity as predicted by classical views of range ecology (Chapter 3; Prior, 1994).

Throughout the 1970s, Somalia and Ethiopia were at war in the Ogaden. During this time 1-2 million Somalis left Ethiopia for Somalia, Kenya and Djibouti. During the 1990s, when Siad Barre fell from power, similar numbers moved back to Ethiopia, with impoverished Somali agropastoralists living alongside the Arssi in southern Bale and migrating to and fro across the perennially contested and war-torn Ethiopia/Somalia border. People and livestock have been killed in the recurrent fighting: many households have lost their male head, and in agropastoralist areas women are increasingly unable to meet the extra labour requirements vital for wet-season transhumance alongside cultivation. Households resort to gathering wild foods in the hungry season, by necessity rather than by choice. The wars have meant internal displacement, cross-border refugee movements (*The Economist*, 2001), and the disruption of lives and livelihoods on a massive scale

> since the late 1970s, the region has been awash with modern automatic rifles and ammunition, thousands of people have been almost continuously displaced and separated from their means of livelihood. (Getachew, 1996).

Recurrent outbreaks of violent conflict have continued to disrupt pastoralist movements and trade in complex and rapidly changing ways. Within the major divisions of Somali kinship and clanship, interrelations of representation, alliance and conflict change continually as coalitions emerge and new regions and groups break away. Identities are continuously being constructed and negotiated, and strategies shift in response to the new opportunities, not least those created by Western interventions, peace negotiations, and donor-driven NGOs (Little, 2003; de Waal, 1997). Somaliland and Puntland have broken away as self-styled independent regions. The livestock economy has undergone enormous fluctuations as well:

> A 16-month ban on the import of its livestock by Saudi Arabia, its chief market, resulted in a collapse in government revenues from $45m to $27m last year. The ban, now lifted, was ostensibly imposed because Somaliland's veterinary certificates, giving the animals a clean bill of health, were not internationally recognised. The main reason why the world will not accept Somaliland's independence is that the rest of Somalia does not want it, and its other neighbours are wary. The second problem is that livestock farming, the backbone of the economy, is in trouble. The nomads, who look after the animals, are the poorest people in the country and there is no government assistance for them or their flocks.... Free enterprise, the government's philosophy, is encouraging people to enclose huge areas of common grazing land. Somaliland's tough nomads, survivors of drought, pestilence and wars, have never faced more difficult times. (*The Economist*: 5 August 1999)

Despite the collapse of the state, other Somali livestock exports to northern Kenya built up to compensate at least in part for the decline of the Gulf export trade (Little, 2003). However resilient the livestock export economy overall, the average pastoralist family within Somalia continues to face insecurity and violence. Conflict and raiding lead to loss of livestock, lives and key labour resources; they constrain mobility, impacting on livestock performance, disrupt markets and pastoral commodity chains. This chapter focuses on pastoral ecological strategies but is unable to analyse the extent to which these preferred movements have been disrupted by war in Somalia.

With the twin influences of the ITCZ and the ITF/monsoon systems, Somali rangelands experience different climates according to location. In the more arid north, average annual rainfall may be of the order of 100-200mm, with frequent single-year droughts, and serious multi-year droughts about one year in ten. Somali pastoralist systems survive in these harsh conditions by concentrating on camels and by making use of the alternation of the seasons to exploit the grazing and water resources of different land units. Lewis (1961) and Cassanelli (1982) described the Somali rangelands as broadly divided into the arid coastal strip (*guban*), the mountains immediately inland (e.g. the Ogo in the North) and the rolling plateau pastures of the hinterland (the *haud* in the north (Hogg, 1997b)), and the *mugud* in the south, continuous with the Ogaden and Bale regions of Ethiopia (Hogg, 1996). Baumann et al. (1993) give a more detailed breakdown.

Each clan or lineage group (see below) had its own home wells, where the herds concentrated during the *jilaal* or long dry season. In the north these were on the *guban* or coastal strip, or in the Ogo highlands. The rolling sandstone *haud* plateau has few permanent water sources. In northern and central Somalia, groups with coastal home wells would spend *jilaal* on the coastal strip, their camels browsing on *Suaeda fruticosa* saltbush and *Salvadora persica* trees (Lewis, 1961; Cassanelli, 1982). With the spring rains they would move up the escarpment and into the rainfed pastures of the Ogo highlands. At the same time, groups that spent the *jilaal* around their home wells in the Ogo would penetrate further inland into the rainfed pastures of the *haud*. In each case, the camel herds would cover hundreds of km in a single season. With a good wet season and relatively prolonged rains, the camel herds would stay away through the short dry season and short rains, returning only with the onset of *jilaal*. Groups migrating inland from the coast might overlap in the Ogo during the short summer dry season with groups whose home wells were located there. With poor rains, they would return to their home wells correspondingly earlier. In drought years, with spiralling competition for dwindling grass and water, conflicts would multiply and erupt into violent confrontations.

Drought responses include temporary destocking (distress sales); temporary outmigration of all but those needed to manage the remaining livestock; and the successively less attractive and more forced options of negotiating client status, resorting to cultivation or urban migration, or relocating to entirely new territories (Cassanelli, 1982). Seeking clientship would mean renouncing political autonomy, and pledging political and military support as well as labour to another group, in exchange for access to water and/or grazing to ensure livestock survival. Outmigrating dependants, temporarily sloughed off from the herding unit, might try to farm, or attach themselves to urban kin with some livelihood, or seek temporary urban employment themselves. Relocation to entirely new territory meant the combined hazards of losing long-established alliances, entering into conflict with new neighbours with whom no alliances would yet exist, and facing the unfamiliar disease foci and other dangers of a new environment. At the beginning of the twenty-first century, essentially the same strategies still apply, though these options are constrained by the aftermath of war, with continuing violence and lack of security, and the collapse of the urban economies. Alternative options have emerged: enlisting in one or other urban warlord's militia, or moving into dependence on relief and international refugee status.

Three types of camel rearing have been described as associated with the three zones (cf. Beja – Hjort and Dahl, 1991). As for Beja camels, coastal *Suaeda* saltbush range is said to produce the best milk yields, although it necessitates daily watering. On the Ogo plateau *caroog* camels graze on mainly *Chrysopogon* pastures, developing a heavy build and a thick coat. The more lightly built *qyuun* or *cayuun* camels of the montane region are mainly *Acacia* browsers, and are relatively poor producers of milk and meat.

The importance of camels in Somali culture is made clear in the great depth of technical and environmental knowledge surrounding their husbandry, and in the way that camel values are embedded in every aspect of customary law, particularly blood price and inheritance, as well as in moral and cultural ideals (Lewis, 1961; Rirash, 1988; see Hjort and Dahl, 1991 for parallels with the Beja). This is expressed in a wealth of poems and song cycles, reflecting every stage of seasonal movement and every aspect of camel lore and management, and describing the arduous life of the camel herders and their physical endurance and courage (Andrzewski and Andrzewski, 1986; Rirash, 1988). Watering the camels during the dry season commonly involves a three-week trek. This entails 7-8 days spent walking to the wells, a week watering the animals, and a similar length of time moving back to distant pastures so as to optimise the use of both grazing and water resources. At the wells the shafts must be repeatedly dug out and water must be raised by a human chain from varying depths. Shallow wells must be cleared night and day to get enough water for all the animals (Talle and Abdullahi, 1993). In the most arid areas herders' families move with them in the wet season, with the women moving and pitching camp as well as herding and milking the small stock. Other than in times of war or feud, these mobile groups form and dissolve a series of short-lived fission-fusion hamlets, with little structure other than the temporary, pragmatic but essential logistical agreements they negotiate over herding and watering arrangements. The wet season is a time of relative plenty, when commonly town-based senior kinsmen may move inland to join the camel herds, and advise on their management and on policy over alliances and conflicts.

Somali pastoralist resource use is inextricably bound up with kinship and its manipulation for ecological, political and economic expediency (Lewis, 1961; Cassanelli, 1982). The clan-families divide into patrilineal clans, each of which may have 100,000 or so men, and which are in turn subdivided into lineages of 5–10 generations depth. Individual Somalis can commonly trace their own ancestry back 20–25 generations and can rapidly establish their degree of kinship with others. Within each lineage there are '*dia*-paying' groups, whose members share the responsibility of underwriting the blood debts any member of the group may incur. Conversely, any such compensation paid for the killing of a member of the *dia*-paying group is also shared within the group. Corporate responsibility and contractual agreements work most effectively at this level (e.g. Prior, 1994). The *dia*-paying group is the basic resource-use group and is also the basic unit of military action. Feuds continually erupt between groups, lineages and clans over access to scarce resources, or over non-payment of compensation, and higher-order alliances are continually renegotiated to suit the case. In particular, recent opportunities presented by Western interventions, with peace negotiations and donor-supported NGOs, triggered a proliferation of groups claiming separate and independent status as a new manifestation of the increasingly complex, constructed, continuously shifting and renegotiated interrelations of lineage, alliance and conflict (Little, 2003). Particularly in more arid areas like northern Somalia, coordination of groups customarily using the same well is a matter of sophisticated management, with any mishandling potentially sparking violent conflict. Personal rights, access to resources, and political power have commonly been acquired and defended by force rather than by land tenure and right of ownership (Lewis, 1961).

Southern Somalia has rather more predictable climate, grazing and water resources, and the character of Somali pastoralism changes progressively further to the south. Livestock breeds, management techniques and production characteristics here are all rather different from the north. Southern Somali have a mix of camels, cattle, small stock and donkeys, with a greater emphasis on more regular, short-range, cattle transhumance as opposed to opportunistic and far-ranging camel migrations, and a denser network of farming settlements. Where possible, different species are kept with different wives, and animals divided into dry (*ureni*) and milking (*werra*) herds. With the higher and more predictable rainfall, camels increasingly give way to cattle. Cultivation is more reliable and more permanent and widespread. Women, children and older men are more likely to be based in relatively permanent farming settlements, while young men herd cattle on wet-season transhumance away from riverine and other areas of permanent water (where disease vectors multiply in the rains) to wet-season plateau pastures. These are much shorter-range movements than those undertaken by the camel herds. Men use ox-ploughs to prepare the fields, and women grow riverine or rainfed crops of cereals, including the distinctively Ethiopian *tef,* pulses and tubers. Livestock are pastured on crop stubble in the dry season, and manure the fields in the process (Baumann et al., 1993). The livestock economy of southern Somalia has changed over the last decades, but persists (Little, 2003).

Compared with other Somali regions, these communities seem to have more developed mechanisms of negotiation and cooperation regulating resource use within their mixture of kinship groups. Their longer traditions of shared rights and responsibilities are established on the basis of common and long-term occupation of a valley or sub-catchment, as much as on kinship. The tradition of a more structured and less fluid control of resources in the south goes back several centuries. Particular groups are recognised as the first occupants of given areas, and as having allowed access to particular client groups, in a relationship that still restricts client rights and confers political power on the nobles with right of tenure. In the nineteenth century many individuals imported slaves to work the land for them, thus accruing individual wealth without involving traditional kinship obligations, in a foretaste of twentieth century individual wealth accumulation and land privatisation (Helander, 1999). Islamic *cadis* became increasingly involved in mediating land transactions (Cassanelli, 1982). Many slaves freed by encroaching colonial powers settled and cultivated in riverine areas, and were progressively assimilated into local clans. These factors all contribute to a distinct pattern of land use in southern Somalia.

Pastoralists in wetlands II: peoples of the Sudd

Throughout the arid and semi-arid rangelands of Africa, pastoralists are dependent on local wetlands to get through dry periods. Local systems operate around wetlands such as Lakes Chad (Schelling, 2002); Baringo (Homewood, 1994; Anderson, 1988, 2002; Little, 1983); Amboseli (Western, 1975); Omo River Mursi and Dassanetch (Turton, 1988; Carr, 1977), El Kala in Algeria (Homewood, 1993). Such wetlands form the focus of competition between farming and herding, smallholder and agribusiness (Scoones, 1991; Landais, 1994; Niamir-Fuller, 1999; Legrosse, 1999; Duany, 1999; Woodhouse et al., 2002; Southgate and Hulme, 1999). Like the Inland delta of the Niger, other large African wetlands such as the Sudd sustain complex interplays of people, animals and production systems involving enormous numbers and movements over a regional scale.

As the White Nile flows from its source in Lake Victoria in the East African highlands it comes to a stretch where the overall gradient averages only 10cm/km over 400 km from south to north (Howell et al., 1988). Here the river and its annual flooding create a vast swamp, grading into drylands on either side. The main channels flowing through the swamp are the Bahr-el-Ghazal, the Bahr-el-Jebel and Bahr-el-Zeraf which merge and join together with the Sobat at Malakal (Fig. 2.1). With the influence of the ITCZ, rains fall from April to November, decreasing from around 900mm in the south to ca. 800mm in the north. The rains coincide with rising flood levels, fed by earlier rain in the catchment areas around Lake Victoria and south-west Sudan. From December to March, the river falls, the rains cease, the floods recede, and the land away from the main channels becomes arid and waterless, with late dry-season temperatures rising to 45°C (Howell et al., 1988). Flood levels have changed over the long term with external changes (drought and rainfall patterns affecting East African lake inflow) as well as local factors (local rainfall; local changes in channel patterns and vegetation blockages generating floods upriver or draining areas downstream – Howell et al. (1988) and Johnson (1988, 1991). High flood years are more difficult for the farming, fishing and herding peoples of the Sudd than are drought years, because in the latter riverine grazing and water are still available, while flooding limits cultivation (Johnson, 1991). In the early 1960s, high inflow to the East African lakes meant that flood levels doubled. The overall swamp area was measured as 7–8000km^2 in the 1930s; 1950s surveys recorded ca3000km^2 permanent swamp and ca11000km^2 seasonal swamp. By the 1980s, permanent swamp covered ca17000km^2 and seasonal swamp ca14,000km^2, forcing considerable reorganisation of settlement and resource use. This has been compounded by the disruption and devastation caused by the civil war that has dominated southern Sudan since the 1980s, displacing large populations of former pastoralists (Chapter 2; Johnson, 2003, 2004).

The term *Sudd* refers to the papyrus and bulrush swamp itself. This vegetation formation, associated with the main waterways, grades into flooding grasslands (*toic*). These rise gradually to rainfed perennial grasslands, which become waterless plains of cracking clay in the dry season. The wetlands support a mix of Nilotic farming, fishing and herding peoples: Dinka, Nuer, Shilluk, and Anuak, who exploit the mosaic of soil, water and vegetation conditions generated by the microtopography and the seasonal cycle of flood and drawdown. For all the Sudd peoples, livestock and particularly cattle are of fundamental importance, not only in their broad-based contribution to the economy, but more generally in the way livestock underpin social relations – marriage, inheritance, compensation, and personal identity (Hutchinson, 1992, 1996). The floods are predictable in timing, but erratic from year to year in behaviour. This unpredictability has fostered a much broader system of social interdependence among different Nilotic peoples of the Sudd than is portrayed by the classic picture of a uniform, predictable ecology, and distinct, mutually hostile ethnic groups (Evans-Pritchard, 1940).

Colonial indirect rule emphasised an oversimplified dichotomy of 'Arab' (equated with northern/Islamic) as separate from 'black' (southern/Christian), accentuating differences in infrastructure, services and education and laying the basis for future rift (Kurita, 1994). As the post-Independence period unfolded, the peoples of the Sudd lost what political representation they initially held in Nimeiri's government in Khartoum (Keen, 1995; de Waal, 1997; Johnson, 2003) and the region has been drawn into civil war (Kurimoto, 1994; Salih, 1993, 1994). This book's focus on the ecology of pastoralist societies cannot begin to deal with the devastation that civil war and famine have brought about in southern Sudan (Allen, 1996; Johnson, 1996; James, 1996; Keen, 1995; Hutchinson, 1996). However, conflicts over tenure and access to natural resources, pastoral land and livestock, have been exacerbated by the pressures that Sudanese agricultural policy placed on the Baggara Arabs (Salih, 1990). This led to the savage attacks, government-backed and perpetrated by Arab militias, on the southern Sudanese (Keen, 1995; de Waal, 1997; cf. Darfur – de Waal, 2004), the backlash of Southern rebellion (Kurimoto, 1994; Salih, 1993, 1994), the current turmoil of displacement, repatriation, relief attempts (Allen, 1996) and the attendant self-serving politics, both local and international (de

Waal, 1997). The development of the oilfields of southern Sudan, and the associated battle for their control, widened the field of conflict and intensified it, but the disruption that has resulted over vast areas and for hundreds of thousands of people is beyond the scope of this book.

Settlements of Sudd peoples have typically been sited on ridges or small raised outcrops of porous sandy soil, high enough to be above the floods, with access to the river or feeder channel and its papyrus swamps, to the flooding riverine *Echinochloa* pastures of the *toic*, and to the rainfed *Hyparrhenia* grasslands on marginally higher-lying, impervious, cracking clays that waterlog in the rains and then rapidly dry out. Dinka, Nuer and Shilluk have all used these four main land units in rather similar ways, though the geographical spread of resources has entailed different patterns of transhumance and degrees of mobility in each case (Howell et al., 1988). The Shilluk largely inhabited a lower rainfall area, with less flooding, and were more sedentary, with structured, permanent settlements. They had a greater concentration of population, more emphasis on cultivation and fishing, and a division of labour that took the cattle herds to riverine pastures under the care of young men for the duration of the dry season. Dinka and Nuer were generally more mobile, with more scattered and temporary settlement patterns and more flexible transhumant movements. The wet season was and is a time of cultivation around settlements. Two or sometimes three crops of sorghum can be staggered to make use of different field sites at different stages of flood and drawdown. At the beginning of the rains livestock graze the rainfed flush of *Hyparrhenia* pastures on the impervious clay plains. Lower-lying pastures flood rapidly, often with a dangerously swift creeping flow. Cattle are kept ever closer to the settlement as the floods rise, so rainfed pastures become inaccessible at their time of peak growth. With the cereal harvest, farming people's diet centres on sorghum porridge and on beer, and calorie intake peaks. As the rains cease and the floods recede, rainfed pastures rapidly become waterless drylands. In the early dry season, rank growth is burned off them and the new green flush that follows provides good grazing for a brief period. There are few permanent sources of water inland, and these vary from year to year, depending for example on the relative height of the Sobat, and whether the gullies feeding it back up to create water points inland. The rainfed plains rapidly become barren. Cattle follow the dry-season drawdown, and by mid-January all concentrate in the *toic* or riverine swamp grazing.

For the Nuer, the *toic* cattle camps of February and March were customarily major social gatherings of people with their animals. Many villages are more or less abandoned for the dry season, particularly as they may have no permanent water source. As the dry season progresses the herds penetrate ever deeper into the *toic* and may be forced to enter the papyrus swamp. The herds lead a grazing succession, with a progression of ever more selective wildlife species – tiang, reedbuck and finally gazelles – from fired rainfed grasslands to *toic*, each following and grazing or browsing the successive layers of sward exposed by the passage of the earlier herds (Homewood and Rodgers, 1991:199). In the dry season, Dinka and Nuer pastoralists of the Sudd eat little or no cereal. As well as relying largely on livestock products, they hunted for food, with wildlife making up 25% of the annual meat intake (Howell, Lock and Cobb, 1988). Fishing also peaked with the dry-season move to the *toic,* as well as during the initial rise of the floods and again when the floods recede at the end of the rains. Poor families might subsist mainly on fishing, in the hope of trading enough to eventually rebuild their herds. With the onset of the wet season, a new grass flush appears on the dry rainfed plains and forage nutrient content peaks (Howell et al., 1988). The livestock benefit, their milk production doubling compared with yields on the abundant but less nutritious *toic* pastures. The herds retreat rapidly to their permanent villages, keeping ahead of the rising floods. There would be little if any stored grain in the settlement, and a hungry season follows, until the first crop can be harvested.

Each settlement has its own particular combination of microtopography, soil and water relations, with different potential depending on the changing patterns of flooding in any given year, and different degrees of vulnerability to famine. Each year would present different combinations of accessible water, pasture and cultivable land; each year, different pockets of settlement would manage adequate or even surplus production, while others faced famine. Some groups, like the Twic Dinka, might build low mud dykes to protect areas of fertile soil against flooding. More often, these measures were of little use in the unpredictable and periodically overwhelming floods. The shifting conditions of water, soil and pasture were compounded by the periodic scourge of rinderpest, contagious bovine pleuropneumonia (CBPP) and trypanosomiasis epidemics (Chapter 6), raiding and warfare (Chapter 3). In this mosaic of risk and opportunity, viability was secured 'not so much by occupation and possession of land and water resources, as by regular access to alternate resources' (Johnson, 1991).

The possibility of access to alternative resources has in the long term been assured by developing and maintaining reciprocal relations of trade, exchange, intermarriage and intermigration, as well as by occasional raiding. Terms of trade for cattle, grain and wives within and between the Nuer and the relatively cattle-poor Dinka have periodically been affected by government policies imposed throughout the twentieth century, restricting patterns of settlement, resource access and trade. The long-term increase in the flooded areas, together with changing internal security and external relations, meant an expansion of the fish trade, and a shift to greater labour migration to North Sudan and the Middle East in the 1980s. The cash economy, cattle and grain trade were all growing and there was periodic involvement in ivory and arms trade. Even before the present nadir, civil war had for decades affected the pastoralist systems of the Sudd in fundamental ways – for example, through the arming of rival Murle[6] raiders by the Sudanese government – with particular impact on the people of the eastern areas, more accessible than the west (cf. Hendrickson et al., 1998). Currently, a precarious coalition of local and international interests is attempting to construct a new social order governing resource use in and around the Sudd (Salih, 1994; Kurimoto, 1994; de Waal,

[6] The Murle are a formerly Omotic-speaking agropastoralist group, estimated as numbering 300-400,000, inhabiting Pibor County in Jonglei, south-eastern Upper Nile, southern Sudan.

1997; Johnson, 2003; Duany, 1999). The powerful rhythm of flood, draw-down and drought in this ecosystem will continue to play a major part in shaping whatever system of land-use management may emerge.

East African pastoralists

East African pastoralist ecosystems are illustrated here through Turkana, Boran and Maasai, though to be comprehensive it would be necessary to include the many other well-studied East African peoples such as the Ariaal, Rendille, Mursi, Dassanetch (Turton, 1988; Fratkin, 1991, 2001; Fratkin and Smith, 1994), and agropastoralist systems such as the Kalenjin-speaking pastoralist communities of the East African Highlands (Pokot, Sebei, Nandi – e.g. Dietz, 1987; Goldschmidt, 1976) as well as the Datoga (Sieff, 1997,1999; Lane and Scoones, 1993).

Maasai

The area now informally termed Maasailand and the people seen as Maasai are very much artefacts of the boundaries drawn up by colonial administrations and also of the progressive loss and excision of other areas of land formerly occupied by Maa-speaking pastoral peoples. Maasailand is now an area covering some 200,000 km² occupying the Central Rift Valley, and areas of the highlands to either side. This area abuts on other pastoralist and agropastoralist Maa-speaking groups (Samburu, Il Chamus – Spear and Waller, 1993; Anderson, 1988; Brockington, 2002). The Maasai also border on the mainly farming and agropastoralist communities of Kikuyu, Chagga, Pare and other Bantu-speaking peoples in Northern Tanzania and southern Kenya. The Maasai have emerged as a recognisable group over the last couple of centuries, and reached their peak expansion in the late nineteenth century. The resource-use patterns described here are those observed during the mid-late twentieth century (Homewood and Rodgers, 1991; Potkanski, 1994). The contrasting development pathways of Kenya and Tanzania are driving progressive diver-gence between the two parts of Maasailand (Homewood et al., 2001 and forthcoming; Thompson and Homewood, 2002).

Straddling the Equator, Maasailand has a bimodal pattern of rainfall. There is a great diversity of local climates, with individual sites variously affected by the presence of the highlands of the Rift (Crater Highlands, Mau), by their rainshadow (Rift Valley sites; Serengeti Plain), and by proximity to Lake Victoria (Western Serengeti). This diversity is further enhanced by the mosaic of geology, topography, soils, surface water patterns and hence of growing conditions. Vegetation types range from short grass associations on the relatively arid plains, through intermediate altitude and montane tussock grass associations (*Pennisetum; Eleusine*) or grassland with *Acacia - Commiphora* shrubs (as for Mkomazi – Coe et al., 1999) to Acacia woodland (Ngorongoro Crater; Amboseli) and high montane forest with cedar stands interspersed with bamboo. Many of the soils associated with the Great Rift Valley are derived from the recent volcanic rocks and are highly fertile, with a rich mineral nutrient content. Rift Valley topography includes volcanic peaks rising to over 3000m, highland plateaux, steep scarps and low-lying plains falling to 500m. The highlands are drained by permanent or seasonally flowing ravines, and inland drainage feeds saline lakes in the central Rift Valley.

The bimodal rainfall pattern, the widespread occurrence of good soils, and the diversity of physical environment and vegetation types mean firstly that there is a relatively long growing period and high primary production in many parts of Maasailand. Secondly, the mosaic of conditions means that all the pastoral requirements of forage, water, minerals and disease avoidance can be met within a relatively shorter radius of movement than is the case in many other African rangeland systems. Thirdly, calving and milk production are potentially spread out over a relatively longer period. This makes possible a heavier reliance on milk-based diets than is the case for many other pastoralists. In the 1980s, studies of a range of Maasai communities showed that pastoral products, particularly milk, made up around half the dietary energy intake across a wide range of circumstances (Homewood, 1992a). All Maasai communities trade pastoral products for grain and other foods, and many cultivate as well (Homewood, 1992a; Homewood et al., forthcoming; Nestel, 1986, 1989).

Historical and archaeological research make it clear that specialised pastoralism has been only one aspect of the Maasai network of subsistence activities (Galaty, 1982; Berntsen, 1976; Spear and Waller, 1993). Maasai systems of land use and livestock production have thus centred on relatively short-range transhumance. Maasai herds are commonly pastured on the plains during the wet season when these relatively arid areas put out a brief but fast-growing and highly nutritious flush of new grass. As the rains come to an end, the pastures dry out and the lack of forage and surface water force a move towards dry-season refuge areas where the permanent homesteads are typically based. In Ngorongoro Conservation Area (NCA),[7] different Maasai communities used wet- and dry-season camps up to 50 km apart, and often much closer. Depending on the community and the resources available, the dry-season refuge may be a low-lying swamp, or a highland area with permanent water and grazing. Either way, these key refuges carry potential problems of disease vectors (tsetse, ticks); gut parasites and/or respiratory infections, and relatively poor-quality grazing. These problems get worse as the dry season progresses, and the Maasai herds move to the plains again with the first rains and new growth.

This pattern changes with local conditions. Loss of land through privatisation (Rutten, 1992; Galaty, 1999; Igoe and Brockington, 1999; Thompson and Homewood, 2002), expropriation for wildlife conservation estate (Igoe and Brockington, 1999; Homewood et al., 2005) or for agribusiness (Homewood et al., 2001) and the spread of farming communities across migration corridors and around key resources all constrain patterns of movement. For those with

[7] Ngorongoro Conservation Area or NCA is a multiple land-use area in Tanzania, established when Maasai were evicted to create the Serengeti National Park in 1959. NCA seeks to combine wildlife conservation and a major tourist industry with a resident pastoralist population.

capital, water development and fodder supplementation begin to replace transhumance as a dry-season strategy. Still, in periods of dire need, Maasai are often able to negotiate access for their herds to private land (Grandin and Lembuya, 1987; Ndagala, 1990, 1992a) and/or conservation estate (Amboseli – Western, 1993; Tsavo – Berger, 1993). The problems may be more than a question of access. In the western part of NCA (eastern Serengeti), the wet-season immigration of more than a million wildebeest onto the transient but temporarily rich grazing of the short grass plains brings both serious grazing competition and severe disease threat to Maasai herds. The cattle are held back in the highland pastures, before moving onto the plains only when the wildebeest (and the best grazing) have gone. Their dry-season grazing is scraped from the sparse shrub and grass cover of the low hills around the short grass plains. They reveal an almost complete reversal of the usual pattern.

Across Maasailand, pastoralist families are showing a rapid diversification into other types of production system and other livelihoods (Homewood et al., 2001, 2004, forthcoming; Thompson and Homewood, 2002). Livestock remain the time-honoured and culturally valued mainstay for most Maasai, and most households also cultivate some maize for home consumption, but larger-scale cereal farming and intensive irrigation of export crops in swamp and riverine areas are spreading rapidly. Wildlife tourism offers the possibility of high revenues to some individuals, particularly to better-off elites and entrepreneurs, while others are increasingly engaging with off-land work, the better-placed as salaried teachers, officials and businessmen, the less well-off as labourers, miners and watchmen (Thompson and Homewood, 2002; Homewood et al., forthcoming).

Turkana

The Turkana represent a rather recently crystallised ethnic grouping, which grew rapidly by assimilation of neighbouring peoples and the welding of corresponding agesets into a powerful fighting force under an exceptionally innovative, forceful and successful leader (Lamphear, 1993). During the twentieth century, a combination of drought, disease, famine and predatory raiding has seen them much reduced (McCabe, 2004; Hendrickson et al., 1998). The Ngisonyoka are one of some 15 subgroups of Turkana peoples, and have been the subject of long-term multidisciplinary research (Little and Leslie, 1999). Many other Turkana live as agropastoralists, as traders, as migrant workers and as refugees dependent on relief (Brainard, 1986, 1991; van den Boogard, 2002). Recent estimates range from ca30-45% of a possible 300,000 Turkana living outside Turkana District (Hendrickson et al., 1998; Little and Leslie, 1999). The picture of land use and livestock management given here focuses on the most arid land and the most remote and most purely pastoralist end of the spectrum of East African pastoralism.

At the time of the South Turkana Ecological Project (STEP – Little and Leslie, 1999) around 10,000 Ngisonyoka Turkana inhabited around 10,000 km^2 of the Rift Valley in the north-west corner of Kenya (Coughenour et al., 1985; Coppock et al., 1986, 1988; Ellis and Swift, 1988). This part of Turkana

District is arid (mean annual rainfall for different localities ranges from 150mm to 600mm), with over half falling between April and June. In good years, there is a second short rains in October–November. The expected bimodal rainfall is relatively rarely achieved, and there is commonly a 9–10-month dry season. Inter- and intra-annual variabilities are high. Droughts are frequent, with rainfall less than one-third of the long-term mean occurring once in every 3-4 years on average, and with several multi-year droughts on record in the last 50 years. During these periods of drought, primary production can fall to one-third or one-quarter of its average value. The central mountains rise to >2100m, and are made up of ancient basement complex rocks, abutting on lava hills and extensive lava plains. Sandy plains stretch away from the central mountains at an altitude of around 370m, carrying a seasonal flush of annual grasses (*Aristida, Eragrostis*) and dissected by drainage lines running from the central highlands. These give wet-season surface or well water, and their woody vegetation (*Acacia, Boscia, Commiphora* trees and shrubs) provides shade and green browse through the year as well as seasonal crops of seeds and seedpods (Scholte, 1992). Dwarf shrubs (e.g. *Indigofera* spp) are important in drier areas. The central mountain grasslands carry a higher biomass and retain permanent water. The Ngisonyoka people use this geological, topographical and ecological diversity together with their range of livestock species to exploit different vegetation resources (McCabe, 2004).

During the April-June wet season, Ngisonyoka Turkana people converge on the sandy plains adjacent to the central mountains, pasturing their livestock on the drainage lines and interdrainage areas. As the forage and wells become depleted towards October, herds and human groups split up and disperse. In recent studies, Turkana homesteads moved on average 8km every 24 days throughout the year, and treks of over 70 km were documented during the transitional seasons. The cattle were progressively moved up into the lava hills and the grasslands of the central mountains. Between them, the camels, cattle, sheep, goats and donkeys made use of an increasingly diverse range of habitats and vegetation types. There was a strong seasonality in forage diversity and abundance, and quality of the livestock, as well as in their feeding habits, activity budgets and water intakes. Overall, the Turkana livestock showed a greater separation of habitat use than was the case for the Maasai. For example, in the Turkana studies 95% of camel intake was browse, and for cattle 95% was graze. By contrast, cattle in Maasailand and many other pastoral systems have commonly been shown to make extensive use of browse. This difference is due both to the predominance of thorny shrubs in arid Turkanaland, not easily used by cattle, and also to deliberate separation by the herders so as to optimise use of all the vegetation types available. Turkana decisions as to when and where to move on transhumance were determined by biophysical environment and security considerations (McCabe, 2004), with lesser consideration of social and other dimensions.

The aridity and strong seasonality of the Ngisonyoka Turkana system means a low population density (1 person/km^2) and relatively few livestock per capita (2.5 TLU/person or approximately 1 camel, 1 cow, 6 goats and 3 sheep per person according to aerial counts in the 1970s: these numbers would be expected to vary dramatically with a run of good or bad years, and averages do not represent the distribution of livestock holdings among households). STEP calculated that stocking rates were well below the theoretical maximum and that livestock numbers were unlikely to affect plant biomass. It found no detectable impacts of grazing on plant production, though livestock do shape shrub growth and may foster the germination and establishment of forage trees, for example through seed dispersal. The Ngisonyoka Turkana, remote from trade and inhabiting an area too arid to cultivate, derived an annual average of 76% of their dietary energy intake from pastoral products: a further 16% came from foods obtained through trade for pastoral produce. In dry seasons and years the temporary shortage of good-quality forage meant that all livestock went into nutritional deficit (even camels, although they were less seriously affected).

Different STEP papers record the extent of Ngisonyoka exploitation as varying between 7000 km^2 and 9600 km^2 (cf. Turner, 1999a: point-centred key resources with varying radius of use). In bad seasons and years, people expanded their area of exploitation, and both herds and human groups split into smaller units and dispersed. People lost weight, shifted to wild resources, and/or emigrated to find food relief or wage labour in towns. In periods of drought, livestock fertility dropped to zero and in multi-year droughts livestock mortality rose to 50–70% (McCabe, 1987a). Herds were rapidly rebuilt through natural fertility (particularly of small stock), immigration and sometimes through raiding. STEP concluded that there could be some density-dependent limitation of livestock numbers in certain high-density areas, but that across most of the region most of the time mortality was density-independent. The Turkana ecosystem is not an equilibrial system where a build-up of livestock numbers brings about long-term degradation, but is rather a dis-equilibrium system driven by a highly variable climate (Ellis and Swift, 1988; McCabe, 2004). Within this the Ngisonyoka have established an efficient and sustainable system of exploiting natural vegetation for human food.

Oromo-speaking peoples of Southern Ethiopia: Borana and Arssi

Borana people extend across the Borana Plateau of Ethiopia, south through the northern part of Kenya to the Tana River. Different Boran groups have had very different trajectories over the last decades, according to their interaction with different nation states. In Ethiopia, the state enlisted and armed (non-Muslim) Boran as allies against other, generally Muslim Oromo-speaking pastoralists (Hogg, 1993; Bassi, 1997), despite initial Boran support for fellow Oromo, and their part in the wider Oromo identity (Baxter, 1994). By contrast, in Kenya the Boran, along with other Oromo-speakers in Kenya, were caught in the political and military fallout of the 'Shifta' wars centred on Somalis in Kenya. The Kenya Boran were interned and most of their stock were lost (Dahl, 1979; Baxter, 1991).

The Borana plateau comprises some 100,000 km^2 of uplands in southern Ethiopia, rising from an altitude of around 1000m near the Kenya border to 1600m at the northern edge of the Borana range, and to 2-3000 m in the Arssi areas further north. The Boran have been seen as typical of specialised East African pastoralism (Cossins and Upton, 1987). The Arssi have been more constrained by land tenure and more diversified into cultivation and trade (Baxter, 1991) and both groups have been radically affected by war in the Horn (Hogg, 1993, 1997a; Farah, 1997; Getachew, 1996). The Borana plateau varies from arid in the south (160mm annual rainfall and 1000m altitude) through semi-arid (5-600mm at intermediate altitude) and subhumid (1000mm or more rainfall and an altitude of over 1600m). The rainfall is bimodal, with 60% falling in the long rains (March-May) and the rest in October-November. On average, one year in five is a drought year, with a run of drought years about once in 20 years. Overall the length of growing season varies from around 90 days in the south through 140 in the semi-arid parts of the Borana area to longer growing seasons in the north. Soils vary from recent, thin volcanic or granitic soils in the most arid zones (nutrient-rich but water-limited) to nutrient-poor basement complex soils in upland areas and fertile clays in bottomlands. The semi-arid rangelands have wooded savannas (*Acacia, Combretum* and *Commiphora* trees with up to 40% canopy cover in many places) and an understorey of *Cenchrus, Cynodon, Pennisetum* and *Themeda* grassland. The plateau is high enough to be largely free of vector-borne diseases – East Coast fever (ECF) and trypanosomiasis.

Borana herds observed during the 1980s were divided into management units typically separating milking cattle with calves and small stock (*worra* herds) from dry and immature stock (*fora* herds). The *worra* herds were kept throughout the year near relatively permanent settled *olla* or villages (usually of 10-30 families). These herds grazed a radius of 16km around the *olla*, generating a patchy distribution of grazing pressure, nutrient stripping and deposition. This was thought to encourage a progressive encroachment of woody vegetation and spread of soil erosion ultimately affecting pastoral production (Coppock, 1993), though *olla* were moved every 5-8 years. The *fora* herds ranged much more widely and had access to better forage, particularly temporary growth in nutrient-rich areas with transient surface water. As female stock matured and became pregnant they were moved to the *worra* herd. As they aged and ceased calving, they were transferred back to the *fora*. Salt earths of various sorts were seen as essential supplements for Borana stock. These salts were collected from volcanic craters in the Borana plateau rangelands (Cossins and Upton, 1987), from deposits round hot salt springs (as in the Arssi areas) or in desert pans (as collected by the Marsabit Boran from the Chalbi desert in Kenya), or more rarely were bought in the market (Baxter, 1991).

Boran pastoralists have long used complex wells to water their stock across most of their plateau range. In this they resemble the Somali of the Ogaden, rather than other East African pastoralists (Cossins and Upton, 1987). In the deeper traditional wells, ramps were dug leading down to specially engineered watering ponds up to 10m below ground level. Water was lifted from a depth of around 30m by means of a human chain using hide buckets. These wells have always required tremendous feats not only of engineering and mainte- nance, and of labour to operate them, but also of management to coordinate watering rights and rotas in general and the schedule of arrival, watering and turnaround at the well itself (Cossins and Upton, 1987; Dahl and Megerssa, 1990; Baxter, 1991). Some see the social organisation of the *olla* as having evolved to deal with the labour and management requirements of operating the wells.

Borana pastoralists based on the plateau in Southern Ethiopia depended for over 90% of their income on their herds of camels, cattle, sheep, goats and donkeys (Cossins and Upton, 1988). Over 65% of their dietary energy intake came from pastoral products, with the rest based on cereals and other foods, mostly purchased with income from the sale of livestock and pastoral products (ibid.). These areas reach densities of 25 cattle and 1.4 families or 6-7 persons/km^2 (Coppock, 1993), comparing very favourably with commercial pastoralist systems in Kenya and elsewhere (Cossins and Upton, 1987). Since the 1990s, Borana pastoralists have come under intense pressure to settle, having lost much of their pastureland to cultivation and facing considerable security risks from armed raiding (e.g. SOS Sahel, 2002).

Southern Africa

Pastoralist societies of Southern Africa have been radically transformed by the region's complex history (see Chapter 2). Indigenous South African livestock production systems have been transformed, in many cases beyond recognition, by cultural and religious crises (Peires, 1989), massive land expropriation (Hall, 1990), genocidal war (Namibia − Pennington and Harpending, 1993, 1990), apartheid which crowded 75% of the population into 10% of the land, betterment schemes (Beinart, 1994; Jacobs, 2003; Turner and Ntshona, 1999), and rural land use based on a migrant labour economy (Jacobs, 2003). Botswana has developed a livestock industry dominated by commercial, fenced ranching concerns, though these are buttressed by smaller, subsistence-level, indigenous production enterprises (Behnke, 1985) still strongly structured by ethnic exclusion (Hitchcock, 1996). In South Africa, Xhosa societies which at one stage sacrificed their stock (Peires, 1989) nonetheless retained economic and cultural ideals centred on cattle-keeping, as have the Zulu, not least because of their long exclusion from so many other forms of production (cf. MacKinnon, 1999). At present, however, rural economies driven by migrant labour remittances and pension payments have drastically constrained livestock-keeping, despite its lasting significance in South Africa's communal lands (Ainslie, 2005). In Namibia, Himba, Herero and Damara people draw their living from a mix of livestock, farming, natural resource use, migrant labour and local employment, which on the face of it bears little resemblance to indigenous pastoralism. Studies of livestock-keeping in Namaqualand (Baker and Hoffmann, 2003) and agropastoralist systems in the communal homelands of Bophuthatswana (Jacobs, 2003) show the extent to which resource use is constrained by social and historical circumstances. However, detailed study shows patterns of land use and livestock movement whose roots lie in customary pastoroforager patterns of natural resource management, rather than the boundaries established in official land registers (e.g. Behnke, 1999; Sullivan, 1999c, 2005). Given the major disjunction between most of these systems and the more mobile, economically and ecologically less constrained forms of pastoralism found elsewhere across Africa, this book does not deal in any detail with South African livestock-keeping.

5

Pastoral Livelihoods & Economy

The seasonal nature of the milk supply, the associated reliance on other cultivated, purchased or gathered foods, and the calorific and monetary terms of trade between pastoral and cultivated produce are the main determinants both of the food system and of the broader economy of those people who rely primarily on their herds for their sustenance. Pastoralist systems are characterised by the flexibility and diversity of their economic as well as ecological strategies, and around these core determinants other activities may take on considerable importance: farming, hunting and fishing by pastoralists of the Southern Sudan (Johnson, 1988, 1991); trade caravanning (Tuareg – Bernus, 1981); urban wage labour (Beja and Somali – Morton, 1990, 1993; Pantuliano, 2002); mining for gold or gems (Sachedina, forthcoming); gathering and processing karité nuts to make shea butter (Peul women in Bénin – Schreckenberg, 1996); artisanal leatherwork (agropastoralist Tamasheq, Mali, Niger and Burkina). Over the last few decades, pastoral groups have experienced the same trend of increasing diversification into non-farm occupations shown by rural populations across sub-Saharan Africa, with intensification where inputs allow (BurnSilver, forthcoming) and increasing rural-urban interaction (Bryceson, 1999; Bryceson and Jamal, 1997; Ellis, 2000). The diversity of additional income-generating activities is limited only by opportunity and access. The wider topic of pastoral diversification into non-farm employment and other rural and urban activities is tackled in Chapter 9. The present chapter focuses on the pastoral economy in terms of land, labour and livestock as the basic factors of livestock production.

The chapter begins by considering a number of different approaches to the analysis of pastoral economies. Classical models of herd growth and household formation are outlined and more recent individual, actor-oriented decision-making models reviewed, which are better able to deal with flexibility in herd structure, household composition, and the wider economy. The great variety

132

of pastoralist response to external change is illustrated through both cross-sectional survey and also long-term case studies of pastoral lineages through changing times. The chapter goes on to look at the range of forms of organisation and division of labour in different groups through caste, ageset, gender and other determinants. It then deals with land – access to, tenure and control of resources in different systems and different circumstances. Sub-Saharan African systems of land tenure and access are diverse, complex, continuously evolving mixes of customary practice, foreign land laws imposed during the colonial period, and post-Independence state interventions, which have commonly been driven by Western political and economic theories rather than by local debate or self-determination. Access to wet- and dry-season grazing resources, to transhumance routes, water resources and tree products has been managed in different ways, creating site-specific outcomes for different pastoralist systems, and shaping their prospects in locally and historically specific ways, which nonetheless show some generalisable parallels.

The last part of the chapter deals with livestock as capital; with their ownership and allocation. Livestock are both the currency and the social medium whereby the individual, the household and the group shift between herding, farming, gathering and hunting and/or off-farm activities. Livestock mediate the continuous turnover driving movements between different castes, socio-economic and occupational classes, stages of household formation and relations between different ages and genders within these categories. Livestock operate as a wealth store that accrues interest in the form of new animals and that underpins the economic rationality of pastoralism. The essential ingredient of the pastoralist economy is not merely livestock ownership *per se*, but the manipulation of rights of access to livestock through patronage and risk-spreading.

Analysis of pastoralist economies

Classic structural/functionalist approaches (e.g. Stenning, 1958) have been superseded by more flexible actor-oriented approaches which build on individual trade-offs and decision-making (e.g. Hodgson, 2000a). Structural/functionalist approaches conceived of social institutions interlinking as functional systems which in turn interacted with the natural environment. These approaches analysed customs in terms of their contribution to the (assumed) stability of any given system. For example, Stenning's analysis of household viability in the pastoral Fulani of Bornu took the household as the major source of labour in a 'traditional' pastoral society. Stenning expected household formation to be adjusted to the economic requirements of pastoralism, and household requirements to be met from the household herd. His analysis of Fulani customs argued a linkage between household and herd structure and formation, using the concept of a developmental cycle of domestic groups. Among the Wodaabe Fulani of Bornu this cycle was short: the marriage dissolved when the last child was old enough to become independent, and Stenning's analysis suggested that this was related to the formation of an independent viable herding unit (see section below on property rights in livestock).

Dahl and Hjort (1976) took the understanding of pastoral economies well beyond this heuristically useful but mechanistic analysis. They drew together and reviewed the great range of variation in African pastoralist communities. Together with their use of simulation models to explore the possible trajectories of herd and household formation, their work made it possible and necessary to think in terms of behavioural responses to social and environmental variability, rather than rigidly self-perpetuating cultural systems. They laid the basis for a wide range of approaches centring on ideas of individual choice and informed decision, rather than ideas of individuals acting out programmed social norms. This novel view saw social customs not so much as rigid constraints but as opportunities or arenas within which people negotiate and validate individual choices and behaviours with respect to society. Dahl and Hjort laid the basis for a growing understanding of the importance of uncertainty and risk in pastoralist societies and of the crucial feature of flexible responses, whether social, spatial or economic, that commonly result.

The strength of this framework is made clear by later work ranging from highly individualised qualitative case-studies through quantitative and statistical to theoretical modelling approaches. *Dudal* (Bonfiglioli, 1988) focused on the changing circumstances of a particular Fulani family over 150 years, illustrating the diversity of factors and their changing relations over time. The case-study set out strategic changes adopted by this Wodaabe family in response to the sequence of political events in the Sokoto Caliphate, and the decimation and reconstitution of their herds during and after the epidemics of the turn of the nineteenth/twentieth century. In the early twentieth century as the French began to tighten their grip on Niger and the Foreign Legion subdued the Touareg, the Dudal family penetrated the Dallol Bosso of South-western Niger, and thence moved on through these newly available territories to the margins of the Sahel, where Fulani and Touareg overlap. The relative independence portrayed by Stenning as the goal each unit strove to achieve represented a possibility that existed for Fulani in this area in the twentieth but not the nineteenth century. Dudal's changing opportunities, constraints and strategies in marriage, politics, land tenure, resource control and religion challenge notions of a normative pastoral society living in adaptive equilibrium with its environment. Beyond this emerging understanding of continuously shifting possibilities, and individual trade-offs and decisions, the enormous diversity and flexibility of pastoral economies, and the enormous number of possible factors influencing their dynamics, present a major problem for any unifying analysis (cf. configurational analyses of smallholder cultivators – Guyer, 1997; Berry, 1993).

Modelling pastoral economic decisions

Modelling approaches have attempted to handle analysis of the diversity of strategies and the determinants and outcomes of decision-making in pastoralist economies.

Modelling approaches have much to offer the analysis of decision-making strategies, and are becoming progressively better able to add significantly to the existing understanding of pastoralist ecology. Modelling seeks generalisable regularities, and useful simplification which clarifies the relative importance of different possible contributing factors, distinguishing driving factors from associated effects. There is always the danger, on the one hand, of oversimplification limiting the validity of the exercise, and, on the other, of undermining the model's wider applicability while making it able to deal with significant complexity (Homewood, 1999). This section looks at some of the attempts to analyse pastoral economies through different modelling approaches.

Empirical approaches: Statistical modelling. Statistical modelling of large data sets can establish empirical, quantifiable regularities across subsets of pastoral systems, identifying factors influencing households, and evaluating their relative importance in economic choices (e.g. Hampshire, 1998; Buhl and Homewood, 2000; Coast, 2000; Homewood et al., 2001, 2004; Thompson and Homewood 2002; Homewood et al., forthcoming). Current studies of pastoralism can disentangle for specific populations the social, economic, ecological and cultural determinants and correlates of access to land (Homewood et al., 2004), of undertaking transhumance or seasonal labour migration (Hampshire and Randall, 1999), of engaging in commercial cultivation and/or wildlife based enterprises alongside pastoralism (Homewood et al., 2001; Thompson and Homewood, 2002; Homewood et al., forthcoming). For example, in a recent study combining in-depth work on land-cover change, demography and household economy in Maasailand, conversion of conservation-compatible rangeland to commercial cultivation incompatible with wildlife emerged as an activity strongly associated with households headed by community leaders, as opposed to ordinary group ranch members (Thompson et al., 2002).

Statistical modelling on large datasets can give a very precise understanding of the factors influencing decisions within the sample represented, but the variability of pastoralist environments (social, economic, political, biophysical) is such that it is hard to generalise from even large and relatively long-term datasets to a wider relevance. There is often a fundamental difficulty in trying to relate environmental to economic and other variables in a quantitative and statistical way for pastoralist environments and populations. Households and individuals are so mobile, their livelihoods are potentially so diverse, and their strategies draw on such a spatially extensive network of resources, that it is difficult to find realistic ways of relating decisions made by particular households to particular spatially explicit environmental measures and *vice versa*.

Indicators commonly used as hard measures of environmental condition are all useful where populations are settled and where primary economic activities are carried out mainly within a specified radius from the settlement. However, when people are in any one location for only a brief period, where they have a range of choices of different types of environment and where they diversify their land use and have fields, herds and household members in different places at considerable distances from each other, it becomes progressively less meaningful to try to relate their decision-making and strategies to the environmental conditions immediately surrounding the site where they happen to have been observed. Any one year's behaviour, and the places visited, may represent a response to patterns of production over a brief period (though constrained by other factors such as social conditions of access) but cannot represent patterns of use of past or future sites. Qualitative and quantitative analysis of transhumance and seasonal labour-migration decisions by different Fulani groups and individual households in Burkina Faso showed the complexity of cultural, economic, demographic and ecological factors entering into play (Hampshire, 1998; Hampshire and Randall, 1999). In this major study of 8,785 Fulani, ethnicity, production system, and household demography were as or more important than environmental trends in driving decisions over transhumance and short-term migration, while poverty *per se* did not emerge as a significant determinant.

In addition to the difficulty of relating specific people to the environmental characteristics of specific places, there are problems with using the household as the basic unit of analysis. The flexibility of household composition (with high rates of transhumance, seasonal labour migration, child fostering and divorce) and economic occupation (with rapid, opportunistic non-farm diversification) is such that the concept of the household becomes difficult to pin down for many pastoral economies. Using the household as a discrete analytical unit in modelling may not be straightforward, and using long-term persistence of a specified 'household' within a specified economic system of 'pastoralism' as an outcome measure of success or failure is particularly problematic (cf. Mace, 1993a), given the great variety of other potential strategies, income-generating activities, and household compositions.

Theory-driven modelling: Cost/benefit, optimality and stochastic dynamic models. Cost-benefit and other optimality models attempt to refine analytical frameworks for household choices further into rigorous and predictive decision-making models (Borgerhoff-Mulder and Sellen, 1994). Working from theoretical expectations, these models specify factors affecting decisions, and then test the validity of the postulated decision rules from observation of responses to changing economic and ecological circumstances. Models of this type have been used to analyse household decisions over livestock management (Mace, 1988, 1990; Mace and Houston, 1989), seasonal transhumance (Ruttan and Borgerhoff-Mulder, 1999), daily herd movements (de Boer and Prins, 1989; Edwards et al., 1994), and to look at household viability through changing economic and ecological conditions (Mace, 1993).

Mace (1988, 1989, 1990, 1993a, b) explored the conditions under which pastoralists might choose to herd or farm, settle or move, sell or store, allow rapid herd increase or adopt a conservative stockbreeding strategy. She used household 'survival' within the pastoralist system as the measure of success of decisions. Building on examples from Il Chamus, Maasai, Turkana, Barabaig, Zaghawa and Fur, Baggara, Zeyadiya, Wodaabe Fulani and Malian Fulani, Mace (1993a) explored the way agropastoral households in different circumstances invest in livestock or crops across successive years in order to maximise their chances of survival in the pastoral system. The model output gave the combination of herding livestock and growing grain most likely to lead to long-term survival of the agropastoral household. The model suggested that as household wealth increased, so it makes increasingly good sense to invest in more animals rather than in stored grain. In areas of high agroecological potential, wealthy households have considerable freedom of choice of strategy. With progressively less favourable environments, 'pure' pastoralism is only possible given a certain threshold of livestock wealth. For a given wealth, progressively larger families do better investing more labour and capital in farming. These predictions are consistent with commonly observed behaviour (e.g. Fulani of CAR – Boutrais, 1988; ch 4; Maasai – Homewood et al. forthcoming). Below a certain threshold, agropastoralism is the most viable strategy, as is indeed the case across much of the Sahel. For seriously poor households in poor-potential environments, the model suggested persistence within the agropastoral system is best served by retaining a few animals rather than converting them to stored grain. The model suggested that with a deteriorating environment, herders would settle and farm, as is commonly observed. With an improving environment, farmers might begin to invest in livestock. Thresholds vary according to labour and family size, with bigger families needing to be wealthier to remain as pastoralists.

Systems and simulations. Building on decades of work exploring empirical relations in specific cases, developing insights on factors and processes governing pastoral economic decisions, postulating and testing rules of behaviour, models are now managing increasingly robust simulation of pastoral economies, and prediction of the impacts of specific interventions. Inevitably such simulations are only as good as the work upon which they are based. Where they are derived from crude statistical associations, insufficiently informed by local knowledge, predictions are likely to be misleading. However, sophisticated and sensitive modelling processes which build on considerable local knowledge are being developed to explore the implications of changing climate, policy and practice for agropastoral economies, ecologies and livelihoods.

The Savanna-PHEWS models draw together the work of decades modelling on the one hand East African rangeland ecosystems as production context, and on the other, the flows of cash and calories through different types of agropastoral household economies (Thornton, et al., 2006; Boone et al., 2006). 'Savanna' is an extremely sophisticated systems model which pulls together rainfall, agroecological conditions, primary production, domestic and wild herbivore populations and the various factors impacting upon them (such as disease) so as to reproduce with a high degree of accuracy the workings of the particular rangeland ecosystem it is set up to simulate in a given run (e.g. POLEYC 2002). PHEWS is a rule-based model which categorises and tracks different types of agropastoral households through iterations of successive months and years in terms of their wealth (stocks) and in terms of their income streams (in cash and in calories) from different pastoral, agricultural and off-farm activities (flows). Where production does not suffice to feed the household (calculated in terms of adult equivalents and international dietary requirements) households meet their needs by selling livestock, or from gifts into the household. The proportion of such "externally derived" calories is used as a measure of food insecurity. By contrast where successive months and years bring a surplus this accumulates as wealth (Thornton et al., 2006).

Linking the two models makes it possible firstly to simulate the conditions which people in a specific system have dealt with over the last decades (using actual rainfall, crop and livestock yields, prices etc. for specific runs of years) and to test the validity of the combined models' outputs against observed outcomes. It also becomes possible to explore the likely outcomes of particular biophysical or political and economic changes. Savanna-PHEWS has been used to explore the implications for pastoral households and livelihoods of privatization of formerly communal rangelands, of livestock 'improvement' with higher-yielding but potentially less resilient breeds, of water development and of expanding cultivation in arid and semi arid Kajiado District of Kenya (Thornton et al., 2006; Boone et al., 2006).

Through modelling of this type, more precise definition of factors, processes and linkages, and more rigorous statements of generalisable continuities are continually sought within the immensely fluid and flexible range of pastoral and agropastoral economic behaviours. At the other end of the disciplinary spectrum, social anthropologists stress the diversity, the variability, and the particularity of individual cases, as defying the reductionism and generalisation that models impose. Little by little, these two perspectives are coming closer together, as social scientists tease out broad generalisations that remain robust across variability, and as modellers use those insights to deal with ever greater complexity. The very precision with which these models specify factors under investigation, and measure decisions and changes observed, may limit their scope and validity. The rest of this chapter focuses on the factors of land, labour and capital as they shape production.

Labour

Labour needs, strategies and returns

There are some tasks inevitably associated with livestock and pastoralism: herding, watering, milking, care of stock, construction and maintenance of dwellings, provision of fuel, food and water for the household, processing and marketing. These are interwoven with the management of political, legal, social and ritual affairs (largely expressed through, and in terms of, livestock in many pastoralist systems).

Herding labour needs depend on herd size as well as on the species herded, as each species has different requirements. Dividing up the herds by species, age, sex, class or reproductive condition to deal with their different requirements means that more labour is needed. Herding labour is a factor in choice of species, and in the choices of progressively wealthier pastoralists to convert large numbers of small stock into smaller numbers of individually more valuable large livestock (Mace and Houston, 1989). Labour requirements change with the management goals of the herd. Commercialisation commonly entails a shift away from labour-intensive herding with a close man-animal relationship and extraction of marginal products (Chapter 9) to management for meat and/or numbers with more animals per herder, and less individual contact, forfeiting the diversity of subsidiary products (Behnke, 1983, 1985). Labour requirements may seasonally become very heavy, for example in systems where water must be raised from deep wells. Among the Kel Adrar studied by Swift, watering the herd involved raising water by hand from wells 100m deep. Collaboration was necessary for any one family to be able to carry this out adequately for several species of livestock. In other cases, intensive and skilled herding is needed to keep livestock from damaging crops (cf. Hagberg, 1994) or to control herds at watering points (Borana – Cossins and Upton, 1987; Dahl and Mergessa, 1990; Baxter, 1991; Maasai – Homewood and Rodgers, 1991), for reasons of security, or where cross-border movements contravene official laws.

Most extensive pastoral systems show considerable flexibility, moving animals and/or people rapidly in response to changing conditions, so the temporary structure and composition of the household meet the labour requirements of the herd, and herd production sustains the household. This may be achieved through stock friendships and loans that redeploy animals to where there is labour, joint herding (Homewood and Rodgers, 1991), seasonal out-migration of one or more members of the household (Hampshire and Randall, 1999), hire of herding labour (Little, 1985; Hagberg, 1994), and/or institutionalised child-fostering arrangements (Shell-Duncan, 1994), re-deploying labour to where there are animals. Household structures show great diversity and flexibility. Living, working and eating units do not always correspond, nor does the economic occupation of the group that is observed necessarily represent the full economic complex from which they draw their livelihoods. Economic occupations change, as do household composition and functioning, while gender-specific responses may diverge and conflict (e.g. Fulani – Hampshire, 1998, Buhl, 1999).

In most African farming systems, labour input determines output. In pastoralist systems, it is possible to carry on increasing the number of animals herded by one person (increasing output:input ratios and therefore productivity) up to a given threshold when a single herder can no longer control or protect the herd effectively. Additional labour is then needed to minimise such problems as loss of animals to wild predators (Homewood and Rodgers, 1991), loss of crops entailing compensation, conflict and loss of access (Hagberg, 1994). Agropastoralism dictates a different pattern again. Labour bottlenecks create a major problem for these mixed ventures. In particular, the main harvest at the beginning of the dry season is both a period of concentrated work in the fields and a time when it is vital to keep the animals well away from them. Conversely at the end of the dry season and the beginning of the wet season there is a need to break the soil and get the crops planted as rapidly as possible to make the most of the limited rains ahead, while there may also be the need to herd animals to distant grazing areas, to lop branches for fodder and/or to use skilled herding knowledge to optimise livestock use of different range types so that they regain condition as rapidly as possible. All of this must be undertaken at a time when stored grain is running low and disease challenges for both people and livestock are spiralling as vector populations increase (Chambers et al., 1984; Swift, 1983).

Decisions as to whether (and to what extent) to invest labour in farming or herding are crucial. The equation changes from year to year and from family to family depending on rainfall, on labour available, and on terms of trade as well as on livestock holdings, stored crops and other assets, themselves reflecting conditions over the run of past years. In real life the alternative strategies are many, diverse and contingent (Hampshire, 1998). There is no single answer: individuals and households are continually evaluating, predicting and responding to shifting tradeoffs among the ecological and economic determinants of the best returns to their labour. Their decisions are as much affected by considerations of long-term viability as of short-term profit, and by cultural values and personal preferences as by simple economic payoffs.

Stratified societies and socio-economic class

Some pastoralist groups are (or have been) strongly stratified, and have structured labour according to these internal hierarchies. Tuareg noble men and women were served by their Bella slaves (Bernus, 1981; Chapter 4). The Bella were members of the Tuareg household, but of distinct ('captive') physical ancestry (generally sub-Saharan, as distinct from the Berber nobles), and were owned as property of individual 'noble' men and women. Bella carried out all the physical work of camp construction, maintenance, herding, milking, food preparation, fuel and water collection, child care and any cultivation. In a comparable system in the Macina empire of the Inland Delta of the Niger, noble Fulani established villages of Rimaibe slaves to cultivate the cereals pastoralists needed (Chapter 2).

These stratified systems with their institutionalised slavery were steadily eroded by the changes brought about through colonial administration, Independence and the levelling effects of repeated major droughts since the 1970s (Chapter 2). In the cases both of Tuareg and of Fulani, much of the terminology and associated structures and differentials remain (Hill, 1985; Randall, 1985). However, most formerly noble Tuareg have become long-term refugees, no longer able to command Bella labour (Randall, 2002). At the beginning of the twenty-first century, these societies are structured as much by recent political and socio-economic factors as by past history of conquest and slavery. On the fringes of all pastoral groups, poor people who have lost their livestock provide hired labour to the better-off. In many systems this position of hired labour would once have brought social membership of the household, often bound by the social currency of shared milk, and rewarded by gifts of stock which would eventually permit a valued shepherd to rebuild his own herd (e.g. White, 1986, 1991). This has changed: a large literature on hired herders, the individuals who are driven to take this employment, the conditions under which they work, the dangers they face and the poor returns they make suggests that hired herders are increasingly the poorest of the poor, and trapped in that poverty (e.g. Little, 1985; White, 1986; Bassett, 1994; Hagberg, 1994; Heffernan et al., 2001). Where outsiders access communal pasture resources through exploiting the social affiliations of hired herders, the effects impact on the whole pastoral system as well as on the individual herder (Bourbouze, 1999).

Gender

> Pastoral production is almost always clearly structured by gender and age, although there is of necessity flexibility in the assignment of duties to accommodate individual and household exigencies. (Hodgson, 2000a)

Clear divisions of labour may exist by age and gender as well as by caste and class. The earliest studies of pastoralist societies tended to focus on largely male aspects of kinship systems, inheritance, marriage negotiations, resource control and herd management. These earlier views of pastoralist groups as economically, politically, socially and culturally male-dominated have shifted with the emergence of studies of the role of women in pastoralist groups (Chieni and Spencer, 1993; Talle, 1988; Monimart, 1989; Waters-Bayer, 1985; Sikana et al., 1993; Dahl, 1987; Oboler, 1985; Hodgson, 2000a). 'Women's status' is not a useful analytical concept *per se* (Hodgson, 2000a). There is no general principle governing gender relations in pastoralist societies. Women's roles emerge as diverse, differentiated, complementary and overlapping with those of men.

> women are never simply women: they are daughters, widows, married mothers of small children, unwed mothers, wives of migrant labourers, mothers in law. The authority, autonomy, responsibility, obligation and workload they have in the family vary accordingly. (Ostergaard, 1992:9)[1]

In some groups the gender division of labour is underlined by the existence of women who are treated as honorary men in terms of the responsibilities they are given in herding and caring for livestock, the autonomy they are accorded (Roth, 1994 – *sepaade* women of the Rendille; see Chapter 8), and sometimes a social role as women 'husbands' and herdowners. This differentiated view makes it clear that women in different households, and different women within any one household, are subject to very different opportunities and constraints. It is important to disaggregate household production, consumption and wealth by status as well as by gender (Buhl, 1999; Buhl and Homewood, 2000). Hodgson (2000a) reviews the heterogeneity and fluidity of pastoralist women's roles, their progression with age (see below) and the historical and social continuities that have influenced women's labour and its control.

That variation between the situations of individual women is nonetheless bounded by broader social and cultural structures. The position of women varies between pastoralist societies according to religion and kinship systems. For example, pre-Islamic Berber matrilineality and inheritance rules persist in Toubou and Tuareg societies. Women's roles are also affected by social organisation, which may be structured by caste, by ageset or by marital and parity status, and systems of tenure influencing women's rights in livestock and in land. For example, Islam, by defining women's position with respect to polygyny and divorce, has affected the extent to which men may control their

---

[1] I am grateful to Solveig Buhl for drawing my attention to this quote.

labour. By influencing codes of conduct, particularly the ideal of female seclusion, it has constrained women's ability to trade in the market and consequently their economic autonomy. On the other hand, it confers certain rights (such as inheritance – Buhl and Homewood, 2000). The colonial period in some cases precipitated a major decline in women's autonomy and rights, by focusing on men as the heads of households and by extension as legal owners of land and livestock, with women increasingly cast as juridical minors (Hodgson, 1999, 2000a). Similarly, state laws and their enforcement have affected women's property rights – often adversely (see below) but sometimes for the better – again bearing on their economic autonomy and their own control of their own labour.

Despite the variety of systems, some common generalisations emerge as to the gender division of labour. Pastoralist boys are commonly responsible for most daily herding and also the main labour of constructing of wells. Young men undertake the more complex, difficult and dangerous herd movements such as cross-border movements, long treks to distant markets, and dry-season watering (which may require considerable herding skills to manage large herds of thirsty animals converging on and queueing at a communal waterpoint, and/or where water is raised from deep below ground). Older men progressively withdraw from heavy labour if it is possible for them to hand over. Instead, they increasingly focus on management and negotiations over trade, marriage agreements, sanctions for infringement of customary institutions of resource access (see section below on age).

Pastoralist women are typically responsible for house-building and for moving camp in more mobile groups (e.g. Turkana, Fulani, Maasai, Tuareg). They are responsible for child care and for the domestic chores of ensuring that daily food, fuel and water needs are met. They also work with the livestock. In particular, they are responsible for managing milk yields. However, societies differ as to whether or not women actually carry out the milking, and if so which animals they milk. Milking may be carried out by men or by women, according to the particular group, but rarely by both, a decision that is often affected by whether the economy is primarily milk- or meat-based. Among Maasai, women both milk and allocate the yield (Homewood and Rodgers, 1991; Grandin, 1988; Talle, 1990; Nkedianye et al., forthcoming). Among Fulani, men commonly milk, while women allocate the yield and may manage dairy sales (Buhl and Homewood, 2000). Where milk and other products are sold or exchanged for grain, this activity may be entirely the responsibility of women.

Dairying by pastoral women has become a major prop of women's and more generally pastoralists' livelihoods in peri-urban Nigeria (Waters-Bayer, 1985), Somalia (Herren, 1990; Little, 1994), East Africa (Nkedianye et al., forthcoming) and in other populations where sufficiently good transport networks exist for pastoralist women in the rural hinterland to organise regular deliveries to urban areas (see Waters-Bayer, 1985 for a description of an established trading system based on Fulani women supplying and Hausa women retailing milk products). Marketing may be expressly denied to women in more orthodox Islamic groups. This varies according to religious and cultural values, and the extent to which people's socio-economic position allows them to conform with those ideals. Among the more orthodox Islamic Fulani, women are excluded from milking or selling milk: the combined driving forces of wealth and piety dictate seclusion of women, constrain dairying and entail a shift to livestock sales catering particularly for urban demand. Among the less orthodox and/or less well-off, older women and their young daughters will be more or less active in marketing milk and other dairy products, but young women will be under pressure to remain in seclusion in the compound and forgo trading (Buhl and Homewood, 2000; de Bruijn and van Dijk, 1994, 1995). In the more humid zones of West Central Africa, where farming populations place little value on milk or other dairy products, pastoralist women may channel their products through middlemen (CAR: Boutrais, 1988).

In other cases pastoralist women shift from the characteristic dairy marketing enterprise into convergent enterprises based on gathering, preparing and selling wild products. For example, as milk yields decline in the dry season Fulani women milk-sellers in Nigeria adulterate their limited supplies with a liquid preparation of the baobab fruit (Waters-Bayer, 1985). In Bénin dairying is largely replaced by processing and sale of locally culturally preferred 'butter' from the *karité* shea butter-nut tree (Schreckenberg, 1996). Where livestock losses have impoverished households, it is the women who feed the family by gathering wild grains (*fonio* or *cramcram* – SSE, 1992; Legrosse, 1999). Pastoralist Parakuyo women impoverished by eviction from Mkomazi Game Reserve in Tanzania worked as itinerant peddlers, gathering, processing and selling medicinal plants (Brockington, 2001a).

Societies differ in the extent to which women join in the care of animals, herding (Maasai – Hodgson, 1999a), cleaning (Fulani in CAR, deticking – Boutrais, 1988), and watering them (Dahl and Megerssa, 1990). Pastoralist women have long-established roles in healing (Hodgson, 2000a). They may develop specialist knowledge of plant-related medicines (for example, Tamasheq noble women, relieved of any domestic duties, become knowledgeable about plant medicines (Randall, 1991); at the other end of the socioeconomic scale, so do poor Il Parakuyo women collecting plant medicines for sale (Brockington, 2001a). Sullivan (2000a) describes women's creative and individual use of plant perfumes among Damara of Namibia. Women are also creators and guardians of other aspects of culture and society, for example, where they are literate, as poets (Boyd, 1986), through their inputs to participatory action research (e.g. Heffernan et al., 2001) and as peacemakers (Elmi et al., 2000).

Age

For much of the time herding labour is not energetically demanding. Children can do much of it, and child labour is commonly used. Households lacking enough herding labour may borrow children for this purpose (Shell-Duncan, 1994; Maasai – Coast, 2000). In many pastoralist groups labour (among other dimensions) is structured according to an ageset system (Kurimoto and Simonse, 1998). For example, among Maasai, uncircumcised boys have customarily been responsible for most of the herding, and this in itself constituted a phase of training in their apprenticeship towards becoming a herdowner in due course.

> A boy's upbringing is geared towards the unremitting care of stock. From the time he can barely walk, he may try his hand at herding, clutching an upraised stalk as he tumbles towards the smallest stock as if to round them up. When he is first left by himself in charge of calves near the village, he has to learn to master a situation that constantly tends to get out of hand, as the calves spread out in search of grazing. His father or his older brothers teach him to control the herd and to respond to any situation that may arise, developing an awareness of the opportunities and hazards of the bush. The more he can be trusted, the greater his responsibility. As he becomes more involved with mature stock further afield, he is left to interpret the broad directions given him in the morning, and to make his own judgments during the day.
>
> The skill of the herdboy is confined to this daily experience, and does not extend to decisions concerning migration or survival during a serious drought, which clearly demand the experience of an older man. Even so, this wider understanding grows out of the intimate knowledge of cattle, goats and sheep acquired during boyhood. (Spencer, 1988: 51)

Among Maasai, the circumcised youths and young men of the warrior ageset take responsibility for difficult and dangerous herd movements. Senior elders make grazing management decisions, and negotiate the social, political, legal, religious and also commercial matters making up the context within which grazing and livestock management must operate. The hard physical work pastoralist labour involves changes with age for women as for men (Hodgson, 2000a). Girls help with all the domestic chores, care for young and sick livestock, and help with herding and with marketing pastoral produce. As girls become wives, and young women become mothers, they become responsible for organising as well as executing all these tasks, and also for building and maintaining their houses. As women age and their children grow up, they become senior figures managing extended households, and their responsibilities shift from the chores of collecting, preparing and providing food, fuel, and water to progressively more social, cultural and political roles in teaching, advising, managing and negotiating, parallelling the changes undergone by men.

Factors affecting division of labour: summary

A concrete example shows how labour allocation tradeoffs integrating these many factors were managed by different Fulani groups in Burkina Faso, and by different types of household within any one group (Hampshire, 1998). In-depth qualitative and large-scale quantitative analyses showed that different groups responded to different factors in making decisions as to whether or not one or more family members should take herds on transhumance. The factors influencing the decision ranged from environmental (availability of forage) to the need to keep herds away from maturing crops, to the desire to camp near a settlement where pastoral produce could be sold or exchanged on temporarily favourable terms of trade. Decisions as to whether or not a man should go on seasonal labour migration depended on household demography (and the amount and type of labour therefore available), cultural affiliation to a particular subethnic group, and household wealth. Decisions over whether a Fulani woman should engage in economic activities like cultivating crops, or selling milk in the market, were similarly complex, depending on ethnic and economic as well as demographic (a woman's age and parity), and sociocultural factors (the potential impact of the activity on her reputation and thus on her position within a social network that ultimately represents her safety net – Buhl, 1999; Buhl and Homewood, 2000). Among Maasai, decisions over allocation of labour (and other resources) to herding or farming are finely calculated and change in response to political as much as economic tradeoffs (Thompson and Homewood, 2002). The overall picture is of dynamic and responsive systems far removed from past perceptions of peasants and pastoralists locked into rigid social and agro-ecological systems, unwilling and unable to learn, adapt or respond to change. Decision-making models can tackle part of this diversity and flexibility (Mace, 1993a); statistical modelling can tease out the relative importance of different determinants of observed choices under different circumstances within a given dataset (Hampshire, 1998; Coast, 2000; Thompson, 2002).

Land

Pastoralist enterprises, pastoral livelihoods and the pastoral economy all depend on access to grazing, water, mineral and gathered plant materials. This section reviews the implications and trajectories of different systems regulating access to these resources. Any system of pastoralist land tenure and access we see today is a palimpsest reflecting pre-colonial histories, colonial legacies, post-Independence policies, and prevailing economic as well as ecological pressures and opportunities. For clarity of analysis, the discussion here separates ecological from historical, political and social influences.

Current analyses stress the distinction between common pool resources and common property regimes, confusingly often designated by the same acronym CPR (Ostrom et al., 1999; Adams et al., 2001). Common pool resources – renewable natural resources like grazing, water, fuelwood – are all finite resources whose consumption affects availability for other users. Common pool resources can be managed under a number of different systems ranging from communal to private. Common property regimes are systems of joint ownership and management, where a group of local users jointly own, regulate, monitor, police and exploit a common pool resource. Under private ownership and management, these functions are carried out by the private individual (or company), or conversely under state control, by central, regional and/or local government agencies.

Ecological influences

Spatial mobility is related as much to political strategy and security as to environmental availability of resources, and sometimes these factors act against one another. For example, the immediate ecological disadvantages to pastoralists of settling into sedentary occupation of the Adamawa Plateau have been clearly outweighed by the long-term social and political pay-off in terms of control and tenure of key resources (Burnham, 1975, 1985). Nonetheless, ecological influences constrain resource management systems (Chapter 3). Where grazing land productivity per unit area is low, primary production variable, and inputs few, mobility is essential for a successful pastoral economy (but see Baker and Hoffman, 2006 and Jacobs, 2003 for South African examples where mobility has been constrained). The costs of enforcing exclusive private use are likely to become disproportionately high in transhumant and semi-nomadic systems. Instead, tenure systems focus on specific, and strongly enforced, tenure of point-centred key resources (water points, pockets of high-potential land – for example, the Saharan massifs of the Tuareg – Bernus, 1981). Around these key resources, territories are defended and/or controlled within a radius which in the Saharo-Sahelian context changes from season to season and year to year (Turner, 1999a). When the resources involved are sufficiently abundant and the need is sufficiently great, other users may negotiate access. Rights over sub-Saharan arid and semi-arid land resources have often been exercised as rights of priority (rather than exclusive) access and use. Control of the central limiting resource can mean regulated access to the broader array of resources, so that a system apparently open to access by a large number of different users is in fact controlled:

> ...control over access to a traditional water point in some pastoral regions of the Sahel can be a matter for a very restricted group, or even a family, who have priority in using the water. However, access may also be offered to passing herds, in accordance with precise rules which are designed to control the rate of consumption of the surrounding pasture by the animals. (Thébaud, 1995a:7)

'Land rights become more diffuse as occupation of a given region becomes more sporadic' (Galaty, 1994) and in progressively more arid areas, diffuse general tenure may operate over broad areas. At the other end of the spectrum, as in apartheid South Africa where very high densities of livestock and people were concentrated into low-potential communal areas, rights of access to the commons have become complex and differentiated, requiring frequent movements based on factors other than range condition (Baker and Hoffmann, 2006).

Within point-centred and concentrically graded common property resource systems (Turner, 1999a), there are also bundles of situation- and individual-specific rights to the use of particular waterpoints, mineral licks and other resources such as trees. For example, individual Ngibocheros Turkana families own access to specific *Acacia tortilis* trees, whose pods are valued as high-quality forage (especially for goats – McCabe, 2004:218-19). Different users may exist side by side (with differential allocation of rights to graze, to use mineral deposits, to gather, to lop, to fell, to burn), whether timesharing (as in the Inland Delta of the Niger's tightly regulated seasonal succession of fishing, farming and herding – Chapter 2; Gallais, 1984; Legrosse, 1999; Vedeld, 2003) or simultaneous occupation (e.g. intensively used *fadama* and *bas-fonds* wetlands of the Sahel, with permanent family fields clearly demarcated, and communal grazing shared among multiple groups (Thébaud, 1995a).

Specific water or mineral resources of special importance to livestock, as opposed to grazing, commonly constitute the key factors that limit pastoral production, and as such they become the focus of tenure and access. Various authors describe as common property regimes the well construction, maintenance and management by Tuareg (Bernus, 1981), Borana (Cossins and Upton, 1987; Dahl and Mergessa, 1990; Baxter, 1991), and Somali (Cassanelli, 1982). Similarly, mineral resources have often been managed as common property regimes (Bernus, 1981) but sometimes with an added dimension of private exploitation (Baxter, 1991). Where key resources are strongly localised and easily defensible, they may be managed by common property regimes, but are also open to being ringfenced as private resources for pastoral or other production, and private ownership can more readily emerge. For example irrigated plots (Bisson, 1989) or valuable trees (such as gum arabic in the north of Senegal – Thébaud, 1995a and Sudan – Kibreab, 1997) may be individually owned. Bisson (1989) describes *foggara* systems of water provision and irrigated oasis agriculture in the Algerian Sahara, where the person who constructed and maintained the system had considerable rights over the resource. Similarly, Joffe (1989) describes *khattara* and other gravity-fed systems of irrigation and water provision in Morocco. Dating back to the Almoravids or before, *khattaras* are constructed, maintained and controlled by the landowner and/or by *habous* religious foundations owning the catchment lands on which the *khattara* depends. In East Africa, Maasai constructing their own waterpoints control access to those sources (Potkanski, 1994), as do Tuareg in the West.

Throughout sub-Saharan Africa, there has been widespread disruption to established CPR regimes. This has led to considerable confusion over access to and rights over government- or aid-constructed watering points in arid and semi-arid rangelands, as often their construction cut across the broader common property resource (CPR) rights of the pastoralist group formerly using the area where they were sited, creating an effectively open access resource. In other cases, well-placed individuals or groups have been able to co-opt aid-driven water development and use this to extend their control over such resources.

Various levels of access, from communal to private and/or state-controlled, often come together as a nested system. In the Maghreb of North Africa, subject to Arab and Islamicised Berber states from AD 1100 on, land was commonly categorised as *beylik* (belonging to the bey or the Islamic ruler of the state), *melk* (individual privately-owned wealth or land) and *arch* (CPR grazing – Homewood, 1992b) as well as *habous* (land deeded to Islamic religious foundations). Common land might be winter lowland grazing (e.g. El Kala: forest reserves) or summer highland grazing (as in the Moroccan Atlas). Fertile, accessible valley-floor land was commonly privately owned farm or fallow land. CPR systems persist in the High Atlas and elsewhere in the Maghreb, but they are vulnerable both to pressures from outsiders entrusting livestock to legitimate users increasing competition for grazing, and also to increasing privatisation. Though still more mobile than many other Mediterranean pastoralist systems, the Moroccan Atlas pastoralists are increasingly dominated by a few large owners moving their livestock by truck (Bourbouze, 1999). Comparable systems operated in Bedouin pastoralist groups where CPR grazing was managed as *hima* or *qidal* lands (Shoup, 1990) alongside privately owned farmland and communal areas.

Gathered plant resources from trees and other wild plants are of considerable importance to pastoralist groups for house and corral construction, fuel, foods, medicines and utensils (Kalahari pastoroforagers – Wilmsen, 1989; Namibian Damara – Sullivan et al., 1995, Sullivan and Konstant, 1997; Somalia – Cassanelli, 1982; Beja – Hjort and Dahl, 1991; Samburu – Perlov, 1984, Heine et al., 1988; Orma – Ensminger, 1984; Turkana – Little and Leslie, 1999; Maasai – Maundu et al., 2000). Gum arabic and frankincense (Kibreab, 1997) shea butter nut and other tree foods (Schreckenberg, 1996), palm frond baskets and mats (Konstant et al., 1995) and many other gathered tree products (Heine et al., 1988; Niamir-Fuller, 1990) have been important and even central to pastoralist diets and economies. Similarly, wild cereals like *fonio* and *cramcram* (SSE, 1992; Legrosse, 1999) remain regular and even major dietary components for Sahelo-Saharan groups, and Namibian pastoralists make considerable use of wild grass seeds gathered directly or taken from harvester ants' nests (Sullivan, 2001; Kinahan, 1991). These products may customarily buffer hungry seasons and times of disruption, drought or epidemic (de Waal, 1989a) and strong cultural values and preferences underpin their present-day use (e.g. Sullivan, 2000a). These resources may be sparsely and patchily scattered, and commonly gathered from common lands. Access and availability are declining in many areas, with intensification of production and privatisation of rangelands (Sullivan, 2001 – Namibia; Schreckenberg, 1996 – Bénin).

Historical changes in land tenure and access

Until recently, the basic conditions for pastoralism across sub-Saharan Africa were access to animals (owned or loaned through social networks of reciprocity) and entitlement to use of CPR grazing and water (through social ties with a group controlling those resources). At the outset of the twenty-first century, the basic condition for pastoralism is becoming private ownership of enough land to keep animals year-round, or at least to allow negotiation of reciprocal individual access to enough key resources to cover year-round needs.

Throughout Africa, most areas of rangeland have in the past been managed on the basis of complex, negotiable and continuously evolving systems of access and use that do not correspond easily with Western notions of property (Thébaud, 1995a; Galaty, 1994). In general, arid and semi-arid rangelands were in the past held by the group rather than the individual. Priority access established through *force majeure* and/or customary use by a particular group allowed others to negotiate for access, depending on present need in relation to resource availability, and often built on the possibility of reciprocal access. In the nineteenth century pastoralist societies exercised politico-military control of key land and water resources in many parts of sub-Saharan Africa, often as competing systems separated by no man's land areas, without clear political boundaries (Chapter 2). Major waves of pastoralist expansion asserted control over new grazing lands through military action (Chapter 2: *mfecane*; Hall, 1990; Maasai: *Iloikop* Wars – Waller, 1985; Spear and Waller, 1993; *jihad* in the Inland Delta of the Niger – Adamu and Kirk-Greene, 1986). Early twenty-first century Fulani movements and resource access in the Inland Delta of the Niger are, albeit modified, still an outcome of nineteenth-century statutes on successional land use set up by the Macina state. These statutes were themselves formal compromises between Islamic Fulani victors and the fishing, farming and trading peoples under their hegemony (Chapters 2 and 4).

Pre-colonial common property regimes in different pastoralist groups involved consultation, decision-making and enforcement within hierarchical systems often structured by caste (Tuareg – Bernus, 1981), by chiefly lineage (Botswana – Hitchcock, 1990), by age or generation set (Maasai – Potkanski, 1994; Parakuyo – Brockington, 2002; Barabaig – Lane and Scoones, 1993; see also Adams et al., 2001; Scoones et al., 1993; Niamir -Fuller, 1999) or simply by residence and prior customary use. Within such systems, rights of access have depended on birth, kinship, investment of labour and wider social contracts. In Botswana, where the powerful expansion of the *kgamelo* system in the nineteenth century put the chief and his royal family in conrol of all land-use allocation, the chief held the land in trust for the people of the tribe rather than owning it in the sense of being able to dispose of it (Hitchcock, 1990). Land decisions could not be made without consultation. As an extreme example, the dispossession of the BaSarwa and Bagkalagadi in Botswana was accomplished by stripping them of their livestock assets while nomenclature still acknowledged their original residence and firstcomer status (Wilmsen, 1989).

The important corollary of such common property resource systems of access to grazing and water was that rights of access were flexible and 'fuzzy', socially, temporally and spatially. Unlike Western property rights systems, where ownership is clear-cut and property implies complete and legally enforceable exclusion of others, social and spatial boundaries were to some extent dependent on open-ended, ongoing negotiation, adjudication and political manoeuvre (cf. Berry, 1993; Turner, 1999a). During the colonial period, such negotiated systems were largely swept aside and replaced by the land law of newcomers who saw themselves as introducing a legal framework where none had previously existed. The concept of 'eminent domain' made alienation of land to settlers possible within colonial legal structures.

The twentieth-century colonial period and its post-Independence aftermath saw a proliferation of strictly demarcated boundaries and borders, whether local, regional, national or international, cutting through areas that were seen as no man's land. Almost by definition, this means that boundaries were drawn through pastoralist rangelands (Nugent, 1996; Homewood, 1996; Galaty and Bonte, 1991). Pastoralist groups who try to retain their mobility, and their cultural and economic links across those borders, are seen as threatening political and military security. Their fragmentation across modern international boundaries has weakened pastoralist groups politically and economically, and contributed to their marginalisation, which has in itself meant that they have often lost out on the process of formalising land claims. Post-Independence African governments carried out a variety of land-tenure changes in pursuit of economic growth, sustainable management and/or poverty reduction. Whether land reform (seeking to redistribute land and assets more equitably) or tenure change (seeking to integrate customary and official systems of rights within a formal code), these changes were largely driven by Western political and economic theories rather than by any process of local debate or self-determination (Toulmin and Quan, 2000). At the free-market end of the spectrum of development models, many governments, influenced by the prevailing Tragedy of the Commons view of African rangeland dynamics, chose to privatise land. Former CPR-managed resources have been parcelled out as individual freehold under free-market models. This is linked to privatisation of key resources other than rangeland by wealthier pastoralists or outsiders. For example, the construction and individual control of wells or other water points by Tuareg in the Saharo-Sahelian region and by Somali in the Horn have led to privatisation of range resources made accessible by those waterpoints (Prior, 1994). In Northern Nigeria large areas of river basin have been claimed by farmers for dry-season *fadama* cultivation, meaning the loss of dry-season grazing. Elsewhere, fencing means that migration corridors are progressively harder to maintain (Niamir-Fuller, 1999). Pastoralists may deliberately limit their own mobility, and/or cultivate, in order to stake claim to particular areas (Kenya Maasailand – Homewood, 1992a).

Where CPR systems have survived, they come under enormous pressure from outside investors. In semi-arid Baringo, the boom-and-bust, drought-and-plenty swings of the environment drive a spiral of encroachment by outside investors (who have alternative sources of income) at the expense of the Il Chamus pastoralists. The Il Chamus are progressively dispossessed and increasingly remain as hired herders tending livestock of absentee herdowners who exploit their customary right of access to Il Chamus CPR grazing (Little, 1985; Homewood, 1994). Similar pressures are described for the Moroccan High Atlas CPR systems (Bourbouze, 1999). In Botswana, privatisation, fencing and ranching of high-potential areas by the elite have gone alongside their continuing to exploit the common property grazing lands, which thus carry the burden year-round, while private ranchlands are being rested (Hitchcock, 1990). In Northern Somalia, the privatisation of key resources drove the majority of herders to concentrate livestock in areas that were formerly used on a seasonal basis, with dire results in geomorphologically vulnerable areas (Prior, 1994).

It was generally assumed by international development agencies that privatisation of rangeland and associated resources would encourage investment, leading to sustainable management and economic growth. Instead, privatisation has often resulted in a general impoverishment alongside enrichment of the few. Privatisation of rangelands has given rise to serious difficulties, particularly for the poorer pastoralists and for secondary rights holders – women and dependants (Platteau, 2000; Rutten, 1992). More than any other group, poor pastoralists have lost the benefit of customary systems allowing flexible access. Land titling programmes have demonstrated 'the dominance of economic theory over a careful consideration of how things work in practice' (McAuslan, 2000). Where CPR grazing land underwent a planned transition direct to private ownership, as was the case with the parcelling out of Kenya Maasailand into individual and group ranches, many individuals have been unable to maintain their pastoral enterprise and have ended by losing their private land and thus their foothold in the pastoral production system altogether (Rutten, 1992; Homewood, 1992; Galaty, 1999). This process has often been mediated through male spheres of grazing access and livestock management, but ends up having its major impact on women and children (Talle, 1988; Hodgson, 1999a).

Although the process was different, the outcome is much the same for those areas where, without formal processes of establishing private land claims, wealthier families were able to co-opt aid inputs, establish water developments, fence off the range around those developments, and ultimately privatise their ownership of those areas while dispossessing their neighbours (e.g. Somalia – Swift, 1977; Behnke, 1988; Prior, 1994). The privatisation of part of the range puts intolerable pressures on the remainder (e.g. apartheid South Africa, and its aftermath of extreme social (Jacobs, 2003), practical (Baker and Hoffmann, 2006) and ecological implications (Hoffmann, 1999; Turner and Ntshona, 1999; Hoffmann et al., 2003)).

In addition to the impacts of privatisation and intensification, states have in many cases imposed laws restricting the use and products of trees and other wild resources in ways that have hampered both their sustainable use in common property areas and even their use by owners of the land who planted the trees in the first place (Elbow and Rochegude, 1990). The upshot is that there is a strong disincentive to invest in and manage such resources, despite their potential importance in pastoral economies and diets.

Burkina Faso, Ethiopia, Tanzania and Mozambique went through strongly socialist periods during which the state nationalised and/or moved to redistribute all land. Common pool resources formerly managed by common property regimes, and taken over by the state under an egalitarian socialist banner, often proved beyond the capabilities of African states to manage effectively, given relatively poor systems and generally weak accountability. With dwindling state resources for enforcement, resistance by local users, and the universal ability of well-placed individuals to corner key resources for personal gain, the resulting scramble of competition meant that *de jure* state-owned rangelands became *de facto* open access tragedies of the commons (Berkes, 1989; Bromley and Cernea, 1989). Formerly CPR rangelands which originally were a reliable source of food for immediate consumption and of goods which could be sold directly or after processing (e.g. charcoal), were increasingly commoditised by elites and entrepreneurs as well as by the rural poor. Land redistribution by succeeding governments in the wake of nationalisation creates many complexities, with customary ownership reasserting itself alongside *de facto* occupation by new users (e.g Shivji, 1998). These new users may be subsistence farmers (as with settlers on agricultural schemes in the Fulani dry-season grazing areas of river valleys opened up by onchocerciasis control – McMillan, 1995). In other areas new users include powerful entrepreneurs investing in agribusiness or conservation (wheat and seed bean enterprises; tourist lodges in areas formerly used by pastoralists and now set aside for wildlife conservation (such as in Northern Tanzania – Igoe and Brockington, 1999; Brockington, 2001; Shivji, 1998).

However well-intentioned, state attempts to devolve control to user communities in some more equitable manner have sometimes been to the serious disadvantage of mobile pastoralist groups, who may be completely overlooked, despite long-standing customary seasonal use. In Burkina Faso, the nationwide *Gestion de Terroirs* programme of devolving control of land and natural resources was drawn up and implemented on the basis of the needs of settled farming communities and made no provision for mobile pastoralism, despite the overwhelming and long-standing importance of transhumant livestock throughout this Sahelian nation (Thébaud, 1995a; Niamir-Fuller and Turner, 1999: 29; Turner, 1999a: 120). The concept of *mise en valeur* (developing land use) was framed entirely in terms of farming; pastoralist land use is not seen as putting the land to productive use (Scoones et al., 1993). Current moves to draw up and implement a *Code Pastoral* alongside the extant *Code Rural* attempt to tackle some of these issues in parts of West Africa (Toulmin et al., 2002); however, in East Africa and elsewhere the rapid dispossession of pastoral people by both quasi-legal and illegal means has reached epidemic proportions (Igoe and Brockington, 1999; Galaty, 1999; Galaty and Ole Munei, 1999). In Tanzania, local residents' rights are recognised in the Village Land Act 1998, but pastoral rangelands are defined in general land law as empty, so pastoralists are unable to assert rights of occupation or use (Nelson et al., forthcoming).

South Africa and Namibia have initiated land redistribution programmes relatively recently (Turner and Ntshona, 1999), as to some extent has Zimbabwe (Wolmer et al., 2003), where population densities in communal areas mean herding and farming compete for land (Wilson, 1990). Livestock remain an economically as well as culturally important strategy (MacKinnon, 1999; Ainslie, 1998; Hoffmann, 1999; Hoffmann et al., 2003). Communal lands are grazed by herds built on pensions and remittance earnings (Ainslie, 2005; Baker and Hoffmann, 2006). Common property areas in Botswana are subject to manipulation of access by absentee herd-owners, often outside investors rather than local pastoralist users.

Throughout sub-Saharan Africa, these trajectories have meant that pastoralists experience common problems of securing rights of access, and of harmonising customary tenure systems with imposed alien legal systems of property rights, against a backdrop of recurring policy shifts. Plural legal systems overlap, foster competing claims, invoke conflicting sources of legitimacy and lead to contradictory outcomes (Shivji, 1998; Toulmin and Quan, 2000). There is an urgent need to develop ways of supporting CPR systems, mobility and flexibility of access and different types of forum for negotiating flexible access (Toulmin and Quan, 2000; Scoones et al., 1993; Niamir-Fuller, 1999).

Livestock

Livestock as capital and as commodity

In their most general sense the factors of production are taken as land, labour and capital. Capital is the productive output that is not consumed, but is rather set aside and used to generate more productive output. There has been some debate as to how best to approach the analysis of capital in pastoral systems. In effect, the livestock themselves are the capital,[2] in that they are the product, the means of production and the means of subsistence. At the same time, it has become clear that labelling the herd as capital does not make pastoralism a capitalist system, nor does it make the direct application of Western economic analyses necessarily appropriate in understanding African pastoralist systems (cf. Schneider, 1979). The extent to which livestock are linked to the market, and the ways in which this takes place, are central to pastoral economies. The terms of trade between livestock and cultivated products are fundamental determinants of pastoral economies as subsistence (<25% gross returns from pastoral produce), semi-commercialised (25-50%) and commercial (>50% –Swift, 1986). Even subsistence pastoral economies have a component of sale and exchange of pastoral for other produce, and in most groups there is a long-established and major market involvement with cultivators.

For much of the twentieth century, pastoralists have been seen by Western observers as not responding to pressures of supply and demand in an economically rational way. They were seen as being dominated by a cattle complex dictating irrational accumulation of numbers without consideration of quality, environmental sustainability or economic profit (Herskovits, 1926). Dahl and Hjort's work has been followed by many other investigations of the true economic and ecological costs and benefits of pastoralist enterprises (Sandford, 1983; Brockington, 2001; Brockington and Homewood, 1999; Homewood et al., forthcoming) and in particular of the different goals and therefore the different types of cost and benefit that accrue to subsistence versus commercial systems (Behnke, 1985). Pastoralist groups tend to show a supply response when the price is right, where they can dispose of less valued categories of animals (old females and a wider range of male animals), and where they have need of the cash or exchange product. However, the price is often not right, and it becomes difficult to carry out a rigorous analysis, given the many shifting values involved (Nkedianye et al., forthcoming). Depending on the society and subgroup in question, people will use progressively less milk as greater proportions and numbers of animals are marketed. This is as much affected by religious and cultural considerations constraining marketing behaviour as by market opportunities (Burnham, 1980; Orthodox Islamic Fulbe *vs* pastoral Fulani – Hopen, 1958). Behnke (1983) documented a shift from hardier camels and goats to the more risk-prone but commercially valuable sheep and cattle with the commercialisation of pastoralism in Somalia. Bernus (1981) documented the shifting economic

---

[2] The very word 'capital' derives from the French *cheptel*, or livestock; both trace back to the ancient French *chatel* – moveable inheritance, or chattel.

tradeoffs between Tuareg camel caravans and their replacement with motor transport.

Herds are both the product and the means of subsistence, and offtake for subsistence must affect the ability of the herd to grow. Pastoral production has the potential to far exceed agricultural production. Herds can potentially increase exponentially (though this is not always nor even often the case). However, poor pastoralists will eat into their own capital literally in a way that is not directly comparable with agricultural peasants. The implication is that within the pastoral economy there is scope for substantial wealth differentials between economic units, despite any egalitarian ethos and social institutions of risk spreading and redistribution that may exist. The wealth and subsistence functions of livestock are emphasised differently by different societies and by the different strata within a society. In some groups, livestock assume a quasi-monetary role. They may represent 'special purpose' money – a sphere of exchange in which only cattle circulate, as in those agropastoralist societies where only cattle can function as bridewealth (Tswana – Kuper, 1982). The ways in which such systems change is illustrated by the Fulani (Dupire, 1962a, 1970, 1972; cf. Burnham, 1987), the Mursi (Turton, 1988, 1996), the Nuer (Evans-Pritchard, 1940; cf. Johnson, 1988, 1991; Hutchinson, 1992, 1996) and Zulu (MacKinnon, 1999). Some analyses have suggested that the more pastoral the economy, the less monetary the role of cattle and the less punitive the cattle payment. In those societies with little dependence on cattle, the elders may extract the maximum payment for marriage settlements in terms of a non-subsistence resource. This is not borne out by pastoral Turkana, who exact perhaps the highest livestock payments and simultaneously depend most on them (McCabe, 2004).

Livestock ownership: concepts and mechanisms

Property rights can only be understood in terms of concepts of ownership, on the one hand, and systems of livestock acquisition, on the other. Rights in livestock are differentiated not just between rich and poor, but by caste, age and gender, and have changed through time under the influence of Islam, colonial rule, capitalist economy, development interventions (Hodgson, 1999a, 2000a). In very stratified pastoralist societies some classes may be excluded from ownership of livestock (Chapter 2: Bella slaves among the Tuareg; Rwanda/Burundi Hutu commoners by the Great Lakes Tuutsi pastoralists; BaSarwa and Bakgalagadi in Botswana – Wilmsen, 1989; Hitchcock, 1996).

Monetisation and commoditisation may have weakened women's rights to livestock, turning cattle from what had been historically a shared good in which men and women held shared rights and responsibilities into a commodity bought, sold and 'owned' by men (Hodgson, 2000a). Colonial indirect rule 'consolidated and expanded the power of men', and post-Independence development interventions targeted men as the owners and experts. Islam has also influenced the extent to which women might inherit particular categories of livestock. Such differentiated impacts may in part account for the divergence in the literature between accounts of West and East African livestock tenure systems, with individual ownership being more commonly seen in West Africa and 'bundle of rights' approaches more common in East African pastoralists. West African systems, in particular many of the more conspicuous Fulani and Tuareg systems, have long been strongly market-oriented (see e.g. Kerven, 1992). This divergence between East and West African pastoralist systems was encouraged and perpetuated by the very different structures of taxation, pricing and incentives to market livestock in the two regions (Kerven, 1992), and individuated stock ownership may have become increasingly common with increasing commercialisation.

Cattle and other livestock are acquired in a number of ways by different categories of individual. Most if not all pastoralist groups have a system whereby, on repeated occasions, through the birth and growth of a child livestock are placed in trust for that child (Dahl and Hjort, 1976; Buhl, 1999). Normative practice described for many pastoralist groups would involve clan and kinsmen giving animals into trust for a child on significant occasions (Fulani naming ceremony; circumcision – Stenning, 1958,1959; Dahl and Hjort, 1976). Those animals, cared for by older relatives, with luck survive and multiply to form the basis of the grown child's herd. With the droughts and impoverishment of the last few decades, many pastoralists are no longer able to fulfil the ideal of livestock gifts (e.g. Fulani of Northern Burkina Faso – Buhl, 1999). Depending on the group, female children may in any case not qualify for such gifts, or may be the first for whom the practice is dropped.

> At the naming ceremony one week after birth, girls and boys are given animals by their mother and/or father. Depending on how well off the parents are this may be a small ruminant or a cow. In many cases of course it is 'not even a chicken', as some Fulani expressed it. All depends on whether parents have animals at all. At this stage parents do not usually differentiate between male and female offspring. Whether this animal then reproduces and multiplies the child's holdings is, according to the Fulani, solely in the hands of God. … Later on a father might allocate animals to his children during their childhood and youth. At this stage he usually prefers to give to his elder sons than to his daughters, as his daughters will in the long run leave the household and will not have to support a family. (Buhl and Homewood, 2000)

Commonly gifts of livestock are made at ceremonies marking birth, naming, circumcision, manhood, betrothal and marriage. Beyond this, the details vary greatly from group to group. Among the Fulani each life-stage of the growing male child is marked by his acquisition of cattle. Betrothals are made at an early age, but the actual establishing of an independent household takes place only after the weaning of the first child. Again, this process involves series of elaborate stages, each of which requires gifts of stock to build the independent herding unit, the simplest being a man who herds and milks with his wife who sells the milk, buys cultivated foods in exchange and looks after house, food and children.

There are other channels for acquisition of stock. Wodaabe Fulani of Bornu practised anticipatory inheritance with an early transfer of stock to the next generation (Stenning, 1959). As each son grew up and married, he received his own proportional share of the paternal herd. After the last child came of age, it was common for the parents to separate and each live with a different offspring. More generally, when a herdowner dies his livestock move along pathways of inheritance that trace and recreate social relations (Broch-Due, 1999; Goldschmidt, 1969). In Muslim groups, women are entitled to inherit, though their portion may be half that of their brothers, may exclude particularly valuable livestock like camels, and may be waived altogether on pain of losing the wider support women could normally expect from their natal kin (Buhl, 1999). Other means of acquiring livestock include gifts sealing stock friendships, expressing a man's appreciation of a favoured wife (pers. obs. Maasailand) and loans from clansmen to households in serious need (Fulani – *habbanae*; Maasai – *ewoloto*).

In a case study of the legacy of one herdowner's death (Goldschmidt, 1969: *Kambuya's Cattle*) 20% of the livestock in the herd were implicated in some form of exchange or stock friendship arrangement quite distinct from the now increasingly common commercial arrangements of hired herding. Stock deployment often formalises political patron/client relations (e.g. *kgamelo* – Tswana; numerous other examples include Great Lakes and Lesotho agro-pastoralists). Livestock, particularly cattle or camels, change hands to set seal on marriage agreements or as compensation for contraventions.

East African pastoralists of the Plains Nilote groups (Maasai, Samburu, Turkana) tend to have a house-based allocation of livestock. The herdowner/husband allocates individual animals to each of his wives, supposedly according to the numbers of children each has to care for, though in practice other personal factors enter in. The male head of the polygamous household keeps a residual herd, and there is commonly a conflict of interest between payments for his own additional marriages and those of other male relatives. Among these groups the opportunities and constraints are intensified by a structured ageset system. Young men were expected not to marry until they had graduated from the warrior ageset, in which they were expected not only to defend the herds of their group but to add to them, raiding cattle as the basis for establishing their own herds. Raiding continues (Kuria – Heald, 1999; Fleischer, 1999; Turkana – McCabe, 2004; Hendrickson et al., 1998; Lamphear, 1998; Mirzeler and Young, 2000; Maasai/Barabaig – Ndagala, 1990; Samburu, Orma, Il Chamus, Tugen – Heffernan et al., 2001) as one avenue to building up a herd, marrying, establishing stock friendships and operating as an independent economic unit.

Sustainable livelihoods framework

This chapter has used as a framework for understanding pastoral economies the classical factors of production: land, labour and capital. Currently, donors and development workers are more likely to use the sustainable livelihoods framework to analyse pastoral economies and livelihoods in terms of natural, physical, social, human and financial dimensions of capital (Carney and Farington, 1998), a refinement on the classical factors of production. Detailed expositions of the sustainable livelihoods framework can be found elsewhere (Ellis, 2000) but in brief, and in the pastoral context, natural capital is represented primarily by land for cultivation, grazing, and other natural resources (poles, woodfuel, etc.). Physical capital is represented by roads, waterpoints and other infrastructural developments. Social capital comprises the network of social relations on which households can draw to gain access to land, labour and livestock. For the Maasai, for example, the framework of section, location, clan, and ageset all structure customary entitlements. Alongside this are the powerful factors of position as, or relation to, local leaders (group ranch chairmen or treasurer; councillor; chief; district or Provincial administration; Member of Parliament). Human capital is represented by access to and investment in education and health services. Finally, financial capital in the context of the pastoralist populations of sub-Saharan African rangelands encompasses income (a flow) and wealth store (a stock) in terms of holdings of livestock and/or land, as well as longer-term consideration of livelihood diversification and security (Homewood et al., forthcoming). Types of employment include secure (often government) jobs, which are generally skilled and often with business connections; moderately reliable though poorly paid non-farm jobs; and the poorest options of sporadic, casual and unskilled employment (cf. Iliya and Swindell, 1997). This pentagon of assets – natural, physical, social, financial, human – is used to ensure a holistic understanding of the different facets of livelihoods. A later chapter explores the diversification of pastoralist livelihoods, a process in which the expanded analytical structure offered by the sustainable livelihoods framework becomes particularly useful.

The present chapter has considered analytical approaches including possibilities for modelling elements of pastoral economies. It has focused on access to land (natural capital) for a variety of purposes, including cultivation, livestock grazing and as an investment through the ownership and rental of property. Secondly, it has considered human capital, largely in terms of labour availability and organisation. Thirdly, it has dealt with access to livestock as representing financial capital. The additional dimensions of socio-political networks and physical infrastructure are dealt with in other chapters.

6
Biology
of the Herds

Decades back, Dahl and Hjort (1976) outlined a comprehensive approach to understanding the dynamics of pastoralist herds. They based that understanding on a detailed review of fertility, mortality and production in a wide range of pastoralist livestock, and on a sound empirical knowledge of pastoral economies. None of the work that has emerged since then has faulted the broad analysis and insights they presented. This chapter uses their approach as a framework within which new research on the biology of pastoral herds and its interaction with pastoralist ecology and economy can still be best organised and understood.

Herd composition

Pastoralist and agropastoralist systems have on the whole operated with different aims and methods from Western livestock ranching systems. Those differences in management dictate some major differences in herd biology. Western commercial ranching systems aim to maximise profit through production of meat or milk. Commercial ranches run on Western lines operate at the conservative end of the spectrum (Chapter 3), maintaining relatively constant stocking rates on usually privately owned, fenced land. Western commercial ranchers invest considerable capital in water development, food supplements and veterinary inputs. They specialise in particular species, breeds and age/sex classes – for example, breeding stock, or weaners, or fattening for slaughter. High-yield milk or meat breeds are used, often crossbred with considerable exotic blood. Unproductive animals are rapidly culled and the herd managed for an age and sex class composition maximising output of the desired product. Slaughter stock are sold for meat once they reach their peak weight (ca. four years old).

These inputs and constraints guarantee that a certain type and level of output are maintained, despite fluctuations in climate, forage availability and disease challenge. Herd age structure, fertility, mortality rates and production reflect these intensive inputs, and a 25-30% offtake can be sustained from commercial sub-Saharan ranching operations managed in this way (Williamson and Payne, 1984). By contrast, indigenous sub-Saharan pastoralist systems range from primarily subsistence-oriented to strongly market-oriented (Chapters 3 and 9). Either way, indigenous livestock production systems tend to have lower capital investment than the Western-style ranches, and rely more on managing herd biology to buffer environmental fluctuations. They often have a lower offtake of around 5-10% per annum (Sandford, 1983). These differences become apparent in the demography and dynamics of pastoralist herds.

Species

Pastoralist herds typically have a broader range of livestock species – cattle, sheep and goats throughout much of the Sahel and further south, with camels an additional important component throughout the more arid Saharo-Sahelian systems (Chapter 4). This characteristic breadth of species within any one pastoralist system allows complementarity in rangeland use (e.g. Coppock et al., 1986; McCabe, 2004); in production (growth rates; reproductive rates; lactation timing and duration: Williamson and Payne, 1984; Dahl and Hjort, 1976); in disease management and drought recovery (e.g. McCabe, 1987); in wealth storage for management of income and expenditure (Mace, 1990; Broch-Due, 1998); and in the long-term switching strategies, described in many empirical studies and modelled in optimality and cost-benefit terms by Mace (1990, 1993a and b). Given the variety of breeds and the range of conditions under which any one is kept, it is only possible here to outline broad comparative indices for different species, representing performance under good conditions (Table 6.1).

Poor pastoralists can build their herds through their rapid-reproducing small stock. As their herd increases, they begin to trade small stock for slower-reproducing but less risk-prone large stock. Over a wide range of pastoralist

Table 6.1 Indicative production characteristics of livestock species

	Camels (dromedaries)	cattle	sheep	goats
Adult female body weight (kg)	450-600	250-450[a]	30-50	25-45
Age at 1st calving (yrs)	4-6	3	1	0.5-1
Longevity (yrs)	20-25	12-15	5-9	5-6
Minimum inter-birth interval (yrs)	2	1	0.75	0.75
Gestation (months)	12-13	6	5	5
Peak daily milk yield (kg)	9	2	0.5-1	0.5-1

[a] breeds ranging in size from small East African zebu to large Boran; pastoralists are unlikely to keep the very small or dwarf trypano-tolerant breeds – see text

systems, particularly those with boom-and-bust fluctuations, small stock represent a demonstrably viable strategy both to rebuild herds after disaster, and for long-term survival of the poorer households (Heffernan et al., 2001). Both empirical observation and modelling predict that large stock are only taken on once a certain threshold of wealth has been passed in terms of livestock units (e.g. Mace, 1990).

Breeds

Past classifications have distinguished three groups of cattle breeds in Africa: the humpless (or taurine), the humped (or zebu) and various crosses between the two groups (e.g. Mason, 1984). This classification was expanded through the osteological work of Grigson (1991) who identified in large, longhorned (*Bos taurus*) breeds the descendants of indigenous African domestications, including a number of longhorned breeds such as the Ankole cattle of the Great Lakes (e.g. Hima cattle of Lake Mburo) and the Kuri cattle of Lake Chad (with distinctive, giant, pear-shaped horns thought to act as floats), among others. More recently, genetic work has taken our understanding of the interrelations of African cattle beyond ideas of stable breeds. A study of 15 microsatellite loci in 50 indigenous cattle breeds from across the continent suggests an indigenous domestication of African *Bos taurus*, probably from a single point of origin, which spread through the continent reaching southern Africa by an eastern rather than a western route (Chapter 2; Hanotte et al., 2002). This ancestral indigenous African *B. taurus* mixed with Near East and European *Bos taurus* genetic influences and, more recently, zebu (*B. indicus*). Genetic studies have shown that zebu males (not females) were introduced over the last few centuries through the Horn and all along the east coast of Africa. The earliest known *B.indicus* and/or *taurus/indicus* hybrid remains are from the Hyrax Hill Kenyan site, and date to the sixteenth century AD (Marshall, 2000). There is a gradient of time depth of zebu spread across the continent, with older admixture in the south, more recent hybridisation in the northwest (MacHugh et al., 1997; Freeman et al., 2006), and zebu genetic influence still spreading.

Along with *in situ* adaptation to strong local selective pressures, particularly of disease, these crosses have given rise to the present-day wide diversity of African breeds, some of which are considered stable. For example, there are two main groups of trypano-tolerant cattle, the longhorned dwarf N'Dama breed and the West African shorthorns, which include both dwarf and Savanna forms of Muturu (Hausa for shorthorn). Zebu cattle, along with the majority of longhorn *Bos taurus*, are generally considered susceptible to trypanosomiasis, and the aggressive spread of the zebu genetic influence is seen as a threat to these West African disease-tolerant taurine cattle. African breeds, characterised by size, horn length, presence or absence of hump and/or dewlap, and colour, thus constitute a fluid, dynamic and continuing mix of cross-breeding, natural and artificial selection among the genetic influences outlined above, with more or less admixture of zebu. For example, indigenous West African pastoralist breeds selected for long transhumance treks tend to be larger, longer-legged and heavier than the arid-adapted East African zebu common to Maasai and

Samburu. Boran cattle, from the higher, more temperate Borana plateau, are larger than zebu. Wealthier Maasai pastoralists increasingly experiment with Boran seed bulls and/or other 'improved' breeds with a large admixture of exotic blood.

No attempt is made here to develop a comprehensive classification of local breeds, though some are cited (and see e.g. Poland and Hammond-Tooke, 2004). Since the colonial period, a range of 'improved' breeds (e.g. pure or crossbred Friesian dairy cattle) have been introduced for particular intensive production enterprises. These animals are highly valued by mixed farmers operating relatively intensive crop-livestock systems in comparatively cool humid areas such as the East African highlands. Agropastoralists wanting to use ox-ploughing and ox-drawn carts, and farming areas with tsetse disease vectors and trypanosomiasis, have to find a compromise between disease resistance and the capacity of the animal for farmwork, as indigenous trypano-tolerant breeds tend to be physically very small (adult female N'dama and dwarf Muturu weigh 120-200 kg: Williamson and Payne, 1984). As human population densities rise throughout the Sahelian zone, vegetation suitable for tsetse vectors may be declining, and as trypanocides become more readily available, the possibilities for larger stronger breeds in agropastoralist systems increase (Bourn and Wint, 1994). However, introduced breeds have shown poor survival and production under the constraints of pastoralist management in arid and semi-arid areas, and many herdowners unable to access or afford supplements and veterinary inputs prefer to keep to local breeds that can more reliably deal with the stresses they are likely to encounter (e.g. disease challenge – Homewood et al., 2006; heat stress, water shortage, poor forage). This is particularly important where structural adjustment has meant a decline in availability of water provision, feed supplements and veterinary services.

Age/sex composition

Pastoralist herds managed on extensive transhumant systems commonly have a characteristic age/sex composition. Table 6.2 summarises data from one major review: other studies confirm the general pattern that, for cattle, around 60% of the herd is commonly made up of female animals, of which a further 60% (i.e. around 40% of the total herd) are commonly adult females. This guarantees considerable reproductive potential and hence resilience, as livestock losses can be relatively rapidly replaced. Agropastoralist herds are different, with a much higher proportion of adult males (steers) that are useful for farmwork. Compared with Western commercial herds, pastoralist herds have tended to retain older animals that are past their prime in terms of weight gain (and market value) as well as in terms of calf and/or milk production. These animals are those which have been exposed to – and survived – disease and drought. To the pastoralist, their lower productivity is more than balanced by their hardiness. This difference in perception between cultures and production systems is nicely conveyed by the term 'old cow'. Among the Turkana, this expression is an honorific laden with respect and acknowledgement of virtue and achievement (Broch-Due, 1999).

Table 6.2 Age/sex structure of agropastoral and pastoral cattle herds

	Mali agro-pastoral	Mali pastoral	Kenya pastoral
All males	47	33	33
<1yr	6	7	10
1-3 yr	8	11	15
> 3yr	33	15	8
All females	53	67	67
<1yr	6	8	10
1-3 yr	11	16	15
> 3yr	36	43	42

Source: Data from De Leeuw and Wilson (1987)

Biology of livestock production

Pastoral products

Pastoralist herds, particularly at the more subsistence end of the spectrum, tend to be used for a much wider range of products than is the case for Western commercial ranching concerns. At the more subsistence end of the scale, small stock are often milked – a labour-intensive and low-yield process in most cases (Dahl and Hjort, 1976; Behnke, 1980; Williamson and Payne, 1984). As well as milk when it is available, blood, dung and hair are used from the living animals and meat, fat, hides, sinews, horn and hooves once they are dead. These animal products continue to be used for a wide range of purposes including food, utensils (e.g. snuff boxes commonly made from horn), construction (Maasai houses are plastered with dung mixed with mud; Tuareg tents until recently used hide coverings), clothing (until recently Maasai women commonly wore embroidered kidskin skirts), medicines, cosmetics (animal fat is often used as a softening and moisturising cream and as a base for mixing and applying ochre to the body). The animals also represent the focus of cultural, emotional, religious and legal values above and beyond their direct economic worth (Kuper, 1982; Hutchinson, 1992, 1996; Broch-Due, 1999; MacKinnon, 1999). As pastoralist systems become more commercialised, they often shift away from this breadth of product use towards more specialised production (Chapter 4; Behnke, 1980, 1983, 1985).

Variation in herd performance

These characteristic differences in management goals between pastoralist, agropastoralist and specialised ranching concerns are reflected in the composition, biology and dynamics of the livestock. Herd composition, fertility and mortality all show correlates of the different styles of production system. By comparison, commercial ranching concerns show high fertility, low mortality, and high meat and milk production. This performance must be seen against the background of the capital investment, recurrent inputs and the manipulation of herd age and sex structure, as well as the fact that many commercial ranches buy in their young stock from pastoralist concerns (Sandford, 1983), which confuses the production statistics. By contrast with Western commercial ranching concerns, pastoralist operations, whether more subsistence- or more market-oriented, tend to maintain lower levels of fertility, higher mortality, and lower milk and meat production per animal (Behnke, 1985; Table 6.1). Again, this contrast must be seen in the light of low inputs, maintenance of risk-averse herd structures, and production of other outputs. Where all these measures are taken into account, indigenous livestock production systems commonly show higher returns per unit area (though lower per animal – Scoones, 1995b: 12).

Cattle fertility, mortality and offtake provide useful indices of herd performance, revealing periods of stress. Livestock fertility and mortality rates can be calculated using a register of animals present in the herd, and relating numbers of births, deaths and transfers to the number of 'cow-years at risk' for a particular event (Hadgu et al., 1991; Rodgers and Homewood, 1986; Brockington, 2004; Homewood et al., 2006), whether for animals present during the period of the study, or historically, using retrospective data. Historical data are biased against clusters of related animals dropping out of sight: respondents are less likely to remember dead cattle that have left no live offspring. Mortality rates calculated from these data are therefore *minimum estimate* mortality rates. By contrast, fertility rates are biased towards more fertile animals (barren cows leaving no offspring are less likely to appear in the register). Fertility rates are therefore *maximum estimates*. In Mkomazi, where such data demonstrate the livelihoods impacts of eviction, these biases act to obscure rather than create worsening trends consequent upon exclusion from key resources (Brockington, 2001, 2004). The same problem affects data for other populations, making comparisons legitimate.

On the basis of such figures, fertility and mortality rates can be evaluated in relation to drought, disease and other types of disruption. For example, cattle in East African systems with bimodal rainfall have better year-round forage and water availability for relatively more circumscribed transhumant movement, and show high fertility rates as a result. By contrast, cattle in Sahelian systems, with a 9-month dry season, tend to show lower fertility, as animals that fail to regain condition and conceive within the brief period of abundant water and good forage are unlikely to get a second chance in any one year. In other cases, management interventions leave their mark through mortality and fertility changes. Some authors report lower fertility and higher mortality from non-transhumant agropastoralist cattle compared with transhumant herds (Dahl and Hjort, 1976). This has been interpreted as the penalty of being resident year-round in the same area with continuous exposure to disease (and no period of reduced parasite transmission cycles); no possibility of regaining condition on the fresh, nutrient-rich forage of the wet-season transhumance; and possibly the implications of farm work without sufficient supplement.

As an extreme illustration, all the Fulani cattle left to spend the wet season on islands in the Inland Delta of the Niger, to provide milk for the permanent settlements isolated by rising floodwaters (Chapter 2), are expected to die during or shortly after the wet season (Gallais, 1984). In a very different situation, comparatively low-fertility and high-mortality estimates around Mkomazi Game Reserve in Tanzania, backed up by interviews with pastoralists, suggest that eviction concentrated cattle into areas close to mountains where tick-borne diseases are particularly prevalent, affecting fertility and calf mortality adversely through loss of mobility and shortage of grazing and through transmission of infectious disease and parasites (Brockington and Homewood, 1999).

Management of herd reproduction

As well as the wide range of empirical observations on which Dahl and Hjort's qualitative insights are based, work with stochastic dynamic models confirms their analyses of pastoralist decision-making over livestock species choice (Mace, 1990) and breeding strategies (Mace, 1993b), in response to changing economic and ecological conditions. Models investigating choice of species confirm the management rationale of the widely-reported empirical observation that herders shift from small stock to large stock as they accumulate more animals, and *vice versa*. Small stock are high-risk, high reproductive rate, high mortality, short-lived animals. Nonetheless, a poor herder is better-off with several head of small stock than with one or a few large stock to the corresponding economic value, for three reasons. Firstly, small stock represent more convenient units for sale or exchange if it becomes necessary to purchase grain or pay taxes, fines or school fees. Secondly, the loss of one camel or cow to drought, disease or accident means a major dent in the capital of a poor herder, while the loss of a single sheep or goat would be a lesser blow. The larger numbers of small stock mean that there is a better chance that some proportion will survive disaster. Thirdly, the rapid reproductive rate of small stock means there is a better chance for a poor herdowner to establish a more substantial herd.

As small herdowners accumulate progressively larger numbers of small stock, so they become increasingly likely to exchange part or all of their herd for a smaller number of large-bodied livestock (camels or cattle). These are easier to manage, longer-lived and potentially lower-risk than are small stock. Empirical data and models investigating decisions to allow or limit rapid breeding focus on the relative wealth of different pastoralist households living in the same highly variable and drought-prone environment (Mace, 1993b). They bear out Sandford's suggestion that relatively better-off herdowners tend to choose a more conservative strategy, while poorer households may 'gamble with goats' (Mace, 1988, 1993b). Translated into terms of breeding strategies, this is seen in the fact that in some groups, in line with predictions, poor households do not restrict breeding male access to females. By contrast, wealthier households either separate the males physically or fit them with a harness that prevents breeding. The upshot is that fast-breeding females belonging to poorer households have higher fertility, but also show depletion and higher mortality in drought and at the onset of the rains. The herds of wealthier households show a lower fertility but better survival.

Impacts of drought and disease on herd biology and performance

Table 6.1 and the previous section document pastoral cattle-herd performance figures for 'normal' non-drought, non-epidemic circumstances, to some extent comparable with mean long-term ranch figures (ranches invest inputs to buffer herds from the potential impacts of drought or disease). However, pastoralist herd performance changes dramatically during drought or epidemic (Rodgers and Homewood, 1986; Homewood and Lewis, 1987; McCabe, 1987a, 2004: see implications for pastoral economies in Chapters 5 and 9; also Hesse, 1987; White, 1986; Homewood, 1994; Hendrickson et al., 1998; Little and Leslie, 1999; McCabe, 2004).

As a severe dry season stretches into drought, particularly where this comes after a run of bad years, herds move to areas that have relatively better forage and water. These are often areas which at other times have disease-vector populations to be avoided at all costs, but where those vector populations and the associated disease challenge are temporarily low. Security issues may make these movements doubly difficult and dangerous (McCabe, 2004). As the drought progresses, animals become concentrated at very high densities in small areas of key dry-season resources. Mortality of the very young animals jumps to 50-100%. Mortality also rises among adult animals, particularly lactating females that are already nutritionally depleted. Fertility drops to zero as starving animals fail to conceive or to carry their calves to term. Now a year into the drought, the reduced numbers of animals that are left survive on the limited key resources still available. While fertility remains at zero, mortality drops back to normal levels: the vulnerable have already died, and those that are left are likely to survive. Fertility remains at zero, but there is a steady trickle of new animals being brought into the system, whether as distress migrants or as investment in the anticipation of improving conditions (Homewood and Lewis, 1987; Homewood, 1994).

If the drought breaks with heavy rains, there may be dramatic mortality among small stock as severely depleted animals die of hypothermia (McCabe, 1987, 2004; Little and Leslie, 1999). Once the drought has broken, there is a rapid growth of new mineral-rich forage in formerly barren areas. The herds disperse and there is a speedy recovery of condition with the rich grazing, abundant water, minimal competition and effective absence of infectious disease which are all correlates of the aftermath of drought mortality. All the female stock conceive. Fertility rates the year after the drought run at 90-100%, well above the values for a 'normal' run of years. There is an explosive increase in the herds, with all the female stock bearing young, and anyone who can afford to do so brings or buys in additional stock from outside the drought-affected area. Simulations show that cattle herds would take 30 years to grow back to their original size after a drought or disease die-off of 50-80% (Dahl and Hjort, 1976). Empirical observation shows that recovery from stock losses of that magnitude takes only a few years from a regional point of view (Home-wood, 1994), although individual herd-owners may never recover.

Table 6.3 Major infectious diseases of sub-Saharan livestock (see text for full names represented here by acronyms)

Disease, cause	Transmission	Incubation	First symptoms	Outcome	Preventative measures	Other domestic stock/wildlife
Trypanosomiasis *Trypanosoma vivax/congolense* protozoan	Tsetse fly *Glossina*	1–3 weeks	Intermittent, progressive anaemia, anorexia, wasting	Acute cases die in a week. Animals that recover are premune[a] but prone to relapse	Tsetse control, drug prophylaxis, avoidance of tsetse areas	Other stock affected to different degrees, wildlife reservoir
ECF – *Theileria parva* protozoan	3-host tick[b] *Rhipicephalus appendiculata*	14 days	Lymph nodes round tick bite swell; wasting, rapid distressed breathing	Non-zebu/no prior exposure: 90%+ die. If recover, keep immunity for life + periodic challenge	Tick control by dipping/by environmental management + avoidance	None, but others are also host to the tick vector?
Rinderpest myxovirus	Droplet infection; contact and inhalation	6–15 days	Fever, anorexia, abscesses inside lower lip and in gut, bloody diarrhoea	Rapid death from dehydration in high proportion of non-immune	Highly effective JP15 vaccination programme has reduced impact	Domestic and wild ruminants
CBPP – *Mycoplasma mycoides*	Direct contact droplet infection and inhalation	3–6 weeks (2 weeks – six months)	Loss of appetite, rapid breathing, painful cough	Up to 50% die, 25% become carriers,	Slaughter of affected and vaccination of the rest	None
MCF–virus	Contact/droplet infection, congenital transmission	2–8 weeks up to several months+	Lymph glands swell; inflammation; mucous pus discharge from mucous membranes and eyes; bloody diarrhoea; skin sores	High mortality	Avoid contact with carriers	Wildebeest and sheep
FMD – virus	Direct contact with discharge from lesion; inhalation of windborne particles	3–8 days	Stomatitis; salivation; vesicles and ulcers on tongue and feet; anorexia, lameness	Not fatal; ulcers heal in 2–3 weeks loss of condition productivity decline	Slaughter affected; segregate exposed; mass vaccination but effect is strain-specific and short-lived; quarantine	All domestic livestock affected

[a] A subclinical symptomless infection with circulating antibodies that stop the disease developing further unless the animal comes under severe stress.

[b] Tick vectors have different life-cycles, with different implications for their transmission of disease and their control. In 'one-host' ticks, such as the Boophilus tick that transmits babesiosis and anaplasmosis, the adult female takes a blood feed, lays thousands of eggs and then dies. After weeks or months the eggs hatch into tick larvae that climb up a grass blade or shrub stem, and attach to a new host. They remain on this host on which they spend the full larval, nymph and initial adult stages. The adult female tick eventually drops to the ground after a blood meal, lays her eggs, and the cycle begins again. Two-host tick species spend a couple of weeks on the first host, during which time they change from larva to nymph, then drop to the ground as engorged nymphs and moult. They must then find a fresh host for the adult feed. The control of two-host ticks needs more frequent dipping or spraying. In the 'three-host' tick, the newly hatched larva finds a host, feeds, drops, moults to emerge as a nymph which again finds a new host, feeds, drops, moults and emerges as an adult. The adult finds the third host, feeds, drops, lays eggs and dies. In the transmission of ECF, Theileria organisms transmitted by the bite of the tick multiply asexually in the lymph cells of the cow and are ingested by a new tick vector. The disease organism completes sexual reproduction in the tick and gives rise to large numbers of infectious forms (sporozoites) in the tick mouthparts and salivary glands, whence they are injected into the next cow. There is some debate as to whether the infection survives the vector tick moulting from larva to nymph or nymph to adult, but most agree firstly that the infection is not carried in the egg, and that when an infected nymph feeds on an immune host, the infection is lost and the adult tick is 'clean'. This fact is exploited by Maasai management of the disease.

This boom-and-bust pattern stands in sharp contrast to the relatively much more stable stocking rates and returns of the Western-style ranching systems, where the shocks of drought and disease are buffered not by redeploying animals, nor by allowing numbers to track conditions, but by intensive inputs of fodder, water and veterinary care. Pastoral strategies are less able to use such inputs, which are both expensive and rarely available. They are continually working for the next phase of the boom-and-bust cycle. In good periods, herds are built up and diversified, the better to survive the next collapse. During periods of disaster, decisions are made as far as possible to ensure that, when conditions improve, the household and its herds will be in the best possible position to take advantage of the boom.

Livestock diseases

Infectious diseases cause high mortality rates in pastoralist herds. Western vets commonly consider that African pastoralists define diseases according to different taxonomies, and aggregate and disaggregate symptoms 'wrongly' (cited in McCorkle and Mathias-Mundy, 1992). Historians of science would see this more in the light of a struggle for power between different systems of knowledge and control (Waller and Homewood, 1996). However, current reviews show the breadth and depth of disease knowledge and practical control measures underpinning African pastoralist ethnoveterinary management (Schillhorn van Veen, 1996; Nigerian agropastoralists – Ibrahim, 1996; Samburu pastoralists – Heffernan et al., 1996; Ferlo FulBe – Bonfiglioli et al., 1996). The present work focuses on two main issues. It deals firstly with the array of major livestock diseases as identified by Western veterinary knowledge (Williamson and Payne, 1984; Norval et al., 1992; Bourn et al., 2001). Secondly, it looks at the different approaches to disease control, the conflicts between those approaches and their contrasting epidemiological outcomes (Ford, 1971; Birley, 1982; Giblin, 1990a, 1990b, 1993). Patterns of livestock disease, and pastoralist response, can be understood not only in terms of the biology of pathogens and vectors, but also as a product of the synergies and conflicts between pastoralist and Western veterinary models of disease. Strategies based on the different systems of knowledge lead towards different biological/ecological outcomes, and modern as well as historical epidemiological events should be interpreted in the light of conflicts between state policy and pastoralist strategy (Scoones and Wolmer, 2006). In this light it is interesting that recent major reviews of livestock diseases of economic importance in Africa have been compiled by a wide panel of international experts, but with little if any consultation with the pastoralists and other livestock-keepers themselves (Perry et al., 2002; Bourn et al., 2001; but see e.g. Catley, 1999).

Trypanosomiasis

Trypanosomiasis is a major vector-borne disease caused by a parasitic proto-zoon. The tsetse fly vector breeds in woody vegetation, so the disease is associated with particular habitats (Chapter 3). There are several tsetse vector species with different habitat needs, and several different species and strains of trypanosome with different abilities to infect and cause disease symptoms in different livestock species and human groups. This makes for a complex epidemiology with varying risks of human and livestock disease across the 10 million km^2 of tropical Africa infested with the tsetse vectors. Some forms of the trypanosome cause sleeping sickness in humans. In the aftermath of the rinderpest epidemic at the turn of the nineteenth/twentieth century, the massive losses of 90-95% of most grazers and browsers allowed woody vegetation to grow back across areas that had been maintained as pasture and cropland (see Table 6.3 and rinderpest section below). This woody vegetation offered habitat for tsetse vectors of trypanosomiasis to breed. Belts of disease-vector habitat created a new landscape of risk for pastoralists and agropastoralists (Chapters 2 and 3; Ford, 1971). Human and livestock trypanosomiasis spread rapidly with drastic impacts. About two-thirds of sub-Saharan Africa (including much higher-potential land) are now infested. Indigenous cattle breeds have varying degrees of resistance to trypanosomiasis and, with mild disease challenge, commonly develop sub-clinical infections which may not become apparent until the animal is under stress, but exotic breeds are at much greater risk (as are camels, which are acutely susceptible). Past control schemes involved clearing large areas of bush, eliminating wildlife populations (as in Zimbabwe or former Rhodesia) and resettling huge numbers of people and their livestock.

Ford (1971) was the first Western scientist to recognise generalisable regularities in the bewildering and rapidly shifting mosaic of human and livestock epidemics, to grasp the patterns of calculated risk, graded exposure, physiological resistance and acquired immunity exploited by African pastoralists, and to see the implications of limiting seasonal mobility in such systems. Since his seminal work, others have adopted similar explanations, firstly of adaptation to the presence of disease foci (and their calculated use in building immunity through graded exposure of stock), and secondly of the far-reaching effects of disrupting established patterns of exposure and immunity (Ford, 1971; Kjekshus, 1977; Giblin, 1990a, b, 1992; Birley, 1982). In the early twenty-first century, trypanosomiasis control and eradication remain a major industry attracting ever higher technology interventions (Bourn et al., 2001).

Colonial and post-colonial governments have attempted a double strategy of control: reducing the vectors and tackling the pathogen with drugs. There is a great diversity of tsetse control methods ranging from ultra-low-volume pesticide spraying to using tsetse traps made of local materials such as cloth and cow's urine (Dransfield et al., 1990). Table 6.4 shows the difference in potential efficacy and relevance to governments and individual herd-owners of different techniques of tsetse control. Vector control through environmental measures is often seen by pastoralists as a lower priority (and a public good vulnerable to free-riders) compared with treatments which are applied directly to the individual animal (and therefore a private good). It has been hard to sustain local involvement in even highly effective and low-technology, low-cost tsetse trapping methods (DFID, 2001; Bourn et al., 2001). This is all the

Table 6.4 Trypanosomiasis control methods and their applicability

	Sterile insect	Aerosol technique	Ground spray	Traps and targets	Insecticide-treated cattle
Nation/ Region 0.5-1 x 10⁶km²	+++++	++++	++	+	+
Province/nation 100,000 km²	+++++	++++	++	+	+
Province 10,000 km²	+++	+++++	+++	+++	++
District 1,000 km²	+	++	++++	+++++	++++
Village group 100 km²	-	+	++++	+++++	+++++
Village <10 km²	-	-	+++	+++++	+++++

Source: Modified from DFID (2001)

more so because government and international research institutes have tended to focus on high-tech, 'scientific' approaches to vector-insect population control. By contrast, intensive use of pour-on insecticides and prophylactic drugs in high-potential areas (Boutrais, 1988) means that pastoralist systems may operate in high-risk zones, albeit at considerable cost in terms of medication and the associated intensive care of individual animals, as well as a growing problem of pathogen resistance (Bourn et al., 2001). Recent analyses suggest a significant and steady increase of people, areas farmed and numbers of livestock throughout the Sahel, both a cause and a result of trypanosomiasis decline (Bourn and Wint, 1994).

East Coast Fever

East Coast Fever (ECF) has been endemic to parts of Maasailand since before the colonial era, although it was first recorded for Kenya in 1904 (Waller, 1979; Norval et al., 1992; Giblin, 1990b). It has since spread and is now one of the most serious cattle diseases in East Africa. ECF is a tick-borne protozoan disease which causes high mortality in susceptible animals which have not been able to acquire or maintain immunity through exposure to disease challenge as calves. It is vector-borne, and thus associated with those areas where the tick vector can complete its life-cycle including the off-host life stages. ECF may therefore be considered as an 'ecosystemic' disease involving land as well as the herd (Giblin, 1990b). This accounts for its regionally very different epidemiologies. In Southern Africa, marginal conditions for tick vectors make it possible to control the disease (and eliminate it altogether for long periods over wide areas) by reducing vector populations through dipping or in some cases by range management (Norval et al., 1992; Giblin, 1990b).

East Africa forms a shifting patchwork of endemically stable areas where vector populations maintain transmission, and unstable areas where there is temporarily no transmission. Quarantine procedures were set up early in the twentieth century to protect the settler exports by stopping the disease spreading through susceptible herds and uninfected tick populations. At the end of the colonial period and in the first decades of Independence, regular and sometimes compulsory cattle dipping with acaricides was established in both Kenya and Tanzania. However, growing numbers of susceptible exotic and cross-bred animals, rapid emergence of acaricide resistance in ticks, and inability to deal with carriers and disease reservoirs caused mounting costs and declining efficiency of dipping. The result was a treadmill of pesticide use, spiralling expense, increasingly disastrous impacts of the disease and an increasingly vulnerable stock population (Raikes, 1981; Kariuki, 1990).

Animals in the carrier state show no clinical symptoms themselves, but can transmit the protozoon to feeding ticks which can then infect other, susceptible animals (Norval et al., 1992). This understanding gave rise to the Infection and Treatment Method (ITM) for managing ECF in East Africa (Norval et al., 1992; Webb, 1996). This involves deliberate inoculation of the animal with the pathogen alongside a course of antibiotic protection. Substantial numbers of animals died in the early days of ITM, while inoculation strains and antibiotic cover regimes were being developed. However, the current system is outstandingly successful (Homewood et al., 2006). ITM echoes the customary management of the disease by Maasai, manipulating exposure to challenge of young calves under the partial protection of maternal antibodies, and maintaining protection of non-exposed non-immune animals (Potkanski, 1994). Detailed work on impacts of ITM on calf survival, livestock numbers, turnover and offtake, and household economy, for a total of 72 households and 1528 cattle, suggests that the vaccine improves calf survivorship dramatically (2% of vaccinated calves died in the first two years of life, cf. 50-80% of unvaccinated calves: Homewood et al., 2006).

Throughout East Africa, ECF challenge and mortality peaked after the 1997-8 El Niño event. In 1999, Tanzania used ITM to immunise over 10,000 animals against ECF, mainly improved dairy stock on smallholder mixed farms, and began extending immunisation to Maasai pastoralists' indigenous calves. Pastoralists prioritise investment in animal health, and there is currently a dramatic uptake of ITM at a cost of $8-$12/head, with ca.3000 indigenous calves immunised against ECF in the Arusha region from May 1999 to June 2000. The survival rate over 10 months' monitoring exceeded 90 %, and cost-recovery ran at around 91% , showing pastoralists' willingness to pay for the perceived benefit. At the same time, thousands of indigenous young stock were immunised as part of a donor restocking programme in Ngorongoro Conservation Area. ITM has until recently not been available in Kenya, and Kenyan herds are said to cross into Tanzania seeking ECF immunisation in

Monduli and Ngorongoro Districts. However, vaccine uptake and the extent of its use by any one herd-owner is closely linked to wealth and livelihood security, and in particular to their involvement with the commercial livestock trade. If anything, vaccination is driving socio-economic differentiation as poor households, unable to buy vaccine and its benefits, progressively lose their share of the livestock production system to wealthier herd-owners able to vaccinate their stock (Homewood et al., 2006). For ITM to fulfil its potential for improving the livelihood security of poor households, the benefits of enhanced livestock production need to be more equitably distributed, and to outweigh commercial cultivation and wildlife tourism. Potential environmental effects also need further research.

Rinderpest

Rinderpest is a viral infection transmitted through contact (much as is Contagious Bovine Pleuro Pneumonia or CBPP) and causing high mortality in non-immune cattle and in some wild animal species. It has been known in Europe since the time of Charlemagne, but never penetrated to sub-Saharan Africa until the end of the nineteenth century. During the late 1880s, infected animals were brought to Eritrea from Aden by invading Italian troops, and others were brought down the Nile to Khartoum by the British forces belatedly sent to relieve General Gordon. They triggered a disastrous pandemic throughout sub-Saharan Africa, killing 90% or more of all cattle as well as many other ruminants both wild and domestic. This massive ecological shock, and particularly the consequent re-growth of under-grazed/ under-browsed woody vegetation and vector habitat, paved the way for other diseases, notably trypanosomiasis.

Rinderpest was thus the trigger responsible for the collapse of many African societies in the late nineteenth century (Kjekshus, 1977; Maasai – Waller, 1988; Great Lakes, Nigeria – Ford, 1971). The combined shock of pandemic and colonial impact ensured that pastoralist groups lost their former military and economic dominance. At first, the disease's extreme virulence ensured that outbreaks burnt themselves out, but as rinderpest established itself it evolved milder strains to which animals could develop some immunity. Rinderpest has been controlled by a highly successful vaccination programme (Scott, 1985). Despite occasional minor recurrences, its effective control among livestock had the knock-on effect of protecting the large wildlife populations of the East African savannas, and triggering the ungulate eruption whereby, for example, wildebeest increased from around 200,000 to ca.1.8 million in the Serengeti in the 1960s-70s, setting off ecosystem-wide changes (Sinclair and Norton-Griffiths, 1979; Sinclair and Arcese, 1995; Sinclair et al., 2006).

Contagious Bovine Pleuro-Pneumonia

Contagious Bovine Pleuro-Pneumonia [CBPP] is a mycoplasma disease which spreads by droplet infection from breathing in the nasal discharge of infected animals within the herd. Although acute cases may die within two weeks of fever and respiratory distress, other animals recover, either completely or as 'lungers', apparently healthy animals which may still carry and transmit the disease. The presence of carriers, together with the long incubation period of up to six months, means that the disease may spread undetected through a herd, or remain dormant for long periods. It prompted one of the most unpopular of veterinary interventions, the inspection of herds and the slaughter, often without compensation, of all suspect animals – a measure with consequences to the owners potentially more damaging than the disease itself.

In view of its political repercussions, the colonial authorities in Kenya decided not to apply the most drastic method of CBPP control to African herds, slaughtering only visibly affected animals and imposing preventive quarantines and inoculations in contact cases (Waller and Homewood, 1996). In East Africa, CBPP reached Maasailand from the south in the early 1880s. Its impact was severe, but negligible by contrast with the great rinderpest pandemic ten years later which struck and virtually destroyed the Maasai herds in early 1891 (Waller, 1988). In the case of CBPP, a form of variolation was used, perhaps based on a similar technique for smallpox, in which matter taken from a diseased animal was rubbed or bound into an incision made in the nose or tail of a healthy animal (Merker, 1910:170, cited in Waller and Homewood, 1996). Both rinderpest and CBPP recurred at intervals and have become endemic in East African herds.

Epidemiological implications of conflicting knowledge systems

The interaction between indigenous and imported Western models of animal health has major implications for the widely observed gap between animal health policies supporting local livelihoods and those driven by international economic interests (Scoones and Wolmer, 2006). These issues are explored here with special reference to Maasai, using material summarised from Waller and Homewood (1996).

Maasai management of disease is based on the way their knowledge of live-stock health is gained and on the way they value their herds. Practical knowledge and skills, gained through learning and experience, mean that many if not most men (and women – Hodgson, 2000a), become expert managers and diagnosticians. Western science sees health as the normal state, and disease by contrast as abnormal, requiring medical intervention and, ideally, eradication. By contrast, pastoralists often regard disease as a natural, inevitable, but potentially manageable part of the environment. Ailments are diagnosed by their characteristic external symptoms and effects, not through a micro-biologically-based germ theory of disease. Steps may be taken to limit losses, but disease cannot simply be eradicated, nor is a disease-free state necessarily desirable. Animals without acquired immunity are known to be vulnerable, and herd movements and controlled exposure to endemic disease are established ways of protecting herds against epidemic outbreaks (Potkanski, 1994). Herd size and composition buffer unpredictable mortality, while management seeks to minimise it. Western and indigenous management sometimes coincide, though rarely because of shared models of causation.

Often they conflict. It is by no means always the case that indigenous models and their associated outcomes lead to less successful management of disease (in terms of the goals of the pastoral enterprise) than does Western veterinary intervention. At the same time, pastoralists are quick to recognise and adopt veterinary inputs which suit their purpose.

While pastoralist groups such as the Maasai have long understood the importance of immunity, and themselves practised forms of immunisation, they have historically been highly sceptical of the value of infecting an otherwise healthy adult animal directly with disease. Calves infected with ECF and mild rinderpest might recover and then be immune to further attacks, but adult animals that were infected usually succumbed. Pastoralist scepticism was justified by the dangerously unstable behaviour of early inoculations (and some recent ones), which have killed as often as they cured. Herd-owners have become willing to pay for ECF immunisations (Homewood et al., 2006) and trypanosomiasis treatments, but not for all other interventions. Their selectivity has been guided by cost, by experience and by the relative contribution immunisation may make to the survival and subsistence value of the herd as a whole. Treatment against anthrax, for example, was sought when cases occurred in the herds (Waller and Homewood, 1996). Not surprisingly, treatment for Foot and Mouth has commonly been ignored, since the disease has little obvious effect on the well-being of the herd. Similarly, while Maasai reluctantly submitted to CBPP inoculations, they have historically resisted testing for carriers, since this might lead to the slaughter and loss of an animal which would otherwise contribute to the household economy.

Conflicting political, economic and practical priorities mean that pastoralists and veterinary services have often been divided. The example of attitudes to Foot and Mouth Disease (FMD) makes clear the contrast between grassroots producer and veterinary viewpoints, and the 2001 outbreak in the UK shows that this is generalisable far beyond African pastoralist contexts. FMD is rarely lethal. It tends to be mildly debilitating and to reduce productivity. From the viewpoint of the pastoralist, it is a mild disease of relatively little consequence for the viability and functioning of the indigenous livestock-production enterprise. From a veterinary viewpoint, FMD is a listed disease. The European Union and the United States ban the import of meat from affected areas. Meat exports from sub-Saharan countries have been important both to their governments and to their politically influential large-scale commercial producers. Governments have, therefore, concentrated on creating disease-free zones protected by an outer ring of compulsorily vaccinated animals. Not only the outbreak of FMD, but the mere passage of potentially infected animals through areas occupied by export-grade animals means the immediate loss of lucrative foreign export markets for their meat. As was the case in the UK in 2001, it becomes a priority for governments and vets to control the disease. In the UK, this led to a programme of mass slaughter and quarantine which had incalculable impacts on the rural economy. In the light of that experience, there is now a strong move to change the administrative framework and the official management of FMD from quarantine and culling to vaccination, formerly considered unacceptable.

In Africa, highly disruptive quarantines are imposed on local pastoral producers in order to block the movement of infected animals which might jeopardise the national livestock export trade (Raikes, 1981). It then becomes a priority for pastoralists (with little or no share in the profits of those official export markets) to evade quarantine restrictions and optimise their herd movements both for grazing and for trade. Foot and Mouth is commonly seen by pastoralists as an external lesion to be treated externally, not as requiring quarantine or worse. State-driven quarantine and prophylactic measures are geared to the needs of the protected export market, not to those of subsistence pastoralism and the local market.

More generally, pastoralist cultures tend to see the herd as considerably more than the aggregate economic worth of individual animals. Disease threatens social disaster, not just the loss of valuable markets or capital investment. Exactly parallel feelings of social disaster were expressed very strongly by UK livestock farmers in the face of the mass slaughter of their stock in the 2001 FMD outbreak, despite the economic compensation they stood to receive. By contrast, veterinary authorities work within a framework of economic policy emphasising the market value of stock, protection of valuable animals and general improvement of stock quality, defined in market terms (Scoones and Wolmer, 2006). Subsistence and social values of herds in pastoral areas are seen by official agencies as being of secondary importance.

Drought and disease continue to take a regular toll of the herds in sub-Saharan Africa, and livestock development schemes from the late 1930s onwards have not compensated for losses of grazing and water resources. Prudent stock-owners have made cautious and selective use of what Western veterinary science had to offer, based on an assessment of how it might contribute to the continuation of pastoralist livelihoods and the survival of the herds, and of whether its rationale accorded with their own knowledge and experience. For example, Maasai resisted reducing their herds, as the people of Bophuthatswana resisted the donkey cull (Jacobs, 2003). Individually owned numbers remain the best protection against disaster. Exotic breeds may increase productivity, but are still too vulnerable to disease and poor range conditions, though grade (cross-bred) cattle may be incorporated into the herds where their viability and value have been proven by experience, and where the necessary inputs can be accessed relatively reliably (BurnSilver, forthcoming).

Policy implications

African pastoralists have generally welcomed veterinary inputs which visibly improve the health of their animals, to the point where human health interventions, which are otherwise hard to deliver in remote pastoralist areas, may be pegged to the incentives and logistics of animal health delivery (Zinsstag and Weiss, 2001; Zinsstag et al., 2006). However, interventions that treat the individual animal or cordon off the land into protected spaces, may, in the pastoralists' view, fail either to address the important manifestations of disease or to make use of the environmental constraints within which it operates. In such cases pastoralists may perceive that commercial farmers and international entrepreneurs benefit from animal health policies at their expense, as with FMD quarantines. In some cases the political implications may be unacceptable, quite apart from the economic impacts (e.g. dipping in pre-Independence Zimbabwe – Wolmer et al., 2002: 156).

The ways indigenous stock-owners have attempted to deal with disease may conflict with state policy. Indigenous strategies have centred on the use of space and movement to control or avoid outbreaks. Selective use and management of pasture was commonly used in the past to maintain the health of the herds by rotating them seasonally through different types of rangeland (e.g. Schillhorn van Veen, 1996; Maasai – Waller, 1979; Potkanski, 1994). Pastoralists are widely aware of the connection between some diseases and the insects that carry them, and of how this vector relationship fits into, and is affected by, the wider ecosystem. Maasai connected trypanosomiasis with the tsetse fly and either avoided areas of tsetse bush or took cattle through them only at times that represented minimum risk (Waller and Homewood, 1996). The development of such indigenous knowledge through trial and error is thought to have played a major role in the spread of pastoralism across Africa (Chapter 2; Gifford-Gonzalez, 2000).

The creation and enforcement of colonial boundaries and their consolidation and further spread in the postcolonial period have undermined the use of natural checks within the ecosystem. In the case of trypanosomiasis, flexible use of the rangeland mosaic can maintain partial immunity and endemic stability, but this presupposes access to a wide range of pastures and the ability to move freely between them. These choices become ever less available. The pressures of development and wildlife conservation (Homewood and Rodgers, 1991; Homewood et al., 2005) mean less space and restrictions on movement, undermining use of controlled grazing to manage shifts in vegetation patterns and associated disease vectors (Waller, 1979, 1990; Giblin, 1990a, 1993; Niamir-Fuller, 1999).

Pastoralist modes of land use and management have conflicted as much with recent Western perceptions of landscape and its value as with veterinary orthodoxies (Knowles and Collett, 1989; Brockington and Homewood, 1996). Grass burning and close grazing by a succession of different animals have in the past been an effective method of cleaning pasture of ticks and other parasites[1] and of preventing the spread of tsetse bush, but it has been condemned by outsiders as ecologically destructive (Birley, 1982; Sutherst, 1987 citing Branagan, 1974; Laris, 2002, 2003). Pastoral land use has been conventionally seen as involving overgrazing and poor management inimical to the interests of conservation and economic development alike (Arhem, 1985; Bell, 1982; Fratkin, 1991). It is not surprising that dipping for vector control has usually prevailed over burning. The result has been, ironically, a real if gradual deterioration in pasture resources in rangelands across many areas, caused not by pastoralist land use but by its interdiction (Laris, 2003).

More recently, 'expert' and pastoralist opinions on grazing management

---

[1] When ticks feed on a resistant animal with circulating antibodies, they lose their capacity to infect in the case of particular diseases and vector species.

have begun belatedly to converge. Some of the former now give a cautious but still sceptical reception to methods of disease and pasture control derived from indigenous knowledge, including naturally acquired immunity (e.g.Norval et al., 1992: 307, 335). Current scientific thinking on ECF is both a vindication of, and compromise with, indigenous systems of control.

Strategies based on such understandings run counter to prevailing trends in land use and tenure policies and would require a re-assessment of many national livestock health policies and priorities (Scoones and Wolmer, 2006; UNOCHA-PCI, 2007). Though national livestock health policy documents pay lip-service to pro-poor development and local livelihoods security alongside their interest in international markets, it is clear that there is a deep-rooted divergence between the different animal health needs of these two sets of goals (Scoones and Wolmer, 2006). Supporting local livestock-related livelihoods means prioritising mobility alongside infrastructure and inputs which encourage local production and trade. It also means using decentralised networks of (private) paravets and (state) community animal health workers (CAHWs) alongside private suppliers of appropriate, low-cost veterinary products, to focus on easily treatable, high impact diseases and those affecting multiple livestock species. By contrast, animal health policies focused on high-value international trade and export markets prioritise transboundary animal disease control, eradication and compliance with international standards. These are primarily achieved through investing in export zones, quarantine systems, registered abattoirs and certification, with centralised disease reporting, mass vaccination and eradication systems (rolled out through CAHWs). These measures in most cases run at least partly counter to pastoralist interests, and the divergent goals and priorities mean recurrent conflicts over national policies towards the management of livestock disease.

7

Pastoralist Food Systems,
Diets & Nutrition

Pastoral produce has been estimated to account for 25% of food production in sub-Saharan Africa (expressed as monetary grain equivalents – Jahnke, 1982). The great majority comes from indigenous breeds managed in pastoralist and agropastoralist systems with minimal fodder or veterinary inputs, though an increasing number are managed as peri-urban dairy stock dependent on such inputs. Livestock numbers have kept pace with and in some areas exceeded the spread of cultivation throughout the Sahelian and Sahelo-Sudanian zones (Bourn and Wint 1994), and this estimate is now likely to be if anything on the low side. However important the contribution of their livestock to feeding Africa, pastoralists' own food security is often precarious. Africa's population growth rate has exceeded growth in food production for some decades, and food-purchasing power has declined throughout the same period. Of 88 low-income food-deficit countries listed by the FAO, 44 are in Africa, and of these 37 are famine-prone. The deterioration in food production and availability[1] has been driven largely by political and economic factors (Raikes, 1988; Dyson, 1994) but agro-ecological correlates of global warming and climate change in African arid and semi-arid lands mean that trends are predicted to worsen (Rosenzweig and Parry, 1994; IPCC, 2001; Hoffmann, 1999). Recent estimates suggest that 33% of the African population are undernourished, with 50% food-insecure (FAO 2001; Downing et al., 1996). Pastoralist groups, who make up a disproportionate share of famine-prone arid-land populations, as well as of displaced and refugee populations (NOPA, 1992; Chapter 3; Hendrickson et al., 1998), and who commonly have the least secure rights of tenure and

---

[1] See counter-stories of success, eg. Mortimore (2005): Kano-Maradi region of Nigeria and Niger. Despite rural populations and their subsistence requirements doubling, rainfall declining by 25-35% 1960s-1980s, and wildly fluctuating economic and policy contexts, intensification and diversification have allowed producers to keep feeding consumers at declining real prices through this period.

access to common pool resources on which pastoral production depends, also make up a disproportionate share of Africans vulnerable to hunger.

The literature on pastoralist food systems, diet and nutrition begs a number of questions. First, given the enormous variability between systems, environments, years and seasons, is there any such thing as a characteristic pastoralist diet centred on the consumption of pastoral produce? Second, are there recognisable health and growth correlates of pastoralist diets? How do pastoralist indices and trajectories of physical growth compare with those for other sub-Saharan populations, and what causes the contrasts? Third, how do pastoralist food systems respond to stress? What coping systems come into play in the face of famine and hunger? What circumstances make pastoralists nutritionally more vulnerable? Are pastoralists consistently less well-buffered against such shocks than people depending on other production systems? Finally, what are the implications of change, whether impoverishment or improvement of economic and development status, for pastoralist food systems, diet and nutrition?

Pastoralist diets have often been assumed to consist of meat and milk. Deviations from such a diet have tended to be seen as recent changes in response to impoverishment or acculturation. Calculations of herd sizes necessary to support a pastoral household on a diet of meat and milk were until quite recently used as evidence arguing for pastoralism being ecologically irrational and environmentally inappropriate (Brown, 1971; Jewell, 1980). More recently, this stereotype has been thrown into question by detailed studies of the diets of a wide range of pastoralist groups (Galvin, 1991; Nestel, 1985, 1986, 1989; Benefice et al., 1984; Holter, 1988; Sellen, 2003). Gathered wild foods, and cultivated products obtained by exchange or purchase, are important even to the 'purest' pastoralist systems (Coughenour et al., 1985; Little and Leslie, 1999). Many pastoralists experience major transitions in food systems through livestock loss and poverty-driven sedentarisation (Brainard, 1990; Campbell et al., 1999), or, on the other hand, through increasing involvement in trade, wealth accumulation and urban living. The present chapter uses these studies together with recent syntheses (Galvin, 1992; Galvin et al., 1994; Galvin and Little, 1999; Little and Leslie, 1999) as a basis for understanding pastoralist diets, patterns of physical growth and nutritional vulnerability (Galvin, 1992), nutritional strategies (Galvin et al., 1994) and their implications for health and welfare (Pelletier, 1994), and other aspects of pastoralist ecology and development.

The chapter begins with a survey of methods and methodological problems involved in the study of pastoralist diets. It goes on to look at the range of food systems of different pastoralist groups. It outlines regional variation, differences arising from production system and market strategy, seasonality, age, sex and socio-economic status through differences of caste, class or life-cycle stage. Calorific, protein and micronutrient values for typical diet items, and estimates of pastoralist activity levels and nutritional requirements, are outlined. The nutritional implications of the diet are examined in terms of energy and protein adequacy. Anthropometric profiles characteristic of pastoralist groups, and their significance and implications are reviewed. Food security and famine strategies are examined. Exploiting favourable calorific terms of trade by exchange of pastoral for cultivated produce, flexible household composition, out-migration of household members, alternative occupations, gathering wild foods, are all strategies used by pastoralists for coping with food-deficit periods.

Overall, this chapter attempts to link patterns of nutrition in pastoralist groups to interannual variation, social stratification, interactions of nutrition and infection, and to the impacts of development, acculturation, sedentarisation and a growing market orientation.

Pastoral diets

Methods and methodological problems

Sample design is a major consideration in approaching studies of pastoralist systems, particularly food systems, diet and nutrition. Regional, seasonal and socio-economic variability is the hallmark of the arid and semi-arid ecosystems with which most sub-Saharan pastoral systems are associated, and any study can only be understood in terms of the specific conditions under which it was carried out. The particular subjects chosen inevitably determine the type of results obtained, and may reinforce preconceptions where studies emphasise an extreme of 'pure' pastoralists (such as Ngisonyoka Turkana as opposed to other 'pastoral' Turkana, or recently settled Turkana groups – Coughenour et al., 1985; Little and Leslie, 1999), or age/sex or socio-economic classes that have a more purely pastoral diet than is characteristic for the rest of the society (as with Maasai *moran* – Homewood and Rodgers, 1991; Tuareg noblewomen – Hill 1985). Choice of population within an ethnic group, site within a population, household within a site will all affect results.

Most recently, studies seek to disaggregate not just by household characteristics (e.g. wealth – Sellen, 2003), but by an individual's position within the household. Family structures rarely if ever correspond to the Western notion of a nuclear family. Families may, for example, be polygamous and dispersed over several sites. Where the household is taken as the unit of consumption, this could range from (as in the Maasai) a woman with some of her own children, her foster children and the occasional presence of a husband (who also periodically eats with his other wives, whose houses may be in the same and/or distant homesteads), to groups which (as in the case of the Tuareg) include biologically unrelated but 'family' slaves or dependants as well as kin, affines and friends of the household head.

There is a perennial problem of defining the food consumption unit; is it those who eat from one pot? In most pastoralist families and households, a substantial proportion of people are at any one time travelling for transhumance, trade, marriage negotiations and social or ritual occasions. Visitors are common and make up a large part of the group to be fed at any time. Food sharing and communal eating may make it harder to measure individual intakes and intra-household allocation. The frequency of eating away from the hearth makes for further difficulties, whether in estimating the use of wild foods (Ngisonyoka Turkana – Coughenour et al., 1985; Galvin, 1985; Damara –

Sullivan 1999a; Fulani – Schreckenberg 1996; Buhl, 1999; SSE, 1992) and/or foods shared in other households, which may involve a considerable proportion of the overall food budget. Among Tanzanian Maasai in Ngorongoro in the 1980s, food shared out accounted for a mean of 40% of milk production in households with a high food adequacy, and 10% of milk production in low food-adequacy households (Homewood and Rodgers, 1991). Food sharing is even more central to the Ngisonyoka Turkana (Johnson, 1999:103).

There are also potential complications with social norms and taboos making it inappropriate to witness or discuss consumption of certain foods by particular groups (e.g. consumption of cultivated foods by Maasai *moran*). In some cases, it is not appropriate to show any interest in or enquire about food types and quantities eaten (Fulani – Buhl, 1999). Even in households prepared to have their food patterns observed, an investigator repeatedly questioning food consumption soon becomes a nuisance, and prestige effects may readily distort results (e.g. Schelling, 2002: 67). Sampling problems associated with extreme and unpredictable variability inevitably affect the time and duration of study. The characteristic seasonality of pastoralist habitats makes year-round observation important, but in very mobile groups, and in groups that undergo extremes of dispersal and aggregation and/or have a highly flexible household composition, this presents major practical problems.

Special circumstances arising from the characteristics of pastoralist lifestyles may constrain methods for collection of data on diet and nutrition. Twenty-four hour dietary recall (e.g. Nestel, 1985, 1986) may entail problems with accuracy, but becomes progressively more accurate and easier to carry out where there is a relatively simple diet, as may be the case with more milk-based pastoralist systems, remote from markets. Self-recording techniques depend on literacy, which is low in many pastoralist groups. Weighed larder methods and direct observation are problematic because of their intrusive nature, and because of the potential difficulties of standardising measures, but have been used in conjunction with 24-hour recall. Anthropometry and energy expenditure studies using work diaries, time budgets, and/or double-labelled water have all been used to complement work on pastoralist diets. The present chapter focuses on food-system aspects of diet and nutrition, but more physiological aspects have been explored in detail by Galvin and other researchers (see Little and Leslie, 1999). Anthropometric studies commonly use indices of height and weight related to age. In pastoralist populations with low literacy and no birth records, ages can be estimated through event calendars (e.g., Little and Leslie, 1999), and weight-for-height indices are independent of age.

Pastoralist diets

Despite the methodological problems set out above, there have been several in-depth studies, and pictures of a wide range of pastoralist food systems are now emerging. The chapter does not attempt to review the many different combinations of pastoral produce, cultivated cereals, pulses, root and vegetable crops, gathered foods (wild meat, fish, wild plants, honey) and shop-bought items like tea and sugar observed in different pastoralist diets. It also makes no attempt to present a catalogue of methods used by different pastoralist groups to process and (where there is any surplus) preserve pastoral foods, such as production of soured milk, clarified butter, cheese, blood products and preserved meat. Instead, it focuses on fundamental dietary composition in terms of basic categories of nutrient (protein, fat and carbohydrate), the implications for protein and energy adequacy, and the patterns of growth that result.

Some of the main case studies include detailed work on Maasai (Kenya: Nestel 1985, 1986, 1989); (Tanzania: Arhem et al., 1981; Homewood 1992; McCabe et al., 1992); Turkana (Galvin, 1985, 1988, 1992; Little and Leslie, 1999; Galvin and Little, 1999; see van den Boogard (2002) for studies on less isolated Turkana); Rendille (Fratkin et al., 2004); Fulani (Hill, 1985; Mali:

Table 7.1 Percent dietary calories derived from different diet items (after Galvin 1999)

Region	Group	Meat	Milk/ milk products	**Total pastoral**	Grain	Other	Reference
East	Maasai	10+	34+	**44**	50	4	Homewood &Rodgers, 91
	Maasai	4	64	**68**	16	16	Nestel, 85
	Maasai	12	31	**43**	34	23	Nestel, 89
	Turkana	18	62	**80**	8	12	Galvin, 99
	Borana	6	31	**38**	58	5	Galvin, 92, 94
North -east	Baggara	5	16	**21**	57	22	Holter, 88 (Galvin, 99)
	Awlad Hamid	1	8	**9**	58	33	Holter, 88
West	Tuareg	3	51	**54**	47	–	Swift, 76, 86
	Tuareg	8	68	**76**	24	–	Swift, 76, 86
	Tuareg	–	45	**45**	53	2	Bernus, 88
	Tamasheq F	8	45	**53**	48	–	Wagenaar-
	Tamasheq M	8	28	**36**	65	–	Brouwer, 85
	Bella	14	20	**34**	66	–	
	Tamasheq (Mali)	12	33	**45**	55	–	Galvin, 99[1] from WB 85
	Fulani	2	39	**41**	58	–	Swift, 76, 86
	Fulani (Niger)	–	36	**36**	63	1	Bernus 88
	Fulani AP[2]	–	25	**25**	75	–	Swift, 76, 86
	Fulani AP	2	24	**26**	74	–	Swift, 76, 86
	Fulani AP	3	12	**15**	85	–	Swift, 76, 86
	Fulani AP	3	18	**21**	62	17	Benefice et al., 84
South-west	Herero	16	22	**38**	55	7	O'Keefe et al., 88

[1] Galvin appears to have averaged these data across Tamasheq men and women and also noble and Bella, who combine to form households but who have very different diets and energy expenditures.
[2] AP = agropastoralist

Wagenaar-Brouwer, 1985; Niger: Loutan, 1985; INSEE/SEDES, 1986; Senegal: Benefice et al., 1984); Tuareg (Bernus, 1981, 1988, 1990, Wagenaar-Brouwer, 1985; INSEE/SEDES 1986; Claude et al., 1991). Others look specifically at interactions of disease with micronutrient and other aspects of diet (Schelling, 2002). Where available, quantitative estimates are summarised in Table 7.1.

It is clear that there is no single characteristic pastoralist diet, nor is there a characteristic diet for any particular pastoralist group. To get an even moderately representative picture for any of these groups it is essential to look at more than one study and site. To take an obvious example, the diet and nutrition of agropastoral Fulani in Senegal are quite different from those of the Wodaabe Fulani in Niger. The Ngisonyoka Turkana eat a quite different diet from that of irrigation scheme settler Turkana. Despite the fact that the blossoming of studies for new groups and situations has tended to point up the overall variability within and between groups, it has also begun to make it possible to derive some more robust generalisations. These diets, averaged across wet and dry seasons, show a wide range of dependence on pastoral produce, from <10% to >75 % of dietary energy intake. 'Pure' pastoralists could perhaps be taken as those who derive more than a certain percentage of their dietary energy from pastoralist produce, but such definitions break down on closer inspection. For example, Tuareg households include noble women with a very high milk intake, and noble men and Bella slaves with a greater reliance on cereals. Ngisonyoka Turkana and Kel Adrar Tuareg emerge as the 'purest' pastoralists, with 80% and 76% dietary energy from pastoralist produce respectively. By contrast, among several migratory peoples with a strong pastoralist ethic, and powerful cultural values attached to meat and milk and pastoralist lifestyles, pastoral produce makes a relatively small contribution to dietary energy, such as the Awlad Hamid (Holter, 1988: 9% dietary energy from pastoral produce; see also Schelling, 2002: 67-72, 142). Even groups with commonly high contributions of pastoral produce to the diet periodically face temporarily severe conditions undermining this dietary norm (e.g. Zaghawa – de Waal, 1989a).

Protein and energy in pastoral diets: calorific and monetary trade-offs

The nutritional composition of pastoral diets, and in particular the presence of at least some milk in the diet, has certain predictable corollaries. In the first place, all these pastoral diets have a protein intake well in excess of the international recommended minimum dietary intake. This general character-istic of a diet with even a small meat or milk component is important in understanding patterns of growth and disease in pastoralist groups. Where the diet contains at least some milk and meat, this also provides a relatively balanced intake of vitamins, essential fatty acids and minerals.

A second striking generalisation concerns seasonal variation in dietary composition and calorific intakes. If anything, it is the trade-off equation between products of the herd and foods obtained by purchase, exchange or diversification, that characterises pastoralist food systems, rather than the composition of the diet itself. Table 7.2 indicates the calorific values of the

Table 7.2 Nutritional and calorific values of pastoral foods

	Milk	Meat	Fat	Blood	Grain
Kcals/100g	60–80★	100–150	900	33	350
% protein	4★	15–20		10	5
% fat	5★	5	100	+	+
%carbohydrate	5★	<5		+	95
Vitamin A	+		+		
Vitamin B	+	+			
Vitamin C	+				
Iron		+		+	
Calcium	+				
Phosphate	+				

★seasonal variation

different components commonly encountered in a range of pastoralist diets. Precise calorific values tend to change with the season. For example, the fat content of milk varies according to species and the condition of the animals. Among the Ngisonyoka Turkana, camel's milk has the lowest and cow's milk the highest fat content (Galvin and Little, 1999); conversely in these herds protein content is highest for goats and lowest for cattle. However, these species characteristics and rankings will be affected by local and seasonal forage, water and energy expenditures, and rank order cannot be assumed to remain constant across different pastoralist herding systems and range conditions. Fat content in milk tends to be high at the beginning of the dry season (when the animal is in peak condition) and then fall progressively as the dry season continues. In a bimodal climate like that of East African Maasailand, fat content may fluctuate (see, for example, Galvin and Little, 1999) but remain quite high year-round. In a Sahelian climate with a 9-month dry season, fat values may drop very low. In any pastoralist system, milk production will eventually cease altogether where the dry season stretches into drought. Some groups fall back on gathered foods, but in most cases cereals and other cultivated staples then fill the energy gap, obtained by sale or exchange or by more or less opportunist agropastoralist cropping. The calorific (and monetary) terms of trade therefore become fundamental to understanding pastoralist diets and economy.

The third generalisation concerns the absolute value of caloric intakes. At the more purely pastoral end of the scale, energy intakes commonly recorded for East African pastoralists such as the Maasai and Turkana are very low, commonly around 70-80% of the international recommended values (Homewood, 1992; Galvin and Little, 1999). As a result, these pastoralists tend to have low mean BMI values, in the region of 18-19 even during 'normal' periods (Maasai – Homewood, 1992a; McCabe et al., 1992; Turkana and Borana – Galvin et al., 1994, Little et al., 1999; Galvin and Little, 1999). Similar average BMI values of 18-19 can be estimated from the data reported for Wodaabe Fulani in Niger (Loutan, 1985). West African Fulani had higher energy intakes, with energy balances and BMIs closer to international averages

(Galvin, 1992). Though this may be more typical for established agropastoral populations with reliable supplies of complementary pastoral and crop foods, those more recently settled through poverty are, not surprisingly, likely to show worse anthropometric status than related populations still in the pastoral sector (Turkana dependent on food aid – van den Boogard, 2002; sedentarising Rendille – Fratkin et al., 2004).

Conditions may rarely be 'normal'. Many populations face prolonged periods of shortage through drought, poverty, raiding or warfare (Keen, 1995; van den Boogard, 2002; Hendrickson et al., 1998). For the last decade or more many Tamasheq have lived as displaced people in refugee camps, with far-reaching effects on diet and nutritional status impacting on an already complicated picture of nutritional status, with extreme contrasts between men and women, noble and slave, resident and refugee (Wagenaar-Brouwer, 1985; Randall, 2001, 2004).

Seasonal variation

Unimodal vs bimodal rainfall climates. West African pastoralists may have a more regular dependence on grain, as the short Sahelian and Saharo-Sahelian rainy seasons mean that milk production is unlikely to feed households year-round. By contrast, equatorial East Africa's bimodal rains, and use of drought-tolerant zebu cattle, make it possible for Maasai and Turkana to rely primarily on milk for more of the year. Pastoralists alternating seasonally between more milk-based and more grain-based diets commonly take in fewer calories during periods of milk consumption. This is partly due to the pastoralist perception of competition between people and calves for cow's milk. The more milk stripped from the cow for human consumption, the less left for the calf, the more fragile its chances of survival and growth, and the worse the long-term prospects for herd increase. Many pastoralist groups have a strong ethos of self-restraint, particularly as regards food intake, forming part of their concept of self- and mutual respect (Fulani *pulaaku*; Maasai: *enkanyit*).

Complementary food sources and energy adequacy. Seasonal variation in pastoral diets depends on the timing of seasons of deficit and surplus in pastoral produce (themselves dependent on rainfall patterns outlined in Chapter 3). Seasonal trade-offs in terms of dietary adequacy or deficit depend on the complementary food types in any one group. Among Ngisonyoka Turkana, the milk diet is supplemented with gathered and hunted foods in uncertain supply. In the wet season, Ngisonyoka caloric intake rises with abundant milk, while in the dry season there is a deficit despite their foraging activities. By contrast the Kenya Maasai are closely tied into local market and exchange systems. During the wet season they may use their own milk production (although this means an energy deficit, and although they could get a higher calorie intake by exchange or sale). In the dry season they trade livestock for grain, and although this may be culturally less valued as a diet, their calorie intake often rises (Grandin, 1988; Nestel, 1985, 1986). Among many Fulani groups wet-season milk consumption rises, while in the dry season stock are traded for grain and calorie intake rises (Galvin, 1992). For transhumant Fulani, this pattern may be partly the product of their wet-season distance from markets and from any chance of sale or exchange for grain.

Seasonal stresses: workload, disease challenge and energy balance. For many pastoralists, late dry-season workloads peak in terms of distances travelled to find grazing and water, and in terms of lopping forage and watering animals from deep wells. It is also the time of least milk availability. For some groups, such as the Ngisonyoka, this means dietary deficit, while for others it means a temporary transition to a higher calorie diet based on cultivated foods (Galvin, 1992). Disease challenge varies substantially, depending on the extent to which the area has year-round malaria transmission or a seasonal increase in vector populations (Schelling, 2002: 64; Hill, 1985). In the latter case, disease challenge peaks in the wet season. Malaria has a particularly marked effect on energy intakes, expenditures and anthropometric status. Other infections (e.g. respiratory diseases) have a different seasonal pattern of occurrence (interacting with vitamin A levels – Schelling, 2002) and can also affect energy balance (Tomkins, 1993). Pastoralist patterns of seasonal energy stress differ from those of farming groups, for whom the worst time is the rains when work loads are high, the previous year's harvest is running out, and the next harvest is not yet in, as well as there being peak challenge from vectors and water-borne diseases (Chambers et al., 1984; Swift, 1983).

Seasonal swings in pastoral food systems, diets and nutritional status are therefore complex and situation-specific. The commonly very low energy intakes, combined with superimposed seasonal swings, mean that for many groups there is a hungry season when they are nutritionally very vulnerable. Galvin (1988) has shown a time lag of several months among the Ngisonyoka between energy balance and anthropometric status. There is a late wet-/ early dry-season period of catch-up (with high food intake, low energy expenditure and low disease challenge translating into weight gain), followed by a progressive decline through the late dry-/ early wet-season, with minimum intakes and maximum workloads and disease transmission.

Growth patterns & anthropometric status

Growth trajectories, height for age and weight for height

Where studied, pastoralists follow NCHS growth standards well up to two years (Nestel, 1989 – Maasai; Galvin and Little, 1999 – Ngisonyoka Turkana; Loutan, 1985 – Fulani; Turkana – Little and Leslie, 1999). There is then a progressive fall-off in weight gain for older children, especially girls aged 5-15 and males aged 5-20. In the mid-teens pre-marriage period, girls' nutritional status improves. The same applies to males in the post-herdboy stage. There is commonly no clear adolescent spurt: adolescents remain below the 50th centile for height until the age of 15 for girls (20 for males). Their average height is thus at or below the bottom 50% for NCHS standards. As young adults, they catch up to rival US adult heights, but mean weight remains at the 5th centile

(Galvin, 1992; Galvin and Little, 1999; Little et al., 1999). Even allowing for pastoral lifestyles, which may involve lower energetic expenditure than farming, the low energy intakes of many pastoral groups suggest significant nutritional vulnerability. Low weights-for-height in African pastoralist under-fives are unlikely to be due to genetic endowment, as subsets of children from high-income families achieve NCHS standards. Genetic endowment certainly plays a part in the highly linear physique of the Dinka and Nuer of south Sudan (cf. Diamond, 1991), but it is clear that low anthropometric status correlates with mortality risk in a wide range of sub-Saharan African populations (Pelletier, 1994), and it is unlikely that pastoralists are displaying a 'thin but healthy' state. Shell-Duncan (1999) found a high proportion of pastoral children both under- or malnourished and also unable to produce a competent immunological response, associated with high incidence and prevalence of malaria, respiratory infections and diarrhoea among Turkana.

Growth outcomes: pastoralists vs cultivators

The more purely pastoral diets are commonly relatively low in energy, high in protein, and balanced in terms of micronutrient intake. Agropastoralist diets tend to be higher in energy, adequate in protein, and balanced in terms of micronutrient intake. By contrast, many cultivator groups with few or no livestock, and no use of milk, may have a rather low protein intake, particularly among children. These patterns are reflected in the patterns of growth seen in the three groups. It has long been recognised that pastoralists tend to be relatively tall compared with cultivators (Galvin, 1992; Galvin and Little, 1999: 189). The Turkana are extremely tall, the Borana and Maasai less so. Dinka pastoralists are among the tallest adults in the world. This is achieved, despite the lack of an adolescent spurt, through prolonged adolescent growth and late maturation. East African pastoralists are taller than cultivators but have low weight for height, while West African Fulani, whether pastoral Wodaabe or more settled Senegalese agropastoralist Fulani, are both taller and heavier than cultivators, with the Fulani approaching US standards (Galvin, 1992). It has been suggested that the enhanced dietary protein (especially at weaning and in childhood) somehow supports more linear growth, with greater final height in pastoralist groups. Farming groups where weanlings suffer a transition to a lower protein diet may be relatively stunted, while agropastoralists with adequate intakes of both protein and energy grow tall and achieve a weight-for-height that matches NCHS standards.

Children of destitute Turkana who had been resettled on irrigation schemes, and for whom school meals were provided, had better intakes and nutritional status than Ngisonyoka pastoral Turkana (Little et al., 1993). However, a longer-term study found that settled Turkana showed shorter stature among adults, compared with nomads; nutritional status was better among children receiving supplementation at school, but worse among schoolchildren who were not supplemented (Campbell et al., 1999; Little and Leslie, 1999). A three-year study of 488 Rendille children under the age of 10 showed that the pastoralist children were heavier and taller than their sedentary contemporaries.

Height and weight for age were a direct function of milk intake; morbidity and poverty were major determinants associated with poor anthropometric status in the sedentary populations (Fratkin et al., 2004).

Although patchy, the data in Table 7.3 give some indications of variation with age/sex class and caste. The term '80-90% weight for height' (WFH) represents the percentage of the sample who fall between 80 and 90% of the international standard weight for a given height. People falling in the 80-90% WFH category are undernourished; those <80% WFH are malnourished. Among the Maasai, two independent studies found around one-fifth of under-fives to be less than 80% weight for height (WFH). Over one-third of under-fives were between 80 and 90% WFH. Adult women showed a similar distribution, but 5-18-year-olds showed even more markedly low anthropometric status (one-third below 80%WFH; over 40% 80-90%WFH). Adolescence is a time of hard physical work and few regular meals for boys who are herding. Girls have similarly high expenditure and low intake. The greatest contrast is between warriors (18-30 yrs) and elders (>30 years). While nearly half the 18-30-year-old men were <80%WFH, fewer than one-fifth of men over 30 were in this very low anthropometric category. Similarly one-third of 18-30-year-olds were in the 80-90% WFH category, as opposed to fewer than one-fifth of men over 30. This pattern reflects the change in lifestyle from herder/warrior (physically active, competing in athletic and

Table 7.3 Percentage of each age/sex class in different weight-for-height categories

WFH	Group	Males 18–30	Adult male	Adult female	5–18yrs	<5yr	Reference
(Annual means from two or more measurements on each sample)							
80-90%	Maasai	35	18	34	42	34 [38]	{Nestel, 89
<80%		45	18	21	34	19 [19]	{[McCabe et al., 92, 97]
Turkana data not available in this form: Little and Leslie, 99							
80-90%	Fulani	–	–	–	–	–	
<80%	(WoDaaBe)	–	–	–	–	9	Loutan, 85:218
80-90%	Fulani AP	–	–	–	48	23	Benefice
<80%		–	–	–	19	4	
80-90%	Fulani AP	–	–	–	–	30	{Wagenaar-
<80%		–	–	–	16	7	{Brouwer, 85
80-90%	Fulani AP	–	40	4	?	79★	
<80%	[Seno-Mango]	–	51	32	?	18★	
80-90%	[Rimaibe]	–	43	42	?	★	
<80%		–	18	10	?	★	
80-90%	Kel Tamasheq	–	–	–	35	14	{Wagenaar-
<80%		–	–	–	5	0	{Brouwer 85:239

★ Seno Mango FulBe and Rimaibe children under-5 pooled

military pursuits, travelling long distances and undertaking complex and dangerous herding tasks) to elder (based at the homestead, controlling but not physically working with the herd, taking a diet with more cultivated foods, waited upon by wife and children).

Table 7.3 shows higher percentages of Maasai than other groups in the lowest anthropometric category (<80% WFH). This is the case for all age/sex classes, particularly under-fives (most groups have fewer than 10% <80% WFH). Pastoral Fulani of the Seno-Mango, however, have large numbers in very low anthropometric categories, similar to or more vulnerable than Maasai in those categories. The only Tamasheq studied show relatively low vulnerability, with no under-fives and few 5-18-year-olds in the <80%WFH, and with >85% of under-fives and 60% of 5-18-year-olds above 90% WFH. Among both the Fulani and the Tamasheq of the Inland Delta of the Niger, the nutritional status of former slaves was better than the average among their former nobles. Tamasheq noble women were above the standard, while many noble men, but no Bella, fell below the 80% cutoff. Only 10-20% adult Rimaibe were in the lowest category, compared with 30-50% among the pastoral Fulani of the Seno Mango. Table 7.3 bears out the expected contrast between more purely pastoral versus agropastoral diets, and underlines the peculiarities of distribution in the Tamasheq system.

Intra-household, socio-economic class and caste variation

Grandin (1988) found no meaningful differences in the dietary energy intake or composition for Maasai households of different wealth. Homewood (1992a) found no difference in dietary energy intakes or anthropometric status of under-5s between Tanzanian and Kenyan Maasai. Members of wealthier pastoralist households do not necessarily show better WFH than poorer households (McCabe et al., 1989, 1997; Homewood, 1992a; Nestel, 1986.1989; Sellen, 2003).

A number of reasons could account for this. Firstly, pastoralist households may include relatively privileged individuals who are lineal descendants of the herd-owner as well as relatively disadvantaged dependants. This tends to produce as much variation within the household as between households and obscures wealth-related differences where these are analysed at the collective household level. Secondly, in many groups there is an obligation to share with visitors and households that may have a temporary shortfall. Milk is a social currency that maintains social networks and ensures reciprocity in time of need. Thirdly, many pastoralist societies have an ethic of self-discipline and self-denial as far as food is concerned (*pulaaku:* Fulani; Maasai - *enkanyit*). To eat more than the bare minimum is seen as 'eating the herd'. People are in competition with calves for milk (Grandin, 1988). A wealthy herd-owner may have a herd producing more milk than does an individual with only a few animals, but it is in the long-term interests of the herd to invest that milk in calf growth and survival rather than satisfying hunger that could be endured (Maasai – Grandin 1988). Finally, household composition is flexible and children or other dependants may go to households which need additional

Table 7.4 Dietary composition and energy intake for wealthy and poor Maasai

Wealth ranking:	<5LU/AE poor	5-13 LU/AE mid	>13 LU/AE rich	mean
% Dietary energy from:				
milk/milk products	63	62	66	64
meat/fat	2	4	4	4
maize	21	20	12	16
sugar	8	8	9	8
other	6	6	9	8
Dietary energy as % recommended dietary intake	70	74	70	70
Calories from milk as % recommended dietary intake	43	46	45	45

Source: Data from Grandin (1988); LU/AE = Livestock units per adult equivalent

labour and have the wherewithal to feed them (Bishop, 2003, 2007).

Among the Tuareg, the cultural ideal attached to milk, and the pastoral ethic, emerge in a different way. Among noble Tuareg, for most of the twentieth century, wealth was displayed by enormously fat womenfolk, force-fed milk, butter and millet to the point where they were so handicapped as to be entirely dependent on their Bella slave women. This expression of prestige through the cultural value of milk and its apportionment created major contrasts in diet and anthropometric status between Tuareg noble women and noble men, and also between Tuareg noble women and Bella slaves (Wagenaar-Brouwer, 1985:235). The calorific value of the diet was if anything generally better for Bella overall, because of their more regular grain intake. However, food entitlements change drastically in times of famine. As milk supplies dwindled, Bella slaves were turned out to support themselves, and noble Tuareg called on settled Bella ex-dependants for grain supplies and hospitality. With long-term climatic downturn and civil disruption, patterns of entitlement and vulnerability have shifted. Many formerly noble Tuareg have lost all their herds and exist as displaced, dispossessed and destitute refugees (Randall, 1988, 2001, 2004). Some former Bella are established as landed farmers with little obligation to Tuareg nobles, while others maintain their ties and provide support. Still others eke out a hand-to-mouth existence, farming and foraging in marginal areas (e.g. Gourma Bella – SSE, 1992).

Livestock per person ratios in evaluating food security

Attempts to evaluate changing patterns of food security in pastoral societies have built on the sorts of livestock per capita calculations set out by Brown

Table 7.5 Alternative systems for summing livestock holdings across species

	Unit	Camel	Cow	Sheep/goat
Galvin 1992 (after FAO, 1967)	TLU	1.25	1.0	0.125
Dahl and Hjort, 1976			0.8	0.1
ILCA, 1981			0.71	0.17
NCDP, 1987	SSU		0.67	0.1
Brown, 1971	SSU	where 1 SSU = 500 kg liveweight		
Thompson, 2002	LE		0.71	0.17

(1971) and Jewell (1980), using standardised units for both livestock and people. Livestock of different species can be summed in a single agro-ecological currency by converting to standard stock units (SSU), or tropical livestock units (TLU) or Livestock Equivalents (LE) (Table 7.5). Each of these systems involves different multipliers, with different implications.

Similarly there are several different standard systems for summing people of different age/sex classes and activity patterns, using a common currency of metabolic equivalents (Table 7.6)

Table 7.6 Systems for summing households as consumer or reference adult units

	Unit	Adult male	Adult female	Adolescent		Infant/child
Sellen, 2003 (after NRC 1989)	Consumer units	1.0	0.76	Boys 4-15 yrs	Girls 4-15 yr	0-3 yrs 0.38
ILCA, 1981	Reference adult	1.0	0.86	M/F 11–15 0.96	M/F 6–10 0.85	0-5 yrs 0.52
Little, 1985	Adult unit	1.0	1.0	M/F 7-14 (or >60) 0.67		<7 yrs 0.25
Homewood & Rodgers, 1991	Adult equivalent	1.0	0.9	M/F 10-14 0.9	M/F 5-9 0.6	2-4 yrs 0.52

These variants illustrate the difficulty of comparing livestock holdings per person across systems, or within a system across time, with different studies using indices calculated in different ways. Nonetheless, some studies have compared average holdings in different systems against estimates of livestock per person necessary to maintain pastoral food systems (Sellen, 2003; Homewood, 1992a, McCabe et al., 1992).

These comparisons suggest three main conclusions. First, there are multiple ways of measuring livestock holdings relative to people dependent on them, and this can be a major source of confusion in making comparisons within or between systems. Second, the measures presented here as mean values mask enormous variation between households in any given area, from those with no livestock at all, to those with very high ratios. Means are notoriously skewed

Table 7.7 Livestock per person ratios for East African pastoralists

	Theoretical minimum	Observed mean ratio	Units/ notes	Reference
	2.5-4.5		SSU/person	Brown, 1971
General	7.1		TLU/person	Jewell, 1980
Barabaig	5		Cattle/capita	Kjaerby, 1979
Borana		3.0	TLU/person	Galvin, 1992
Rendille		3.1	TLU/person	Galvin, 1992
Maasai (Kajiado ranch)		12-16 (pre-1960) 8.3 (1980s)	LE/RA	Grandin, 1988
Maasai (Mara)		8.2 (1990s)	LE/RA	Homewood et al., 2001
Maasai (NCA)		8 (1970)	SSU/AAME	Homewood & Rodgers, 1991
		5 (1977)	SSU/AAME	Homewood et al., 2001
		4.4 (1990s)	LE/RA	Thompson, 2003
Turkana		3.5	TLU/person	Galvin, 1992
Datoga		4.2	LU/AE	Sieff, 1999
		5.7	TLU/AU	Sellen, 2003

far upwards by small numbers of very well-off households. It is really the variation between households, and in particular the long tail of households with few or no livestock, which is important in understanding comparative livelihood implications of change. Furthermore, even for individual households, an aggregate 'household wealth' measure conveys little about the distribution of livestock production between (and therefore relative food security of) different individuals within the household (Sellen, 2003). Third, the absolute value of the ratio (whether across a household, or across a community, or across a population) in itself conveys little about the food security of the group to which it refers. This is both because it conveys little about the production indices of the animals concerned, which will differ depending on herd composition and on local spatial and temporal variation in range ecology, and more importantly, because the absolute value of the ratio conveys little or nothing about the way in which those livestock holdings are being used to support pastoral livelihoods. Are families seeking to live primarily off their animals' produce? How much of that produce – milk, live animals – is being sold or exchanged for cereals? What are the terms of trade (Zaal and Dietz, 1999)? Measures of the livestock per person ratio are most useful as a means of comparing households within a community, or comparing trends within a community across a period of years, but are problematic as a means of comparing across groups or sites, and taken alone give a limited indication of food system or food security.

Food crises & famine

With drought, grain availability drops and prices rise at the same time that livestock lose condition, cease bearing or giving milk, and in many cases die. The vulnerability of pastoralist systems lies in the rapid collapse of the terms of trade for livestock, and the disappearance of milk products, at the very time when income is most needed to buy food (cf. Chapter 3). During such times, pastoral produce is by definition scarce and low-value. What there is may have to be sold to buy more calories in the form of cultivated foods, but is unlikely to fetch much in return. Pastoralists seek alternative sources of food – moving out of the pastoral system to find paid work or if necessary to beg. In a classic study, de Waal (1989a, b) showed that agropastoralists in Darfur dealt with prolonged drought and serious regional famine by voluntarily restricting intake (while protecting children, but not the elderly). They sought alternative sources of income and food, and tried everything to put off having to sell their means of future production (agricultural tools, seed grain) in expectation of the onset of the rains and the return of agricultural possibilities.

Elsewhere, even during good times, many pastoralist groups use supplementary foods by gathering wild plants (Gourma – SSE, 1992 ; Damara – Sullivan, 2005), hunting (Howell et al., 1988; Johnson, 1988) and fishing (eg. Turkana – Sobania, 1988; Broch-Due, 1999; Nuer – Johnson, 1988). Wild foods may be highly valued for the diversity they bring and may carry important cultural connotations (Sullivan 2005) though for some their use is considered a shameful admission of poverty (Buhl, 1999 – Burkina Faso Fulani). As pastoral produce dwindles, particularly where cultivated foods are also in short supply, these complementary foods may gain in importance. Among poor Tamasheq, women would spend a whole day gathering wild grass seeds (*cramcram; fonio* – Randall 1988) so that, winnowed and pounded, they could yield a single meal for the household once in two days. In Namibia, Damara agropastoralists manage the underground nests of harvester ants so that the ants' gleanings can be removed periodically without killing off the colony in the longer term (Sullivan, 2005). Fulani women gather and process the fruit of the *karité* (shea butter nut tree) to extract the butter, valued locally and internationally in cooking, confectionery and cosmetics (Schreckenberg, 1996). They also gather and process *néré*, the fruit of *Parkia biglobosa,* into an essential relish to be used at home or traded in the market.

Fulani women maintain the volume of their milk sales despite seasonal fluctuations in supply by watering down the milk, mixing it with the juice of baobab fruit, or preparing it with cereals so that volumes, prices and incomes remain the same while the product undergoes seasonal change. Schreckenberg (1996) describes a similar sequence with wild products marketed by Fulani women in Bénin, such as the *néré* relish (volumes and prices are kept constant but the product is adulterated with ash to a greater or lesser extent depending on the season). With karité butter and palm oil butter prepared by Fulani women, portions are sold for a constant price but vary seasonally in size. Other fruits (e.g. doum palm; *Boscia senegalensis*; *Balanites aegyptiaca*), roots (e.g. water lily bulbs) and products such as honey from wild beehives are all foods whose perennial value or potential become critically important in times of famine.

Factors other than drought can precipitate famine. Epidemic disease triggered the cataclysmic famine and disruption of the 1890s (Waller, 1988). Eviction from customary resources, whether because of agribusiness (Lane 1996a, b – Barabaig), conservation-induced displacement (Brockington, 2001; West et al., 2006), raiding or warfare (Keen, 1995; Allen, 1996; Kurimoto and Simonse, 1998; de Waal, 2004) are as much a cause of collapse of pastoral production systems and loss of pastoralist food security and livelihoods as any climatic downturn. Often it is the marginalisation and isolation of pastoralist groups, their fragmentation between different hostile neighbouring nation-states, and the suspicions that accrue to them as a result, that both set the scene for their vulnerability to drought-induced famine and also exacerbate its impacts (Galaty and Johnson, 1990; Galaty and Bonte, 1991; Keen, 1995; Johnson, 2003). Recent reviews suggest that predatory raiding has been a major element in precipitating famine among pastoral groups, and that not uncommonly situations attributed to drought (which is politically neutral) can only be understood in terms of deliberate, sometimes state-driven attacks (Hendrickson et al., 1998, Keen, 1995; Johnson, 2003; de Waal, 2004).

This has fundamental implications for the management of aid and famine relief, which generally has to operate with and through national governments (de Waal, 1997). In some cases, pastoralist social networks, long adapted to coping with drought and epidemic, may be sufficiently strong to buffer even prolonged periods of deficit (Seaman and Holt, 1980; McCabe, 2004; Johnson, 1999). Some authors see customary redistribution as better able to manage food shortages than, for example, market and wage systems (Seaman and Holt, 1980). Hill (1988) has argued that, partly as a result of these internal safeguards, the impacts of even apparently drastic Sahelian droughts and famines have been less severe than is widely supposed. He suggests that famine tends to concentrate and make visible high-risk families and individuals, as much as or more than actually creating them. On the other hand, many observers see increasing commercialisation as undermining customary social networks and leaving poorer pastoralists more vulnerable, at the national, regional (Baringo – Homewood, 1994) household and individual level (Talle 1990, Ndagala 1990, 1992b – Monduli). Although large numbers continue within pastoral production systems, the rate of drop-out from these systems suggests the extent to which pastoralist households are vulnerable.

Nutrition & health in pastoralist groups

Nutrition and infection

Malnourished people are more susceptible to infection, because their nutritional status affects their ability to maintain physical and immunological barriers against invasion by and proliferation of pathogens (Ulijascek, 1990; Shell-Duncan et al., 1999). Chronically low anthropometric status among pastoralists is probably associated with vulnerability to TB and respiratory infections. Where there is still a milk component to the diet, this may confer some protection (high circulating vitamin A levels are protective against respiratory infection). However, a number of pastoralist populations seem to have at least seasonally extremely low vitamin A, and a concomitantly high incidence of respiratory disease (Schelling, 2002; Little and Leslie, 1999). Until recently it was thought that low nutritional status might also limit the most serious effects of malaria infection, particularly the 'stickiness' and often lethal clumping of red blood cells commonly caused by *falciparum* malaria (Edirisinghe, 1986). Recent reviews show the complexity of interaction between malaria and nutritional state, and the dimensions on which poor nutritional status generally exacerbates the disease (Shankar, 2000). It has also been suggested that a diet relatively high in pastoral produce, and relatively low in grain, may protect against malaria infections, because pastoral produce is deficient in the para-amino benzoic acid (PABA) which the *plasmodium* malaria organism needs to grow and multiply (Edirisinghe, 1986; Shankar, 2000). However, malarial incidence among pastoral Turkana (Shell-Duncan et al., 1999), Fulani and Aran cattle-keepers (Schelling, 2002), together with seasonal, interannual, and household or individual variation in consumption of pastoral produce, suggests that non-dietary methods of managing malaria are far more important.

Lactose intolerance

Adults of most populations have low levels of the intestinal enzyme lactase, necessary to digest the disaccharide milk sugar lactose (Stinson, 1992). High lactase activity is common to all infants (evolutionarily adapted to use a milk diet) but as children grow they commonly lose these high levels of lactase and with it the ability to digest and absorb fresh milk. With low lactase levels, individuals drinking fresh milk or eating other products high in lactose get severe intestinal discomfort with bloating, flatulence and diarrhoea. In a small number of populations, including several sub-Saharan pastoralist groups alongside Northern European and Middle Eastern groups, high levels of the enzyme are maintained throughout adolescence and adult life, and individuals with this trait can easily digest and absorb lactose.

There has been considerable controversy over the origin of this genetic difference. Most authors relate it to some combination of the selective advantages to pastoralist and/or dairying groups of being able to use fresh milk as a food. It is also possible that lactose tolerance has been selected for among more northerly groups because of the physiological corollary of increased intestinal absorption of calcium (as effected by vitamin D). Vitamin D is normally synthesised in the skin under the action of sunlight, and its regulation of calcium uptake and metabolism is essential to prevent rickets. Northern European groups in low insolation environments, and using insulating clothing, are at risk of vitamin D deficiency and rickets. This is thought to be one of the driving forces behind the loss of (ancestrally dark) skin pigmentation in European populations. Lactose-tolerant individuals in such a population might have a selective advantage with their additional calcium-absorption capacity. Finally, it is possible that the genetic polymorphism for lactose tolerance was established long before animals were domesticated or milked, and that it has persisted and spread in some populations as a result of random genetic drift effects unrelated to milk consumption (see Stinson 1992, for review). A comparative phylogenetic approach that takes account of the shared ancestry of many of the lactose-tolerant populations suggests that the ability for adults to continue to digest lactose evolved after the emergence of dairying and not in relation to high latitude vitamin D requirements (Holden and Mace, 1997).

Lactose tolerance and its underlying lactase activity are common in many pastoralist groups, but others (including the Maasai) appear to have little if any lactose tolerance. Even where lactose tolerance is common, it is present as a polymorphism, and a proportion of individuals in the population are unable to use fresh milk without discomfort. Most pastoral groups, however, make milk products such as sour milk, yoghurt and/or cheese in which the milk sugar lactose is altered by fermentation to more digestible nutrients.

High animal-fat diets and CHD

It is a common myth that pastoralist groups such as the Maasai have a special physiology enabling them to live off a diet high in animal fats without suffering the atheroma build-up and cardiovascular complications of a high cholesterol intake (e.g. Casimir, 1991). The review of diets here has made it clear that pastoralists are not using foods high in animal fats as commonly as has been assumed. Secondly, pastoralists are commonly living off around 70% of internationally recommended dietary energy intakes on average, and high proportions of individuals have very low anthropometric status. This means that, even if their diets are in relative terms high in animal products, in absolute terms their energy intakes are so low relative to their expenditures that they are not likely to be able to accumulate the atheromatous deposits associated with high-fat and high-animal-product diets in Western populations.

Change in pastoralist food systems

Shifting trade-offs in pastoral food production, consumption, sale and exchange

Simple economic terms and analyses help make clear the shifting trade-offs for households in different economic and ecological circumstances and help structure analysis of household decisions as to whether to sell, consume or store milk, meat and other pastoral produce. (see Box 7.1)

While the 'use value' of livestock (whether for milk, draught, manure, wealth store, as social currency underpinning networks of reciprocation, risk-spreading and patron-client relations, or some combination of these) exceeds their exchange value in the market, pastoralists are not surprisingly unwilling to trade (Behnke, 1985; Sikana et al., 1993). As exchange values rise in relation to use value so pastoralists reorient towards markets. This shift may be because of an improvement in the monetary terms of trade; because the cash profits to

---

Box 7.1 Economic values of milk for consumption, exchange or investment in the herd

- A use value: the value of the milk (or other pastoral produce) when consumed directly, both for its nutritional value and also its worth as a social currency in creating and maintaining networks of reciprocity and obligation
- Exchange value: calorific or monetary terms of trade, which change with seasonal supply and demand
- Growth value: the exchange value of milk converted into calf growth.

---

be had and the possibility of low-paid hired labour begin to outweigh the worth of social networks maintained by milk and livestock as social currency; because pressing cash needs force pastoralists to sell; or because calorific terms of trade make sale of slaughter animals or pastoral produce, and purchase of cereals with the proceeds, a more efficient way of meeting food needs. Pastoralists are continually weighing up whether to consume milk directly, sell or exchange it for cereals, or invest milk into calf growth so that animals may be produced for sale (Sikana et al., 1993). Pastoralist diets and food systems change accordingly on a seasonal basis, through time, and between different households in different economic, ecological and sociocultural circumstances.

Other things being equal, the use value of milk decreases as milk production becomes more abundant. It may do so more rapidly for smaller households with less labour (meaning both fewer people to maintain on milk, as well as fewer to process the surplus milk into some less perishable product). When exchange value equals use value, milk is exchanged or sold rather than consumed. The thresholds shift with the season and with household wealth, leading to different combinations of outcomes: milk may all be consumed, may be consumed in the wet season and sold in the dry, may be sold in both, or left for the calf. Any one pastoralist household will use one or more of these strategies depending on the conditions of supply, demand and the terms of trade as well as the type of labour needed and the options open for supplying that need. For households using milk as a dietary staple and maintaining their domestic and herding labour requirements by incorporating adopted, fostered or boarded children and protégés into the household as quasi-kin, milk is worth more as a valued food with strong social significance, and it is all consumed. In such systems milk may be given, never sold, as experienced by the author in remote parts of Tanzania Maasailand (Homewood and Rodgers, 1991). Where market demand for milk is high, for example where dry-season prices mean that household food needs are more readily met by trading milk for cereals, exchange value effectively exceeds use value and milk may be sold or exchanged, as is now the case for many Kenya Maasai communities (Grandin, 1988; Nkedianye et al., forthcoming) and some Fulani (Galvin, 1992; Buhl and Homewood, 2000). With the relative abundance of milk in the wet season, prices decline. Wealthier pastoralists may cease trading milk in the wet season as prices fall, preferring to consume their milk themselves, while poorer families must continue to exploit the calorific terms of trade to meet their food needs through grain, despite the relatively low prices fetched by their dairy products (Sikana et al., 1993). Where exchange values are consistently high at least some milk is sold year round, as is the case for many pastoral Fulani systems (Stenning, 1958; Hopen, 1958; Buhl, 1999; Buhl and Homewood, 2000), as well as more fundamentally market-oriented Fulani systems (e.g. Waters-Bayer, 1985 for Nigeria), and dairying systems elsewhere (Somalia – Herren, 1990; Little, 1994).

In practice decisions are made on still more complex grounds. In a study of three different sub-ethnic groups of Fulani in Burkina Faso, the decision as to whether or not to sell depended on supply – though prices were high in the dry season, many households simply had no milk to sell. The location of the camp at any given time influenced access to markets, and some transhumant moves were primarily determined by this consideration rather than by grazing and water resources (Hampshire, 1998; Homewood, 1997). Finally, milk selling could only be carried out by women whose age, parity and socio-economic status made this appropriate (Buhl, 1999; Buhl and Homewood, 2000). Decisions depended on the circumstances of individual households. It is seen as inappropriate for wives of well-off men to trade in the market, and these households will not sell milk though they have enough to do so. By contrast, poor households with little milk are driven to exploit the calorific terms of trade by selling or exchanging that milk for grain. Wealthy pastoralist households with many animals and a lot of milk consume part of their own milk production, while selling or exchanging part when terms of trade are profitable and also milking relatively less from relatively fewer animals so as to invest more into calf growth for live animal sales (Maasai – Grandin, 1988). They are able to move in and out of markets as terms of trade fluctuate. They can choose to invest less in social networks and to hire labour at a relatively low cost, rather than incorporating labour as additional household members to be fed milk from the herd.

Similar trade-offs apply for meat. Where pastoralists' needs are best met by selling animals, milk offtake for sale or consumption is commonly reduced or ceases altogether. The resulting improved survival and growth of calves is used as the basis of an increased animal offtake for market (wealthier Kenya Maasai – Grandin 1988; settled orthodox Islamic FulBe in Cameroon – Burnham, 1975; Burnham and Last, 1994). Conversion of milk to calf growth represents a relatively low 'sale' price, as around 9kg milk are necessary to produce around 1kg calf weight (Bekure et al., 1991), not all of which is saleable meat, and the value must be further discounted by the time taken for the animal to reach marketable size and by the possibility that it will die before it can be sold. Poor or wealthy, commercialisation results in a decline in the use of milk in the diet, whether because of the need to exploit the calorific terms of trade or because of maximising calf survival and growth.

Pastoral food systems and development

From the 1960s on, development interventions in pastoralist systems have primarily focused on trying to intensify livestock production to boost milk and meat offtakes. Sub-Saharan African livestock have among the lowest production indices in the world, and improving their performance was seen as the key to all other forms of development throughout African rangelands. Upgrading livestock meat and milk production was to produce food, generate wealth and encourage the settlement of previously mobile pastoralists, who would then be better able to access food, health and education as well as generally coming within easier reach of the government administration. Between the 1960s and 1980s hundreds of millions of dollars went into range and livestock development programmes throughout pastoral areas of sub-Saharan Africa, with little improvement in livestock production or pastoralist development in general or in pastoralist food systems in particular (Homewood, 1992a). Development attempts which emphasised intensification of pastoralist livestock production systems have commonly meant a change in the ratio of livestock to people (Chapters 3 and 9). Ultimately this is brought about by a movement of former pastoralists out of the system, at best through temporary or permanent labour migration, and at worst as displaced people dispossessed of their livelihoods (Chapter 9). Increasing commercialisation of pastoral produce affects its availability to the wider pastoralist population through social networks of sharing. Studies in Monduli (Ndagala, 1990, 1992b) and Kenya group ranches have suggested a decline in the availability of milk to be shared, and potentially increasing vulnerability (Talle, 1988, 1990). Management of milk can be central to women's social and economic as well as cultural roles (Talle, 1990). In many though by no means all cases, pastoralist women control the cash from milk sales (see Chapter 5; Buhl and Homewood, 2000; Grandin, 1988; Nestel, 1986). In some cases this means that they can access new and shop-bought foods. In other cases women may lose control of formerly shared resources of milk production, animals, and land to male heads of household (Hodgson, 1999, 2000a, 2001), and women and children may be made destitute by alcoholic husbands.

More recently the whole basis of development in pastoralist societies has been reassessed. Post-Independence development programmes emphasised high-tech, capital-intensive interventions based on exotic livestock breeds, Western-style commercial ranching and intensive dairy production. Food security is now recognised as a priority goal of equal importance for development in pastoral systems (Chapter 9).

8

African Pastoralist Demography*

SARA RANDALL

This chapter examines the evidence for a characteristic African pastoralist demographic regime by first considering different theories about pastoralist demography, followed by a detailed examination of the key demographic parameters: fertility, nuptiality, mortality and migration.

Much of the literature on pastoralist demography is somewhat confused because the terms pastoralist and nomad are often used interchangeably. Many theories about pastoralist demography are in fact theories about the demography of nomadic populations, and many of the demographic characteristics of pastoralists may be a direct function of their mobility rather than consequences of herding animals. There are also pastoralist populations who are either semi- or totally sedentary, often with some agriculture integrated into their production system. The boundaries become very blurred about who is a pastoralist. Is the man from a traditional cultivating population who has 20 goats and a cow a pastoralist? Is the man from a traditionally nomadic pastoralist group no longer a pastoralist when all his animals die in a drought? Such definitional problems make an examination of the demography of contemporary pastoralists difficult, especially because over the last 40 years increasing numbers of previously agricultural specialists have acquired animals (Toulmin, 1992) and former pastoralists have taken up agriculture (Fratkin and Roth,

* This chapter would never have been written without many discussions and debates on pastoralist demography with Kate Hampshire and Ernestina Coast. By deciding that they too were interested in these issues and by committing themselves to months of discomfort, bad food, illness, loneliness and exhaustion in order to collect demographic data under difficult field conditions they have contributed substantially to the ideas and the results presented here.

All Tuareg / Tamasheq studies discussed in the chapter were undertaken by the author. Studies carried out in 1981 and 1982 were commissioned by the International Livestock Centre for Africa (ILCA) and were funded by ILCA, Population Council and an SSRC studentship. The 2001 repatriated refugee study was financed by ESRC (grant R000238184) and undertaken in collaboration with ISFRA, Bamako.

2005). In considering evidence for the demography of pastoral populations, we focus here on studies that have analysed demographic dynamics in particular ethnic groups renowned for being pastoralists, even if not all members of these groups actually own animals. Where the nomadic aspect of the lifestyle is important, statements will be qualified.

Interest in the demography of nomadic pastoralists stems from two main sources. African colonial administrators were interested in the demography of their subject populations in order to extract taxes and labour. Colonial preconceptions about nomadic demography in both Francophone and Anglophone Africa coloured and continue to influence how nomads' demographic behaviour is perceived (Coast, 2001a). Nomads were generally believed to have low fertility and high mortality and were often associated with a high prevalence of sexually transmitted diseases. These ideas were rarely based on reliable data (sometimes on no data at all), and reflect the general colonial mistrust of these populations with this alien mobile lifestyle. Apparently low population growth rates may simply have reflected the inability of colonial administrators to find and count these elusive people who were adept at concealing both animals and people. The general idea that nomads have low fertility persists today.

Evolutionary anthropologists focus on nomadic pastoralism as an intermediate state between hunter-gatherers and settled farmers. According to Pennington and Harpending (1993; 102) '*the goal of finding a relationship between subsistence regime and the fertility and mortality of groups has been at the core of much population research in anthropology*'. The intensity of the production system is thought to impact on population growth through differential exploitation of natural resources, population densities which can support such production systems and different labour demands (Campbell and Wood, 1988; Bentley et al., 1993). The general expectation is that hunter-gatherers have the lowest population growth rates and settled cultivators the highest, with nomadic pastoralists intermediate. Several cross-cultural studies have examined this issue, encountering substantial problems because of diverse data collection methods, small sample sizes, different outcome indices and different periods of data collection. Few conclusive patterns emerge.

Few demographers are interested in the demographic dynamics of contemporary pastoralist populations because such populations are generally small national minorities, difficult to study and not appropriate domains for studying the dominant issues in demographic research. In fact, Guilmoto's (1997) study of migration in the Senegal River Valley excluded transhumant migrations '*because they are a different sort of thing altogether*' – a statement which typifies the general attitudes to pastoralists in demographic literature.

Data quality

In assessing any general account of pastoralist demography, data quality is a key theme, and nomadism becomes a major issue. Most contemporary nomadic pastoralists live in marginal arid areas, unsuitable for agriculture and often far removed from capital cities and areas of high population density and good infrastructure. Such environments can support only a very low population density which itself makes data collection difficult and expensive, and population mobility makes sampling virtually impossible (see République du Niger 1966 for attempts at different ways of sampling nomads). Isolation and underinvestment in services mean that nomadic pastoral populations usually have low levels of school attendance and literacy and poor knowledge of ages and dates. Agesets and the use of local event calendars can help improve dates but are time-consuming.[1] On a national scale most pastoral nomads are minorities, exceptions being Mauritania and Somalia, and often perceive themselves to be subject to a range of political and economic discriminations. This makes them mistrustful and wary of responding to questionnaires about numbers of people or animals, since previous experience has led them to associate such studies with taxation. Hence there are far fewer demographic data available for nomadic pastoral populations compared with sedentary groups, and those data that do exist tend to be for small communities and of relatively poor quality.

The extent of this data-deficit on a continent-wide scale can be evaluated when we consider that Kenya, probably the country with the best demographic data in sub-Saharan Africa and many nomadic pastoralist populations, excluded the 7 northerly districts (where most Kenyan pastoralists apart from Maasai live) from all DHS surveys up until 2000. Things have changed, and the national sampling frame developed from the 1999 census now includes clusters from the whole country, although more mobile and isolated groups are still more likely to be excluded from surveys. Sample sizes for pastoralist groups remain small and, with the exception of ethnicity, the questions do not allow pastoralists to be identified for analysis (CBS et al., 2004).

In Mali, a 1960-61 national sample survey only sampled from the 5 southern regions, excluding the then 6th region (now Tombouctou, Gao and Kidal Regions) where the majority of Mali's pastoral nomads live (République du Mali 1961): in 1987 and 1996 the DHS only took small urban samples from the regional capitals of Gao and Tombouctou regions and no rural sample (Mali, 1989, 1998). The Mauritanian World Fertility Survey only covers the 30% of the population who were sedentary in 1976, not the 70% nomadic pastoralists. In Tanzania the 25% research sample from the 2002 census (and the 10% sample from the 1988 census), for which detailed individual and household data were collected, does not include the migratory population, which includes nomadic pastoralists, fishing camps, miners and the homeless (National Bureau of Statistics, 2003). There are numerous other examples from both Demographic and Health Surveys and censuses. Either nomadic groups are excluded or data collected do not allow pastoralists to be identified separately. Hence, the few demographic studies of mobile pastoralist populations tend to be small community studies undertaken by anthropological demographers,

---

[1] Events themselves are often difficult to date. One Tuareg knew he was born the year his uncle was bitten by a snake!

rather than representative samples of larger populations. These community studies form the basis for most of the discussion below.

A pastoralist demographic regime?

Why might one expect pastoralists to have a different demographic regime from agriculturalists or from urban populations? Various theories have been put forward, though not all distinguish clearly between nomads and pastoralists. A particular nomad demography was apparently confirmed by Henin's research in the Sudan (Henin, 1968, 1969), focusing on two ethnic groups, Kawalha and Baggara, and the comparative fertility of different sub-populations who were nomadic to varying degrees. Henin demonstrated that the more nomadic groups had lower fertility than the sedentary populations, although his samples were smaller for more nomadic groups and the data quality evidently poorer. Henin concluded that there were intrinsic aspects of being nomadic which hindered reproduction, but he did not consider the nature of the pastoral economy.

Four main themes emerge relating to either pastoralism or nomadic pastoralism, and to specific demographic regimes.

Livestock demography

For continual economic well-being pastoralist human population growth cannot exceed herd growth, as Stenning (1958) identified in considering the developmental cycle of Fulani households and the need for adequate livestock numbers to allow new independent households to form. Spencer (1973) showed how, for Kenyan Rendille camel herders, younger sons in households with inadequate numbers of slow breeding camels left the group and became Ariaal goat herders. Such transformations, along with out-migration, are one way of coping with imbalance between people and resources; another may be lower population growth by controlling fertility.

Labour requirements

In subsistence populations the future household labour supply is largely ensured through reproduction. In extensive agricultural production systems where land is not limited, the increasing returns from more labour inputs has contributed to pro-natalist regimes with wives and children welcomed to build up a household's economic and political power. For pastoralists, once a certain minimum labour force has been achieved, economies of scale mean that more labourers do not necessarily lead to increased production (Swift, 1977): more children mean more consumers and herd division, although labour requirements do depend somewhat on herd-management strategies and herd composition. Turkana mixed herds and herding strategies are very labour-intensive, with labour shortages a production constraint, and women contributing substantially to daily herd management. In contrast, West African

Tuareg not only have less intensive herd management, but also, until recently, a dependent servile labour force (Bella) who did much of the herding and domestic work, further reducing any economic advantages of many children. High-status Tuareg did not need children because they had access to dependent Bella labour: Bella children just became labour for others. Another pastoralist group with low labour requirements are the Herero whose cattle management has been described as 'laissez-faire' (Vivelo, 1977 cited in Pennington and Harpending, 1993)

Once pastoralists diversify into other activities such as agriculture or seasonal labour migration, the need for several adult men in a household becomes critical if the herds are to be managed effectively throughout the year, and substantial numbers of cooperating adults are a significant advantage (Hampshire and Randall, 1998,1999; White, 1986). Animals need to be tended throughout the year and although intensity of labour fluctuates by season, pastoralist households with only one adult male cannot execute other income-generating activities alongside herd production.

Environmental stress

Environmental stress has been claimed to influence pastoralist demography. Contemporary pastoralists, especially nomadic groups, generally live in marginal, arid areas far from population centres. These areas are harsh, food availability and disease fluctuate seasonally and health services are rare. Livestock herding exposes people to accidents and infections and many pastoralist populations practise risky raiding (Gray et al., 2002). One could expect high mortality from accidents and seasonally variable patterns of birth and death, although low population density limits transmission of infectious diseases (Loutan and Paillard, 1992).

Isolation and marginalisation

Spatial marginalisation, coupled with the political marginalisation faced by many pastoral populations, may have other impacts on contemporary demography. Mobile, sparsely populated groups rarely receive the same health-care provision as those in settled, more central communities. Dispensaries are small, ill-equipped, often unstaffed and difficult to access (Sheik-Mohamed and Velema, 1999). Similarly, although family planning and contraception are now widely available in many African countries, they are much less likely to be accessible to remote pastoralist populations. Whereas, in the past, the harsh environment and isolation may have had direct impacts on both fertility and mortality through direct stresses, now it is the relative lack of health-care services which is more likely to influence pastoralist demography.

In examining the three major demographic parameters, fertility, mortality and migration, each of these four influences will be kept in mind and emphasised where appropriate.

Table 8.1 Fertility estimates for pastoralist populations

Population	nomadic/ sedentary (sed.) / semi-nomadic (s-n) pastoralist/ agropastoralist	Data quality and age reporting **p**oor **m**edium **g**ood	TFR or completed parity		Sample size (aged 15–49 unless otherwise stated)	Source and comments
			TFR	CP		
Tuareg						
Delta Mali 1981 (TFR: 1976-81)	nomad / past.	p/m	5.4	5.2	1265 women	Randall, 1984 (TFR reworked
Gourma Mali 1981 (TFR: 1976-81)	nomad / past.	p/m	5.6	5.3	1440 women	using original data)
Mema Mali 2001 (TFR 1996-00)	some nomads / past. + other	m/g	5.4	5.7	1888 women 15-54	
Fulani						
Delta Mali 1982	Sed. + nomad	m	7.1	6.4	1615 women	Hill, 1985
Seno Mali 1982	agropast.	m	6.6	7.1	1214 women	
Transhumant Fulbe Mali Delta 1988	transh. past.	v. small no.	8.8	8.9	55 women <45 9 women >40	Marriott, 1993: (pp. 68, 72)
Seno Mali 1989						
Fulbe	s-n agropast.	small no.	6.7		87 women	Castle, 1992
Rimaibe	sed. cultivators	small no.	8.1		94 women	Table 3.1
N.Burkina Faso 1995						
Liptaako	sed agropast.	m	6.4	7.2	395 women	
Gaobe	s-n agropast.	m	6.3	6.7	570 women	Hampshire,
Djelgobe	nomadic past.	m	9.2	7.8	302 women	1998
Mauritania nomads						
1965	nomadic	m	5.6		ns v. large sample	Traoré, 1984
1976	nomadic	m	6.1		118,390 women 12-49	
Turkana						
1985-90	nomadic	good	7.1		217 women	Leslie et al, 1999
	long settled	small no.	6.4		66 women	Campbell et al., 1999
Nakwamoru	long settled	small no.	5.5		60 women 45+	Brainard, 1991 (p. 113)
Nakwamoru	recently nomadic	small no.	6.8		28 women 45+	
Maasai (1998)						
Kenya	s-n agropast	m	7.8		594 women	Coast, 2000:
Kenya	s-n past.	m	8.3		807 women	(p. 185)
Tanzania	s-n agropast	m	6.9		1701 women	
Tanzania	s-n past.	m	4.4		208 women	
Rendille						
non –*sepaade*	sedentary	indirect	6.04		111 women	Roth, 1993
sepaade	sedentary	from men	3.69		101 women	
Baggara (1961-2)						
Muglad	settled nomads	m	4.6	5.5	335 women	Henin, 1968
Baggara	nomadic	p	3.5	4.6	1157 women	

Table 8.1 cont.

Population	nomadic/ sedentary (sed.) / semi-nomadic (s-n) pastoralist/ agropastoralist	Data quality and age reporting **p**oor **m**edium **g**ood	TFR or completed parity TFR	CP	Sample size (aged 15–49 unless otherwise stated)	Source and comments
Kawalha (1961–2)						
Gezira	sed.	m		6.1	1027 women	Henin, 1968
Managil	recently settled	m		5.4	878 women	
Blue Nile						
nomads	nomads	p	3.6	4.9	733 women	
Datoga 1987–9	s-n	m		6.9	102 post-menopausal women	Borgerhoff-Mulder, 1992
Toposa 1984	agro-past.	?		6.7	not stated	Roth, 1994
Gabbra 1993	nomadic camel pastoralists	?	5.89		1142 women direct birth histories	Mace & Sear, 1996 underreporting of dead children?
Herero 1909-56	sedentary	p?	2.65		611 birth histories for all periods combined Retrospective reconstructed fertility	Pennington & Harpending, 1993
1957-66	pastoralists	p-m?	3.98			
1967-76		g	5.41			
1977-86		g	7.02			

Fertility

Low pastoral nomad fertility is the most persistent theme throughout accounts of pastoralist demography, reinforced by Henin's comparative Sudanese studies (Henin, 1968, 1969). In looking at available data on fertility it is essential to consider issues of data quality and, if there is evidence of low fertility, how this is achieved. Although pastoralist populations may have used traditional forms of contraception, we have no evidence of effective medicinal fertility control. Thus, if they do have lower fertility than expected, we assume that it is achieved through the action of other proximate determinants of fertility: marriage, spousal separation, involuntary sterility, breastfeeding and serious energetic stress being the most likely candidates.

In those groups for which we have both completed fertility and Total Fertility there are substantial differences between the two, pointing to data problems and/or considerable interannual fluctuations in fertility. Compared with other populations worldwide (Wilson, 2001), these pastoralist groups all have relatively high fertility (Table 8.1), with three exceptions: early Herero

Total Fertility Rates where retrospective and indirect data collection suggest some underreporting, Henin's two nomadic Sudanese populations, and Rendille *sepaade* women (see below). None of these populations have been exposed to contemporary family planning campaigns and modern contraception, and most have very low levels of female education. Compared with non-contracepting agricultural populations, there is no obvious pattern of variation, and there is no systematic effect of nomadism. In Sudan, the more nomadic Baggara and Kawahla had lower fertility. In Burkina Faso, more nomadic Fulani had higher fertility. In a dual-country study of Maasai (Coast 2000), more nomadic pastoral Maasai in Kenya had higher fertility than agro-pastoral women; the opposite was true for Tanzania. In Mali, Tuareg in the early 1980s had much lower fertility than sedentary Bambara farmers: in 2001 a restudy of the same Tuareg population, many of whom had sedentarised, showed no fertility differences between sedentary and mobile Tuareg, but fertility was lower than for other rural Malian populations (Randall, 2004).

The principal theme of contemporary pastoralist fertility is that these populations remain natural fertility populations. This is a function not of pastoralism *per se*, but of the fact that contemporary pastoral (nomadic) populations are now among the most marginalised in the modern political economy, with low levels of schooling, poor access to information and services and little incentive to change, and these characteristics have most impact on their demographic regimes. Nevertheless, there are subtle aspects of fertility which may be related to a pastoral economy and the environments in which it is practised.

Seasonal stress

Leslie and Fry (1989) use reproductive histories of Turkana women to examine environmental influences on fertility. Their detailed data allow them to look at seasonal patterns of birth and conception which show a peak of conceptions at the end of the wet season and in the early dry season – the period corresponding to peak milk production and nutritional intake – although they point out that because conception is a probabilistic event, this coincidence may be '*a fortuitous product of the distribution of waiting times with a return to fecundity a few months earlier*'. No other pastoralist dataset has sufficiently accurate timing of events to allow for an examination of birth and conception seasonality but, since most groups experience similar fluctuations in food availability and energy expenditure, it is likely that most will experience similar seasonal stresses. The Turkana data are also sufficiently accurate to be able to calculate past fertility rates, and the authors say that, in periods of good rainfall and animal production, fertility is higher than in poor periods. This may also be true for other populations and could explain the extraordinarily high fertility observed for the Burkina Djelgobe Fulani population in the year preceding the survey (Hampshire, 1998). There is some evidence for Malian Tuareg of a deficit of births in 1988 (1987 had very poor rainfall), followed by an excess of births in 1989 which could be a function of both a catch-up of delayed births and an extremely good rainy season in 1988 (Randall, 2004).

Sexually transmitted diseases and infertility

Despite little concrete evidence, pastoralists are rumoured to suffer badly from sexually transmitted diseases, said to be one of the reasons for high levels of infertility and subsequent low population growth rates and low fertility (though as shown above this low fertility itself is a myth). The perception that Maasai had a serious problem with STDs was strong in the British colonial period (Coast, 2001). In Mali in the 1980s many people believed that Tuareg had a problem with syphilis (they did, but it was endemic syphilis, not sexually transmitted syphilis). Pennington and Harpending (1993) interpret the slow Herero population growth before 1950 and the fast subsequent growth as a consequence of the beneficial effects of antibiotics on STDs and infertility. They cite various forms of evidence to reinforce their interpretation that the Herero were part of the African low fertility belt. However, the small sample sizes for the early years, the indirect data collection, and the age-specific fertility rates which are lower for every age group further back in time suggest that the effect of STDs may be somewhat exaggerated. Henin cites clinic-based data on venereal disease, with 11% of women saying they had had a venereal disease and 20% saying their husband had (Henin, 1969:188, but Henin explains that many other diseases are interpreted by nomadic women as syphilis). In a self-selected sample examined by a gynaecologist in one of his study sites, of 130 women interviewed 98 complained of sterility or repeated abortion, 26 had syphilis and 17 signs of gonorrhoea. None of these studies were properly designed epidemiological studies.

It is plausible that this frequent association of nomads with sexually transmitted disease is just part of the social marginalisation and moral disdain with which such mobile groups are treated by the sedentary majority. Henin (1969: 189) mentions the 'relaxation of sexual morals especially amongst unmarried men and women'. Humans have a long tradition of condemning, and treating as dirty, diseased and inferior, groups who behave differently from them: in Europe gypsies and Roma have long been despised and perceived to be dirty and disease-ridden. Mobile populations in much of Africa suffer the same attitudes. Physical mobility may be associated in people's minds with sexual mobility and therefore with sexually transmitted disease. However, there are few epidemiological studies demonstrating that nomads are disproportionately affected by STDs. Clinical records in Turkana show little indication of venereal disease (Campbell et al., 1999) and there is certainly no objective reason why pastoralists should be more susceptible than non-pastoralists, except that contemporary groups are less likely to receive treatment for the reasons outlined earlier. The idea that production mobility leads necessarily to sexual mobility is absurd.

Sexual networking and infertility

There are probably as many patterns of sexual networking as there are different pastoral populations. Some groups, at least traditionally, did have patterns of sexual behaviour which other groups may have found unacceptable, but extensive networking is by no means a ubiquitous feature of pastoralist society. The two populations with the lowest recorded levels of infertility (Maasai and Turkana) are in fact those for whom pre-marital and extra-marital sexual activity are most acceptable. Pre-pubertal Maasai girls have considerable sexual freedom, but after menarche they are circumcised and married. The nature of the ageset system means that a married woman may legitimately have sexual relations with other members of her husband's ageset, although all children belong to the husband (Coast, 2000). Turkana marriage is a long-drawn-out affair with a substantial number of children born outside marriage (Dyson-Hudson et al., 1998). Their pro-natalist attitudes mean that such children are welcomed into their mother's family.

Hampshire's study of Northern Burkinabe fertility in three Fulani subgroups with different degrees of mobility and dependence on pastoralism demonstrates the complexities of trying to understand the relationship between fertility, infertility and pastoralism. Here, the populations which are least mobile and least pastoralist have slightly higher levels of infertility, both primary and secondary (Hampshire and Randall, 2000). It is thought that this may be a consequence of high levels of seasonal male labour migration to the Ivory Coast among the less nomadic groups, with consequent changed sexual networks. It is difficult for nomadic pastoralists to participate in seasonal labour migration because herd management is a year-round activity with no slack season. This behavioural pattern contributes to the lower fertility observed in the Liptaako and Gaobe populations (Table 8.1).

Malian Tuareg in the 1970s and 1980s did have higher levels of infertility and secondary sterility than neighbouring agricultural populations (Randall, 1996). Unlike the Burkinabe Fulani, this is probably not a consequence of labour migration which was rare at that time. Many of the women with no children had never married, but even within marriage there were higher levels of infertility than expected. It was thought this might be related to the substantial female obesity subsequent to forcefeeding which occurred for some high-status women, although there are no data to link the phenomena, and in the recent 2001 Tuareg re-study ever-married women maintained high levels of infertility for younger women, despite the abandonment of force-feeding (Randall, 2004).

Henin claims that lower fertility and much infertility amongst Kawalha and Baggara women are due to miscarriages and the general hardship of nomadic life as well as STDs (see above). Apart from the somewhat unrepresentative and unreliable evidence for STDs, he has little data to back up his conclusions, and the apparently low fertility may also be a function of poorer data quality.

Although several of the sub-groups in Table 8.2 do have slightly high levels of infertility, there is no consistent pattern associated with pastoralism. It is possible that many of the differences in infertility are actually a consequence of reporting errors and selection bias. Although most Tuareg want some children, unmarried individuals and childless married people are not considered particularly anomalous or problematic people; they are fully integrated into daily life. This is not the case for Fulani and Maasai for whom childlessness is a major social problem for both men and women, and people will go to

Table 8.2 Percentages of women reporting no live births (primary sterility)

Population	Percentage sterile	Number of women	Comments	Source
Herero cohorts				
1894-1921	12.0	92	includes	Pennington &
1922–31	7.2	65	retrospective	Harpending,
1932–41	5.9	82	data on	1993
			dead women	
Maasai			Coast suggests	Coast, 2000
Kenya 30-39	2.7	293	infertility is	
40-49	0.9	213	underreported	
50-59	2.2	93	especially in	
60+	5.8	103	Tanzania because	
Tanzania			children fostered	
30-39	0.8	486	by infertile	
40-49	1.0	311	women were	
50-59	0	224	classified as theirs	
60+	6.6	106		
Datoga	3.0	102	post-menopausal	Borgerhoff-Mulder, 1992: 391
Turkana				
settled	0.6	160	selectivity/	Campbell et al.,
nomadic	0.9	114	emigration of	1999,
			nulliparous	Table 17.1
			women may	
			explain very low	
			infertility	
Kawalha				
BN nomads				
30-9	16.1	151		
40-9	12.0	125		
newly settled			ever-married	Henin, 1969:
30-9	3.1	218	women	179
40-9	2.0	97		
long settled				
30-9	3.5	246		
40-9	4.7	142		
Baggara				
nomads 30-9	15.5	272	ever-married	Henin, 1969:
40-9	11.5	192	women	179
Muglad 30-9	7.5	74		
40-9	14.0	49		

Table 8.2 Percentages of women reporting no live births (primary sterility)

Population		Percentage sterile		Number of women		Comments	Source
Tuareg 1981/2		EM	all	EM	all		
Gourma	30-39	3.8	8.6	363	383	EM=ever-	Randall, own
	40-54	4.7	8.7	297	310	married	data
Delta	30-39	4.5	9.0	308	324	All= all women	
	40-50	4.2	8.4	167	179	High levels of	
Tuareg 2001						childlessness	
30-39		6.3	15.6	411	463	largely due to	
40-49		5.3	11.7	303	341	non-marriage	
50-59		2.9	7.8	207	219		
60+		4.2	11.9	215	236		
Fulbe (N Burkina)						women 25-54	Hampshire,
Djelgobe		1.2		163		married at least	1998: 274
Gaobe		4.4		297		5 years. Similar	
Liptaako		7.6		237		levels for men	
						by sub-groups	
Mauritania 1977							Mauritanie, 1977: 99
nomads	30-39	8.2		26146			
	40-54	6.7		30119			
	55+	8.5		24426			

extraordinary lengths to treat it. Childless women are often given other children to care for, partly in the hope that this will stimulate pregnancy. This means that, in a single-round demographic survey, there may be an underestimate of primary infertility because children are ascribed to the wrong mothers.

In conclusion, there is some evidence of excessive infertility in some pastoralist groups and extraordinarily low levels of infertility in others. There is no evidence that nomadic pastoralists in general have sexual networking patterns that lead to a higher than usual incidence of STDs, although each population has its own traditions which may be condemned by other neighbouring groups.

HIV and AIDS

Recent evidence does suggest that pastoralists may have low prevalence of HIV compared with other sub-groups in the same country. The 2003 Kenya *DHS* undertook HIV testing, with overall prevalence by province ranging from 0 to 15.1% of adults aged 15–49 (CBS et al., 2004, Table 13.4). In the isolated and underdeveloped North Eastern province where a substantial proportion of the population is nomadic pastoralist, prevalence was 0%. This may be a situation in which the isolation is beneficial to pastoralists. This benefit is also reflected in mortality changes in Kenya. Using census data, life expectancy at birth was calculated for each Kenyan district and the changes in life expectancy from 1979-89 and 1989-99 calculated (CBS, 2002: 29). Overall life expectancy in Kenya declined between these two decades by about 5 years for both males and females, and the same was true for most provinces and districts. However, there was substantial variation and in many pastoralist districts life expectancy improved.[2] If pastoralists remain isolated, then their mortality advantages may increase in countries with a substantial HIV burden. Coast's research suggests that, although Maasai sexual networking patterns in rural Maasailand might indicate risky behaviour, male Maasai migrants in urban areas are largely celibate, avoiding sexual relationships with non-Maasai women and thus reducing risks of urban-rural transmission of HIV and other STDs (Coast, 2006).

Marriage

The factor with most impact on pastoralist fertility is marriage. This is hardly surprising since, along with migration, marriage is the demographic parameter over which people have most control; and it is also very sensitive to negative feedback, especially where bridewealth is paid, which is the case for most nomadic pastoral populations. It is easy to imagine how an absence of animals could inhibit a man from amassing the necessary bridewealth to marry and reproduce, and could thus help maintain population growth in line with herd growth. Because most African pastoralists use animals for paying bridewealth, marriage is also an important way of redistributing wealth and creating the alliances which are an essential lifeline in times of crisis and herd loss.

There is substantial variation in the tolerance of unmarried individuals. For Fulani and Maasai, unmarried individuals, be they men or women, are anomalous members of society and both marriage and childbearing are essential parts of being adult and a full member of society. For the Turkana, Tamasheq, Maures and Herero the situation is very different, with some men and women never marrying yet still participating fully in social life, albeit in very different ways. Many Turkana women reproduce outside marriage and Herero women continue to reproduce for their husband long after he is dead, and many also reproduce outside marriage. In contrast, Tuareg extra-marital births are almost entirely confined to the Bella social class (Randall and Winter, 1985).

Marriage regimes within African pastoralist populations are extraordinarily diverse. East African Maasai are highly polygamous, with women almost continuously exposed to childbearing from puberty, although older widows do not remarry but may continue to reproduce with their husband's agemates for their dead husband's patriline. There are few illegitimate children, because women marry immediately after puberty and marriage is universal for men and women. There is some evidence that education is linked to a lower likelihood of marriage (5% of women aged 25–39 with primary schooling were never married, compared with just over 1% of uneducated women, Coast, 2000). The variability in the number of children Maasai men achieve is substantial and

---

[2] For women, there were improvements in Isiolo, Marsabit, all of Northeastern province, Baringo, Kajiado, Samburu, West Pokot and Turkana; for men, improvements in Northeastern province, Samburu, West Pokot and Turkana.

depends on the numbers of wives they manage to acquire. West African Fulani also have universal marriage, but unlike Maasai, divorce and remarriage are fairly frequent. Fulani are only mildly polygynous, with 7.6% of currently married men and 13.5% of currently married women in polygynous unions (Hampshire, 1998: 251), and the majority of polygynous men have only two wives. Turkana are much more polygamous but have a relatively late age at marriage for both women and men and about 10% of women and slightly fewer men who remain pastoralists in the area never marry (although they may have children). Turkana data on the marital status of out-migrants show that many were never married (Little and Leslie, 1999: 284), and it is likely that their failure to marry precipitated their departure.

The Tuareg have a very different marital regime. Although Muslims, they are monogamous and this, combined with frequent divorce, large spousal age differences and high adult mortality, means that women may spend a substantial proportioden of their reproductive years outside marriage. No more than 70% of any reproductive age-group of women are currently married (Randall, 1984; Fulton and Randall, 1988). Unlike Turkana, childbearing outside marriage is strongly condemned and the impact of the marriage regime is the principal reason why Tamasheq fertility continues to be substantially lower than that of other rural Malian populations.

The Rendille marriage system had the most obvious impact on fertility and can best be interpreted as an (albeit unconscious) attempt to restrain human population growth. According to Roth (1993), of the different men's agesets, the daughters of every third set were *sepaade* who should not marry until all their brothers have married. Many *sepaade* women did not start reproducing until their late twenties or early thirties; their age-specific fertility rates peaked in their early thirties, unlike the other two groups for whom fertility was higher at younger ages and peaked at the 25-29 age group (Roth, 1993: Table 8.1). Although *sepaade* women continued to reproduce longer than non-*sepaade* women their achieved fertility was considerably lower (CP = 3.7 compared with 6.1; Roth, 2004). This tradition was not explained by the Rendille as a means of controlling population growth, but was certainly relatively effective, although not sufficient to stop the transformation of Rendille men into Ariaal goat herders (Spencer, 1973). Even non-*sepaade* women, like Turkana women, marry relatively late compared with the mid to late teens for West African pastoralists and Maasai. Roth (2004: 101) notes '*in the summer of 1998 the Rendille terminated the sepaade tradition*'. His investigations into the motivation for this revealed that the main reason was to stop *sepaade* women from leaving and marrying into other groups. This suggests therefore that, even had controlling population growth originally been a motive for this tradition, by 1998 retaining nubile women and maintaining population growth was more critical.

Herero marriage is largely irrelevant with respect to fertility. About 40% of children are born outside marriage and, although some may be claimed later by their genitors, others are not. Even after marriage there is much marital mobility, but since few Herero know the dates of their marital events, data comparable to those for other populations are absent. Regression analysis by

Table 8.3 Measures of polygamy and attitudes to divorce

Population	% currently married men in monogamous marriages	Mean number wives per polygynist	% of women aged 15-49 with co-wives	Attitude to divorce	% of women aged 40+ never married	Proportions of non-marital and extra-marital children	Source
Toposa	42.8	3.03					Roth, 1994
Rendille	85.2	2.03					Roth, 1994
Maasai							
Kenya	54	2.72		rare	2.0	rare	Coast, 2000
Tanzania	54	2.84			0.5		
Turkana	61	2.66			Surviving women in pastoral sector 11.8	23.6% of births conceived before cohabitation	Adapted from Table 14.4 Dyson-Hudson et al., 1998
Kawalha					women 30-49		Henin, 1969: 184
settled			10.6	frequent	0.7	ns	
new settled			5.7	among	0.2		
nomad			19.2	nomads	1.7		
Baggara				frequent	women 30-49		Henin, 1969: 184
settled			10.3	among	1.6		
nomad			18.9	nomads	3.3		
Herero				frequent		high (40% of births)	Pennington & Harpending, 1993
Mauritania nomads				frequent	3.6	9.7% male births reported to unmarried women	Mauritanie, 1977
Tuareg							
Delta 1981		2	3.7	frequent	4.1	v. rare.	Randall
Gourma 82		2	2.2	no stigma	5.5	More frequent	
Mema 2001	97.8	2	1.7	attached	7.6	among ex-	
Niger 1966					8.8	slave class	
Fulani							
Burkina	92.4	2.27	13.4	quite	0	rare	Hampshire
Niger 1966				frequent	1.5	social disaster	1998: 252

Blank = no data available

Table 8.4 Age at first marriage (mean ± sd)

Population	Measure	Women	Women min-max	Men	Men min-max	Source & comments
Turkana	mean	22.7 ± 4.5	14-38	31.8 ± 6.1	21-47	Leslie et al. 1999 fig 14.1
Maasai						
Kenya	mean	17.0	10-34	25.6	13-50	Coast
Tanzania		17.1	11-32	29.4	13-65	2000, table 6.1
Fulani: N Burkina	mean of					Hampshire
Djelgobe	reported	15.2 ± 2.7	7-24	21.4 ± 3.7	14-32	1998: 251,
Gaobe	agefm	15.0 ± 3.2	7-27	24.0 ± 3.9	13-40	table 7.4
Lipataako		15.4 ± 3.8	9-23	23.4 ± 4.0	14-37	and original data
Djelgobe	median	16.2		21.2		women 25-
Gaobe	reported	15.7		25.2		49
Lipataako	age at first marriage	15.9		23.3		men 25+
Tuareg Mali 2001	mean	17.0 ± 4.3	7-44	27.1 ± 6.0	15-50	Randall data for
	median reported agefm	16		26		women 20-60 men 30+
Rendille 1987-90						Roth, 1993
non-sepaade	mean	22.2 ± 4.92				
sepaade		30.2 ± 8.9				

Pennington and Harpending showed that married women had higher fertility than unmarried women but that '*women who undergo a transition in marital state during their birth intervals have the lowest fertility, whereas women who stay married or unmarried during their birth intervals have identical levels of fertility*' (Pennington and Harpending, 1993:168). Herero men are polygamous and, like Maasai, Turkana and Toposa, tend to accumulate several wives over their lifetime leading to substantial spousal age differences. Apparently it is quite acceptable for younger women married to older men to have lovers and any children will belong to the husband's lineage.

The nuptiality regime is probably the most important determinant of the variation in fertility observed in Table 8.1. African pastoralist nuptiality patterns demonstrate diversity in all aspects of marriage: age at first marriage, polygamy, proportions marrying, prevalence and attitudes to divorce, extra-marital and pre-marital childbearing. Thus whilst for any specific population the marriage regime is an important determinant of overall fertility, there is even less evidence for a pastoralist marriage regime than there is for a pastoralist demography.

Mortality

Mortality data for pastoralist populations are far more limited than fertility and marriage data. All populations are reluctant to talk about dead people, but many East African Maa-speaking pastoralist groups have particularly strong taboos. Even the Turkana birth history data gathered over a long period of time by known researchers appear to show substantial underreporting of child deaths, especially where data were collected from only one parent, with an estimated 40% of child deaths unreported. Coast's study (2000) encountered huge problems in obtaining reports of infant deaths and indirect reports of adult deaths through orphanhood. In West Africa the problem appears to be less acute. Tuareg underreport neo-natal deaths, but an examination of proportions dead of children born, by age of woman, increases with age for Tuareg and Fulani but not for Maasai and Turkana,[3] suggesting less under-reporting for the West African populations.

With such problems all we can do is correct for underreporting where possible and be aware of biases. Table 8.5 shows the estimates of childhood mortality for a range of pastoralist populations. Some publications have measured mortality indirectly (using the Brass methods and proportions dead of children ever born), and some directly. The relationship between infant and child mortality for indirect measures is very dependent on the model lifetable used, so only the estimate for 5q0 (the probability of dying before age 5) is given.

Why might pastoralists have a particular mortality regime? Unlike fertility where there is the possibility of deliberate manipulation to match resources, we assume that there is no such manipulation of mortality through infanticide. This may not have been the case in the past, but most pastoralist societies are organised to allow substantial mobility of children between households (Shell-Duncan, 1994; Castle, 1995; Pennington and Harpending, 1993) and thus infanticide seems unlikely except in the case of inappropriate births (such as extra-marital births for Tuareg). An exception to the lack of information on infanticide comes from Roth (1994: 140), that the Rendille '*are unusual in directing infanticide against specific males eg sons born after the first-born has been circumcised, twin boys and males born on moonless Wednesdays*'. Legesse (1989) also cites a tradition of infanticide amongst Ethiopian Boran and Gabbra but states that this is no longer found amongst the Kenya Gabbra.

Infant and child mortality might be expected to be high among pastoralists because of isolation, inaccessibility of health services, low levels of immunisation, poor water quality, seasonal stress in food availability and mothers' time. On the other hand, it might be lower than in neighbouring sedentary agricultural populations because low population density inhibits maintenance of epidemics of infectious disease (Loutan and Paillard, 1992), and reduces problems of waste disposal and contamination of standing water. Ownership of animals means that children have access to milk as a supplement and as a

---

[3] These should increase with age because on average older women's children have been alive longer and have had more time in which to die. If mortality has been improving then the trend should be even more marked. Only if mortality has been increasing, should proportions surviving remain stable.

complement to other weaning foods which may improve childhood nutrition. Fratkin et al., (1994) and Nathan et al., (1996) showed that nomad children had better nutritional status than sedentary Rendille and Ariaal. Those pastoralists who live in arid and semi-arid areas may have considerably less exposure to malaria than those in more humid zones. In the 1981-82 Mali studies the Fulani who lived in the Inner Niger Delta showed extraordinarily high childhood mortality compared with those (poorer and more isolated) in the much drier Seno Mango. The Tuareg who spent time in the Delta left during the wet season, which may explain why their mortality was lower than that of the Delta Fulani (Hill and Randall 1984). These Tuareg now barely use the Delta for transhumance and the change in disease pathogens probably contributed to the substantial decline in their mortality between 1981 and 2001.

There is substantial heterogeneity in levels of pastoralist child mortality (Table 8.5), much of which can be accounted for by temporal change. Even in those marginal populations with little access to health-care and immunisation, the general time-trend is one of decreasing child mortality. This is clearest for the Delta Tuareg population which was restudied in 2001 after a traumatic period of forced migration, refugee camps, repatriation and substantial sedentarisation in the five years before the survey, despite which mortality had declined substantially. They now experience lower childhood mortality than the rest of rural Mali (Randall, 2005).

Further evidence suggests that neither being nomadic pastoralists nor environmental characteristics are primary determinants of mortality here. The Tuareg in the early 1980s remained a highly stratified society with high-status Berber and free Tuareg, many of whom owned black slaves. Bella, former slaves who had left their masters years previously, tended to be poorer than the high-status groups, but everyone lived in the same environment in similar mobile tents, drinking the same, limited, and often highly contaminated water, eating similar foods, although with different ratios of milk and meat to grain, and with effectively no access to modern health services. If the environment were the major determinant of mortality levels, one would expect little difference between the sub-groups. If wealth were the principal determinant, one would expect the high-status Tuareg to have lower mortality than the black ex-slaves. In fact the opposite was the case (Figure 8.2).

Indirect child mortality estimates for Delta and Gourma Tuareg in the early 1980s consistently show high-status Tuareg with significantly higher mortality than low-status Bella, despite living in the same environment and camps. The differences are thought to be due largely to cultural norms: high-status women tended to be very fat, many having been force fed from an early age. The fatter the woman, the less active child care she undertook and the more her children were cared for by young Bella nursemaids. Bella women cared for their own children and as cooks and domestic workers were more likely to wash their child during the day and provide continuity of care if the child was sick. Bella women were probably healthier than Tuareg women (adult female Bella mortality was much lower). By 2001 the last vestiges of slavery had basically disappeared. Flight, four years in refugee camps and impoverishment had led to the abandonment of force-feeding; high-status women were more active

Table 8.5 Probability of dying before age 5

Population		5q0	Method	Source
Tuareg				
Niger	1966	.37	indirect	Niger, 1966
Mali Delta	1981	.30	indirect	Randall, 1984
Mali Gourma	1982	.34	indirect	Randall, 1984
Mali Mema	2001	.17	indirect	Randall, 2001 data
cohort	1981–90	.21	direct	
cohort	1990–95	.16	direct	
Fulani (Fulbe)				
Mali Delta	1982	.48	indirect	van den Eerenbeemt, 1985
Mali Seno-Mango	1982	.33	indirect	van den Eerenbeemt, 1985
Mali Fulbe (delta)	1988	.30	direct	Marriott, 1993
Mali Fulbe (Seno)	1989	.57	direct	Castle, 1992
Burkina Djelgobe	1995	.18	indirect	Interpolated from Hampshire, 1998
Burkina Gaobe	1995	.29	indirect	Interpolated from Hampshire, 1998
Burkina Liptaako	1995	.29	indirect	Interpolated from Hampshire, 1998
Mauritanian nomads	1977	.23	indirect	calculated from census report
Turkana	1990	.13–.21	indirect	Leslie et al., 1999
Long settled		.22	indirect	Brainard, 1991 (calc. from Table 6.5)
Recently settled				
(20-29)		.23	indirect	Brainard, 1991
Rendille		.22	direct	Roth 1993, Table 3
Datoga boys		.30	direct	Borgerhoff-Mulder,
girls		.26	direct	1992, Table III
Herero pre-1960		.20	direct	calculated from Pennington and
1960-74		.17	direct	Harpending, 1993
1975+		.09	direct	
Maasai		Underreporting of dead children too severe to allow for reasonable estimates		

Note: Indirect measures usually refer to an average of mortality over the 20 years before the survey. Direct measures can be for specific cohorts or an average for women of reproductive age.

and probably healthier. Child care was more continuous, with more recourse to modern medicine. The water supply was cleaner and few now migrated into the unhealthy Inner Niger Delta. Class mortality differentials had declined (Fig. 8.2).[4]

[4] Bella interviewed in 2001 were a small, select sub-group of those still living in mixed communities and were not representative of those surveyed in 1981. However, in 2001 Bella surveyed were likely to be the least well-off and innovative.

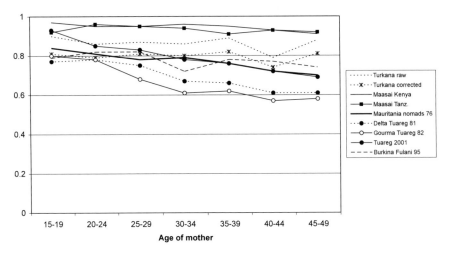

Figure 8.1 Reported levels of proportions of children surviving in different pastoralist populations

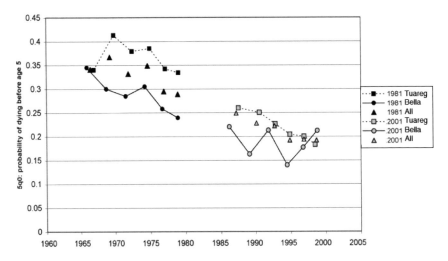

Figure 8.2 Indirect estimates of Tamasheq childhood mortality, 1965–2000

This case-study demonstrates the substantial heterogeneity over space, class and time within just one nomadic pastoralist population, and is further evidence that there is no specific pastoralist demographic regime.

Adult mortality

Data on adult mortality of pastoralist populations are scarce. Adult mortality is hard to study where there is no vital registration. Methods for estimating adult mortality indirectly from questions on the survival of parents, spouses or siblings have been developed, but they are imperfect and require large samples (UN, 1983; Timaeus et al., 2001). Adult mortality, particularly that of men, might be high because of risky behaviour: pastoralists often hunt big game (Herero are said to hunt lions at 'substantial personal risk' (Pennington and Harpending, 1993: 35), and cattle raiding is frequent in East Africa (Gray et al., 2002). Herding animals alone is also risky in terms of accidents, infected wounds and snakebites. Mobile women may be at increased risk during pregnancy and childbirth and have little contact with maternity services. One might therefore expect maternal mortality to be higher than in sedentary populations.

For East Africa the only reasonably viable estimates of adult survivorship are for Maasai men who have similar e_{20}[5] to West African Fulani and substantially higher than Malian Tuareg. It is not clear why this should be. Another source of adult mortality estimates is Kenyan district-level estimates of adult mortality calculated by Blacker using the 1979 census data. These are not for pastoralist groups *per se*, but in 1979 pastoralist districts were largely dominated by populations with a pastoralist production system. The district-level estimates suggest substantial heterogeneity both in levels of mortality and in the ratio between male and female mortality (Randall, 1994).

The series of mortality estimations for West Africa suggest that in the 1970s Tuareg adult mortality was extremely high, especially in the Gourma, where the proportions of children orphaned were so high that for some age groups it was not possible to give the estimates because the model life tables did not go that high. At that time adult mortality appeared to be improving but the 2001 data for repatriated refugee Tuareg suggest that adult mortality has deteriorated recently. This may be because of the rebellion and losses of young adult men in the fighting. The period in refugee camps ultimately had better health and sanitation conditions than previously although we have no data on mental health and chronic disease.

The few estimates available for maternal mortality using siblinghood (Graham et al., 1989) amongst pastoralists are inconsistent (Table 8.7). The estimates for Maasai are improbably low, given that they are lower than national Kenyan estimates and Maasai have little access to obstetric services and maternity clinics. Although Mace and Sear (1996) suggest that Gabbra maternal mortality is high, it is still lower than Kenyan national levels and substantially lower than that recorded for West African pastoralists. Extremely high maternal mortality for Tuareg may partly be a relic of past obesity (the measure is a composite estimate combining deaths over 20-25 years), but seems a realistic representation of particular health difficulties faced by isolated, mobile populations.

Adult mortality estimates for African pastoral populations do not suggest a specific pastoralist adult mortality regime, but the data are scanty and poor-quality. There is evidence of substantial within-population heterogeneity, with

[5] e_{20} = the expectation of life at age 20. i.e. the average number of further years someone would expect to live after age 20.

Table 8.6 Estimates of adult mortality: e_{20}

Population	Women	method	Men	method	Source & comments
Maasai	estimates unreliable	orphan-hood widow-hood		orphanhood data not collected because biological fathers unclear	Coast, 2001 Strong taboo against discussing dead people means there is serious
Kenya			49.9 improving	widowhood	underreporting using orphanhood
Tanzania			50.5 improving	widowhood	
Fulani Burkina 1995	49.5 possible slight improve-ment	sibling-hood	48.4 improving	siblinghood	Data from Hampshire, estimates made by Randall
Tuareg 2001 2001	38.2 deteriorating 40.5 deteriorating	siblinghood orphanhood	37.6 deteriorating 44.0 deteriorating	siblinghood orphanhood inconsistent	Randall. Possible distortion in 2001 because of raised adult mortality in rebellion
Delta 1981	40.1 improving	orphanhood	37.3 improving	orphanhood	Male mortality so high that is off the
Gourma 1981	31.3 deteriorating	orphanhood	27.9 stable	orphanhood	scale of West MLT level 1

high-status Tuareg women in the populations studied in 1981 and 1982 having much higher mortality than Bella (Randall, 1984), whereas the opposite was true for the men. This suggests that specific cultural determinants of adult mortality may be more important than being pastoralists or not.

Migration & movement

In order to consider issues of migration within African pastoralist populations it is essential to have clear ideas about the different types of migration and movement. These populations are largely identified by their mobility, which is an essential aspect of livestock production in semi-arid environments. Movement with animals as part of the production system is totally different from movement out of the production system.

Table 8.7 Estimates of maternal mortality using sisterhood

Population	Lifestyle / production	Maternal mortality lifetime risk	Comments	Source
Fulani 1995 N.Burkina Faso	mobile & sedentary pastoralists & agropastoralists	1 in 18		Hampshire in Mace and Sear (1996)
Tuareg Mali 2001	mobile & sedentary pastoralists	1 in 8	extraordinarily high	Randall
Gabbra 1993	nomadic camel pastoralists	1 in 31	N Kenya	Mace and Sear 1996
Maasai 1998 Kenya Tanzania	agro-pastoralist agro-pastoralist	1 in 59 1 in 33	implausibly low because of extreme dislike of mention of maternal deaths	Coast, 2001: 111 National levels 1 in 20 Kenya, 1 in 18 Tanzania

We can define movement and migration in three ways, using the terms outlined below (not all authors use such terms consistently, but these are the definitions used here).

Transhumance: movements with animals as part of pastoralist production

Ethnographies and geographical studies often document the scale and direction of such movements (e.g. Gallais, 1967; Bernus, 1981). There is evidence that in the pre-colonial and early colonial eras transhumant movements were often over very large distances, but international boundaries and frontiers, expansion of agriculture and colonial attempts to control populations have substantially restricted transhumance movements.

Different populations have adopted different ways of using households to manage and move with animals. Until recently Malian Tuareg households moved as units and were totally nomadic, whereas in other populations (Fulani) young men have always been much more mobile than the rest of the household, although most people move at some time during the year . Some Fulani groups (e.g. Liptaako) are basically sedentary, although young men or paid herders take the cattle far away from the homesteads. Although substantial distances may be covered, these movements form part of the production system and therefore are not a way of adjusting the human population to available resources or employment, but the way in which the humans, along with the animals, exploit the natural environment.

Table 8.8 Animal ownership and animal husbandry after sedentarisation (% of households, 2001)

	Owns animals	Works with animals &/or owns animals
Way of life since 1996		
nomad	82.0	97.2
semi-sedentary	68.4	88.1
site (Tamasheq settlement)	67.3	79.8
village (ethnically mixed)	35.1	49.1
TOTAL	71.2	85.3

Sedentarisation: (only applicable to formerly nomadic groups)

Sedentarisation is taken to mean a change in lifestyle from mobile housing to fixed housing. This is often, but not always, accompanied by a change in production and the adoption of agriculture either as a supplement to or replacement of a pastoral economy. In droughts or epidemics of livestock disease, pastoralist households may lose their entire animal wealth. In order to survive they must adapt, and in rural areas the most common adaptation is to take up agriculture and either gradually build up one's herd again or transform into an agropastoralist (who by cultivating must be settled for part of the year). Evidence suggests that pastoralist individuals, households and populations have always shifted between different balances of animal husbandry and other economic activities (Bonfiglioli, 1990; Cisse, 1981). Relief aid after droughts or other catastrophes has tended to encourage people to sedentarise in order to participate in income-generating projects (Brainard, 1991; O'Leary, 1990; Randall and Giuffrida, 2006).

People who sedentarise do not necessarily move away from the wider territory where they had previously transhumed, but they select a space on it to establish themselves. Sedentarision may in effect be an economic migration – out of pastoralism and into agriculture and other activities (Bovin, 1990) – or it may just be an economic transformation whereby people remain pastoralists but in a different way. This can be seen in a comparison of the 1981 and 2001 Tuareg studies. In 1981 the entire population studied was nomadic. The composition of households might change over a year, the composition of a camp certainly did, and some individuals would move much further than others, yet they were all nomadic and no-one practised any agriculture. The same population studied in 2001 had a much more diverse lifestyle. Some were still nomadic, some semi-sedentary and some were permanently fixed all year round. There were minor attempts at agriculture, but most households were still primarily involved in animal husbandry (Table 8.8).

Sedentarisation under certain circumstances can be a population-level adaptation to maladjustment between herds and people, and waves of sedentarisation often occur after a crisis such as drought. It can also be a function of the political economy. There is evidence that the rapid sedentarisation of repatriated Tuareg refugees in Western Mali is partially a response to strategies and politics of repatriation and decentralisation (Randall and Giuffrida, 2006).

The largest study of national level sedentarisation was undertaken by Traoré for Mauritania using data from 1965 and 1976. He estimates that of just over 1 million Mauritanians in 1965, 73.8% were nomadic, 15.9% were rural and sedentary and 10.2% urban, making this one of the few nations dominated by pastoral nomads. Depending on one's definition of both nomad and sedentary dweller (he demonstrates the numerous categories in between) he shows that by 1976 about 60% of the former nomads had sedentarised (Traoré, 1984: 103). He does, however, qualify this because, as he puts it, *'It seems a bit ambiguous to call sedentarisation, for example, the simple construction of an immovable dwelling in a permanent camp'* (p.104, my translation). He then examines the links between sedentarisation and migration.

Migration

Migration is defined here as a movement away from a person's area of origin *and* a movement away from pastoralism. Thus it is both a spatial and an economic transformation and has long been a way for pastoralist individuals, households and communities to adapt to imbalances between the animal and human population, being a much more immediate response to crisis or change than adjustments to fertility, and a way of avoiding excess mortality. Given the poor educational provision in most pastoralist areas, migration is inevitable for secondary education. There is a lot of evidence that, as in most other rural African communities, the last fifty years have seen a substantial amount of out-migration from nomadic pastoralist communities. The principal macro-evidence is the fact that – with little quantitative evidence – a general picture of rural African semi-arid lands would suggest that there are far fewer nomadic pastoralists than there were 40 years ago, despite the natural fertility and mortality dynamics of these populations which should generate natural growth rates of between 1.5 and 3% per annum.

So what are the patterns of migration? In West Africa different groups have long practised seasonal labour migration from rural areas to coastal cities such as Abidjan, Dakar and Accra, alongside the large urban centres of the interior. Pastoralist populations have generally participated far less in seasonal labour migration than sedentary agricultural populations. In a highly seasonal semi-arid environment, rainfed agriculture is restricted to a few months per year and seasonal labour migration is a useful way of supplementing income, diversifying and reducing the numbers of consumers without compromising production. The same is not true for pastoralism: although labour inputs vary seasonally, with the most difficult season for pastoralists usually being the dry season – heavy demands for watering animals and long treks to find meagre pastures – animals require supervision throughout the year, and the best animal welfare and production require constant inputs. Thus pastoralists have no slack season, and White (1986) paints a clear picture of the downward spiral of poverty and low productivity onceWoDaaBe men resorted to seasonal labour migration. In Northern Burkina Faso, the most nomadic pastoralist group, the Djelgobe, participated least in seasonal labour migration because of these labour constraints. Agro-pastoral Gaobe and Liptaako had already compromised on pastoral production by diversifying into agriculture, and Gaobe men first started migrating to Abidjan after the 1973 drought. Men from large adult sibling groups were most likely to leave, where someone from the family was left behind to care for the herds and ensure their wellbeing, and migration was a further livelihood diversification (Hampshire and Randall, 1999).

Pastoralists' migration to urban areas by young men, or whole families, has been documented in times of drought and also by men who have lost their livestock, have failed to marry or have some other reason for wanting to leave their area and pastoral production. In both East and West Africa many nightwatchmen in large cities originate from pastoralist groups. Turkana genealogical data (with data for twice as many women as men) showed that both women and men who have migrated out were much less likely to have married and established a viable domestic unit than those who remained. Kenyan census data show that, in 1979, 66.2% of people defining themselves as Turkana lived in Turkana District. 33.8% did not, but this had increased to 39.3% by 1989 (Dyson-Hudson and Meekers, 1999). Although some of these Turkana out-migrants may have been pastoralists elsewhere, most will have left pastoralism. Similar patterns could certainly be found elsewhere in both West and East Africa, if census data were appropriately classified. The Turkana genealogical study is able to examine out-migration rates by year and time period, and shows a major acceleration from a low rate in the 1960s, increasing substantially into the 1980s. Annual data for Turkana out-migration demonstrate the effect of drought: the authors state that most outmigrants do not return and few become pastoralists elsewhere.

Studies in West Africa have documented similar patterns, although in less detail. In his analysis of Mauritanian sedentarisation and migration from 1965 to 1977, Traoré considers that drought played little role in the rapid transformation of Mauritanian nomadic society, arguing that these production systems had experienced droughts before and had always maintained their way of life. He blames colonialisation for destabilising nomadic pastoral societies both economically and socially, exacerbated by Independence and the drive to develop a modern economy away from subsistence. In contrast, Pedersen's analysis of out-migration from the Gourma area of Mali concludes that the 1984-5 drought was a major stimulus to out-migration (Pedersen, 1995). Both studies are plagued with data problems: inconsistencies in definitions, underenumeration, poor reporting, confounded in Mali by the 1976 and 1987 censuses being held in totally different seasons so that all the nomadic populations were in different administrative areas (Randall, 2001).

All the studies confirm substantial out-migration from nomadic pastoral populations, but, given relatively high natural growth rates, it is not clear that absolute numbers are declining. Highly mobile groups may be disappearing partly because civil unrest, frontiers and agricultural expansion are limiting mobility, but also because nomadic pastoralists are adapting to the modern world by becoming more fixed in order to benefit from health and education services. Those who go to school almost inevitably leave the region and the sector. But it may be these migrants who help maintain pastoralism in the arid lands. Traoré cites a study undertaken in Mauritania which estimated that nearly half of rural income came from salaries, transfers and gifts, whereas agriculture and livestock-raising contributed one one-tenth and less than one-third respectively (Souleyman, 1981, cited in Traoré 1984: 147). The recent study of repatriated Tuareg in Mali showed the importance of networks with urban centres and with educated people who could tap into development funds (as well as salaries). About 9% of adult male Tuareg siblings lived abroad, mainly in Mauritania or Libya, being a substantial part of the 17% of siblings living outside the study area; slightly fewer women lived elsewhere. Many of the households in the rural areas, particularly the more sedentary ones, are highly dependent on the economic flows generated by these networks. Such flows are not limited to remittances but include much more complex links with development agencies and NGOs and their investments and projects in rural areas.

Most pastoralist populations have long had extensive socio-economic links outside their traditional areas. Thus, although, on the one hand, migration can be seen as an adjustment of human population to the animal and environmental resources, it can also be part of a strategy to extend that exploitable environment through the traditional pastoralist response of mobility and movement. Migration is just another way of spreading risks and extending the spatial boundaries of the potentially exploitable environment in much the same way that pastoralists have always had pastures which were used only in times of crisis.

Is there a pastoralist demography?

There is no one pastoralist demography, but there are common themes. Poor and inconsistent data and small sample sizes are a major issue. Available data suggest that contemporary nomadic pastoral populations have relatively high mortality and high fertility, but this is likely to be because of barriers to accessing services because of isolation and marginalisation. Much of the data on pastoralist demography were collected in the 1960s, 1970s and early 1980s, and where retrospective reports are used, data may refer to even earlier periods. At those times the pastoral groups probably resembled neighbouring sedentary populations in the degree of access to services, and it may be significant that these earlier data often suggest that pastoralists (or nomads) have lower fertility than their sedentary neighbours. We also have to consider the issue that once pastoralists become educated and urbanised, they are no longer included in the rural community studies of pastoralists, although it is very probable that a majority of large livestock (cattle and camels) which are herded by traditional pastoralists actually belong to these urbanites – who should in one sense be defined as pastoralists.

Heterogeneity with respect to mortality, fertility and nuptiality regimes is the main theme. A key issue running through pastoralist demography is the need to find social or demographic mechanisms for adjusting human population growth to livestock population growth and for coping with the often dramatic and quite rapid changes in livestock numbers. Nuptiality regimes which constrain reproduction do exist but are by no means universal, and some pastoral populations appear to be maximising fertility and population growth. This is feasible, given the principal response to economic crisis which is demographic adjustment through movement: movement away from the area where the crisis is occurring; movement away from pastoralism when there are insufficient animals; jettisoning expendable population sub-sections; movement into agriculture or manual labour; sedentarisation and the adoption of new forms of production, either temporary or permanent; and ultimately migration out of pastoral production and regions. Movement and cultural specificities are really the key characteristic of dryland African pastoral demography.

9

Diversification, Development & Change in Pastoralist Systems

One theme that has emerged repeatedly in this book concerns the fluidity of pastoralist societies and economies. Pastoralist societies may have been seen as conservative, 'traditional' and unchanging, but the work of archaeologists, historians, geographers, economists, demographers and anthropologists all points to the fact that pastoralist societies are continuously changing under the pressures, constraints and opportunities thrown up by changing biophysical, political and economic environments. Some pastoralist groups and elites display an adroit manipulation of or adaptation to change, that enables them better to operate within new parameters (Burnham and Last 1994; Markakis 1999, Lewis 2001, Little 2003). In other cases changes are more the result of marginalised people being pushed into ever less tenable situations (NOPA, 1992; Baxter and Hogg, 1990; Galaty and Bonte, 1991; Doornbos, 1993). This chapter considers the many possible trajectories of both development and diversification, and sketches analytical frameworks to help structure their variety.

Development means different things to different people. Development trajectories have been measured by GNP, by wealth holdings and their distribution, by indices of food security, health and education. Development goals for pastoralist groups are ideally defined by the priorities they themselves set, often revolving round the degree of political representation, tenure and access, food security, health, and education that any one group is able to achieve, alongside a perennial interest in animal health. In practice, development pathways fall far short of this ideal. There are three main approaches to understanding rural development trajectories in sub-Saharan Africa in general (Ellis, 2000), and diversification of pastoralist livelihoods in particular. The first is based on a perennial official assumption that 'successful' pastoralist development involves intensification on a Western model of livestock ranching for commercial meat or dairy production. This is a specific case within the more general assumption that rural agricultural systems in developing countries would progress by means of sectoral development to an industrialised economy (Bryceson, 1999). African rural populations and production systems in general, and sub-Saharan pastoralists in particular, have tended to show trajectories very different from those expectations.

The second broad approach is based on political economy, which focuses on the distributional implications of change. In particular, it emphasises the universal ability of well placed individuals and groups to benefit from technological innovation at the expense of the most vulnerable (Raikes, 1988). Land tenure changes (eg Shivji, 1998), animal health and production interventions (Scoones and Wolmer, 2006, Homewood et al., 2006), and structural adjustment have exacerbated the differences between rich and poor in most sub-Saharan pastoralist and agropastoralist groups along with other rural populations (Ellis, 2000). The third main approach emphasises the positive ways in which population growth and increasing rural population density may stimulate agricultural innovation and economic transformation through local solutions (Boserup, 1967; Tiffen et al., 1995).

This chapter picks up current ecological themes in the study of development in pastoralist groups. Firstly, it looks at the issue of commercialisation which dominated development thinking in the post Independence era. Development in pastoralist societies was at one time measured against indices of the extent to which the system was intensifying production for commercial offtake. Pastoralist livestock production development schemes, privatisation and commercialisation, and their ecological correlates are contrasted with case studies of major systems that have shown spontaneous commercialisation. These case studies emphasise the gulf between conventional pastoral development theory and practice, and the reality of change and spontaneous 'indigenous' commercialisation in established pastoralist systems. The chapter goes on to explore sedentarisation and intensification. It develops a discussion of livelihoods diversification among sub-Saharan pastoralist groups, through choice or necessity. Diversification complements and in some cases completely replaces pastoralist livelihoods in different ways depending on relative wealth and opportunity. Finally, the implications of development, diversification, sedentarisation and intensification for gender issues, education and health are examined, focusing on ecological rather than political, economic or social dimensions. The conclusion draws together this overview of the futures of African pastoralists.

Pastoralist production, privatisation & commercialisation

The period 1960s–80s saw concerted efforts throughout African rangelands to change pastoralism into Western-style livestock production systems, intensifying production operations, investing in high-tech water development and veterinary inputs, introducing high-yielding exotic breeds, and producing a commercial offtake for official national and international markets. The most immediate indices of herd fertility, mortality, offtake and the volume as well as the value of trade suggest that attempts at livestock development between the

1960s and 1980s tended to fail at this most basic level, and, if anything, made things even worse in terms of general levels of prosperity, food security and health in pastoralist groups. The three perspectives of development theory, political economy and indigenous innovation each lend insights to trajectories and outcomes of commercialisation in African pastoral systems and help explain the interplay of (and gaps between) grassroots realities and high-level policies (Scoones and Wolmer, 2006). In line with orthodox development theory, certain technical innovations have revolutionised livestock production potential. These include vaccination against rinderpest (and more recently ECF); the use of insecticides and other measures against tsetse and trypano-somiasis; the availability of broad-spectrum injectable drugs such as oxyte-tracycline, and the use of vermifuges. Some aspects of water development and marketing have also increased the potential for specific systems and sectors (Little, 1996; Scoones and Wolmer, 2006). Often commercial ranches established on Western lines do better on indices of productivity per animal, though not per unit area (Scoones, 1995b), and often by virtue of drawing on the indigenous systems, whether buying in stock (Sandford, 1982), or sharing common grazing during the wet season while retreating to private grazing during times of shortage (Hitchcock, 1990). However, the political-economy perspective emphasises that the distribution of benefits from these innovations has been very uneven, with elites and large-scale producers (including the state) able to profit and expand at the expense of smaller concerns. Markets for meat and milk have operated under heavy constraints for local producers, with access to profitable markets remaining the privilege of the few, and punitive taxes or artificially low prices discouraging producers elsewhere (Anderson, 2002; *The Economist*, 1993; Homewood and Rodgers, 1991; Raikes, 1981; Kerven, 1992; Quarles van Ufford, 1999). Despite all the interventions, the commercial systems through which most pastoral animals and produce move have grown up through spontaneous indigenous processes, explored in more detail here.

Spontaneous commercialisation in pastoralist systems

Given the right conditions, commercialisation of pastoralist meat and milk production has repeatedly taken place quite spontaneously. Where pastoralists have been reluctant to engage with commerce, this has generally been due to a whole range of factors making it simply not worth their while to trade their animals or produce.

Milk selling and dairying. Chapter 7 showed how milk selling tends to come about as a result of the need to exploit the calorific terms of trade. The cash or grain obtained makes it possible to meet food needs that cannot be filled by limited milk supplies. Wealthier households may sell milk when the terms of trade are to their advantage, and withdraw when milk prices fall, preferring to drink their milk or invest it in calf growth. Poorer households become obligate milk sellers, continuing to sell through periods when the terms of trade are relatively poor. Some dairying concerns have grown up linking milk production in mobile livestock camps, retaining a form of migratory movement, to urban demand (Buhl and Homewood, 2000; Buhl, 1999). Pastoralists may modify their migration strategies to take advantage of the economic opportunities this offers, though distance of livestock production areas from markets is a perennial constraint (Raikes, 1981). Occasionally, market forces seek out the dairy produce, as has been the case with mobile cheese factories in Northern Sudan. Baggar Arabs are able to maintain year-round production with some modification of their migratory routes so as to maintain access to the cheese factories. More commonly, dairying forces settlement near the market and a loss of mobility that entails a decline in performance and growing expense of feed and veterinary inputs. Sikana et al. (1993) describe cases in Kismayo, Somalia and in Bamako, Mali where mobile pastoralists place some milk animals in peri-urban pastures and rely on fodder purchases in order to take advantage of dairying possibilities.

In Somalia, different dairying enterprises span this range (Herren, 1990; Little, 1994). Before the 1990s civil wars and state collapse, long-term arrangements developed between town-dwelling women traders and women in quite distant, mobile livestock camps, able to maintain migratory movements and retain the benefits of better livestock nutrition and health. Empty containers were sent out and milk brought back on a regular basis by lorry drivers who took a considerable share of the returns. Other milk sellers paid to pasture milch camels on privately owned grazing near the city, the so-called '*seere*' system. Both enterprises largely collapsed during the last decades under the pressure of civil war, as violence between rival factions isolated towns from their rural hinterlands (Little, 2003). In Nigeria, *sabo* sectors of Ibadan city are effectively Hausa settlements, used as depots and distribution outlets for culturally highly valued traditional dairy produce brought by Fulani women traders from more distant mobile camps. In Khartoum, urban milk sellers buy fodder and other food supplements for their milch animals. The inputs are seasonally so expensive as to force them to operate at a loss for some of the year, recouping their deficit when prices improve (Salih, 1985). By contrast, milk sales make up 20% of Maasai income around Nairobi (Nkedianye et al., forthcoming).

The potential for dairying is not determined just by milk production. Market conditions may mean that dairying can become marginal or even fail to be viable, for example where cultural preferences mean that demand is low, where there is competition from alternative formal dairying markets, or where subsidised imports of dairy produce undercut the pastoral producer. Fulani women in CAR, unable to sell milk directly to local farming people, sold to town-based Arab women who in turn acted as middlemen in an international ghee trade (Boutrais, 1988). There is a comparable lack of interest in Fulani dairy produce among many southerners in Nigeria. Here, and in Kenya, the official commercial dairying industry is heavily subsidised and protected and delivers culturally preferred products. In many sub-Saharan countries, the international milk industry set up formal dairying concerns based on imports of cheap dried skimmed milk produced under subsidised conditions in the European Union or the United States. Dried milk is processed locally to be sold as reconstituted milk, yoghurt or ice cream. The dairy factories are able to function year round, unaffected by seasonal availability of local produce. Structural adjustment and changes in EU subsidies mean that, in a number of cases, these formal dairying industries have turned more to local pastoralist sources for milk, though less than 10% of pastoral milk production goes into such formal industries (Sikana et al., 1993).

Commercial dairying tends to conflict with production of animals for sale. Where a family maintains both enterprises side by side, the conflict may become polarised between men (characteristically in control of animal sales) and women (often controlling milk sales). This may reach the point where women are debarred from milking because it is felt that they would strip too much from the cow and jeopardise the calf (Beja – Hjort and Dahl 1991). In other cases, families specialise in either live animal production or milk selling, but not both. Reliance on live animal production is only really possible for wealthier households, while dairying becomes typical of poorer families, in which men and women cooperate over the management and sale of milk, or largely female-headed households focus on dairying as a survival strategy.

Commercialisation of animal sales. There are long-standing indigenous systems of livestock marketing both in West Africa and in East Africa (Nigeria and Niger, Maasai and Samburu in Kenya: Kerven, 1992; Burkina Faso and Kenya: Zaal 1998; Bénin: Quarles van Ufford, 1999; Tanzania: Raikes, 1981). Particularly in West Africa, these systems are exceptional for their economic importance, their geographical extent and their long-established customary structure and organisation. They have responded to modern market opportunities and benefited from new opportunities for disease control. In East Africa, livestock marketing has been constrained by competition from subsidised formal markets, artificially low prices, taxation (whether as a spur to sales, Kenya – Kerven 1992: 9–10, or a disincentive, Tanzania – Raikes, 1981, 1988) and quarantine (Chapter 6). Examples of spontaneous commercialisation from Libya, Somalia and Botswana are developed here, drawing on the insights developed by Behnke (1983), Sikana et al. (1993), Sikana and Kerven (1991), and on aspects of the present-day East African livestock trade (McPeak and Little, 2006).

Commercialisation of animal production in pastoralist systems is characterised by a shift in economic orientation, with a progressive rise in the numbers or proportions of animals for sale, and an increase in the ratio of livestock to people (with a progressive rise in the numbers of livestock per capita for producers), a change in animal management (with less intensive man/animal contact alongside the progressive restriction to a single product), and a change in land tenure (with the progressive increase of private land at expense of common property rights systems; Behnke, 1983). Other changes could involve the age/sex composition of the herd (with greater value placed on male calves) and a shift in the household food system (with a decline in the use of milk and greater use of cultivated products). These features are best understood through case-studies (Behnke, 1983; Kerven, 1992) and long-term trajectories.

Case-studies of commercialisation

North Africa: Libya. During the first half of the twentieth century, Bedouin herders in Cyrenaica maintained sheep and goat herds as small family operations within a wider social system of patronage and stock redistribution, to some extent dominated by the centuries-old network of trade and control maintained by the Islamic Senussi lodges (Kwamena-Poh et al., 1982; Behnke, 1980). Most families produced most of the products they needed, and relatively few animals were sold. Sheep were milked, a labour-intensive activity. During the 1960s, Libya achieved Independence and underwent an oil boom that transformed the national economy. There was a surge of rural to urban migration, with many young men and small herdowners leaving the pastoral system. The spiralling demands of the wage-earning population for red meat gave rise to a new market for animals. At the same time, pastoral producers found themselves decreasingly able to maintain labour-intensive inputs for marginal returns on a whole range of livestock products.

Over a few years there was a spontaneous and rapid restructuring of livestock production and of its domestic organisation in response to the high returns for a single product: meat. After the 1970s the average size of individual herds had risen from 60 to ca.400 animals, the technical limit manageable by a single shepherd (Behnke, 1980). The numbers of families living as pastoralists declined accordingly. By the 1970s, the still outwardly traditional pastoralist system displayed a ratio of livestock to people and an emphasis on a single product that made it a clearly commercial system. National markets and a national police force had largely replaced both customary patterns of social redistribution and traditional systems of alliance, patronage and protection. Outmigration made the commercialisation transition both possible and relatively painless for the Libyan Bedouin in ecological, economic and social terms. A parallel situation has been described for Berber pastoralists in El Kala, North East Algeria (Homewood, 1993).

West Africa: Fulani in Nigeria and Niger. The West African Fulani livestock trade extends across multiple international borders, involving hundreds of thousands of people. In the 1960s, the Nigerian trade alone was already recognised as a multi-million pound industry (Ferguson 1967 in Kerven, 1992). Parallel and linked systems in Niger, Burkina Faso, Mali, and Chad are of similar importance. The West African livestock trade has continued to grow through the ups and downs of drought, the dumping of subsidised foreign meat on West African markets, and devaluation of the CFA franc (Quarles van Ufford, 1999).

The trade developed from long cycles of seasonal transhumance through zones of settled farmers, and offered opportunities for mutually beneficial cooperation. The Sahelian climate, with its short single rains dictating strong seasonality in calving and milk production, and its attendant implications for pastoral food systems (Chapter 7), contributed further incentives for trade. Long interaction between farming groups and herding Fulani saw a vigorous trade in animals coming to extend over ever wider areas from the fifteenth century on. The Fulani livestock trade developed in conflict, competition, and complementarity with equally important indigenous trading systems run by Tuareg in Niger (Lovejoy and Baier, 1975). From the nineteenth century, as Tuareg hegemony was progressively undermined by French colonial interventions, security and economic opportunities improved correspondingly for the Fulani. During the twentieth century the Fulani continued to expand into ever drier, more northerly ranges, through the Dallols to the west (e.g. Bonfiglioli, 1988), the Ader in the centre and the Damergou to the east.

In Sokoto, interaction between pastoral Fulani and established Hausa traders operating from the margins of the Sahara in the north to the coast in the south, dates from the fifteenth century. It became formalised after the nineteenth century Fulani *jihad* into a regular, controlled trade of live animals and dairy products in exchange for cultivated grains, salt and other goods. Islamic alms, taxes, tithes and tribute were paid in livestock. This system was adopted by the British colonial administration in Nigeria, which carried on with a cattle tax (*jangali*) imposed per head of livestock, but avoided establishing settler enterprises that would undermine the revenue of the Native Administrations. The northern more arid areas acted (and still do) as breeding grounds feeding livestock to the south for fattening and market outlets. The British facilitated the trade both through improvement of migration corridors, transport and slaughter facilities and also through veterinary measures, with vaccination against rinderpest, tsetse control, and other inputs. By contrast, French colonial administration (e.g. in Niger) imposed more punitive taxes, customs and barriers to movement, as well as taxing settled farmers in a way that led to the expansion of cultivation at the expense of grazing. French policies hampered the continued development of livestock commerce through French West Africa, while driving pastoralists to unofficial cross-border movements and sales to Nigeria (Kerven, 1992). Terms of trade remained generally poor into the 1950s, and much Fulani production was still not primarily oriented to trade in live animals (e.g. sales were not timed to coincide with seasonally high prices – Dupire, 1962b). The Fulani trade in live animals expanded with the growth of the plantation economy on the West African coast up to the 1960s, and continued to grow with the post-Independence Nigerian oil boom and the spiralling urban demand for meat (Quarles van Ufford, 1999; Kerven, 1992). From the 1960s on, traders sought livestock from ever further north throughout West Africa. In Niger, a decentralised network of collection, bush markets, and livestock movements feeding southern urban markets became established. Its often superficially informal and traditional appearance belies its international scale and commercial value.

Production has become more market-oriented, with changing patterns of sale, cereal acquisition, and dependence on cereals (Kerven, 1992; Sutter, 1982; Swift, 1984; White, 1986, 1991). Changing seasonal patterns of sales indicate growing price responsiveness, and a shift in age and sex structure of herds and of animals presented for sale indicating a change in herd management and market response (Kerven, 1992). The West African pastoralist livestock trade was if anything reinforced by the Sahelian droughts of the mid-1970s and mid-80s. These brought hardship – livestock losses, smaller herds, more difficult access to dwindling grazing – but at the same time drove up meat prices. Importations of cheap EEC beef (subsidised during production, storage, transport and marketing) undercut indigenous pastoral producers throughout West Africa (*The Economist* 1993), particularly in French West Africa with the artificially high CFA franc. Since devaluation of the CFA franc in 1994, the market for local beef has reasserted itself and Fulani producers have come back into their own.

Somalia. Commercialisation was economically and socially more painful in Somalia than in Libya, contributing to civil war and social disruption over recent decades (de Waal, 1997; Lewis, 2001). Somalia's nineteenth-century internal economy was based on pastoralism or pastoroforaging. Urban coastal settlements, linked to but not controlling the interior, acted as channels for the export of wild resources such as ivory and resins. During the late nineteenth and early twentieth centuries, Somalia established an export trade in a wide range of byproducts of subsistence pastoralism, including milk, ghee, meat and hides (Swift, 1979; Behnke, 1983, 1988). Between 1950 and 1970, with the oil boom in the Gulf States, Somalia became the biggest exporter of sheep and goats worldwide, and Berbera the biggest livestock shipping port. Even in the mid-1970s, after massive drought had decimated pastoralist herds throughout north-east Africa, Somalia contributed one-sixth of all livestock exports by value, and animal products accounted for 80% of its foreign exchange (including remittances).

Somalia's trade in livestock centred primarily on live animals exported to Saudi Arabia and other Gulf States. The Gulf continues to be a major (if not the main) destination, despite partial losses of this market during periods of drought and civil disruption, and the periodic reorientation of trade to North Kenya markets when Somali coastal ports are effectively cut off and cease to function (Little, 2003; McPeak and Little, 2006). The Gulf trade also suffered from periodic bans imposed during outbreaks of livestock disease and when civil disruption and/or state collapse interrupted veterinary certification (Chapters 4 and 6). Commercialisation in Somalia meant a major shift in terms of who retained involvement in pastoralism, and how they did so (Swift, 1979; Prior, 1994). Camels and goats, species that underpin risk-avoidance, gave way to relatively risk-prone but highly-priced cattle and sheep. Despite little overt change in land use systems (ch 4) or livestock performance, larger producers were able to build wealth and then invest, especially in private water development, gaining *de facto* private dry-season access to surrounding grazing, despite *de jure* communal tenure. In some areas the rangelands were fenced for private use, ultimately squeezing the majority into ever smaller areas unable to support year-round high densities (Prior, 1994; Little, 1996).

Wealthy producers, particularly from then President Siad Barre's ruling Marehan clan, invested in education for their sons securing further jobs, political influence, and administrative control. Small producers lured into the commercial market restructured their own domestic production, decreasing their labour force and shifting from labour-intensive husbandry (and relative self-sufficiency) to low-input single-product concerns. During drought, with serious fluctuations in the terms of trade, small producers found themselves trapped, while large producers could survive. Traditional redistribution networks were progressively replaced by offtake for commercial trade: where there had been a safety net, none now existed. Land-tenure change led to the crystallisation of historically fluid and transient wealth status. Increasing numbers were forced out of the pastoralist system because of a permanent change in rights of access to the basic means of production. Commoditisation led to the loss of stock without hope of replacement for small producers. Increasing numbers of young men failed to find employment within either pastoral or urban economies. The discontent these changes engendered, in the context of Somali clan-based political networks, played its part in the emergence of militias backing warlords, and in the eruption of civil war.

The Somali state had done so little to support its rural producers that production, exchange and trade survived the explosion of violence and collapse of civil society, with North Kenya markets, producers, herders and traders continuing to function and developing new outlets in place of those cut off by the war (Little, 2003; McPeak and Little, 2006). However, small producers and their families are thought to have suffered intensely from the violence and disruption, for example women whose dairying livelihoods have been lost. The operation of the relief system, its manipulation and failures have compounded the collapse (de Waal, 1997; Allen, 1996; Lewis, 2001).

East Africa: Maasai and Samburu in Kenya. Both the Samburu and the Maasai have long been involved in trade (Spear and Waller, 1993), but Kerven (1992) portrays this as historically relatively local and small-scale. The short transhumance cycles characteristic of the varied East African habitat, the bimodal rainfall pattern that makes year-round milk production possible, and the way pastoralist ranges have bordered on, rather than intermingled fully with, farming peoples, all contrast with West Africa. In Kenya, most wants could be satisfied either within the pastoral system, or with relatively small-scale and short-distance trade. In some cases exchange and trade focused on enclaves of agropastoralist farmers with strong cultural and ethnic ties to pastoralist societies (Spear, 1993a and b, 1997). Longer-distance trade into Somalia and Ethiopia was mediated mainly by Somali, Kamba and other outsiders.

At the same time Maasai and Samburu were relatively remote from the commercial markets that developed during colonial times. Commercialisation of the Maasai and Samburu livestock trade was in many ways held back by colonial administrations. Beyond ensuring enough livestock to supply government needs (including compulsory livestock sales to supply military needs in the Second World War), and establishing payment of poll tax through livestock sales, the administration encouraged settler prospects at the expense of indigenous production, whether by alienation of land, by quarantine measures that protected settler cattle and excluded indigenous animals, and/or by exclusive settler access to profitable markets (Raikes, 1981). Artificially low prices offered by official buyers like the Kenya Meat Commission discouraged sales. Constrained by 'official blockages of indigenous trading patterns as well as passive neglect...' (Kerven, 1992), Maasai maintained unofficial cross-border as well as local illegal sales, smuggling stolen cattle to Kenya through areas such as Engare Naibor in northern Tanzania (Waller pers. comm.), now a vigorous rural trading centre with some comparatively very wealthy herdowners and livestock traders (Homewood et al., forthcoming).

The relative proximity to major urban markets and the rapid expansion of cities like Nairobi meant growing markets (Raikes, 1981), particularly for Maasai livestock. Even where held artificially low, the terms of trade still broadly favour the pastoralist producer (Zaal and Dietz, 1999). Kenya Maasai and Samburu are now dependent on commercial sales for food needs, school fees and livestock acquisition (Zaal, 1998; Homewood et al., forthcoming). An estimated two-thirds of Samburu sales in the mid-1980s took place through official channels (Perlov, 1987, cited in Kerven, 1992), while, in Tanzania, official estimates suggested that 70% of livestock sales were taking place through unofficial cross-border channels (Homewood and Rodgers, 1991). Recent reviews dissect this perennially vigorous cross-border trade (McPeak and Little, 2006).

Southern Africa: Botswana. Botswana has a very long history of the development of commercialisation of pastoralism (Chapter 4). Anthropological, archaeological and historical material suggests a pastoro-forager system supplying wild products to east coast sites from the ninth century AD, and later to Mapungubwe and Great Zimbabwe, themselves centralised states based on cattle and trade (Wilmsen 1989). This export of wild products continued well into the nineteenth century. During this period the rapid expansion of the Tswana polity, already founded on the social circulation of cattle (Kuper, 1982, Hitchcock, 1990), brought the livestock and other resources of the Kalahari under Tswana control. Pastoralist products grew to make up 70% of all officially exported goods by the 1920s–40s. Unofficial trade is estimated to have reached five times the level of officially recorded sales, as livestock are easy to smuggle. After Independence in the 1960s, Botswana's long-established elite made a seamless transition from the exercise of power through *Kgamelo* and *mafisa* networks of animal redistribution and rangeland control (Chapter 4) to a profitable and specialised trade in cattle rearing for export of beef, first to South Africa and more recently to the UK and Europe.

Commercial ranching has developed alongside the growing involvement of Botswana people with labour migration, facilitated by the dispossession of the BaSarwa or San who became a reserve of cheap herding labour in the Kalahari (Wilmsen, 1989). By the 1940s the lack of herding labour in other parts of Botswana was having a noticeable impact on livestock management. Cattle are commonly herded only where there is danger of crop trespass or predation: otherwise they are allowed to roam, with calves often being kept near the homestead as an incentive for cows to return. Cattle-rearing concerns range from very large commercial operations grossing high returns (but showing limited efficiency per animal and an emphasis on single products) to large numbers of small herds (<20 head) where more intensive husbandry extracts a wide range of sometimes marginal products. The small operations are subsistence concerns, with low stock:people ratios, a wide diversity of products, more intimate labour-intensive husbandry, and few animals being marketed (Behnke, 1985). This strategy allows small producers to build their herds. Big producers invest in private water developments (gaining *de facto* control over grazing), and education (monopolising jobs, administrative control and political influence). Their market orientation siphons off animals which would once have been redistributed around the safety net/risk-avoidance/risk-spreading networks. In Botswana, commercialisation and integration with modern global markets have served to reinforce historical antecedents of inequalities in resource access and stock ownership (Hitchcock, 1990).

Conclusions on commercialisation of pastoral production. Changing commercialisation in pastoral production can be best appreciated through the three complementary perspectives of orthodox development theory, political economy and populist theories of indigenous innovation. Major commercial systems in sub-Saharan Africa emerged without technical interventions by development agencies. Commercialisation in the case-studies described here came about as spontaneous indigenous responses to changing opportunities and tradeoffs. In many cases market conditions alone have triggered a transition to more commercial systems over the last century or more. Recent technical interventions have, however, made a difference to those processes. Water development has in many cases extended the productive potential of particular rangeland areas, though the pressures on social institutions managing those changes have often been problematic. Vaccination programmes have eliminated rinderpest as a major threat to livestock, and made major differences elsewhere (e.g. to East Coast Fever/ECF mortality – Homewood et al., 2006). Where inputs have been targeted at established, successful producers, as was the main thrust of donor policies in the 1960s–80s and beyond, those inputs not surprisingly served primarily to enhance the private enterprises of the already well placed, whether through vaccination programmes (eg. ECF – Homewood et al., 2006), water development (eg Somalia – Little, 1996) and quarantine management (eg Foot and Mouth – Raikes 1981; Waller and Homewood, 1996; Scoones and Wolmer, 2006).

Over the last decades commercialisation has tended to go hand in hand with the spread of associated private control over basic productive resources. For any such transition to be relatively painless in social terms, there must be alternative possibilities for those outmigrants dispossessed by commercialisation (e.g. in the oil economy of Libya). In other cases it has brought about impoverishment of the dispossessed (in Somalia, Botswana, and increasingly in Kenya Maasailand and Samburu). On a local and immediate scale, the strategies of wealthy households inevitably change conditions for the poor. Live animals for milk and/or draught power are progressively withdrawn from social networks of patronage, obligation and reciprocity, and key resources including ultimately grazing land itself become harder to access. Poorer households are left with the options of selling their limited milk supply to meet food needs, of becoming hired herders, or of dropping out of the system to take up other livelihoods and/or swell the numbers of impoverished urban migrants (May, 2002; Homewood et al., forthcoming).

Diversification

Livelihoods diversification is the 'process by which rural households construct an increasingly diverse portfolio of activities and assets in order to survive and to improve their standard of living' (Ellis, 2000: 15). Across sub-Saharan Africa, rural people are increasingly diversifying out of and away from primarily agricultural and/or pastoralist activities, whether by choice or by necessity. Pastoralists are no exception. Pastoralist societies and economies have always been subject to change under the pressures, constraints and opportunities thrown up by changing physical environment and by shifting political and economic contexts. The history of any pastoralist group shows families going through long-term cycles of movement into and out of pastoralism as fortunes change. Drought, disease, and raiding have always caused livestock losses, while favourable conditions, good crop years, trading opportunities, and success in raiding and/or war allow re-establishment of herds.

However, many contemporary pastoralists are marginalised people being pushed into ever less tenable situations, rather than well-off households able to choose, or people in temporarily difficult conditions who are likely in the long term to re-establish a pastoral enterprise. Widespread shifts in access to resources of land and livestock are tending to impoverish and dispossess pastoralist groups altogether, or to concentrate ownership in the hands of a few (Bonfiglioli, 1992 ; Prior, 1994; Botswana – Behnke, 1985; White, 1987). It is not only external pressures forcing these changes. Age-group politics, wealth and ethnic identity continue to drive wealth differentiation from within (e.g. Maasai – Southgate and Hulme, 2000) often in synergy with external agencies, aided by the very fluidity and ambiguity of customary processes for continual renegotiation over access and tenure (Peters 2004). In Kenya, the sub-division of group ranches, and the wealth differentials created due to the abuse and misuse of political power, have been well documented (e.g. Galaty, 1999). Across sub-Saharan Africa, the impacts of national policy combine with more local political landscapes to give elites, leaders and gatekeepers opportunities for personal advantage in subdivision and titling of former communal rangelands, at the expense of the wider group.

Trajectories and dimensions of diversification

This section draws on general overviews to look at three dimensions of diversification: poverty strategies driven by necessity; risk-management strategies making the best of difficult, unpredictably changing ecologies and economies; and strategies of wealth investment and accumulation. It explores the implications of diversification for households, individuals and different genders and looks at the relative economic potential and security of the activities into which agropastoralists diversify (Iliya and Swindell, 1997; Homewood et al., forthcoming).

Diversification commonly includes: adjustment of occupation; reorientation of income-earning; shifting social identity and spatial relocation, processes which vary in sequence, rate and timing (Bryceson and Jamal, 1997). These

Table 9.1 Outline of diversification of pastoral livelihoods (TLU numbers indicative only)

	Marginal	Poor	Medium	Well-off	Very wealthy
TLU	None	<average	average	>average	100s–1000s
Land	None	<average	average	>average	Commercial crops, large acreages
Off/ Non-Farm Income: Secure? Regular? Skilled? How Paid?	Live as unpaid dependent or hired hand in another pastoral household or as outmigrant. Any income derives from casual, low paid, 'unskilled' work e.g. charcoal, firewood, casual labour, watchman	Low-paid, occasional, unskilled off-farm work. Household members may sometimes get extra income from e.g. charcoal, firewood, hired labour etc.	Minor, periodic revenue from unskilled or semi skilled work or rents e.g. occasional livestock trade / wildlife dividends	Significant, secure, regular income from skilled work including e.g. established trader, rental property, teacher salary,	Livestock trading, business interests, gem-stone mines; tourist shares; more than 1 individual in the household has regular, well-paid, skilled job
Assets	None	Few/ none	Plough, bike,	Shop, vehicle, business equipment	Farm machinery, property rental, vehicles
Remittances	None	Few/none: sons migrant, low-paid/ casual	Some eg son + regular job	Upwardly mobile sons	Major income rural/urban links
Contacts	None	None: marginalised	Minor	Useful kin/ connections	Traditional leader; government job

may happen in rapid sequence, as in the case of crises such as famine (Ellis, 2000; de Waal, 1989). More generally, different dimensions of diversification have potentially very different implications for individuals and households in different circumstances (Homewood et al., forthcoming). In Longido in Northern Tanzania, and elsewhere, poor individuals and households struggling to make ends meet (Table 9.1, column 2) may show rapid uptake of alternative locally based activities in search of income alongside whatever animals they still have, often through hiring out their labour to other households. They may work as hired herders, or as hired assistants in small local enterprises – shops, market stalls, teahouses, transport services. They may gather, process and sell local natural resources (water, fuelwood, charcoal, construction poles) and work as petty vendors. Women sell small amounts of milk, of garden produce like tobacco, retail small quantities of purchased commodities like tea, sugar and salt at the homestead, or prepare and sell street foods at the market.

As household circumstances deteriorate and where people have exhausted the possibilities of calling in social capital through loans and/or repayments of livestock, food and cash from kin and friends, those individuals who are most able to do so may leave in search of work elsewhere, lessening the demands on the household reserves, and sending back remittances if they do well. The remaining members may, if things continue to deteriorate, be forced to sell moveable assets, and eventually to sell or abandon fixed assets such as land and houses (c.f. de Waal, 1989). Many pastoralists are forced to diversify because individuals, households and whole groups are progressively losing access to the basic resources necessary for pastoral production.[1] Those losing access to the key resources of grazing, water, mineral licks, and gathered plants, and/or losing all their livestock due to drought, disease, theft, or losing labour due to ill health, are increasingly pushed into marginal positions (Table 9.1: column 1). The study of livelihoods at the margins of pastoralism then becomes the study of pastoralist diversification into non-livestock-based poverty strategies. This process has been widely documented, particularly for the pastoralists of Northern Kenya and the Horn (Baxter and Hogg, 1990; Hogg, 1987; Fratkin, 2001; Fratkin et al., 1999, 2004).

The study of pastoralist livelihoods at the margins does not immediately appear part of the study of pastoralism: without livestock, people are effectively invisible as pastoralists. Marginalised pastoralists with no livestock, no land, no herd or farm produce to sell, little education or relevant experience, and few contacts, may gather, process and sell natural resources. In earlier times impoverished pastoralists would live as gatherer-hunters (Spear and Waller, 1993; Anderson and Broch-Due, 1999). Increasingly, this possibility becomes criminalised as former common property resources become private, often fenced land, or state property such as game and forest reserves excluding extractive use. Ironically, wildlife-based livelihoods are now the preserve of the better-off, as African rural landscapes draw tourists who bring lucrative income

---

[1] This is currently happening in Longido as the Tanzanian government implements its current plans for 'wildlife management areas', supposedly community-based conservation areas in which all local habitation and resource use is banned – Homewood et al., 2005; Homewood et al., forthcoming.

to governments and entrepreneurs (Thompson and Homewood, 2002; Homewood et al., forthcoming).

With no assets, no remittances, and no social networks that can provide helpful contacts, individuals become hired hands or unpaid dependants working for their keep in other households, or outmigrants moving to local trading centres, or they move away altogether to mines or distant urban settlements where they may find casual, unskilled, low-paid and often hazardous work (men as watchman or miner; women as brewer or commercial sex worker), or they are reduced to begging. In these cases diversification represents a poverty strategy which is little more than the first stage of a well-documented process of crisis response spiralling into destitution. The activities people pursue are often barely sustainable and offer little opportunity to develop a reasonably secure livelihood as a skilled worker, let alone re-establish as an independent producer. Among pastoral Fulani in Burkina Faso, poverty was most strongly associated with the demographic characteristics of small households, unable to meet the sheer numbers needed to maintain livelihood networks spanning the range of rural (and urban) activities outlined below (Iliya and Swindell, 1997).

By contrast, families of medium wealth can manage risk and secure a buffer against fluctuations by diversifying (Table 9.1, column 3), so that not all income streams on which a given household depends are affected by the same potential shocks of drought or disease or conflict, and so that they can better cope with those shocks. Moderately well-off pastoralists commonly diversify so as to smooth the seasonal fluctuations of production and consumption. Some of the alternative income streams can be generated locally: in Kenya, Maasai landowners in reserves and sites adjacent to parks sometimes earn significant dividends from tourist revenue (Thompson and Homewood 2002; Homewood et al., forthcoming). Other activities require long-range movement: in the West African Sahel, the long 9-month dry season means a slack period in terms of the labour needs of agropastoral systems, and there are long-established patterns of seasonal labour migration (cf. Chapters 5 and 8; Hampshire and Randall, 1999), often to urban areas particularly in the West African coastal cities. The more pastoral the group, the less seasonally fluctuating this pattern of labour needs within the home production system, because livestock require care year-round. More pastoral subgroups of Fulani are less likely to send young men on labour migration than are more agropastoral groups and households (Hampshire and Randall, 1999). Nonetheless, even strongly pastoral groups may show such patterns of seasonal labour migration to urban areas (Somali – Cassanelli, 1982; Beja – Morton, 1990, 1993; Pantuliano, 2002), as much to lessen the consumption needs of the household as in the hope of accumulating profit. Labour migration follows established contacts, and among moderately well-placed families with definite connections people may have reasonably-paid and reliable job opportunities.

In a wide range of pastoral groups, families may increasingly seek to establish and maintain multilocal households with urban and rural branches. Structural adjustment was expected by international financial institutions and Western donor governments to drive a shift of labour from urban back to rural enterprises. In practice, it triggered big price shifts which cannot be matched by comparable shifts in income. In many cases families have responded by diversifying so as to maintain both rural and urban parts of extended households, and by developing diverse livelihood strategies that cross commonly assumed analytical boundaries between sectors and production systems. Rural dwellers produce food and also some crops for cash sales, as well as potentially earning a wage through hiring their labour out to off-farm and/or non-farm work. They are able to send food, and in some cases cash, to help their urban kin, who themselves earn from wage labour, provide a base for young people at school or ill people attending hospital, perhaps qualify for food aid or subsidised purchases, and where possible send remittances back to the rural base, storing (part of) their wealth in family-managed herds. With both rural and urban parts of the extended household earning cash and producing food, there is movement to and fro of goods, money, food, individuals and their labour as well as their consumption needs, and some immunity from drastic shifts in market prices.

The wealthiest households diversify not so much to manage risk as to develop a portfolio of investments and manoeuvre to acquire ownership of high-value resources. Increasing rural population densities and intensifying rural-urban links create opportunities to accumulate cash (Bryceson and Jamal, 1997). With growing rural populations and the spread of urban settlements, there is increasing scarcity of, demand for and commodification of formerly free natural resources, especially water, fuelwood, thatch and construction poles. With structural adjustment, former government provision of social services has dwindled, and local provision, for a fee, of healing, midwifery and other services, expands to fill the gap. The growing rural population means burgeoning rural enterprises, from house construction to trade and transport, and the associated service industries (teahouses, eating houses, small hotels). There is increasing demand for provision of water, firewood, charcoal, fodder; processing and selling of food and beverages; brewing; trade and transport; tailoring; house construction and associated brickmaking, pole-cutting, transport and sale; carpentry and metalwork, leatherwork and pottery. Some pastoral individuals and households acquire the necessary skills and have access to the necessary capital, raw materials and equipment to respond to these opportunities.

Both well-off and poor households may show a wide range of occupations, but the occupations themselves are likely to be of a different nature, and better-off individuals are likely to specialise rather than engage in multiple activities (Iliya and Swindell, 1997; Ellis, 2000). Better-off households are typically big households. It is common to find one son managing the herds, another the agricultural enterprise, while yet others have entered salaried occupations as government employees or businessmen. Individuals engage in high-skilled, high-return activities, requiring qualifications and enjoying the security of a regular wage or salary. These occupations draw on, develop and maintain networks of relatively influential political contacts (as government officials or in other gatekeeper positions). Wealthier pastoral individuals bankroll enterprises as owner or shareholder, paying others to run them, moving beyond customary involvement in large-scale livestock trading and in the politics of local social institutions, to large-scale business and political interests, as national or international entrepreneurs and politicians.

Box 9.1 Poverty and pastoralist diversification: examples from Northern Kenya

The Pastoralist Forum (http://www.ids.ac.uk/eldis/pastoralism/index.htm)
provides an electronic snapshot of current views and concerns about pastoralist
development issues and diversification in particular, with contributions focusing on
pressures to diversify, opportunities for diversification and constraints on the
potential for diversification and the livelihoods that may result. Recent Pastoralist
Forum exchanges on diversification in Northern Kenya illustrate these concerns.

In the Northern part of Kenya, increasing numbers are dropping out of
pastoralism and the viability of pastoralist livelihoods is diminishing (Sandford,
2006a and b; van den Boogard, 2002). Already by the 1980s one-third of the
Turkana were in relief camps or resettled on irrigation schemes (Little and Leslie,
1999). Aid organisations continue to implement projects and programmes which
seek to support the pastoralist system, but have to address the contradictions
between helping pastoralists to diversify, and supporting/preserving pastoralist
livelihoods and pastoralism. On the one hand, there have been two decades of
restocking programmes seeking to re-establish impoverished pastoralists as livestock
owners and keepers. In a recent evaluation, few restocked families in Northern
Kenya had resumed a fully mobile transhumant pastoralist existence (Heffernan et al.,
2001). Most were likely to manage their acquired animals from a settled base as peri-
urban poor, pursuing a variety of other income-generating activities, and prioritising
education and general transferable skills for their children rather than wanting them to
be independent herdowners. The common perception among formerly restocked
pastoralists in Baringo and Samburu, and poor pastoralists in Garissa, is that the future
of pastoralism is becoming one of wealthy urban livestock owners making use of the
labour of poor rural livestock herders (Heffernan et al., 2001).

Non-governmental organisations such as FARM-Africa have helped pastoralists
to diversify and set up butchers shops, eco-tourism camps, and businesses running
trucks in Samburu, Marsabit and Moyale. Elsewhere people dropping out of the
pastoralist economy have diversified into hotel businesses, artisanal mining, and
subsistence farming in areas such as Garissa, Isiolo and Mandera. Others have
developed homecraft industries of basketwork, mat-weaving, beadwork and wood
carving in Marsabit, Isiolo and Turkana Districts. Some are drawn into established
fishing industries on Lakes Turkana (Broch-Due, 1999), Bogoria and Baringo
(Anderson, 1988). There is a steady trade in the valuable narcotic stimulant *miraa*
(*khat*) at local markets in most areas occupied by pastoralists in Kenya.

However, there is limited capacity in Northern Kenya for these activities. Both
education and improved economic growth would be needed for other
opportunities to open up, but Kenya has been in recession. There is a continuing
demand for pastoralists to take low-level jobs as watchmen, both in rural areas
(banditry and cattle rustling are on the increase in the ten districts of Northern
Kenya) and in urban areas. This echoes the situation in Tanzania, where Maasai are
valued as 'fierce' watchmen in Mwanza and Arusha, and where the job carries a
high risk (Coast, 2001).

Despite these trajectories of diversification, and often impoverishment, extensive
pastoralism remains ecologically and economically robust for those able to retain
access to land and livestock (Devereux and Scoones, 2006; McPeak and Little,
2006).

Earlier categorisations of formal versus informal economy, rural versus urban households and agropastoral versus other occupations have given way to an understanding of the more complex nature of diversified on-farm, off-farm and non–farm rural activities. 'On-farm' corresponds to agricultural (including livestock-related) work, with the holdings belonging to the individual or household. 'Off-farm' activities comprise all agricultural (including livestock-related) work carried out for a wage on the farms or herds of other households – for example, as hired herder or farm labourer. 'Non-farm' activities include all other work, whether for a wage, as petty trader or independent entrepreneur, in construction or servicing other rural enterprises. These intergrade with urban-based jobs.

Diversification becomes an enduring transition from primarily pastoralist or agropastoral livelihoods to truly multiple sources of income, with a third to a half of household income coming from non-farm activities (Ellis, 2000; Homewood et al., forthcoming). Diversification of this sort does not necessarily constitute economic development. In economic terms, it does not follow the forward and backward links which would, for example, mesh development in the agricultural sector with food processing and cart-making/ transport systems, etc. Instead there is, for most people, an opportunistic uptake, for example, of petty trade, often of cheap imported goods or secondhand clothes (Bryceson and Jamal, 1997; Bryceson, 1999). In a recent cross-border, multi-site comparative study, the poorest Maasai show the greatest diversification away from livestock-based incomes (Homewood et al., forthcoming). Often the intensification of rural-urban links goes along with processes of globalisation which make it increasingly hard to find positive local compromises. Morton (1990, 1993) has explored the complexities of the Beja petty traders locked into networks of credit and obligation with the big Port Sudan traders, while big agricultural schemes have expanded at the expense of Beja rangelands, particularly in the Gash area. The small tenants on the schemes find it hard, if not impossible, to make cotton pay, and are progressively displaced by major operators, who can consolidate ever larger holdings and who bring in West African labour to work them.

Corollaries of diversification and development

Intensification and sedentarisation

Pockets of high-potential land (Spear, 1997) and cases of exceptional market opportunities (Behnke, 1980) have underpinned success stories of intensification (Mortimore, 2005; Tiffen et al., 1994; though see Murton, 1999). In a number of cases, outside investors have been quick to capture such opportunities (Igoe and Brockington, 1999), often converting key resources to land uses which remove them from pastoralist access (e.g. irrigation for export crops; enclosure as protected areas). More generally, the overwhelming constraints – arid and semi-arid climates, lack of permanent water, low soil fertility, remoteness, lack of capital for veterinary or agricultural inputs – have limited intensification to date.

However, intensification and sedentarisation are taking place alongside diversification away from pastoralism. Sedentarisation was encouraged by colonial and subsequent post-Independence governments, as necessary for effective administration, taxation and provision of health, education and other infrastructure. Apart from wealthier pastoralists commonly settling in urban areas to pursue political and business interests, however, herd-owners have tended to resist the constraints sedentarisation imposes on mobility and management. In Tanzania, for example, Maasai responded to the national drive for villagisation, but retained flexible transhumance little changed by the emergence of village centres (Ndagala, 1982; though see Bishop, 2007 for wider-term impacts). Elsewhere, pastoralists hit by drought, famine, epidemics or warfare, had little choice but to settle, whether as refugees around relief centres, or on state-sponsored agricultural schemes (Turkana – Little and Leslie 1999; Boran – Dahl 1979, Randall 2005). The negative implications often attributed to sedentarisation are correlates of poverty and forced settlement rather than of sedentarisation *per se* (Fratkin and Roth, 2005). The trajectories of different groups of households settled under contrasting circumstances, with different access to resources and opportunities, range from highly positive economic and ecological outcomes achieved through incorporating the activities and opportunities of sedentary life as one part of multi-stranded livelihoods, to situations of near-destitution.

Intensification is a natural corollary of more sedentary land use. As such livelihoods shift from more mobile herding to more settled agropastoralism, and mixed farming (Chapter 3) trajectories follow the patterns identified by Mortimore (1998, 2005). Under favourable circumstances, there is positive feedback between livestock and farming, with increasingly intensive management of soil fertility through manuring and feed supplementation with crop residues, and of traction and draft (McCown et al., 1979). Crop surpluses are invested in livestock, and livestock increases can pay for the hire of additional labour, tractors or other inputs. New breeds, technologies and markets offer new opportunities, as local knowledge and expertise expand to encompass new possibilities. However, these trajectories are not all in the direction of greater integration and intensification (Scoones and Wolmer, 2002).

Gender issues

Women's activities and workloads. The socio-economic position, autonomy, health and education of pastoralist women are changing. Development interventions may create and reinforce inequalities (Talle, 1988; Sullivan, 2000). With sedentarisation, intensification and urbanisation, problems of fuel, water, raw materials, fodder, services, transport and communications are inevitably experienced differently by different types of household and categories of individual. The types of income-generating activities recorded for poor pastoralist women include cultivation, sale of milk/ milk products, brewing, charcoal burning, collection and sale of fuelwood, collection and sale of plant medicines, prostitution, petty trade, craftwork and education leading to employment (Dahl, 1979; Heffernan, et al. 2001; Brockington, 2001a). Diversification can mean a blurring of former gender barriers, but is likely to present more options for men than for women. For example, brewing moves from being traditionally a woman's social role within the household, and women's contribution to community ceremonial and ritual, to being a commercial enterprise managed by men. Men, women, and youth of both sexes engage in petty trade. Women's choices among different activities are constrained not only by opportunity and by relative economic returns, but also by religion and culture which dictate certain codes of behaviour. Fulani *pulaaku* and Maasai *enkanyit* dictate values of reserve, modesty, and self-restraint, though they are interpreted, applied and expressed differently by different ethnic subgroups. They create an arena for negotiation and manipulation as much as a normative straitjacket, but being seen to adhere to the code, as it is locally understood, is central to retaining the respect and support of the social network on which a woman depends (Buhl, 1999; Buhl and Homewood, 2000). Nonetheless, women come to place a monetary value on their labour: Samburu women experiencing a development intervention came away equating development with enhanced individual opportunities for and participation in trade (Straight, 2000).

One corollary of rural sedentarisation in Maasailand and elsewhere (Talle, 1988; Grandin, 1986) has been the progressive shift towards smaller settlements where individual households establish a homestead and cultivate as a strategy to stake private claim to ownership of an area. Many women find themselves dealing single-handed with all the aspects of domestic chores, child care, food preparation, fuel and water collection, alongside cultivation, caring for livestock and maintaining the small income-generating activities on which they depend to keep the household fed. With an effectively nuclear family, or a female-headed household, women may lose possibilities open to them in larger settlements of sharing and implementing economies of scale and division of labour among themselves.

Using spot sampling over a brief period, Fratkin and Smith (1995) measured women's workloads associated with four stages of sedentarisation among the Rendille: mobile pastoralists; settled pastoralists; agropastoralists and town-based ex-pastoralists without livestock. Patterns of work differed among categories but there was no significant increase or decrease with diversification or sedentarisation of mean times spent working by women, though patterns did change for men and children. It is, however, important to disentangle the effects of impoverishment from those of diversification and sedentarisation. Sedentarisation, for example, may often make access to water easier, but access to fuelwood harder, while poverty generally makes both more difficult. While sedentarisation and diversification may adversely affect poor women's workloads and also their control of their own labour (Joekes and Ponting, 1991), this may only become clear where analyses differentiate between households and individual women in different circumstances (Ostergaard, 1992; Fratkin and Roth, 2005). Though sedentarisation *per se* may not affect women's workloads overall, the workdays of poorer women may be intensified: not only do women work for a wage during the day, but they continue to be responsible for the household chores morning and evening.

Access to and control over land, livestock and natural resources. The increasing workloads for poorer women, and in many cases their loss of control over their own labour with impoverishment, diversification and sedentarisation, may be exacerbated by tenure changes, changes in livestock entitlements and by the dwindling availability of and access to natural resources. With sedentarisation and land adjudication, title to land has most commonly been reserved for men. Colonial impacts may have contributed to such gender differences in rights of access and control of land and livestock (Hodgson, 2000a). Pastoralist women in a range of groups have customarily co-owned and managed livestock and land, as well as having important roles in healing and in political negotiation. Colonial assumptions about working through male heads of household, assigning land title and attributing ownership of livestock to men, may have created and exacerbated gender inequalities. Post-Independence development interventions continued to work through male heads of household, entailing major implications for women's rights of ownership, and their social, economic and political disempowerment. Women whose husbands have mismanaged their land and their herd, or who are widowed, find themselves dispossessed and excluded, where their access, use of resources, and livelihoods would have been safeguarded under customary forms of tenure and entitlement (e.g. Talle, 1988; Joekes and Ponting, 1991). Even in systems where women have not owned livestock as property which they themselves can dispose of, they have customarily acted as guardians and managers for the livestock accruing to their male offspring. In a range of pastoralist systems, women were allocated livestock which could not then be reallocated or sold off without the woman's consent (e.g. Maasai – Spencer, 1988). The growing ascendance of market pressures over social obligations make it increasingly common for such livestock to be disposed of by men without consulting their wives (Talle 1988).

At the same time, another prop of women's economic security – their use of gathered resources – is being undermined. With the rapid spread of private and exclusive ownership, with the spread of fencing and with increasing concentration round population centres, access to areas where women can gather wild plants for fuel, foods, fibres, medicines, and other products is becoming increasingly difficult (eg. Namibia – Sullivan, 1999a, 1999c, 2000a; Bénin – Schreckenberg, 1996). This affects women and their dependants at every level of income, workloads and food security (Anon, 1990). As fuelwood becomes more scarce, fewer meals may be prepared, food may be less well cooked, small children and elderly folk may have fewer suitable foods prepared for them at a time when pastoral foods are increasingly replaced by diets centring on cultivated foods (which need more preparation and cooking time). Women may have to spend more time seeking fuel, or may have to find the money to purchase fuel. This last means restructuring domestic activities and perhaps spending more time on producing items that can be sold to finance fuel purchases. A similar chain of knock-on effects surrounds the dwindling availability of gathered foods (*fonio* and *cramcram* (Tamasheq); shea butter nut (West African Fulani); honey (Maasai); seeds (Namibia – Sullivan, 1999a); and also fibres, for example for making mats. These last are necessary as household items (e.g. mobile Fulani houses) as well as providing the basis for women's income-generating activities (Konstant et al., 1995; Sullivan et al., 1995). Now, women are increasingly taking on diverse income-generating activities (e.g. Heffernan et al., 2001) and putting monetary values on labour (e.g. Straight, 2000).

Milk management. Women's management of milk changes as it becomes less easily available, with fewer animals, with animals being resident for more of the year and their production often constrained by poor forage and higher parasite load, and with more milk being diverted from social networks to market outlets. The social redistribution of milk among the Maasai is important not only to poorer individuals, who benefit from the milk as food, but also in establishing the women who manage the milk as central and responsible for matters of importance to the household and to the group as a whole (Talle, 1990). Progressively greater diversion of that milk to market outlets affects the fabric of social relations (Grandin, 1988 for Kenya (Kajiado) Maasai; Ndagala, 1990, 1992 for Tanzanian (Monduli) Maasai).

In some cases, with the commoditisation and commercialisation of milk, women lose control of both the management and the proceeds of milk sales, particularly where there is the possibility of larger-scale dairying enterprises. It has a knock-on effect on nutrition for the household as a whole, and for their dependants in particular. Fulani women manage the proceeds of milk sales to ensure an adequate diet for the family, while feeling more free to use earnings from other sources (mat-making, wild products, etc.) for their own small purchases (Waters-Bayer 1985). As urban agglomerations grow in semi arid and arid areas, the opportunities to sell milk and other pastoral products become progressively greater (e.g. Nkedianye et al., forthcoming). As more and more pastoralist households find themselves dispossessed by the enclosure of the rangelands, and as male labour migration leaves more female-headed households to fend for themselves, urban dairying activities by pastoralist women become increasingly common (Somalia – Herren, 1990; Little, 1994 and Nigeria – Waters-Bayer, 1985). These enterprises are characteristically small-scale individual activities with little capital investment and low profit margins. Sikana and Kerven (1991), Sikana et al. (1993) analyse their effect on the division of labour and on control of income in the domestic economy. Among the Baggara Arabs of Kordofan, the growing importance of milk sales in the domestic economy has meant the continued importance of women's role in processing dairy products, alongside increased status and more input into decisions over migration routes. In other cases, men take control of marketing and revenue, and women's autonomy and income deteriorate with knock-on effects on the food and health of dependants (Salih, 1985 – Khartoum).

Education, development and diversification

Pastoralist areas and populations tend to have very low levels of educational attainment and marked gender differentials. Spatial factors, the physical environment, the production system, mobility, poverty, local attitudes to modern education, and misinformed perceptions of local populations by politically dominant groups from which many teachers and administrators are drawn, all contribute to the widening gap between agropastoralist peoples in semi-arid areas and other economic groups and regions across Africa (Krätli, 2000, 2001; Carr-Hill, 2002).

Levels of formal education among the Fulani of Mali and Burkina are comparably low (Castle, 1992, 1995; Hampshire and Randall, 1999). Within the Burkina population, more settled Liptaako Fulani showed higher literacy levels than did the mobile GaoBe and nomadic DjelgoBe. Mobile lifestyles and the role of children in the pastoral economy combine to limit schooling. Enrolment is low and attendance irregular. Around half or fewer of school-age pastoralist children were enrolled for primary education in Nigerian areas where schools were available (Vereecke, 1989). A survey of 14,925 Maasai showed 9% Tanzanian and 32% Kenyan Maasai children aged 7–12 years enrolled in primary education, significantly below national averages (Coast, 2000, 2002). There are marked gender differences in education in most pastoral groups. More boys than girls are educated: for example, among Tanzanian Maasai, of all children aged 8–10 at the time of a 1998 survey, 28% of boys and 17% of girls were currently attending primary school; 10% of all women and 34% men aged above 20 years had received any education. Maasai comment, that historically, less-favoured children were selected for school attendance, but now the most promising are sent.

Historically, an educated wife was seen as a troublemaker more likely to desert her husband (Coast, 2002). Maasai households are now increasingly choosing to educate daughters as well as sons (Bishop, 2003, 2007), despite persistent concerns about the implications for deeply held cultural ideals. Differentials may change with sedentarisation. Among more settled Fulani, orthodox Islam is strong and Koranic schooling is common. In these families girls may also be taught to read and write. The tradition of highly respected women poets (Boyd, 1986) provides a cultural basis for educating women. Some groups show less gender differential: among Tuareg nobles, the ancient Berber Tifinagh script is still used, and Tuareg noble women as well as men are literate in the Tamasheq language. Across a broad range of societies, maternal education is a very strong predictor of reduced infant mortality. It seems to operate as much through positive effects on women's autonomy, knowledge of health-care options, and ability to seek out and gain access to appropriate forms of health care, as through any specific understanding (e.g. the germ theory of disease). The extent to which a society accords women rights, entitlements, representation and autonomy, is a major predictor of improvement in infant mortality (Caldwell, 1986, 1989).

Education may affect livelihood outcomes, such as retention of rights to land (Galaty, 1992; Igoe and Brockington, 1999) and gender relations, particularly women's livelihoods (Kipury, 1989). Better education could potentially equip pastoralists against impoverishment and, ultimately, open access to more viable alternative livelihood options. Low educational performance has serious implications for poverty, social exclusion, land loss and conflict in these poor and marginalised areas and populations. With increasing levels of social differentiation within pastoral groups (Anderson and Broch-Due, 1999), the consequences of sending children to school differ for poorer and richer households, in terms of the effects on pastoral and agricultural activities, and on other aspects of household livelihood strategies. Wealthier households are more able to afford both the direct and the opportunity costs of sending children to school, which can be high, despite purportedly 'free' education provision in many pastoral areas. Children from poorer families are left behind by this process, or actively removed from it when they are drafted in to fill the labour needs left by the school enrolment of children from better-off families (Bishop, 2007). Attempts in the mid-1980s to establish educational systems for Fulani and other pastoralists in Nigeria were given considerable financial support. Nonetheless, they largely failed to identify pastoralist priorities or to make the educational programme relevant and practicable for mobile families. Together with the low priority pastoralists put on education as opposed to livestock management issues, and the limited nature of the services that were provided, these initiatives had little effect (Ezeomah, 1985; Vereecke, 1989).

At the beginning of the twenty-first century Western donor governments and international agencies are once again putting major financial resources into education for all, and it will be important to learn from past experience. In many cases, and on top of all the other problems of supply and demand, current official curricula denigrate pastoralist land use and livestock management, and pastoralism as a way of life, while failing to take account of pastoralists' specialised knowledge and skills, and denying the economic and ecological contributions of pastoralism (for examples concerning Maasai areas, see Bishop, 2007; Bonini, 1998). Where those biases resonate with the crises people have experienced, as with Turkana refugees from drought and conflict, poor or destitute former pastoralists may prefer to see their children's future as outside pastoralism, and as depending on education, because the only alternative is insecure, poorly paid work as a hired herder (Heffernan et al., 2001).

Education is widely seen by outside agencies as key to finding pathways out of poverty for vulnerable pastoralists, as a basis for diversification into more secure livelihoods. Demand is rising as people recognise the skills and opportunities formal education can bring (Bishop, 2007; Homewood et al., forthcoming). However, conditions in pastoralist areas conspire to undermine educational attainment, and it will be important to develop approaches to education that both value and make it possible to retain the skills pastoralists have developed over millennia in managing their environments and their animals.

Conclusion: the futures of African pastoralism

This book began with the difficulties of defining pastoralism and of estimating the numbers of people and the scale of enterprises involved. African pastoralists emerge as constituting a loose, permeable, highly diverse category that embraces people from a wide spectrum of ethnic groups, ecologies and economies, engaged in an enormous range of livestock-related occupations. They range from mobile transhumant herdowners dependent primarily on pastoral produce, through livestock traders moving animals along the commodity chain from Sahelian producer to urban meat consumer, through landless, stockless hired herders and settled agropastoralists combining livestock and cropping enterprises, to peri-urban, settled households managing a few livestock for dairy trade as one component of a portfolio of income-generating activities. The historical trajectories sketched in this book show that, for millennia, Africans have managed livestock in a variety of economies and societies, often geographically remote but tied into systems of exchange and trade, continually shifting between specialised livestock production and diversified, complementary, sometimes conflicting forms of land use and labour allocation.

This book tries to convey the richness and complexity of social, cultural and economic factors influencing pastoralist systems, while taking the ecological dimension as a central organising theme. Pastoralists respond to biophysical opportunities and constraints so as to make the most of often unpredictable and continuously shifting conditions of forage and water availability, on the one hand, and disease challenge, on the other. In arid and semi-arid environments, livestock offer the chance of turning patchy, sparse, scarce, unreliable rangeland resources into produce supporting whole societies and contributing a considerable proportion of Africa's total food production. At the other end of the ecosystem scale, in the humid highlands and forests, livestock production competes with alternative land uses, and pastoralists compete with other cultures and economic groupings. Nigh on a century of new breeds, and new technologies providing water, forage, veterinary care and global markets, where these have been limiting factors, have altered the details of pastoralist ecology, but made little difference overall to African pastoralist systems and production.

The truly far-reaching change for the ecology of pastoralists has turned on shrinking land areas, on the one hand, and growing population numbers, on the other, changing people's access to the rangeland and water resources that represent the basic factors of pastoral production (Sandford, 2006b; Devereux and Scoones, 2006). Pre-colonial pastoralist societies were often militarily and politically dominant over wide areas of Africa. From the colonial period on, pathways to privatisation of rangeland and water resources have proliferated, and the African commons are fast becoming African enclosures. At the same time, and largely underlying their loss of tenure and access, most mobile pastoralist peoples have fallen politically behind settled populations more able to access education and political representation, and more in tune with centralised national governments.

At the beginning of the twenty-first century, those trends in tenure, access, education and representation dominate pastoralist development trajectories. They underlie the progressive concentration of livestock ownership in the hands of absentee owners, leaving rural herders poor and marginalised, and the dominance of livestock health and production policies that favour national and international elites (e.g. Scoones and Wolmer, 2006). There will continue to be livestock herded on the African rangelands, integrated in mixed farms, and kept in peri-urban areas for dairy purposes. The ways in which those animals are managed may continue to show many of the features of indigenous livestock production systems, notwithstanding the uptake of innovative practices that producers see to be worthwhile. However, transhumant movements are likely to decline further. Most African governments continue to hold entrenched views about pastoralism being environmentally destructive and economically irrational, though (despite debates on the margin) research over the last three decades has repeatedly confirmed the ecological efficacy and sustainability of mobile transhumant pastoral production systems. Where the gulf between people owning and people managing livestock continues to grow, pastoralists who remain rural livestock-keepers in remote areas are unlikely to develop better representation, and governments will remain unwilling to acknowledge the benefits of transhumant pastoral production.

Moves to strengthen and codify seasonal transhumant access to migration routes and rangeland resources are beginning to be adopted in some cases, (eg Mali's *Code Pastoral*), and in some cases pastoralists have retained or regained a measure of political power sufficient to make their voice heard and to keep the issue of pastoral mobility on the national agenda, such as in Kenya (Markakis, 1999) and Nigeria. More commonly, corridors allowing transhumance are becoming harder to access, more difficult for herders to manage with large numbers of livestock, more likely to generate conflict with farmers anxious for their crops, and less able to provide for the grazing and watering needs of the animals. Parallel problems are as important in African agricultural and agropastoral as in pastoral systems (Berry, 1993). All these production systems are geared to surviving unstable conditions of resource access, meaning a great deal must be invested in staying flexible. However, their fluidity and ambiguity not only exact costs in terms of time and resources invested but also offer dangerous scope for expropriation by the well-placed, rapidly intensifying inequalities as a result (Peters, 2004).

Donor policies have hitherto centred either on livestock production and marketing interventions (eg. Scoones and Wolmer, 2006), on natural resources and desertification, or on 'building civil society', targeting institution-building, particularly herders' organisations (Oxby, 1999). These do not necessarily represent pastoralist priorities: up till now, outsiders have tended to dominate the formulation of those policies and the interventions they entail, and nascent local organisations are easily disrupted by external and internal pressures (Igoe, 2003). For most pastoralist societies, local within-group politics are increasingly connecting with processes of expropriation and wealth accumulation, driven by national elites and transnational agencies, to bring about 'the simultaneous creation of privilege and penury, wealth and poverty, political power and powerlessness' that Peters (2004: 285) sees as underlying conflict, exclusion and differentiation across Africa. The many possible futures of African pastoralist societies, and the range of diversity they continue to embrace, will depend on the trajectories of change that are now taking place in tenure and access, and on whether current trends in education and representation are able to shape those patterns of tenure and access in ways that sustain the ecology of pastoralism as a continuing dimension of African landscapes, livelihoods and societies.

Bibliography

Abel, N. 1993. 'Reducing cattle numbers on Southern African communal range: Is it worth it?' in R. Behnke, I. Scoones & C. Kerven (eds), *Range Ecology at Disequilibrium: New models of natural variability and pastoral adaptation in African Savannas.* London: Overseas Development Institute.

Abel, N. and Blaikie, P. 1990. *Land Degradation, Stocking Rates and Conservation Policy in the Communal Rangelands of Botswana and Zimbabwe,* Pastoral Development Network 29a. London: Overseas Development Institute.

Adams, W. 1992. *Wasting the Rain: Rivers, people and planning in Africa.* London: Earthscan.

Adams, W., Brockington, D., Dyson, J. and Vira, B. 2001. *Common Choices: Policy options for common pool resources.* DFID-NRSPSAP R 7073. Dept. of Geography: University of Cambridge.

Adamu, M. and Kirk-Greene, A. (eds) 1986. *Pastoralists of the West African Savanna.* Manchester: Manchester University Press.

Adamu, M. 1986. 'The Role of Fulani and Tuareg Pastoralists in the Central Sudan 1405–1903'. in M. Adamu and A. Kirk-Greene (eds). 1986. *Pastoralists of the West African Savanna.* Manchester: Manchester University Press.

Ahmed, M. 1988. 'Primary Export Crop Production and the Ecological Crisis in Kordofan: The case of Dar Hamar', in D. Johnson and D. Anderson (eds), *The Ecology of Survival.* London: Lester Crook.

Ainslie, A. 1998. 'Managing Natural Resources in a Rural Settlement in Peddie District'. Unpublished Msc. Thesis, Rhodes University, Grahamstown, South Africa.

Ainslie, A. 2005. 'Losing Ground: Cattle and the politics of value in the communal reserves of the eastern Cape Province, South Africa'. Unpublished PhD Thesis, University of London.

Ajayi, J. F. A. and Crowder M. (eds). 1985. *History of West Africa.* Harlow and Ibadan: Longman.

Allen, T. (ed.) 1996. *In Search of Cool Ground: War, flight and homecoming in North East Africa.* Oxford: James Currey, and Lawrenceville, NJ: Africa World Press, in association with UNRISD.

Anderson D. 1984. 'Depression, Dust Bowl, Demography and Drought: the Colonial State and Soil Conservation in East Africa During the 1930s', *African Affairs* 83:321–43.

Anderson, D. 1988. 'Cultivating pastoralists: ecology and economy among the Il Chamus of Baringo 1840–1980'. in D. Johnson and D. Anderson (eds). *The Ecology of Survival.* London: Lester Crook.

Anderson, D. 2002. *Eroding the Commons: The politics of ecology in Baringo, Kenya 1890–1968.* Oxford: James Currey.

Anderson, D. and Broch-Due, V. 1999. *The Poor Are Not Us.* Oxford: James Currey.

Anderson, D. and Grove, R. (eds) 1987. *Conservation in Africa: People, policies and practice.* Cambridge: Cambridge University Press.

Andrzewski, B.W. and Andrzewski, S. 1986. *Somali Poetry.* Bloomington, IN: Indiana University Press.

Anon, 1990. 'The Impact of Fuelwood Scarcity on Dietary Patterns: Hypotheses for research', *Unasylva* 41 (160): 29–34.

Arhem, K. 1985. *Pastoral Man in the Garden of Eden: The Maasai of Ngorongoro Conservation Area, Tanzania.* Uppsala Research Report in Cultural Anthropology. Uppsala University.

Arhem, K., Homewood, K. and Rodgers, W. A. 1981. *A Pastoral Food System: The Ngorongoro*

Maasai in Tanzania. BRALUP Research Paper n° 70. Dar es Salaam: University of Dar es Salaam.

Asad, T. 1970. *The Kababish Arabs: Power, authority and consent in a nomadic tribe*. New York: Praeger.

Aubréville, A. 1949. *Climats, forêts et désertification de l'Afrique tropicale, Vol. 1*. Paris: Soc. d'Edit. Géog. Marit. et Colon.

Ausenda, G. 1987. 'Leisurely Nomads: The Hadendowa (Beja) of the Gash Delta and Transition to Sedentary Village Life'. Unpublished doctoral dissertation, New York: Columbia University.

Azarya, V., Breedveld, A., Bruijn, M. and Dijk, H. (eds). 1999. *Pastoralists Under Pressure?: Fulbe societies confronting change in West Africa*. Leiden, Boston: Brill.

Baier, S. 1976. 'Economic History and Development: Drought and the Sahelian Economics of Niger', *African Economic History* (Spring): 1–6.

Baker, L. and Hoffmann, T. 2006. 'Managing Variability: Herding strategies in communal rangelands of semi-arid Namaqualand, South Africa', *Human Ecology* 34: 765–84.

Barnes, C., Ensminger, J. and O'Keefe, P. 1984. *Wood Energy and Households: Perspectives on rural Kenya*, Uppsala: Beijer Institute and Scandinavian Institute of African Studies.

Barnes, D. L. 1979. 'Cattle Ranching in the Semi Arid Savannas of East and South Africa'. In B. Walker (ed.), *Management of Semi Arid Ecosystems*. Amsterdam and Oxford: Springer.

Barrow, E. 1990. 'Usufruct Rights to Trees: The Role of Ekwar in Dryland Central Turkana, Kenya'. *Human Ecology* 18 (2): 163–76.

Barthelme, J. 1985. 'Fisher hunters and Neolithic pastoralists in East Turkana, Kenya'. *BAR Int Ser* 254, Oxford.

Bassett, T. 1994. 'Hired Herders and Herd Management in Fulani Pastoralism', *Cahiers d'Etudes Africaines* XXXIV: 147–74.

Bassett, T. and Crummey, D. 2003. *African Savannas: Global narratives and local knowledge of environmental change* Oxford: James Currey; Portsmouth, NH: Heinemann.

Bassi, M. 1997. 'Returnees in Moyale District Southern Ethiopia: new means for an old interethnic game', in R. Hogg (ed.), *Pastoralists, Ethnicity and the State in Ethiopia*. London: HAAN/ Institute for African Alternatives.

Baumann, M., Janzen, J. and Schwartz, H. (eds) 1993. *Pastoral Production in Central Somalia*. Berlin: Deutsche Gesellschaft für Technische Zusammenarbeit.

Baxter, P. 1975. 'Some Consequences of Sedentarization for Social Relationships', in T. Monod (ed.), *Pastoralism in Tropical Africa*. Oxford: Oxford University Press.

Baxter, P. 1991. '"Big Men" and Cattle Licks in Oromoland', in P. Baxter (ed.), *When the Grass is Gone: Development intervention in African arid lands*. Uppsala: Scandinavian Inst. African Studies.

Baxter, P. 1994. 'The Creation and Constitution of Oromo Nationality', in K. Fukui and J Markakis (eds), *Ethnicity and Conflict in the Horn of Africa*. Oxford: James Currey/Athens, OH: Ohio University Press.

Baxter, P. and Hogg, R. 1990. *Property, Poverty and People: Changing rights in property and problems of pastoral development*. Manchester: Dept of Social Anthropology and International Development, University of Manchester.

Bayer, W. 1990. 'Use of Native browse by Fulani cattle in central Nigeria', *Agroforestry Systems* 12: 217–28.

Beach, D. 1994. *The Shona and Their Neighbours*. Oxford: Blackwell.

Beaumont, P., Bonine, M. and MacLachlan, K. (eds), 1989. *Qanat, Kariz and Khattara*. Middle East Centre. SOAS. London: MENAS Press.

Behnke, R. 1980. *The Herders of Cyrenaica: Ecology, economy and kinship among the Bedouin of eastern Libya*. Illinois Studies in Anthropology No.12. University of Illinois Press.

Behnke, R. 1983. 'Production Rationales: The Commercialisation of Subsistence Pastoralism'. *Nomadic Peoples* 14: 3–34.

Behnke, R. 1985. 'Measuring the Benefits of Subsistence Versus Commercial Livestock Production in Africa'. *Agricultural Systems* 16: 109–35.

Behnke, R. 1988. *Range Enclosure in Central Somalia*. Pastoral Development Network 25b. London: Overseas Development Institute.

Behnke, R. 1993. *Natural Resource Management in Tropical Africa Workshop on Listening to People: social aspects of dryland management*. Nairobi: UNEP.

Behnke, R. 1999. 'Stock Movement and Range Management in a Himba community in North west Namibia', in M. Niamir-Fuller (ed.), *Managing Mobility in African Rangelands: the Legitimization of Transhumance*. London: IT Publications and Rome: FAO.

Behnke, R., Scoones, I. and Kerven, C., (eds) (1993). *Range Ecology at Disequilibrium: New models of natural variability and pastoral adaptation in African Savannas*. London: Overseas Development Institute.

Beinart, W. 1984. 'Soil Erosion, Conservationism and Ideas about Development: a Southern African Exploration 1900-1960', *Journal of Southern African Studies* 11: 52–83.

Beinart, W. 1994. *Twentieth Century South Africa*. Cape Town: Oxford University Press Southern Africa.

Beinart, W. and MacGregor, J. 2003. *Social History and African Environments*. Oxford: James Currey.

Bekure, S., De Leeuw, P.N., Grandin, B.E. and Neate, P.J.H. (eds) 1991. *Maasai Herding: An analysis of the livestock production system of Maasai pastoralists in Eastern Kajiado District, Kenya*. ILCA systems study 4. Addis Ababa: ILCA.

Bell, R. 1982. 'Effect of Soil Nutrient Availability on Community Structure in African Ecosystems', *Ecological Studies*. 42.

Belsky, J. 1987. 'Revegetation of natural and human-caused disturbances in the Serengeti National Park, Tanzania'. *Vegetatio* 70: 51–9.

Benefice, E., Chevassu-Agnes, S. and Barral, H. 1984. 'Nutritional Situation and Seasonal Variations for Pastoralist Populations of the Sahel'. *Ecol. Food and Nutrition*. 14: 229–47.

Bentley G.R., Goldberg, T. et al. 1993. 'The Fertility of Agricultural and Non-agricultural Traditional Societies', *Population Studies* 47: 269–81.

Berger, D. 1993. *Wildlife Extension: Participant Conservation by Maasai of Kenya*. African Centre for Technical Studies, Nairobi.

Bergeret, A. 1990. *L'arbre Nourricier en Pays Sahelien*. Paris: Ministre de la Coopération et du Développement, Ed. Maison Sciences de L'Homme.

Berkes, F. 1989. *Common Property Resources: Ecological and community based sustainable development*. London: Belhaven Press.

Bernardet, P. 1984. *Association Agriculture-élevage en Afrique: Les Peuls semi-transhumants de Côte d'Ivoire*. Paris: Editions ORSTOM

Berntsen, J. 1976. 'The Maasai and their Neighbours'. *Afr. Econ. Hist.* 2:1-11.

Bernus, E. 1979. 'Le Controle du Milieu Naturel et du Troupeau par les Eleveurs Touaregs Saheliens', in *Pastoral Production and Society*. Paris: Equipe Ecologie et anthropologie des sociétés pastorales, Maison des Sciences de L'Homme and Cambridge: Cambridge University Press.

Bernus, E. 1981. *Touaregs Nigériens: Unité culturelle et diversité régionale d'un peuple pasteur*. Paris: Memoires ORSTOM No. 94.

Bernus, E. 1988. 'Seasonality, Climatic Fluctuations and Food Supplies', in I. DeGarine and G. A. Harrison (eds), *Coping with Uncertainty in Food Supply*. Oxford: Oxford University Press.

Bernus, E. 1990. 'Dates, Dromedaries and Drought', in J. Galaty and D. Johnson (eds). *The World of Pastoralism* New York: Guilford/Belhaven.

Berry, S. 1993. *No Condition is Permanent: The social dynamics of agrarian change in sub-Saharan Africa*. Madison, WI: University of Wisconsin Press.

Biot, Y. 1993. 'How Long can High Stocking Densities be Sustained?' in R. Behnke, I. Scoones and C. Kerven (eds), *Range Ecology at Disequilibrium: New models of natural variability and pastoral adaptation in African Savannas*. London: Overseas Development Institute.

Birley, M. 1982. 'Resource Management in Sukumaland, Tanzania' *Africa* 52(2): 1–30.

Bishop, E. 2003. 'Maasai Schooling Strategies: A Case Study of Engare Naibor', MSc thesis, University College London, University of London.

Bishop, E. 2007. 'The Consequences of Schooling for pastoralism and pastoralists' livelihoods'. Unpublished PhD thesis, Dept. of Anthropology, University College London.

Bisson, J. 1989. 'Origin and Evolution of *foggara* Oases in the Algerian Sahara', in P. Beaumont, M. Bonine, and K. MacLachlan (eds), *Qanat, Kariz and Khattara*. Middle East Centre. SOAS. London: MENAS Press.

Blaikie, P. 2006. 'Is Small Really Beautiful? Community-based Natural Resources Management in Malawi and Botswana', *World Development* 34 (11): 1942–57.

Blanc-Pamard, C. and Boutrais, Jean 1994. *A la croisée des parcours*, Collection Colloques et Seminaires, Paris: ORSTOM Editions.

Blench, R. 1985. *Pastoral Labour and Stock Alienation in the Sub-Humid and Arid Zones of West*

Africa, Pastoral Development Network Paper 19e. London: Overseas Development Institute.

Blench, R. 1994. 'The Expansion and Adaptation of Fulbe Pastoralism to Subhumid and Humid Conditions in Nigeria'. *Cahiers d'Etudes Africaines* XXXIV: 197–212.

Blench, R. and MacDonald, K. (eds) 2000, *The Origins and Development of African Livestock*. London: UCL Press.

Bocquené, H. 2002. *Memoirs of a Mbororo. The life of Ndudi Umaru: Fulani nomad of Cameroon*. Translated by Philip Burnham and Gordeen Gorder. New York and Oxford: Berghahn

Bökonyi, S. 1976. 'The development of early stock raising in the Near East'. *Nature* 264:19–21.

Bonfiglioli, A. 1985. 'Evolution de la Propriété Animale chez les Wodaabe du Niger', *Journal des Africanistes* LV (1–2): 29–37.

Bonfiglioli, A.M. 1988. *Dudal: Histoire de Famille et Historic de Troupeaux chez un Groupe Wodaabe du Niger*. Paris: Edition de la Maison des Sciences de L'Homme and Cambridge: Cambridge University Press.

Bonfiglioli, A.M. 1990. 'Pastoralisme, agro-pastoralisme et retour: itinéraires saheliens'. *Cahiers des Sciences Humaines* 26 (1–2), 255–66.

Bonfiglioli, A.M. 1992. *Pastoralists at a Crossroads: Survival and development, issues in African pastoralism*. Nomadic pastoralists in Africa project (NOPA). Nairobi: UNICEF, UNSO.

Bonfiglioli, A.M, Diallo, Y. D. and S. Fagerberg-Diallo. 1996. 'Veterinary Science and Savvy among the Ferlo Fulbe', in C.M. McCorkle, E. Mathias and T. W. Schillhorn van Veen, *Ethnoveterinary Research and Development*, London: Intermediate Technology Publications.

Bonini, N. 1998. 'Les Maasai et l'école en Tanzanie (Maasai and school in Tanzania)' *Ethnies* 12, (22-23): 71–84.

Bonte, P. 1991. ' "To Increase Cows, God Created the King": The function of cattle in intralacustrine societies', in Galaty, J. G. and P. Bonte (eds), *Herders, Warriors and Traders. Pastoralism in Africa*. Boulder, CO: Westview Press.

Boogard, R. van den (2002) 'Food Insecurity and Entitlements among Turkana Pastoralists, Northern Kenya'. Unpublished PhD Thesis, Institute of Development Studies, University of Sussex.

Boone, R. BurnSilver, S., and Thornton, P. 2006. *Optimizing Aspects of Land Use Intensification in Southern Kajiado District, Kenya*. Final Report to the International Livestock Research Institute, Nairobi, Kenya. Reto-o-Reto Project, DGIC, December. Available at: www.reto-o-reto.org

Borgerhoff-Mulder, M. (1992) 'Demography of pastoralists: preliminary data on the Datoga of Tanzania', *Human Ecology* 20: 383–405.

Borgerhoff-Mulder M. and Sellen, D. 1994. 'Pastoralist decision-making: a behavioural ecological perspective', in E. Fratkin, K. Galvin and E.A. Roth (eds) *African Pastoral Systems: an integrated approach*. Boulder, CO: Lynne Rienner.

Borgerhoff-Mulder M. 1995. 'Bridewealth and its correlates'. *Current Anthropology* 16 (4): 573-603.

Boserup, E. 1967. *The Conditions of Agricultural Growth*. London: Allen and Unwin.

Bourbouze, A. 1999. 'Gestion de la mobilité et résistance des organizations pastorales des éleveurs du Haut Atlas marocain face aux transformations du contexte pastoral maghrébin', in M. Niamir-Fuller (ed.), *Managing Mobility in African Rangelands: the legitimization of transhumance*. London: IT Publications, and Rome: FAO.

Bourgeot, A. 1986. 'L'Herbe et le Glaive: De L'Itinéraire à L'Errance (La Notion de Territoire Chez les Touaregs)', in *Nomadisme: Mobilite et Flexibilite?* ORSTOM *Bulletin de Liaison* 8: 145–62.

Bourn, D., Reid, R., Rogers, D., Snow, B. and Wint, W. 2001. *Environmental Change and the Autonomous Control of Tsetse and Trypanosomiasis in sub Saharan Africa*. Oxford: Environmental Resources Group, (ERGO). Commissioned by the Animal Health Programme of DFID's Rural Livelihoods Department.

Bourn, D. and Wint, W. 1994. 'Livestock, land use and intensification in sub-Saharan Africa'. *Pastoral Development Network* 37a. London: Overseas Development Institute.

Boutrais, J. 1978. *Deux études sur l'élevage en zone tropicale humide*. Paris: ORSTOM (Travaux et Documents ORSTOM, 88).

Boutrais, J. 1986. 'L'Expansion des Eleveurs Peul dans les Savanes Humides de Cameroun', in M. Adamu and A. Kirk-Greene (eds). *Pastoralists of the West African Savanna*, Manchester: Manchester University Press.

Boutrais J. 1988. *Des Peul en savanes humides. Développement pastoral dans l'ouest Centrafricain*. Paris: ORSTOM.

Boutrais, J. 1994a. 'Les Foulbe de l'Adamaoua et l'élevage: de l'idéologie pastorale à la pluri-activité', *Cahiers d'Etudes Africaines* XXXIV: 175–96.

Boutrais, J. 1994b. 'Eleveurs, bétail et environnement', in C. Blanc-Pamard and Jean Boutrais (eds), *A la croisée des parcours: pasteurs, éleveurs, cultivateurs* Collection Colloques et Seminaires, Paris: ORSTOM.

Boutrais, J. 1994c. 'Pour une nouvelle cartographie des Peulhs', *Cahiers d'Etudes Africaines* XXXIV: 137–46.

Bovin, Mette. 1990. 'Nomads of the Drought: Fulbe and WoDaaBe nomads between power and marginalisation in the Sahel of Burkina Faso and Niger Republic', in Mette Bovin and Leif Manger (eds), *Adaptive Strategies in African Arid Lands*. Uppsala: SIAS.

Boyd, J. 1986. 'The Fulani Women Poets', in M. Adamu and A. Kirk-Greene (eds). *Pastoralists of the West African Savanna*. Manchester: Manchester University Press.

Bradley, D., Loftus, R., Cunningham, P. and MacHugh, D. 1998. 'Genetics and Domestic Cattle Origins', *Evolutionary Anthropology* 6 (3): 79–86.

Brainard, J.M. 1986. 'Differential Mortality in Turkana Agriculturalists and Pastoralists', *Am.J. Phys Anthrop.* 70(4): 525–36.

Brainard, J. 1990. 'Nutritional Status and Morbidity on an Irrigation Project in Turkana District', Kenya'. *Am.J. Human Biology* 2: 153–63.

Brainard, J. 1991. *Health and Development in a Rural Kenyan Community*, New York: Peter Lang.

Braun, H. M. 1971. Primary Production of Grasslands and their Utilization by Game in the Serengeti National Park, Tanzania. Netherlands Foundation for the Advancement of Tropical Research. Report for 1970, pp. 35–7.

Braun, H. M. 1973. 'Primary Production in the Serengeti. Purpose, methods and some results of research', *Annales de l'Université d'Abidjan Série E* (Ecologie) IV(2): 171–88.

Breman, H. and de Wit, C. 1983. 'Rangeland Productivity and Exploitation in the Sahel', *Science* 221: 1341–7.

Broch-Due, V. 1999. 'Remembered Cattle, Forgotten People: the morality of exchange and the exclusion of the Turkana poor', in D. Anderson and V. Broch-Due (eds), *The Poor Are Not Us*. Oxford: James Currey.

Broch-Due V and Anderson, D. 1999. 'Poverty and the Pastoralist', in D. Anderson and V. Broch-Due (eds), *The Poor Are Not Us*. Oxford: James Currey.

Brockington, D. 1999. 'Conservation, Displacement and Livelihoods. The consequences of the eviction for pastoralists moved from the Mkomazi Game Reserve, Tanzania.' *Nomadic Peoples* 3: 74–96.

Brockington, D. 2001a. 'Women's Income and Livelihood Strategies of Dispossessed Pastoralists. The case of Mkomazi Game Reserve'. *Human Ecology* 29: 307–38.

Brockington, D. 2001b. 'Pastoralism on the Margins. The decline and dispersal of herding on the Umba Nyika from 1800 to 1919'. Unpublished ms.

Brockington, D. 2001c. 'Communal Property and Degradation Narratives. Debating the Sukuma immigration into Rukwa Region, Tanzania'. Unpublished ms.

Brockington, D. 2002. *Fortress Conservation. The preservation of the Mkomazi Game Reserve*. Oxford: James Currey, African Issues series.

Brockington, D. 2003. 'Myths of Skeptical Environmentalism'. *Environmental Science and Policy* 6 (6): 543–46.

Brockington, D. 2004. 'The Costs of Conservation. Monitoring economic change as a consequence of conservation policy at Mkomazi Game Reserve, Tanzania', in K. Homewood (ed.), *Rural Resources and Local Livelihoods in Africa*. Oxford: James Currey, and Basingstoke: Palgrave.

Brockington, D. 2006. 'The Politics and Ethnography of Environmentalisms in Tanzania'. *African Affairs* 105 (418): 97–116.

Brockington, D. and Homewood, K. 1996. 'Wildlife, Pastoralists and Science. Debates concerning Mkomazi Game Reserve, Tanzania', in M. Leach and R. Mearns (eds), *The Lie of the Land. Challenging Received Wisdom on the African Environment*, London: James Currey in association with International African Institute.

Brockington, D. and Homewood, K. 1999. 'Pastoralism around Mkomazi Game Reserve: the interaction of Conservation and Development', in M. Coe, N. McWilliam, G. Stone and M. Packer (eds), *Mkomazi: The Ecology, Biodiversity and Conservation of a Tanzanian Savanna*. London: Royal Geographical Society (with the Institute of British Geographers).

Brockington, D. and Homewood, K. 2001. 'Degradation Debates and Data Deficiencies. The case of the Mkomazi Game Reserve, Tanzania', *Africa* 71: 179–227.

Bromley, D. and W. Cernea, 1989. *The Management of Common Property Resources: some conceptual and operational fallacies.* Washington, DC: World Bank.

Brown, L. 1971. 'The Biology of Pastoral Man as a Factor in Conservation', *Biological Conservation* 3: 93–100.

Bryceson, D.F. 1999. 'African Rural Labour, Income Diversification and Livelihood Approaches: A long-term development perspective', *Review of African Political Economy* 80: 171–89.

Bryceson, D.F. and Jamal, V. 1997. *Farewell to Farms. De-agrarianisation and employment in Africa.* Aldershot: Ashgate.

Buhl, S. 1999. 'Milk, Millet and Mannerisms: gender and production among pastoral and agro-pastoral Fulbe households in Northern Burkina Faso'. Unpublished PhD Thesis, University of London.

Buhl, S. and Homewood, K. 2000. 'Milk Selling Among Fulani Women in Northern Burkina Faso', in D. Hodgson (ed.), *Rethinking Pastoralism in Africa.* Oxford: James Currey.

Burke, K. 1987. 'Property Rights in "Animals of Strangers": notes of a restocking programme in Turkana, NW Kenya', in P. Baxter and R. Hogg (eds), *Property, Poverty and People: Changing rights in property and problems of pastoral development.* Manchester: Dept of Social Anthropology and International Development Centre, University of Manchester.

Burnham, P. 1975. 'Regroupement and Mobile Societies: Two Cameroon cases', *J. African History.* 16: 577–94.

Burnham, P. 1980. 'Changing Agricultural and Pastoral Ecologies in the West African Savanna Region', in D. Harris (eds), *Human Ecology in Savanna Environments.* London: Academic Press.

Burnham, P. 1987. 'Pastoralism and the Comparative Method', in L. Holy (ed.), *Comparative Anthropology.* Oxford: Basil Blackwell.

Burnham, P. 1996. *The Politics of Cultural Difference in North Cameroon,* Washington, DC: Smithsonian Institution Press.

Burnham, P. 1999. 'Pastoralism Under Pressure? Understanding social change in Fulbe society', in V. Azarya, A. Breedveld, M. Bruijn, and H. Dijk (eds) *Pastoralists Under Pressure?: Fulbe societies confronting change in West Africa.* Leiden/Boston, MA: Brill.

Burnham, P. and Last, M. 1994. 'From pastoralist to politician: the problem of a "Fulbe aristocracy"', *Cahiers d'Etudes Africaines* XXXIV (133–5): 313–57.

BurnSilver, S. (forthcoming). 'Amboseli', in Homewood et al. (eds), *Staying Maasai? Livelihoods, Conservation and Development in East African Rangelands.* New York: Springer.

Cahiers d'études Africaines. 1994, xxxiv: 133–5 *L'archipel Peul.* Paris: Editions de l'Ecole des Hautes Etudes en Sciences Sociales.

Caldwell, J. 1986. 'Routes to Low Mortality in Poor Countries'. *Population and Development Review* 12 (2) reprinted 1989 in J. Caldwell and G. Santow (eds) *Selected Readings in the Cultural, Social and Behavioural Determinants of Health.* Health Transition Series 1. Canberra: Australian National University.

Cameron, N. 1991. 'Human Growth, Nutrition and Wealth Status in Sub-Saharan Africa'. *Yearbook of Phys. Anthr.* 34: 211–50.

Campbell, B., Leslie, P., Little, M., Brainard. J., DeLuca, M. (1999) 'Settled Turkana', in M. Little and P.W. Leslie (eds), *Turkana Herders of the Dry Savanna,* Oxford: Oxford University Press.

Campbell, D. 1993. 'Land as Ours, Land as Mine: Economic, political and ecological marginalisation in Kajiado district, Kenya', in T. Spear and R. Waller (eds), *Being Maasai.* Oxford: James Currey.

Campbell K.L. and Wood, J.W. 1988. 'Fertility in Traditional Societies', in P. Diggory, M. Potts, S. Teper (eds), *Natural Human Fertility: Social and biological determinants,* London: Macmillan Press.

Camps, G. 1982. 'Beginnings of Pastoralism and Cultivation in North-west Africa and the Sahara: Origins of the Berbers', in *The Cambridge History of Africa.* Cambridge: Cambridge University Press.

Carney, D. and Farington, J. 1998. *Natural Resource Management and Institutional Change.* London: Routledge and Overseas Development Institute.

Carr, C. 1977. *Pastoralism in Crisis: The Dasanetch and their Ethiopian highlands.* Chicago: Chicago University Press.

Carr-Hill, R. 2002, *Education for Nomads in Eastern Africa: Djibouti, Eritrea, Ethiopia, Kenya, Tanzania, Uganda.* Study for the African Development Bank.

Casimir, M. 1991. *Flocks and Food: A biocultural approach to the study of pastoral foodways,* Köln and Weimar: Böhlau Verlag.

Cassanelli, L. 1982. *The Shaping of Somali Society: Reconstructing the history of pastoral people, 1600–*

1900. Philadelphia: University of Pennsylvania Press.

Castle, Sarah 1992. 'Intra-household variation in illness management and child care in rural Mali', PhD thesis (unpublished), University of London.

Castle, Sarah 1995. 'Child fostering and children's nutritional status in rural Mali: the role of female status in directing child transfers'. *Social Science and Medicine* 40: 679–93.

Castree, N. 2003. 'Bioprospecting: from theory to practice (and back again)', *Transactions Inst. Brit. Geographers*, NS 28: 35–55.

Catley, A. 1999. *Methods on the Move: A review of veterinary uses of participatory approaches and methods focussing on experiences in dryland Africa*. London: IIED.

Caughley, G., Shepherd, N. and Short, J. 1987. *Kangaroos: Their ecology and management on the sheep rangelands of Australia*. Cambridge: Cambridge University Press.

Central Bureau of Statistics. 2002. *Kenya Census 1999. Analytic Reports: V. Mortality*, Nairobi and Calverton, MD: CBS, MOH, and ORC Macro.

Central Bureau of Statistics (CBS), Ministry of Health (MOH), and ORC Macro. 2004. *Kenya Demographic and Health Survey 2003*. Calverton, MD: CBS, MOH, ORC Macro.

Chabal, P. and Daloz, J.-P. 1999. *Africa Works: Disorder as a Political Instrument*. Oxford: James Currey in association with the International African Institute.

Chambers, R., Longhurst, R. and Pacey, A. 1984. *Seasonal Dimensions to Rural Poverty*. London: Frances Pinter.

Charney J., Stone, P. and Quirk, W. 1975. 'Drought in the Sahara: a biogeophysical feedback mechanism'. *Science* 187: 43–5.

Chatty, D. and Colchester, M. (eds) 2002. *Conservation and Mobile Indigenous Peoples: Displacement, forced settlement and sustainable development*. Oxford: Berghahn Press.

Chieni, T. and Spencer, P. 1993. 'The world of Telelia. Reflections of a Maasai woman', in T. Spear and R. Waller (eds) *Being Maasai*. London: James Currey.

Cisse, S. 1981. 'Sedentarisation of nomadic pastoralists and pastoralisation of cultivators in Mali', in J. Galaty, D. Aronson, P. Salzman and A. Chouinard (eds), *The Future of Pastoral Peoples*, Ottawa: IDRC.

Cisse, S. 1986. 'Le Delta Intérieur du Niger: Organisation Spatiale', in M. Adamu and A. Kirk-Greene (eds), *Pastoralists of the West African Savanna*. Manchester: Manchester University Press.

Claude, J, Grouzis, M. and Milleville, P. (eds) 1991. *Un espace Sahelien, la Mare d'Oursi, Burkina Faso*. Paris: Editions ORSTOM.

Clauzel, J. 1962. 'Evolution de la vie Economique et des Structures Sociales du Pays Nomades du Mali de la Conquête Française à l'Autonomie Interne (1893–1958). [Changes in Economic Life and Pastoral Social Structure in Mali from the French Conquest to Independence 1893-1958]' *Tiers Monde*, 3 (9 & 10): 283–311

Coast, E. 2000. 'Maasai Demography'. Unpublished PhD thesis. Dept. of Anthropology, University College, University of London.

Coast, E. 2001. 'Colonial preconceptions and contemporary demographic reality: Maasai of Kenya and Tanzania'. Paper presented at IUSSP Conference, Salvador, Brazil, August.

Coast, E. 2002. 'Maasai socio-economic conditions: cross-border comparison', *Human Ecology* 30 (1). 79–105.

Coast, E. 2006. 'Local understandings of, and responses to, HIV: Rural-urban migrants in Tanzania'. *Social Science and Medicine* 63: 1000–1010.

Coe, M., McWilliam, N., Stone, G. and Packer, M. (eds). 1991. *Mkomazi: The ecology, biodiversity and conservation of a Tanzanian savanna*. London: Royal Geographical Society with the Institute of British Geographers.

Coppock, D. 1993. 'Vegetation and Pastoral Dynamics in the Southern Ethiopian Rangelands: implications for theory and management', in R. Behnke, I. Scoones and C. Kerven (eds), *Range Ecology at Disequilibrium: New models of natural variability and pastoral adaptation in African Savannas*. London: Overseas Development Institute.

Coppock, D. 1994. *The Borana Plateau of Southern Ethiopia: Synthesis of Pastoral research, development and change*, Systems Study no.5. Addis Ababa: ILCA.

Coppock D., Ellis, J. and Swift, D. 1986. 'Seasonal Nutritional Characteristics of Livestock Diets in a Nomadic Pastoral Ecosystem'. *Journal of Applied Ecology* 23: 585–95.

Coppock, D., Ellis, J. and Swift, D. 1988. 'Seasonal Patterns of Activity, Travel and Water Intake for Livestock in South Turkana, Kenya'. *Journal of Arid Environments* 14: 319–31.

Coppock, D., Swift, D. and Ellis J. 1986. 'Livestock Feeding Ecology and Resource Utilization in a Nomadic Pastoral Ecosystem'. *Journal of Applied Ecology* 23: 573–83.

Cossins, N. and Upton, M. 1987. 'The Borana Pastoral System of Southern Ethiopia', *Agricultural Systems* 25: 199–218.

Coughenour, M., Ellis J., Swift, D., Coppock, D., Galvin, K., McCabe, J and Hart, T. 1985. 'Energy Extraction and Use in a Nomadic Pastoral Ecosystem'. *Science*. 230 (4726): 619–25.

Cowling, R.M. 2000. 'Challenges to the 'New' Rangeland Science', *Trends in Research in Ecology and Evolution* 15: 303–4.

Crognier, E. 1996. 'Behavioural and Environmental Determinants of Reproductive Success in Traditional Moroccan Berber Groups'. *Am.J, Phys. Anthr.* 100: 181–90.

Cunningham, P. 1996. 'DNA Studies Rewrite the History of Cattle Domestication', *Farm and food* (Autumn/winter).

Dahl, G. 1979. *Suffering Grass. Subsistence & Society of Waso Borana.* Stockholm University Studies in Social Anthropology. Stockholm: Stockholm University Press.

Dahl, G. 1987. 'Women in Pastoral Production: Some theoretical notes on roles and resources'. *Ethnos* 52 (1–2): 246–79 (See also other authors in same issue).

Dahl, G. and Hjort, A. 1976. *Having Herds.* Stockholm Studies in Social Anthropology. Stockholm: Stockholm University Press.

Dahl, G. and Megerssa, G. 1990. 'The Sources of Life: Boran conceptions of wells and water', in G. Palsson (ed.), *From Water to World Making. African Models and Arid Lands.* Uppsala: Scandinavian Institute of African Studies.

Davis, S. 1987. *The Archaeology of Animals.* London: Batsford Press.

De Boer, W. and Prins., H. 1989. 'Decisions of Cattle Herdsmen in Burkina Faso and Optimal Foraging Models', *Human Ecology.* 17(4):445–64.

De Bruijn, M. and van Dijk, H. 1994. 'Drought and Coping Strategies in Fulbe Society in the Haayre (Central Mali): a Historical Perspective'. *Cahiers d'Etudes Africaines* XXXIV: 85–108.

De Bruijn, M. and van Dijk, H. 1995. *Arid Ways. Cultural Understandings of Insecurity in Fulbe society, central Mali.* Amsterdam: Thela.

De Garine, I. and Harrison, G. 1987. *Coping with Uncertainty in Food Supply.* Oxford: Clarendon Press.

De Leeuw, P.N., Bekure, S. and Grandin, B. 1988. 'Some Aspects of Livestock Productivity in Maasai Group Ranches in Kenya', in J. C. Tothill, and J. J. Mott (eds), *Ecology and Management of the World's Savannas.* Canberra: Australian Academy of Sciences, and Farnham UK: Commonwealth Agricultural Bureau.

De Leeuw, P. and Wilson, R. 1987. 'Comparative Productivity of Indigenous Cattle under Traditional Management in sub-Saharan Africa'. *Q. Journal of International Agriculture* 26(4): 377–90.

De Waal, A. 1989a. *Famine that Kills: Darfur, Sudan 1984–5*, Oxford Clarendon Press.

De Waal, A. 1989b. 'Famine Mortality, A Case Study of Darfur'. *Pop.Studies.* 43:5-24.

De Waal, A. 1997. *Famine Crimes: Politics and the disaster relief industry in Africa.* Oxford: James Currey:

De Waal, A. 2004. 'Tragedy in Darfur', *Boston Review* November/December issue.

Delgado, C. 1979. *The Southern Fulani Farming System in Upper Volta.* African Rural Economy Paper No.20. Lansing, MI: Michigan State University.

Dennell, R.W. 1982. 'Archaeology and the Study of Desertification', in B. Spooner and H. Mann, *Desertification and Development.* Burlington, MA: Academic Press.

Desanker, P. and Magadza, C. 2001. 'Africa', in IPCC *Climate Change 2001.* Working Group II: *Impacts, Adaptation and Vulnerability*, New York: UNEP and WMO.

Deshler, W. 1965. 'Native Cattle Keeping in Eastern Africa', in A. Leeds and A. Vayda (eds), *Man, Culture and Animals: The role of animals in human ecological adjustments*, Washington, DC: Amer. Assoc. for the Advancement of Science.

Deshmukh, I. 1984. 'A Common Relationship Between Precipitation and Grassland Peak Biomass for East and Southern Africa', *African Journal of Ecology* 22: 181–6.

Devereux, S. and Scoones, I. 2006. *The Crisis of Pastoralism? A response to Stephen Sandford.* www.future-agricultures.org/pdf%20files/The_crisis_of_pastoralism.pdf

DFID, 2001. *Trypanosomoses, tsetse and Africa.* DFID livestock production and animal health programmes: the year 2000 report. London: Department for International Development.

D'Hoore, J. L. 1964. *Soil Map of Africa 1:5 000 000 Joint Project no. 11.* Commission for Technical Cooperation in Africa South of the Sahara. Publication 93. Lagos.

Diamond, J.M. 1991. 'Why are pygmies small?' *Nature* 354: 111–12.

Diamond, J.M. 2002. 'Evolutionary Consequences and Future of Plant and Animal Domestication'.

Nature 418: 700–7.

Dietz, T. 1987. 'Pastoralists in Dire Straits, Survival Strategies and External Interventions in a semi-arid region at the Kenya/Uganda border: Western Pokot: 1900–1986'. *Netherlands Geographical studies*, 49, Amsterdam/Utrecht.

Dietz, T. 1996. *Entitlements to Natural Resources*. University of Amsterdam. International Books.

Doornbos, M., Cliffe, L., Ghaffar, A., Ahmed, M., and Markakis, J. 1992. *Beyond Conflict in the Horn: Prospects for peace, recovery and development in Ethiopia, Somalia, Eritrea and Sudan*. The Hague: Inst. Soc. Studies. London: James Currey.

Doornbos, M. 1993. 'Pasture and Polis: The roots of political marginalisation of Somali pastoralism', in J. Markakis (ed.), *Conflict and the Decline of Pastoralism in the Horn of Africa*. London: James Currey.

Downing, T. 1992. *Climate Change and Vulnerable Places: Global food security and country studies in Zimbabwe, Kenya, Senegal and Chile*. Research Report no.1. Oxford: Environmental Change Unit.

Downing T., Watts, M. and Bohle, H. 1996. 'Climate change and food insecurity: toward a sociology and geography of vulnerability', in T. Downing (ed.), *Climate Change and World Food Security*, NATO ASI series Global Environmental Change Vol. 37. New York: Springer.

Dransfield, R.D., Brightwell, R., Kyorku, C. and Williams, B. 1990. 'Control of Tsetse Fly (Diptera: Glossinidae) Populations Using Traps at Nguruman, south-west Kenya'. *Bulletin of Entomological Research* 80: 265–76.

Duany, W. 1999. 'Customary law and ways of life in transition among the Nuer of South Sudan', in M. Niamir-Fuller (ed.), *Managing Mobility in African Rangelands: The legitimisation of transhumance*. London: IT Publications, and Rome: FAO.

Dublin, H. 1991. 'Dynamics of the Serengeti-Mara woodlands: an historical perspective', *Forest and Conservation History*, 35: 169–78.

Dublin, H. 1995. 'Vegetation Dynamics in the Serengeti-Mara Ecosystem: The role of elephants, fire, and other factors', in A. Sinclair and P. Arcese (eds), *Serengeti II: Dynamics, management and conservation of an ecosystem*. Chicago: Chicago University Press.

Dupire, M. 1962a. *Peuls Nomades: Etude Descriptive des Wodaabe du Sahel Nigerian*. Paris: Institut d'Ethnologie.

Dupire, M. 1962b. 'Trade and Markets in the Economy of the Nomadic Fulani of Niger', in P. Bohannan and G. Dalton (eds), *Markets in Africa*. Northwestern University Press.

Dupire, M. 1970. *Organisation Sociale Des Peul*. Paris: Edition Plon.

Dupire, M. 1972. *Les facteurs humaines de l'économie pastorale*. Etudes Nigériennes, No. 6. Niamey: Centre Nigérien de Recherches en Sciences Humaines.

Dupuy, C. 1992. 'Trois mille ans d'histoire pastorale au sud du Sahara', *Préhistoire et Anthropologie Méditerranéennes* : 105–26.

Dupuy, C. 1999. 'L'art rupestre à gravures naturalistes de l'Adrar des Iforas (Mali)', *Sahara* 11: 69–86.

Dyson, T. 1994. 'Population Growth and Food Production: Recent global and regional trends', *Population and Development Review* 20 (2): 397–411.

Dyson-Hudson, N. 1980. 'Strategies of Resource Exploitation in East African Pastoralists', in D. Harris (ed.), *Human Ecology in Savanna Environments,* London: East African Academic Press.

Dyson-Hudson. R., Meekers, D., Dyson-Hudson, N. 1998. 'Children of the Dancing Ground, Children of the House: Costs and Benefits of Marriage Rules (South Turkana, Kenya)', *Journal of Anthropological Research,* 54.

Dyson-Hudson, R. and Meekers, D. 1999. 'Migration across Ecosystem Boundaries', in M. A. Little and P. W. Leslie (eds), *Turkana Herders of the Dry Savanna*, Oxford: Oxford University Press.

Economist, The 1993. 'The Fat of the Land: Made in Europe, Dumped in Africa', 29 May: 16.

Economist, The 2001. 'Displaced People: when is a refugee not a refugee?' 3 March: 23–5.

Edirisinghe, J. 1986. 'Infections in the Malnourished: with Special Reference to Malaria and Malnutrition in the Tropics'. *Ann Trop. Paediatrics* 6: 233–7.

Edwards, D., Josephson, S. and Coltrain, J.B. 1994. 'Burkina Faso Herdsmen and Optimal Foraging Theory: a Reconsideration', *Human Ecology* 22: 213–5.

Ehret, C. 1974. 'Cushites and the Highland and Plains Nilotes to AD 1800', in B.A. Ogot (ed.), *Zamani: A Survey of East African History*. Nairobi: East African Publishing House.

Ehret, C. 1998. *An African Classical Age*. Oxford: James Currey

Ehret, C. 2002. *The Civilizations of Africa: A History to 1800*. Charlottesville, VA: University of Virginia Press.

Elbow, K. and Rochegude, A. 1990. *A Layperson's Guide to the Forest Codes of Mali, Niger and Senegal*. Madison, WI: Land Tenure Center, University of Wisconsin-Madison. LTC paper no. 139.

Ellis, F. 2000. *Rural Livelihoods and Diversity in Developing Countries*. Oxford: Oxford University Press.

Ellis, J. and Swift, D. 1988. 'Stability of African Pastoralist Ecosystems: Alternate Paradigms and Implications for Development', *Journal of Range Management*. 41:450–9.

Ellis, J. 1995. 'Climate Variability and Complex Ecosystem Dynamics: Implications for Pastoralist Development', in I. Scoones (ed.), *Living with Uncertainty; new directions in pastoralist development in Africa*. London: ITP/IIED.

Elmi, A., Ibrahim, D. and Jenner, J. 2000. 'Women's roles in peacemaking in Somali society', in D. Hodgson (ed.), *Rethinking Pastoralism in Africa*, Oxford: James Currey.

Elphick, R. 1977. *Kraal and Castle: Khoikhoi and the Founding of white South Africa*. New Haven, CT: Yale University Press.

Ensminger, J. 1984. 'Monetisation in the Galole Orma Economy. Change in Use of Fuel and Woodstock', in C. Barnes, J. Ensminger and P. O'Keefe (eds), *Wood Energy and Households: Perspectives on rural Kenya*, Uppsala: Beijer Institute and Scandinavian Institute of African Studies.

Epstein, H. and Mason, I. 1984. 'Cattle', in I. Mason (ed.), *Evolution of Domesticated Animals* Harlow: Longman.

Evans-Pritchard, E. 1940. *The Nuer*, Oxford: Clarendon Press.

Ezeomah, C. 1985. *Land Tenure Constraints Associated with Some Recent Experiments to Bring Formal Education to Nomadic Fulani in Nigeria'*, Pastoral Development Network. London: Overseas Development Institute.

FAO. 2001. *The State of Food Insecurity in the World 2000*. Rome: Food and Agriculture Organisation.

FAO/WHO. 1973. *Ad hoc expert committee on Energy and Protein Requirements*. WHO Technical report series no 522. Geneva: World Health Organisation.

FAO/WHO. 1992. *Nutrition and Development – a Global Assessment*. Rome: Food and Agriculture Organisation.

Farah, A. 1996. 'Plight and Prospects of Ethiopia's Lowland Pastoralist Groups', in T. Allen (ed.), *In Search of Cool Ground: War, flight and homecoming in North East Africa*. Oxford: James Currey, and Lawrenceville, NJ: Africa World Press.

Farah, A. 1997. 'From Traditional Nomadic Context to Contemporary Sedentarisation: Past Relations between the Isaq and the Gadabursi clans of north Somalia and south east Ethiopia', in R. Hogg (ed.), *Pastoralists, Ethnicity and the State in Ethiopia*. London: HAAN/Institute for African Alternatives.

Fleischer, M. 1999. 'Cattle Raiding and Household Demography Among the Kuria of Tanzania', *Africa* 69: 238–55.

Ford, J. 1971. *The Role of Trypanosomiases in African Ecology*. Oxford: Clarendon Press

Franke, R.W. 1984. 'Tuareg of West Africa: Five Experiments in Fourth World Development'. *Antipode* 16(2): 45–53.

Frantz, C. 1975. 'Contraction and Expansion in Nigerian Bovine Pastoralism', in T. Monod (ed.) *Pastoralism in Tropical Africa*. Oxford: Oxford University Press.

Frantz, C. 1980. 'The Open Niche: Pastoralism and Sedentarization in the Mambila Grasslands of Nigeria', in P. Salzman. *When Nomads Settle: processes of sedentarisation as adaptation and response*. New York, Praeger.

Fraser, S. 2003. 'Parks, Pastoralists and Development Policy in the Nigerian Savanna', Unpublished PhD Thesis, University of London.

Fratkin E. 1991. *Surviving Drought and Development: Ariaal Pastoralists of Northern Kenya*. Boulder, CO: Westview Press.

Fratkin, E. 2001. 'East African Pastoralism in Transition: Maasai, Boran and Rendille Cases'. *African Studies Review* 44(93): 1–25.

Fratkin, E. and Roth, E. 1990. 'Drought and Economics: Differentiation Among Ariaal Pastoralist of Kenya', *H.Ecol.* 18(4): 385–402.

Fratkin, E. and Roth, E. (eds) 2005) *As Pastoralists Settle*. New York: Kluwer.

Fratkin, E. and Smith, K. 1994. 'Labor, Livestock and Land: the Organization of Pastoral Production', in E. Fratkin, K. Galvin and E.A. Roth (eds), *African Pastoral Systems: An integrated approach*. Boulder, CO: Lynne Rienner.

Fratkin, E. and Smith, K. 1995. 'Women's Changing Economic Roles with Pastoral Sedentarisa-tion: Varying Strategies in Alternate Rendille Communities', *Human Ecology* 25: 433–53.

Fratkin, E., Galvin, K. and Roth, E.A. (eds) 1994. *African Pastoral Systems: an Integrated Approach.* Boulder, CO: Lynne Rienner.

Fratkin, E., Roth, E. A. and Nathan, M. A. 1999. 'When Nomads Settle: The Effects of Commoditization, Nutritional Change and Formal Education on Ariaal and Rendille Pastoralists', *Current Anthropology* 40(5): 729–35.

Fratkin, E., Roth, E. and Nathan, M. 2004. 'Pastoral sedentarization and its effects on children's growth, nutrition and health among the Rendille'. *Human Ecology* 32(5): 531–59.

Freeman, A., Hoggart, C., Hanotte, O. and Bradley, D. 2006. 'Assessing the Relative Ages of Admixture in the Bovine Hybrid Zones of Africa and the Near East Using X Chromosome Haplotype Mosaicism', *Genetics* 173: 1503–10.

Fricke, W. 1979. *Cattle Husbandry in Nigeria: A study of its ecological conditions and social-geographical differentiations.* Heft 52, Department of Geography, University of Heidelberg.

Frost, P., Menaut, J.C., Walker, B., Medina, E., Solbrig, O. and Swift, M. (eds) 1986. 'Responses of Savannas to Stress and Disturbance. Report of IUBS Working Group 1985', *Biology International* 10 (special issue).

Fry, P. and Leslie, P. 1984. 'Aspects of Turkana Demography: Responses to a Fluctuating Environment'. *Am.J.Phys Anthr.* 63:159.

Fukui, K. and Markakis, J. 1994. *Ethnicity and Conflict in the Horn of Africa.* Oxford: James Currey/ Athens, OH: Ohio University Press.

Fukui, K. and Turton, D. 1977. 'Warfare Among East African Herders', *Senri Ethnography Studies.* No.3.

Fulton D.J.R. and Randall, Sara, 1988. 'Households, Women's Roles and Prestige as Factors Determining Nuptiality and Fertility Differentials in Mali', in J. Caldwell, A. Hill and V. Hull (eds), *Micro Approaches to Demographic Research*, London: J Kegan Paul International.

Galaty, J. 1980. 'The Maasai Group Ranch', in P. Salzman (ed.), *When Nomads Settle: Processes of sedentarisation as adaptation and response.* New York: Praeger.

Galaty, J. 1982. 'Being "Maasai", Being People of Cattle: Ethnic shifters in East Africa', *American Ethnologist* 9: 1–22.

Galaty, J. 1993. 'The rhetoric of rights: construing Maasai land claims', in *Justice and Paradox in the Conflicts and Claims of Indigenous Peoples.* Washington, DC: American Anthropological Association.

Galaty, J. 1994. 'Rangeland tenure and pastoralism in Africa', in E. Fratkin, K. Galvin and E.A. Roth (eds), *African Pastoral Systems: an integrated approach.* Boulder, CO: Lynne Rienner.

Galaty. J. 1999. 'Grounding Pastoralists: Law, politics and dispossession in East Africa', *Nomadic peoples* 3 (2): 56–73.

Galaty, J.G. and Bonte, P. 1991. *Herders, Warriors and Traders. Pastoralism in Africa.* Boulder, CO: Westview Press,

Galaty, J. and Johnson, D. (eds) 1990a. *The World of Pastoralism.* New York: Guilford Press.

Galaty, J. and Johnson, D. 1990b. 'Introduction: Pastoral systems in global perspective', in J. Galaty and D. Johnson (eds) 1990. *The World of Pastoralism.* New York: Guilford Press.

Galaty, J. and Ole Munei, K. 1999. 'Maasai Land, Law and Dispossession', *Cultural Survival Quarterly* 22 (4): 68–71.

Galaty J., Aronson, D. and Salzman, P. (eds). 1981. *The Future of Pastoral Peoples.* Ottawa: International Development Centre.

Gallais, J. 1967. *Le delta Intérieur du Niger, et ses Bordures,* Paris: CNRS.

Gallais, J. 1984. *Hommes du Sahel: espace-temps et pouvoirs, le Delta intérieur du Niger, 1960–1980.* Paris: Flammarion.

Galvin, K. 1985. 'Food Procurement, Diet, Activities and Nutrition of Ngisonyoka Turkana Pastoralists in Ecological and Social Context'. Unpublished PhD thesis, Binghamton: Department of Anthropology, New York State University.

Galvin, K. 1988. 'Nutritional Status as an Indicator of Impending Food Stress'. *Disasters.* 12: 147–56.

Galvin, K. 1992. 'Nutritional Ecology of Pastoralists in Dry Tropical Africa', *American Journal of Human Biology* 4: 209–21.

Galvin, K. and Little. M. 1999. 'Dietary Intake and Nutritional Status', in M.A. Little and P.W. Leslie (eds), *Turkana Herders of the Dry Savanna. Ecology and biobehavioural response of nomads to an uncertain environment,* Oxford: Oxford University Press.

Galvin, K., Coppock, D. and Leslie, P. 1994. 'Diet, Nutrition and the Pastoral Strategy', in E. Fratkin, K. Galvin and E.A. Roth (eds), *African Pastoral Systems: an integrated approach*. Boulder, CO: Lynne Rienner.

Gamaleddin, M. 1993. 'The Decline of Afar Pastoralism', in J. Markakis (ed.), *Conflict and Decline of Pastoralism in the Horn of Africa*. Basingstoke: Macmillan.

Gasse, F. et al. 1990. 'The Arid-humid Transition in the Sahara and Sahel During the last Deglaciation', *Nature* 346: 141–6.

Gautier, A. 1986. 'Quaternary Mammals and Archaeozoology of Egypt and the Sudan: A survey', in L. Kryzaniak and M. Kobusiewicz (eds), *Origin and Early Development of Food Producing Cultures in North East Africa*. Poznan: Polish Academy of Sciences and Poznan Archaeological Museum.

Gautier, A. 1987.' Prehistoric Men and Cattle in North Africa: a Dearth of Data and a Surfeit of Models', in A. Close (ed.), *Prehistory of Arid North Africa*, Dallas, TX: Southern Methodist University Press.

Gellner, E. 1969. *Saints of the Atlas*. Chicago: University of Chicago Press.

Gellner, E. 1992. *Postmodernism, Reason and Religion*. London and New York: Routledge.

Getachew, K. 1996. 'The Displacement and Return of Pastoralists in Southern Ethiopia: A case study of the Garri', in T. Allen (ed.), *In Search of Cool Ground: War, flight and homecoming in North East Africa*. Oxford: James Currey and Lawrenceville, NJ: Africa World Press.

Giblin, J. 1990. 'Trypanosomiasis Control in African History: An Evaded Issue,' *Journal of African History*, 31: 59–80.

Giblin, J. 1990. 'East Coast Fever in Socio-Historical Context: a case study from Tanzania'. *International Journal of African Historical Studies*. 23: 401–21.

Giblin, J. 1993. *The Politics of Environmental Control in NorthEast Tanzania 1840–1940*. Philadelphia: University of Pennsylvania Press.

Gifford-Gonzalez, D. 2000. 'Animal Disease Challenges in the Emergence of Pastoralism in Sub-Saharan Africa', *African Archaeological Review* 17(3): 95–139.

Goldman, M. 2003. 'Partitioned Nature, Privileged Knowledge: Community-based conservation in Tanzania', *Development and Change* 34 (5): 833–62.

Goldschmidt, W. 1969. *Kambuya's Cattle: The legacy of an African herdsman*, Berkeley and Los Angeles: University of California Press.

Goldschmidt, W. 1976. *The Culture and Behaviour of the Sebei*, Berkeley, CA: University of California Press.

Government of Tanzania 1997 *Livestock and Agriculture Policy*. Section 3: Soil conservation and land use planning, Section 4: range management. Policy statements. Dar es Salaam.

Gowlett, J. 1988. 'Human Adaptation and Long Term Climatic Change in Northeast Africa: An Archaeological Perspective', in D. Johnson and D. Anderson (eds), *The Ecology of Survival.Case studies from northeast African history*. London: Lester Crook.

Graham, O. 1988. *Enclosure of the East African Rangelands*, Pastoral Development Network. 25a. London: Overseas Development Institute.

Graham, W., Brass, W. and Snow, R. 1989. 'Estimating Maternal Mortality: the sisterhood method', *Studies in Family Planning*, 20:125–35.

Grainger, A. 1999. 'Constraints on modelling the deforestation and degradation of open woodlands', *Global Ecology and Biogeography* 8: 179–90.

Grandin, B. 1986. 'Land Tenure, Subdivision and Residential Change on a Maasai Group Ranch'. *Bulletin Inst Dev Anth* 4: 9–13.

Grandin, B. 1988. 'Wealth and Pastoral Dairy Production'. *Human Ecology*. 16: 1–21.

Grandin B.E. and Lembuya P. 1987. *The Impact of the 1984 Drought at Olkarkar Group Ranch, Kajiado, Kenya*, Pastoral Development Network, 23e. London: Overseas Development Institute.

Gray, S., Leslie, P. and Alinga Akol, H. 2002. 'Uncertain Disaster: Environmental Instability, Colonial Policy and Resilience of East African Pastoral Systems', in W. Leonard and M. Crawford (eds), *Human Biology of Pastoral Populations*, Cambridge: Cambridge University Press.

Grayzel, J. 1990. 'Markets and Migration: a Fulbe pastoral system in Mali', in J. Galaty and D. Johnson (eds), *The World of Pastoralism*. New York: Guilford Press.

Grigson, C. 1991. 'An African Origin for African Cattle? – some archaeological evidence.' *African Archaeological Review* 9: 119–44.

Grove, A. T. 1975. 'Desertification in the African Environment'. *African Affairs*. 73:137–51.

Guilmoto, C. 1997. *Migrations et Institutions au Sénégal: Effets d'Echelle et determinants.* 1–45. Dossiers du CEPED. Paris: CEPED.

Gulliver, P. 1955. *The Family Herds.* London: Routledge.

Guyer, J. 1997. 'Diversity and Intensity in the Scholarship on African Agricultural Change', *Reviews in Anthropology* 26: 13–32.

Hadgu K., Yisehak M. and Tekle, G. 1991. 'Interviewing Cows', in *Farmer Participatory Research in North Omo, Ethiopia.* October 1991. Farm AFRICA/IIED.

Hagberg, S. 1994. 'A l'ombre du conflit violent', *Cahiers d'études Africaines* 161, XL1: 45–52.

Halderman, J. M. 1985. 'Problems of Pastoral Development in East Africa'. *Agricultural Administration.* 18: 199–216.

Hall, M. 1990. *Farmers, Kings and Traders. The people of southern Africa 200–1860.* Chicago: University of Chicago Press.

Hampshire, K. 1998. 'Fulani Mobility: Causes, constraints and consequences of population movements in Northern Burkina Faso'. Unpublished PhD thesis, University of London.

Hampshire, K. and Randall, S. 1998. 'Pauvrêté et la migration saisonnière chez les Peulhs du Sahel Burkinabè', in Francis Gendreau (ed.), *Crises, Pauvrêté et Changements Démographiques dans les Pays du Sud*, Paris: AUPELF UREF, Editions ESTEM.

Hampshire, K. and Randall, S. 1999. 'Seasonal Labour Migration Strategies in the Sahel: Coping with poverty or optimizing security?' *International Journal of Population Geography* 5: 367–85.

Hampshire, K. and Randall, S. 2000. 'Pastoralists, agropastoralists and cultivators: interactions between fertility and mobility in Northern Burkina Faso', *Population Studies* 54 (4).

Hanotte, O., Bradley, D.G, Ochieng, J.W, Verjee, Y, Hill, E.W. and Rege, J.E. 2002. 'African Pastoralism: Genetic imprints of origins and migrations'. *Science*, 296: 336–39.

Hardin, G. 1968. 'The Tragedy of the Commons', *Science*, 162: 1243–8.

Harpending, H. and Pennington, R. 1990. 'Herero Households', *Human Ecology* 18 (4): 417–39.

Harris, D. 1980. *Human Ecology in Savanna Environments.* London: Academic Press.

Heald, S. 1999. 'Agricultural Intensification and the Decline of Pastoralism: A case study from Kenya. *Africa:* 69: 213–37.

Heffernan, C., Misturelli, F. and Nielsen, L., 2001. *Restocking and Poverty Alleviation: the Perceptions and Realities of Livestock-keeping Among Poor Pastoralists in Kenya.* Reading: Veterinary Epidemiology and Economics Unit, Department of Agriculture.

Heffernan, C. and Rushton, J. 1998. 'Restocking: a critical evaluation'. *Nomadic Peoples* 4.

Heine, B., Heine, I. and König, C. 1988. *Plant Concepts and Plant Use: An ethnobotanical survey of the semi-arid and arid lands of East Africa Part V: Plants of the Samburu (Kenya).* Saarbrucken and Fort Lauderdale: Verlag Breitenbach.

Helander, B. 1999. 'Power and poverty in southern Somalia', in D. Anderson and V. Broch-Due (eds) *The Poor are Not Us.* Oxford: James Currey.

Hendrickson, D., Armon, J. and Mearns, R. 1998. 'The changing nature of conflict and famine vulnerability: the case of livestock raiding in Turkana District, Kenya', *Disasters* 22 (3): 185–99.

Henin, R.A. 1968. 'Fertility Differentials in the Sudan', *Population Studies* 22:147–64.

Henin, R.A. 1969. 'The Patterns and Causes of Fertility Differentials in the Sudan', *Population Studies* 23:171–98.

Herren, U. 1990. *The Commercial Sale of Camel Milk from Pastoral Herds in the Mogadishu Hinterland of Somalia'.* Pastoral Development Network, 30a. London: Overseas Development Institute.

Herskovits, M. 1926. 'The Cattle Complex in East Africa'. *American Anthropologist.* 28: 230–72, 361–88, 494–528, 633–64.

Hesse, C. 1987. *Livestock Market Data as an Early Warning Indicator of Stress in the Pastoral Economy.* Pastoral Development Network paper 24f. London: Overseas Development Institute,

Hilderbrand, K., Hill, A., Randall, S. and van den Eerenbeemt, M.I. 1985. 'Child Mortality and the Care of Children in Mali', in A. Hill (ed.), *Population, Health and Nutrition in the Sahel.* London: Routledge and Kegan Paul.

Hilhorst, T. and Muchana, F. 2000. *Nutrients on the Move: Soil fertility dynamics in African farming systems.* London: IIED Drylands Programme.

Hill, A. (ed.) 1985. *Population, Health and Nutrition in the Sahel.* London: Routledge & Kegan Paul.

Hill, A. 1988. 'Famine in Africa: The most dreadful resource of nature', in E. van der Walle, P.O. Ohadike and M.D. Sala-Diakande (eds), *The State of African Demography*, Liege: International

Union for the Scientific Study of Population.

Hill, A. 1990. 'Demographic Responses to Food Shortages in the Sahel', *Pop. Dev. Review*: supplement to vol. 15 (1989): 168–92.

Hill, A. and Randall, S. 1984. 'Différences géographiques et sociales dans la mortalité infantile et juvénile au Mali', *Population* 6: 921–46.

Hitchcock, R. 1990. 'Water, Land and Livestock: the evolution of tenure and administrative patterns in the grazing areas of Botswana', in J. Galaty and D. Johnson (eds), *The World of Pastoralism*. New York: Guilford Press.

Hitchcock, R. 1996. *Kalahari Communities: Bushmen and the Politics of Environment in Southern Africa*, Document no. 79, Copenhagen: International Working Group for Indigenous Affairs.

Hjort, A. 1982. 'A critique of 'ecological' models of land use'. *Nomadic Peoples* 10: 11–27.

Hjort, A. and Dahl, G. 1991. *Responsible Man: the Atmaan Beja of North-eastern Sudan*. Stockholm: Almqvist & Wiksell International.

Hodgson, D. 1999a. 'Pastoralism, Patriarchy and History: Changing gender relations among Maasai in Tanganyika, 1890–1940', *Journal of African History* 40: 41–65.

Hodgson, D. 1999b. 'Women as Children: Culture, political economy and gender inequality'. *Nomadic peoples* 3 (2), 115–30.

Hodgson, D. L. 1999c. '"Once intrepid warriors": modernity and the production of Maasai masculinities'. *Ethnology* 38: 121–50.

Hodgson, D. (ed.) 2000a. *Rethinking Pastoralism in Africa*, Oxford: James Currey.

Hodgson, D. 2000b. 'Taking Stock: State control, ethnic identity and pastoralist development in Tanganyika 1948–1958', *Journal of African History* 41: 55–78.

Hodgson, D. 2001. *Once Intrepid Warriors: Gender, ethnicity and the cultural politics of Maasai development*. Bloomington: Indiana University Press,

Hoffmann, T. (coordinator) 1999. 'National Review of Land Degradation in South Africa'. SANBI www.sanbi.org/landdeg

Hoffmann T., Dean, W. and Allsopp, N. 2003. 'Landuse Effects on Plant and Insect Diversity in Namaqualand', in N. Allsopp, A. Palmer, S. Milton, K. Kirkman, G. Kerley, C. Hurt, C. Brown (eds), *Proc VIIth International Rangelands Congress*. Durban, South Africa July–August. Available on line at http://www.rangelandcongress.com

Hogg, R. 1986. 'The New Pastoralism: Poverty and Dependency in North Kenya'. *Africa*. 56: 317–33.

Hogg, R. 1987. 'Development in Kenya: Drought, Desertification and Food Scarcity'. *African Affairs*. 86: 47–58.

Hogg, R. 1991. 'Should pastoralism continue as a way of life?' *Disasters* 16: 131–7.

Hogg, R. 1993. 'Continuity and change among the Boran in Ethiopia', in J. Markakis (ed.), *Conflict and the Decline of Pastoralism in the Horn of Africa*. Basingstoke: Macmillan.

Hogg, R. 1996. 'Changing Mandates in the Ethiopian Ogaden', in T. Allen (ed.), *In Search of Cool Ground: War, Flight and Homecoming in North East Africa*. Oxford: James Currey and Lawrenceville, NJ: Africa World Press in association with UNRISD.

Hogg, R. (ed.) 1997a. *Pastoralists, Ethnicity and the State in Ethiopia*. London: HAAN/Institute for African Alternatives.

Hogg, R. 1997b. 'Changing land use and resource conflict among Somali pastoralists in the Haud of South east Ethiopia', in R. Hogg (ed.), *Pastoralists, Ethnicity and the State in Ethiopia*. London: HAAN/ Institute for African Alternatives.

Holden, C. and Mace, R. 1997. 'Phylogenetic analysis of the evolution of lactose digestion in adults'. *Human Biology* 69 (5): 605–28.

Holden, S.J., Coppock, D. and Assefa, M. 1991. 'Pastoral Dairy Marketing and Household Wealth Interactions, and their Implications for Calves and Humans in Ethiopia', *Human.Ecol.* 19 (1): 35–60.

Holmes, D. 1993. 'Rise of the Nile Delta', *Nature* 363: 402.

Holter, U. 1988. 'Food Habits of Camel Nomads in the North West Sudan: Food habits and foodstuffs', *Ecology of Food and Nutrition* 29: 61–81.

Holy, I. 1974. *Neighbours and Kinsmen: A Study of the Berti People of Northern Sudan*, London: C. Hurst.

Homewood, K. 1992a. 'Development and the Ecology of Maasai Food and Nutrition'. *Ecol.Fd.Nutr.* 29: 61–81.

Homewood, K. 1992b. 'Patch Production by Cattle'. *Nature*. 359: 109–10.

Homewood, K. 1993. *Livestock Economy and Ecology in El Kala, Algeria: Measuring ecological and economic costs and benefits in pastoral ecosystems*, Pastoral Development Network 35a: 1–27. London: Overseas Development Institute.

Homewood, K. 1994. 'Pastoralism, Environment and Development in East African Rangelands', in B. Zaba and J. Clarke (eds), *Environment and Population Change*. Liege: Derouaux, ORDINA Editions.

Homewood, K. 1995. 'Development, Demarcation and Ecological Outcomes in Maasailand', *Africa* 65 (3): 331–50.

Homewood, K. 1996. 'Ecological Outcomes of Boundary Formation in Maasailand', in P. Nugent (ed.), *African Boundaries and Borderlands*, London: Mansell Press.

Homewood, K. 1997. *Land Use, Household Viability and Migration in the Sahel*. Final Report to INCO-DC, EU-DGXII, Contract TS3 CT94 –0276

Homewood, K. 1999. 'Comment', in L. Rutten and M. Borgerhoff-Mulder, *Current Anthropology* 40: 64–2.

Homewood, K. 2004. 'Policy, Environment and Development in African rangelands'. *Environmental Science and Policy* 7:125–43.

Homewood, K. and Brockington, D. 1999. 'Biodiversity, conservation and development in Mkomazi Game Reserve, Tanzania.' *Global Ecology and Biogeography* 8:301–13.

Homewood, K. and Lewis, J. 1987. 'Drought Impact in Baringo Region, Kenya. 1983/85'. *J. Applied Ecology*. 24:615–31.

Homewood, K. and Rodgers, W.A. 1987. 'Pastoralism, Conservation and the Overgrazing Controversy', in D. Anderson and R. Grove (eds), *Conservation in Africa: Past Images and Present Realities*. Cambridge: Cambridge University Press.

Homewood, K. and Rodgers, W.A. 1991. *Maasailand Ecology*. Cambridge: Cambridge University Press.

Homewood, K. and Thompson, M. (in press). 'Social and Economic Challenges for Conservation in East African Rangelands: Land Use, Livelihoods and Wildlife Change in Maasailand', in Johan Du Toit, Richard Kock and James Deutsch (eds), *Wildlands or Rangelands?* Oxford: Blackwell Series 'Conservation Science and Practice'.

Homewood, K., Kristjanson, P., and Trench, P. (eds). Forthcoming. *Staying Maasai? Livelihoods, Conservation and Development in East African Rangelands*. New York: Spinger.

Homewood, K, Lambin, E.F., Coast, E., Kariuki, A., Kikula, I., Kivelia, J., Said, M., Serneels, S., and Thompson, M. 2001. 'Long-term Changes in Serengeti-Mara Wildebeest and Land Cover: Pastoralism, population or policies?', *Proc Nat Acad Sci*.98 (22): 12544–9.

Homewood, K., Thompson, M. and Coast, E. 2004. 'In-Migrants And Exclusion: Tenure, access and conflict in east African rangelands' *Africa* 74 (4): 567–610.

Homewood, K., Thompson, M., Trench, P., S. Kiruswa and E. Coast. 2005. 'Community- and State-based Natural Resource Management and Local Livelihoods in Maasailand'. *Gestione della risorse naturali su base communitaria e statale. Ambiente e sviluppo sostenibile in Africa australe*. Special issue *Afriche e Orienti* 2005 (2):84–101; ISSN 1592-6753.

Homewood, K., Trench, P., Randall, S., Lynen, L. and Bishop, E., 2006. 'Impacts of a Veterinary Intervention in Maasai Cattle: Livestock health, socio-economic correlates and ecological implications. The infection–and-treatment vaccine against East Coast fever'. *Agricultural Systems* 89: 248–71.

Hopen, C. 1958. *The Pastoral Fulbe Family in Gwandu*. London: Oxford University Press.

Horowitz, M. 1975. 'Herdsman and Husbandmen in Niger: Values and Strategies', in T. Monod ed., *Pastoralism in Tropical Africa*. Oxford: Oxford University Press.

Horowitz, M. 1979. *The Sociology of Pastoralism and African Livestock Projects*. AID programme evaluation discussion paper 6. Washington, DC: USAID.

Howell, P., Lock, M. and Cobb, S. (eds) 1988. *The Jonglei Canal: Impact and Opportunity*, Cambridge Studies in Applied Ecology and Management. Cambridge: Cambridge University Press.

Huffman, T. 1990. 'Broederstroom and the Origins of Cattle Keeping in Southern Africa', *African Studies* 49 (2): 1–12.

Hulme, D. and Infield, M. 2001. 'Community Conservation, Reciprocity and Park-People Relations; Lake Mburo National Park, Uganda', in D. Hulme and M. Murphree (eds), *African Wildlife and Livelihoods: The Promise and Performance of Community Conservation*. Oxford: James Currey.

Hulme, D. and Murphree, M. (eds) 2001. *African Wildlife and Livelihoods: The Promise and Performance of Community Conservation*. Oxford: James Currey.

Hulme, M. 1992. 'Rainfall changes in Africa: 1931–1960 to 1961–1990', *Int. J. Climatol* 12: 685–99.

Hulme, M., Doherty, R., Ngara, T., New, M. and Lister, D. 2001 'African Climate Change: 1900–2100. *Climate Research* 17:145–68.

Huss-Ashmore, R., 1996. 'Livestock, Nutrition and Intra-household Resource Control in Uasin Gishu District, Kenya'. *Human Ecology* 24: 191–213.

Hussein, K. 1998. 'Conflicts between Farmers and Herders in the Semi-arid Sahel and East Africa: a Review'. IIED Pastoral Land Tenure Series, no 10. London: IIED.

Hussein, K., Sumberg, J. and Seddon, D., 1999. 'Increasing Conflict between Herders and Farmers in Africa: Claims and evidence', *Development Policy Review* 17: 397–418.

Hutchinson, S. 1992, 'The Cattle of Money and the Cattle of Girls Among the Nuer', *American Ethnologist* 19: 294–316.

Hutchinson, S. 1996. *Nuer Dilemmas. Coping with Money, War and the State*, Berkeley, CA: University of California Press.

Ibn Khaldun, A. 2004. *The Muqaddimah: An Introduction to History*. Edited by N. J. Dawood, with Introduction by Bruce B. Lawrence, translated by Franz Rosenthal. (Bollingen Series). Princeton Classic editions. Princeton, NJ: Princeton University Press.

Ibrahim, M.A. 1996. 'Ethnotoxicology among Nigeran agropastoralists' in C.M. McCorkle, E. Mathias and T.W. Schillhorn van Veen, *Ethnoveterinary Research and Development*. London: Intermediate Technology Publications.

Igoe, J. 2003. 'Scaling up Civil Society: Donor Money, NGOs and the pastoralist land rights movement in Tanzania'. *Development and Change* 34(5): 863–85.

Igoe, J. and Brockington, D. 1999. *Pastoral Land Tenure and Community Conservation: a case study from North-East Tanzania*. Pastoral Land Tenure Series No 11. London: IIED.

ILCA, 1981. *Introduction to the East African Range and Livestock Study*. Nairobi: International Livestock Centre for Africa.

Iliya, M. and Swindell, K. 1997. 'Winners and Losers: Household fortunes in the urban peripheries of Northern Nigeria', in D. Bryceson and V. Jamal (eds), *Farewell to Farms. De-agrarianisation and Employment in Africa*. Aldershot: Ashgate.

Illius, A and O'Connor, T. 1999. 'On the Relevance of Non-equilibrial Concepts to Arid and Semi-arid Grazing Systems'. *Ecol. Applic.* 9: 798–813.

INSEE SEDES NIGER. 1986. *Etude Demographique et Economique en Milieu Nomade*. Vols. 1 & 2 Paris: Ministère de la Cooperation.

IPCC. 2001. *Climate Change 2001: Synthesis Report. A Contribution of Working Groups I, II and III to the Third Assessment Report of the Intergovernmental Panel on Climate Change* [R.T. Watson and the Core Writing Teams (eds)]. Cambridge and New York: Cambridge University Press.

Jackson, I. 1977. *Climate, Water and Agriculture in the Tropics*, London and New York: Longman.

Jackson, R. and Latham, M. 1979. 'Lactose malabsorption among Maasai children of East Africa'. *Am. J. Clinical Nutrition* 32: 779–82.

Jacobs, N. 2003. *Environment, Power and Injustice. A South African history*. Cambridge: Cambridge University Press.

Jahnke, H.E. 1982. *Livestock Production Systems and Livestock Development in Tropical Africa*. Kiel: Kieler Wissenschaftsverlag vauk.

James, W. 1996. 'Uduk resettlement', in T. Allen, (ed.), *In Search of Cool Ground: War, Flight and Homecoming in North East Africa*, Oxford: James Currey, and Lawrenceville, NJ: Africa World Press.

Jewell, P. 1980. 'Ecology and Management of Game Animals and Domestic livestock in African savannas.pp 353-382 in D. Harris (ed.) *Human Ecology in Savanna Environments*. London: Academic Press.

Joekes, S. and Ponting, J. 1991. *Women in Pastoral Societies in East and West Africa*. Drylands Programme, Issues paper 28. London IIED.

Joffe, G. 1989. 'Khattara and Other Forms of Gravity-fed Irrigation in Morocco', in P. Beaumont, M. Bonine, and K. MacLachlan (eds), *Qanat, Kariz and Khattara*, Middle East Centre. SOAS. London: MENAS Press.

Johnson, B. 1999. 'Social Networks and Exchange', in M.A. Little and P. W. Leslie (eds) ,*Turkana Herders of the Dry Savanna. Ecology and biobehavioural response of nomads to an uncertain environment*. Oxford: Oxford University Press.

Johnson, D. 1982. 'Tribal Boundaries and Border Wars: Nuer-Dinka relations in the Sobat and Zaraf Valleys c 1860–1976', *J.Afr. History* 23: 183–203.

Johnson, D. 1988. 'Adaptation to Floods in the Jonglei Area of the Sudan: an historical analysis', in D. Johnson and D. Anderson D. (eds), *The Ecology of Survival. Case studies from northeast African history*. London. Lester Crook/Westview Press.

Johnson, D. 1991. 'Political Ecology in the Upper Nile: The twentieth century expansion of the pastoral common economy', in J.G. Galaty and P. Bonte (eds), *Herders, Warriors and Traders. Pastoralism in Africa*. Boulder, CO: Westview Press.

Johnson, D. 1996. 'Increasing the Trauma of Return: An assessment of the UN's emergency reponse to evacuation of the Sudanese refugee camps in Ethiopia 1991', in T. Allen (ed.), *In Search of Cool Ground: War, Flight and Homecoming in North East Africa*. Oxford: James Currey, Lawrenceville, NJ: Africa World Press, in association with UNRISD.

Johnson, D. 2003. *The Root Causes of Sudan's Civil Wars*, Oxford: James Currey. See also addenda in 2004 re-issue of this work.

Johnson D. and Anderson, D. (eds). 1988. *The Ecology of Survival. Case studies from northeast African history*. London: Lester Crook/Westview Press.

Kahurananga, J. 1981. 'Population Estimates, Densities and Biomass of Large Herbivores in the Simanjiro Plains, Northern Tanzania'. *East African Wildlife Journal* 19: 225–38.

Kariuki, D.P. 1990. 'Current status of theileriosis in Kenya – 1989', in A. S. Young, J.J. Mutugi and A.C. Maritim (eds), *Progress Towards the Control of East Coast Fever (Theileriosis) in Kenya*, Nairobi: KARI.

Keay, R.W.J., 1959. *Vegetation Map of Africa South of the Tropic of Cancer*. London: Oxford University Press.

Keen, D. 1995, *The Benefits of Famine: A political economy of famine and relief in Southwestern Sudan, 1983–1989*. Princeton, NJ: Princeton University Press.

Keenan, J. 1977. 'Power and Wealth are Cousins', *Africa* 47: 242–52.

Keenan, J. 1977. *The Tuareg: People of the Ahaggar*. Harmondsworth: Allen Lane, Penguin.

Kerven, C. 1992. *Customary Commerce: A historical reassessment of pastoralist livestock marketing in Africa*, Agriculture Series, No. 15. London: Overseas Development Institute.

Kibreab, G. 1997. *People on the Edge in the Horn: Displacement, Land Use and the Environment in the Gedaref Region, Sudan*. Trenton, NJ: Red Sea Press.

Kimambo, I. 1969. *A Political History of the Pare of Tanzania, c1500–1900*. Nairobi: East African Publishing House.

Kinahan, J. 1991. *Pastoral Nomads of the Central Namib Desert. The people history forgot*. Windhoek: Namibia Archaeological Trust. New Namibia Books.

Kintz, D. 1986. 'Peul Majoritaires, Peul Minoritaires', in M. Adamu and A. Kirk-Greene (eds), *Pastoralists of the West African Savanna*. Manchester: Manchester University Press.

Kipury, N. 1989. 'Maasai Women in Transition: Class and gender in transformation of a pastoral society'. Unpublished PhD dissertation, Temple University.

Kiwasila, H. (forthcoming). 'Natural Resource Management and Livelihood Strategies of Pare Farmers around Mkomazi, Tanzania'. Unpublished PhD thesis, Department of Anthropology, University College, London.

Kiwasila, H. and Brockington, D. 1996. 'Combining Conservation with Community Development around Mkomazi Game Reserve.' *Miombo Technical Supplement* 1.

Kjaerby, F. 1979. *The Development of Agropastoralism Among the Barabaig in Hanang District*. BRALUP Research Paper No. 56, University of Dar es Salaam.

Kjekshus, H. 1977. *Ecology, Control and Development in East African History*. London: Heinemann. (Reprinted 1996 James Currey).

Klein, R. 1989. 'Faunal Evidence for Prehistoric Herder-forager Activities at Kasteelberg, Western Cape Province, South Africa'. *South African Archaeological Bulletin* 44: 82–97.

Klopp, J. 2001, '"Ethnic Clashes" and Winning Elections: The case of Kenya's electoral despotism'. *Can.J. Afr Studies* 35 (3): 473–515.

Klopp, J. 2002, 'Can Moral Ethnicity Trump Political Tribalism? The struggle for land and nation in Kenya', *African Studies* 61: 269–94.

Klugman, J., Neyapti, B. and Stewart, F. 1999. *Conflict and Growth in Africa: vol. 2: Kenya, Tanzania and Uganda*. Development Centre Studies. Paris: OECD.

Knowles, J. and Collett, D. 1989. 'Nature as Myth, Symbol and Action: Notes Towards a Historical Understanding of Development and Conservation in Kenyan Maasailand', *Africa* 59(4): 433–60.

Konstant, T.L., Sullivan, S. and Cunningham, A.B. 1995. 'The Effects of Utilization by People and Livestock on *Hyphaene petersiana* (Arecaceae) Basketry Resources in the Palm Savanna of

North-central Namibia'. *Economic Botany*, 49(4): 345–56.

Krätli, S. 2000. *Education Provision to Nomadic Pastoralists: A Literature Review*. IDS Working Paper. Brighton: Institute of Development Studies, University of Sussex.

Krätli, S. 2001. *Educating Nomadic Herders out of Poverty? Culture, Education, and Pastoral Livelihood in Turkana and Karimoja*. Brighton: Institute of Development Studies, University of Sussex.

Kretchmer, N. 1972. 'Lactose & lactase', *Scientific American* 227(4): 70–8.

Kuper, A. 1982. *Wives for Cattle*. London and Boston, MA: Routledge and Kegan Paul.

Kurimoto, E. 1994. 'Civil War and Regional Conflicts: The Pari and their neighbours in south east Sudan', in K. Fukui and J. Markakis, *Ethnicity and Conflict in the Horn of Africa*. Oxford: James Currey/ Athens, OH: Ohio University Press.

Kurimoto, E. and Simonse, S. (eds) 1998. *Conflict, Age and Power in North East Africa*, Oxford: James Currey/Athens, OH: Ohio University Press.

Kurita, Y. 1994. 'The Social Bases of Regional Movements in Sudan 1960s–1980s', in K. Fukui and J. Markakis (eds), *Ethnicity and Conflict in the Horn of Africa*, Oxford: James Currey/Athens, OH: Ohio University Press.

Kwamena-Poh, M., Tosh J., Waller, R., and Tidy, M. 1982. *African History in Maps*. Harlow: Longman.

Lamphear, J. 1992. *The Scattering Time: Turkana responses to colonial rule* Oxford: Clarendon Press.

Lamphear, J. 1993. 'Aspects of becoming Turkana', in T. Spear and R. Waller (eds), *Being Maasai*. London: James Currey; Dar es Salaam: Mkuki wa Nyota; Nairobi: EAEP; Athens, OH: Ohio University Press.

Lamphear, J. 1994. 'The Evolution of Ateker 'New Model' Armies: Jie and Turkana', in K. Fukui and J. Markakis (eds), *Ethnicity and Conflict in the Horn of Africa*. Oxford: James Currey/Athens, OH: Ohio University Press.

Lamphear, J. 1998. 'Brothers in Arms: Military aspects of East African age class systems in historical perspective', in E. Kurimoto and S. Simonse (eds), *Conflict, Age and Power in North East Africa*. Oxford: James Currey/ Athens, OH: Ohio University Press.

Lamprey, H. 1983. 'Pastoralism Yesterday and Today: The overgrazing problem', in F. Bourlière (ed.), *Tropical Savannas*, Amsterdam: Elsevier.

Landais, E. 1994. 'Des rizières et des vaches', *Cahiers d'Etudes Africaines* XXXIV, (136): 707–16.

Lane, C. 1996a. 'Poverty, Politics and Pastoralists in East Africa'. *Anthropology in Action* 3(3): 11–13.

Lane, C. 1996b. *Pastures Lost: Barabaig Economy, Resource Tenure, and the Alienation of their Land in Tanzania*. Nairobi: Initiatives Publishers.

Lane, C. (ed.) 1998. *Custodians of the Commons: Pastoral land tenure in East and West Africa*. London: Earthscan.

Lane, C. and Moorehead, R. 1995. 'New Directions in Rangeland Resource Tenure and Policy', in I. Scoones (ed.), *Living with Uncertainty*. London: ITP/IIED.

Lane, C. and Scoones, I. 1993. 'Barabaig Natural Resource Management', in M. Young and O. Solbrig (eds), *The World's Savannas*, Man and Biosphere Series, Vol 12. Paris: UNESCO.

Lane, C. and Swift, J. 1989. *East African Pastoralism: Common land, common problems*. London: International Institute for Environment and Development (IIED) .

Laris, P. 2002. 'Burning the Seasonal Mosaic: Preventative burning strategies in the wooded savanna of Southern Mali', *Human Ecology* 30 (2): 155–86.

Laris, P. 2003. 'Grounding Environmental Narratives', in W. Moseley and B. Logan (eds), *African Environment and Development: Rhetoric, Programs, Realities* Aldershot: Ashgate Publishing Ltd.

Last, M. 1985. 'The Early Kingdoms of the Nigerian Savanna', in A.Ajayi and M. Crowder (eds), *History of West Africa*. Harlow and Ibadan: Longman.

Laws, R. M. 1970. 'Elephants as Agents of Habitat and Landscape Change in East Africa', *Oikos* 21: 1–15.

Le Houérou, H. 1980. *Browse in Africa: the Current State of Knowledge*. Addis Abbaba: ILCA.

Le Houérou, H. 1989. 'The Grazing Land Ecosystems of the African Sahel'. *Ecological Studies* 75. Berlin: Springer Verlag.

Le Houérou, H., and Hoste, C. 1977. 'Rangeland Production and Annual Rainfall Relations in the Mediterranean Basin and in the African Sahelo-Soudanian Zone', *J Range Management* 30: 181–9.

Leach, M. and Mearns, R. (eds), 1996. *The Lie of the Land*. Oxford: James Currey.

Leeflang, P. 1993. 'Some Observations on Ethnoveterinary Medicine in Northern Nigeria'. *Indigenous Knowledge and Development Monitor* 1(1): 17–19.

Legesse, Asmarom, 1989. 'Adaptation, Drought and Development: Boran and Gabra Pastoralists of Northern Kenya', in R. Huss-Ashmore and S. Katz (eds), *African Food Systems in Crisis*, Part 1. London: Gordon & Breach,

Legge, K. 1989. 'Changing Responses to Drought Among the Wodaabe of Niger', in P. Halstead and J. O'Shea (eds), *Bad Year Economics: Cultural Responses to Risk and Uncertainty*. Cambridge: Cambridge University Press.

Legrosse, P. 1999. 'Les règles d'accès des troupeaux Peuls aux pâturages du Delta central du Niger (Mali)', in M. Niamir-Fuller (ed.), *Managing Mobility in African Rangelands: the legitimization of transhumance*. London: IT Publications/Rome: FAO.

Leslie, P. and Fry, P. 1989. 'Extreme Seasonality of Births Among Nomadic Turkana Pastoralists'. *Am.J.Phys Anthr.* 79: 103–115.

Leslie, Paul W., Dyson-Hudson, R. and Fry, Peggy. 1999. 'Population and Persistence' in M.A. Little and P.W. Leslie (eds), *Turkana Herders of the Dry Savanna*. Oxford: Oxford University Press.

Levtzion, N. 1985. 'The Early States of the Western Sudan', in A. Ajayi (ed.), *History of West Africa*. Longman: Harlow and Ibadan.

Lewis I.M. 1961. *A Pastoral Democracy . A study of pastoralism and politics among the northern Somali of the Horn of Africa,* London: Oxford University Press.

Lewis, I.M. 1988. *A Modern History of Somalia: Nation and State in the Horn of Africa*. Boulder, CO: Westview Press, reprinted 2002, Oxford: James Currey.

Lewis, I. 2001. 'Why the Warlords Won: How the United States and the United Nations misunderstood the clan politics of Somalia', *Times Literary Supplement* 5123 (8.6.2001): 3–5.

Lewis-Williams, D. 1981. *Believing and Seeing: Symbolic meanings in Southern San rock paintings*. London: Academic Press.

Lhôte, H. 1966. 'Les Peintures Pariétales d'époque bovidienne du Tassili. *Journal de la Société des Africanistes* 36: 7–27.

Little, M. 1989. 'Human Biology of African Pastoralists'. *Yearbook of Physical Anthropology*. 32:215–247.

Little, M. and Leslie, P. (eds) 1999. *Turkana Herders of the Dry Savanna. Ecology and Biobehavioural Response of Nomads to an Uncertain Environment*. Oxford: Oxford University Press.

Little, M, Galvin, K. and Leslie, P.W. 1988. 'Health and Energy Requirements of Nomadic Turkana Pastoralists', in I. de Garine and G. Harrison (eds), *Coping with Uncertainty in Food Supply*. Oxford: Clarendon Press.

Little M., Gray, S. and Leslie, P. 1993. 'Growth of Nomadic and Settled Turkana Infants'. *Am. J. Phys. Anth.* 92: 273–89.

Little M., Gray, S., Pike, I. and Mugambi, M. 1999. 'Infant, Child and Adolescent Growth, and Adult Physical Status', in M. Little and P.W. Leslie (eds), *Turkana Herders of the Dry Savanna,* Oxford: Oxford University Press.

Little M., Leslie, P. and Campbell, K. 1992. 'Energy Reserves and Parity of Nomadic and Settled Turkana Women'. *Am. J. Hum. Biol.* 4: 729–38.

Little, P. 1985. 'Absentee Herd Owners and Part-Time Pastoralists: the Political Economy of Resource Use in Northern Kenya'. *Human Ecology* 13: 131–51.

Little, P. 1994. 'Maidens and Milk Markets: The sociology of dairy marketing in Southern Somalia', in E. Fratkin, K. Galvin and E.A. Roth (eds), *African Pastoral Systems: an Integrated Approach*. Boulder, CO: Lynne Rienner.

Little, P. 1996 'Conflictive Trade, Contested Identity: The Effects of Export Markets on Pastoralists of Southern Somalia,' *African Studies Review*, 39 (1): 25–53.

Little, P. 2003. *Somalia: Economy Without State*. Oxford: James Currey.

Little, P., Smith, K., Cellarius, B., Coppock, D. and Barrett, C. 2001. 'Avoiding disaster: diversification and risk management among East African herders'. *Development and Change* 32: 410–33.

Livestock in Development. 1999. *Livestock in Poverty-focused Development*. Crewkerne: Livestock in Development.

Loftus, R., MacHugh, D., Bradley, D., Sharo, P. and Cunningham, P. 1994. 'Evidence for Two Independent Domestications of Cattle'. *Proc Nat Acad Sci* 91: 2757–61.

Loutan, L. 1985. 'Nutrition amongst a group of WoDaaBe (Fulani Bororo) pastoralists in Niger', in A. Hill (ed.), *Population, Health and Nutrition in the Sahel*. London: Routledge & Kegan Paul.

Loutan, L. and Paillard, S. 1992. 'Measles in a West African nomadic community' *Bull. WHO* 70

(6): 741–44.

Lovejoy, P. and Baier, S. 1975. 'The Desert Side Economy of the Central Sudan'. *International J. of African Historical Studies*. 8: 551–81.

Lowe, P., 1983. 'Values and Institutions in the History of British Nature Conservation', in A. Warren and F. B. Goldsmith (eds), *Conservation in Perspective*, Chicester: John Wiley.

Ludwig, J.A. 1987. 'Primary Productivity in Arid Lands: Myths and Realities', *J.Arid Environments*, 13: 1–7.

Luikart, G., Gielly, L., Excoffier, L., Vigne, J-D., Bouvet, J. and Taberlet, P. 2001. 'Multiple Maternal Origins and Weak Phylogeographic Structure in Domestic Goats'. *Proc Nat Acad Sci* 98: 5927–32.

Mabogunje, A. and Richards. P. 'The Lands and Peoples of West Africa', in A. Ajayi and M. Crowder (eds), *History of West Africa*. Harlow and Ibadan: Longman.

MacDonald, K. 2000. 'The origins of African livestock: indigenous or imported?', in R. Blench and K. MacDonald (eds), *The Origins and Development of African Livestock*. London: UCL Press.

MacKenzie, J.M. 1987. 'Chivalry, Social Darwinism and Ritualised Killing: The hunting ethos in Central Africa up to 1914', in D. Anderson and R. Grove (eds), *Conservation in Africa: People, Policies and Practice*. Cambridge: Cambridge University Press.

Mace, R. 1988. *A Model of Herd Composition that Maximises Household Viability, and its Potential Application in the Support of Pastoralists Under Stress*. ODI Pastoral Development Network 26b. London: Overseas Development Institute.

Mace, R. 1989. *Gambling with Goats: Variability in herd growth among restocked pastoralists in Kenya*, Pastoralist Development Network 28a. London: Overseas Development Institute.

Mace, R. 1990. 'Pastoralist Herd Compositions in Unpredictable Environments: A Comparison of Model Predictions and Data from Camel-keeping Groups', *Agricultural Systems* 33:1-11.

Mace, R. 1991. 'Overgrazing overstated'. *Nature* 349: 280–1.

Mace, R. 1993a. 'Transitions between cultivation and pastoralism in sub-Saharan Africa', *Current Anthropology* 34(4): 363–81.

Mace, R, 1993b. 'Nomadic Pastoralists Adopt Subsistence Strategies that Maximize Long-term Household Survival', *Behavioural Ecology and Sociobiology* 33, 329–34.

Mace, R. and Huston A. 1989. 'Pastoralist Strategies for Survival in Unpredictable Environments: A Model of Herd Composition that Maximises Household Viability', *Agricultural Systems* 31:185–204.

Mace, R. and Sear, R. 1996. 'Maternal Mortality in a Kenyan pastoralist population', *International Journal of Gynaecology and Obstetrics* 54:137–41.

MacHugh, D. and Bradley, D. 2001. 'Livestock Genetic Origins: Goats buck the trend'. *Proc Nat Acad Sci* 98 (10) 5382–4.

MacHugh, D. Shriver M., Loftus, R. T., Cunningham, P. and Bradley, D. G. 1997. 'Microsatellite DNA Variation and the Evolution, Domestication and Phylogeography of Taurine and Zebu Cattle (*Bos taurus* and *Bos indicus*)', *Genetics* 146: 1071–86.

MacKinnon, A. 1999. 'The Persistence of the Cattle Economy in Zululand, South Africa 1900-1950', *Canadian Journal of African Studies* 33: 98–136.

MacNab, J. 1985. 'Carrying Capacity and Related Slippery Shibboleths', *Wildlife Society Bulletin* 13: 403–10.

Maley, J. 1996. 'The African rain forest: main characteristics of changes in vegetation and climate from the Upper Cretaceous to the Quaternary', *Proc Roy Soc Edinb. Biol Ser* 104B: 31–73.

Maley, J. 2001. 'The Catastrophic Destruction of African Forests around 2500 Years Ago Still Exerts a Major Influence on Present Vegetation Form and Distribution'. Paper presented at Workshop on 'Changing Perspectives on Forests: Ecology, people and science/policy processes'. 26–7 March, IDS, University of Sussex.

Maley, J. 2001. 'Si la forêt tropicale m'était contée'. *Canopée* 19: 6-9, *Journal du Programme Européen*. ECOFAC, Libreville.

Mali, République du. 1961. 'Enquête Démographique au Mali 1960–61'. Bamako: Service de la Statistique et INSEE.

Mali République du. 1989. 'Enquête Démographique et de Santé au Mali 1987'. Bamako: CERPOD.

Mali, République du. 1998. 'Enquête Démographique et de Santé au Mali 1996'. Bamako: CERPOD.

Manger, L. 1988. 'Traders, Farmers and Pastoralists: Economic Adaptations and Environmental Problems in the Nuba Mountains of the Sudan', in D. Johnson and D. Anderson (eds), *The*

Ecology of Survival. London: Lester Crook.

Markakis, J. (ed.) 1993. *Conflict and the Decline of Pastoralism in the Horn of Africa.* Basingstoke: Macmillan.

Markakis, J. 1999. 'Pastoralists and Politicians in Kenya', *Review of African Political Economy* September: 293–6.

Marriott, H. 1993. 'Determinants of Natural Fertility Differentials: a Comparative Survey of the Rural Populations of the Inner Niger Delta of Mali'. PhD thesis (unpublished), University of London.

Marshall, F. 1989. 'Rethinking the Role of *Bos Indicus* in sub-Saharan Africa', *Current Anthropology* 30:235–40.

Marshall, F. 1990. 'Origins of Specialized Pastoral Production in East Africa', *American Anthropologist* 92: 873–94.

Marshall, F. 1994 'Archaeological Perspectives on East African Pastoralism', in E. Fratkin, K. Galvin and E.A. Roth (eds), *African Pastoral Systems: An integrated approach.* Boulder, CO: Lynne Rienner.

Marshall, F. 2000. 'The Origins and Spread of Domestic Animals in East Africa', in R. Blench and K. MacDonald (eds), *The Origins and Development of African Livestock.* London: UCL Press.

Marshall, F., Stewart, K. and Barthelme, J. 1984. 'Early Domestic Stock at Dongodien in North Kenya', *Azania* 19: 120–7.

Mason, I. (ed.) 1984. *Evolution of Domesticated Animals* Harlow: Longman.

Mathias-Mundy, E. and McCorkle, C. 1989. *Ethnoveterinary Medicine: An annotated bibliography,* Ames, IO: Iowa State University Foundation.

Maundu P., Berger, D., Ole Saitibau, C. Nasieku, J., Kipelian, M., Mathenge, S., Morimoto, Y. and Höft, R. 2001. 'Ethnobotany of the Loita Maasai: Towards community management of the Forest of the Lost Child', *People and Plants,* Working Paper No 8. Paris: UNESCO.

Mauritanie, République Islamique de. 1977. *Recensement générale de la population* vols 1&2, Nouakchott.

May, A. 2002. 'Unexpected Migrations: Urban labour migration of rural youth and Maasai pastoralists'. Unpublished PhD thesis, University of Colorado.

McAuslan, P. 2000. 'Only the Name of the Country Changes: the Diaspora of "European" land law in Commonwealth Africa', in C. Toulmin and J .Quan (eds), *Evolving Land Rights, Policy and Tenure in Africa.* London: DFID/IIED/NRI.

McCabe, J.T. 1987. 'Drought and Recovery: Livestock Dynamics Among the Ngisonyoka Turkana of Kenya', *Human Ecology.* 15(4): 371–89.

McCabe, J.T. 1987. 'Inter-Household Variation in Ngisonyoka Turkana Livestock Production', *Research in Economic Anthropology* 8:277–93.

McCabe, J.T. 1990. 'Success and Failure: The Breakdown of Traditional Drought Coping Institutions Among the Pastoral Turkana of Kenya', *J.Afr and Asian Studies.* XXV(3-4):146–60.

McCabe, J.T. 1990. 'Turkana Pastoralism: A Case Against the Tragedy of the Commons', *Human. Ecol.* 18(1):81–104.

McCabe, J.T. 2004. *Cattle Bring Us to Our Enemies: Turkana Ecology, History, and Raiding in a Disequilibrium System,* Ann Arbor, MI: University of Michigan Press.

McCabe, T., Perkin, S. and Schofield, C. 1992. 'Can Conservation and Development be Coupled among Pastoral People? An examination of the Maasai of the Ngorongoro Conservation Area, Tanzania', *Human Organisation* 51 (4): 353–66.

McCabe, J., Schofield, E. and Pederson, G. 1997. 'Food Security and Nutritional Status', in M. Thompson (ed.), *Multiple Land Use: The experience of the Ngorongoro Conservation Area, Tanzania.* Gland Switzerland and Cambridge: IUCN.

McCorkle, C. and Mathias-Mundy, E. 1992. 'Ethnoveterinary Medicine in Africa', *Africa* 62(1): 59–93.

McCown, R., Haaland, G. and de Haan, C. 1979. 'The Interaction Between Cultivation and Livestock Production in Semi-arid Africa'. *Ecological Studies.* 34:297–332.

McCracken, R. (1971). 'Lactase Deficiency: An example of dietary evolution', *Current Anthropology* 12: 479–517.

McDougall, A. 1998. 'Research in Saharan History', *Journal of African History* 39: 467–80.

McIntosh, S. and McIntosh, R. 1988. 'From Stone to Metal: New perspectives on the later prehistory of west Africa', *J. World Prehistory* 2: 89–133.

McMillan, D. 1995. *Sahel Visions: Planned settlement and river blindness control in Burkina Faso,*

Tucson, AZ and London: University of Arizona Press.

McNaughton, S. 1985. 'Ecology of a Grazing Ecosystem: the Serengeti', *Ecol.Monographs* 55: 259–94.

McNaughton, S.J. 1988. 'Mineral Nutrition and Spatial Concentrations of African Ungulates', *Nature* 334: 343–5.

McNaughton, S., Banyikwa, F. and McNaughton, M. 1990. 'Promotion of the Cycling of Diet-enhancing Nutrients by African Grazers', *Science* 278: 1798–800.

McPeak, J. and Little, P. (eds) 2006. *Pastoral Livestock Marketing in Eastern Africa. Research and policy challenges*. London: Intermediate Technology Publications.

Menzies, N. 2004. 'Communities and Their Partners: Governance and community-based forest management', *Conservation and Society* 2(2): 449–56.

Milburn, M. 1988. 'On the Identity of the Tuareg and the Moors', *Sahara* 1: 93–4.

Mirzeler, M. and Young, C. 2000. 'Pastoral Politics in the Northeast Periphery of Uganda: AK47 as a change agent', *Journal of Modern African Studies* 38: 407–29.

Moda, G., Daborn, C., Grange, J. and Cosivi, O. 1996. 'The zoonotic importance of Myco-bacterium bovis', *Tubercle and Lung Disease* 77: 103–8.

Monimart, M. 1989. *Femme du Sahel. La Desertification au quotidien*. Paris: Editions Karthala.

Monod, T. 1975. 'Introduction', in T. Monod (ed.) *Pastoralism in Tropical Africa*. Oxford: Oxford University Press.

Moore, H. and Vaughan, M. 1994. *Cutting Down Trees: Gender, nutrition and agricultural change in the northern province of Zambia, 1890–1990*, Oxford: James Currey; Lusaka: University of Zambia Press; Portsmouth, NH: Heinemenn.

Moorehead, R. 1991. 'Structural Chaos: Community and state management of common property in Mali'. PhD Thesis, Institute of Development Studies, University of Sussex.

Moris, J. 1981. 'A Case in Rural Development: The Maasai Range Development Project', in J. Moris (ed.), *Managing Induced Rural Development*, Bloomington, IN: International Develop-ment Institute.

Mortimore, M. 1989. *Adapting to Drought, Farmers, Famines and Desertification in West Africa*. Cambridge: Cambridge University Press.

Mortimore, M. 1998. *Roots in the African Dust: Sustaining the drylands*, Cambridge: Cambridge University Press.

Mortimore, M. 2005. 'Social Resilience in African Dryland Livelihoods: Deriving Lessons for Policy', in Q. Gausset, M.Whyte and T. Birch-Thomsen (eds), *Beyond Territory and Scarcity: Exploring Conflicts over Natural Resource Management*, Stockholm: Nordisker Afrikainstitutet.

Morton, J. 1990. *Aspects of labour in an agro-pastoral economy: the Northern Beja of Sudan*, Pastoral Development Network 30b: 1-14, London: Overseas Development Institute.

Morton, J. 1993. 'Pastoral Decline and Famine: the Beja Case', in J. Markakis (ed.), *Conflict and Decline of Pastoralism in the Horn of Africa*. Basingstoke: Macmillan.

Murton, J. 1999. 'Population Growth and Poverty in Machakos District, Kenya', *Geographical Journal* 165(1): 37–46.

Muzzolini, A. 1991. 'Les Débuts de la Domestication au Sahara', *Bull. Soc. Préhistoire Ariègeoise* XXVI: 211–33.

Nathan, M., Fratkin, E., and Roth, E.A. 1996. 'Sedentism and Child Health Among Rendille Pastoralists of Northern Kenya', *Social Science & Medicine* 43 (4): 503–15.

National Bureau of Statistics 2003. *2002 Population and Housing Census*, Volume 1, Methodology Report, Dar es Salaam: United Republic of Tanzania, Central Census Office.

NCDP, 1987. *Wet Season Ground Census: Preliminary Report*. Ngorongoro Conservation and Development Project, NCAA, PO Box 1 Arusha or IUCN Regional Office, Nairobi.

Ndagala, D. 1982. 'Operation Imparnati; the Sedentarisation of the Pastoral Maasai in Tanzania', *Nomadic Peoples* 10: 28–39.

Ndagala, D. 1990. 'Pastoral Territoriality and Land Degradation in Tanzania', in G. Palsson (ed.), *From Water to World Making*, Uppsala: Scandinavian Institute of African Studies.

Ndagala, D. 1992a. *Territory, Pastoralists and Livestock: Resource control among the Kisongo Maasai*. Uppsala: *Acta Universitatis Uppsaliensis*.

Ndagala, D.K. 1992b. 'Production Diversification and Community Development in African Pastoral Areas', in A.H.Ornas (ed.), *Security in African Drylands. Research, development and policy*. Uppsala: Reprocentralen HSC.

Nelson, F., Gardner, B., Igoe, J. and Williams, A. forthcoming. 'Community-based conservation and Maasai livelihoods in Tanzania', in Homewood et al. (eds), *Staying Maasai? Livelihoods,*

Conservation and Development in East African Rangelands. New York: Springer.

Nestel, P. 1985. 'Nutritional Status of Maasai Women and Children in Relation to Subsistence Food Production', PhD Thesis, London University.

Nestel, P. 1986. 'A Society in Transition: Developmental and Seasonal Influences on the Nutrition of Maasai Women and Children', *Food and Nutrition Bulletin.* 8(1):2–18.

Nestel, P. 1989. 'Food Intake and Growth in the Maasai'. *Ecol. Fd. Nutr.* 23:17–30.

Neumann, R.P., 1996. 'Dukes, Earls and Ersatz Edens: Aristocratic nature preservationists in colonial Africa', *Environ. Plann. D: Soc. Space* 14: 79–98.

Neumann, R. 1998. *Imposing Wilderness: Struggles over Livelihood and Nature Preservation in Africa.* Berkeley, CA: University of California Press.

Niamir-Fuller, M. 1990. *Herders' Decision Making in Natural Resources Management in Arid and Semi Arid Africa*, Community Forestry Note 4. Rome: FAO.

Niamir-Fuller, M. (ed.) 1999. *Managing Mobility in African Rangelands: the Legitimization of Transhumance*, London: IT Publications and Rome: FAO.

Niamir-Fuller, M. 1999b. 'Towards a Synthesis of Guidelines for Legitimizing Transhumance', in M. Niamir-Fuller (ed.), *Managing Mobility in African Rangelands: The legitimization of transhumance.* London: IT Publications, and Rome: FAO.

Niamir-Fuller, M. and Turner, M. 1999. 'A Review of Recent Literature on Pastoralism and Transhumance in Africa', in M. Niamir-Fuller (ed.), *Managing Mobility in African Rangelands: The legitimization of transhumance.* London: IT Publications and Rome: FAO.

Nicholson, S. 2002. 'What are the Key Components of Climate as a Driver of Desertification?' in J. Reynolds and D. Stafford-Smith (eds), *Global Desertification: Do humans cause deserts?* Dahlem Workshop Report 88. Berlin: Dahlem University Press.

Nicholson, S. and Entekhabi, D. 1986. 'The Quasi-periodic Behaviour of Rainfall Variability in Africa and its Relationship to the Southern Oscillation', *Archiv. für Meteor. Geophys. Bioclimo. Ser. A Meteorology and Atmospheric Physics* 34: 311–48.

Nicholson, S. and Flohn, H. 1980. 'African Environmental and Climatic Changes and the General Atmospheric Circulation in the Late Pleistocene and Holocene', *Climatic Change* 2: 313–48.

Nicholson, S.E., Some, B., and Kone, B. 2000. 'A Note on Recent Rainfall Conditions in West Africa, including the Rainy Season of the 1997 ENSO Year', *J Climate* 13: 2628–40.

Nicholson, S., Tucker, C. and Ba, M.B. 1998. 'Desertification, Drought and Surface Vegetation an Example from the West African Sahel', *Bull Am Meteorol. Soc* 79: 815–29.

Nicolaisen, J. 1963. *Ecology and Culture of the Pastoral Tuareg.* Copenhagen: National Museum.

Niger, République du. 1966. *Etude Démographique et Economique en milieu nomade: démographie, budgets et consommation.* INSEE, SEDES, Paris: Ministère de la Cooperation.

Nkedianye, D., Radeny, M., Kristjanson, P., Herrero, M. Forthcoming. 'Assessing Returns to Land and Changing Livelihood Strategies in Kitengela', in Homewood et al. (eds), *Staying Maasai? Livelihoods, Conservation and Development in East African Rangelands.* New York: Springer.

NOPA 1992. *Pastoralists at a Crossroads: Survival and development issues in African Pastoralism.* Nairobi: UNICEF/UNSO Project for nomadic pastoralists in Africa.

Norval, R., Perry, B. and Young, A. 1992. *The Epidemiology of Theileriosis in Africa.* London: Academic Press.

Noy-Meir, I. 1982. 'Stabilisation of Plant-herbivore Models and Possible Applications to Savannas'. *Ecological Studies* 42: 591–609.

Nugent, S. (ed.) 1996. *African Boundaries and Borderlines.* London: Mansell Press.

O'Leary, M. 1990. 'Drought and Change amongst Northern Kenya Pastoralists: The case of the Rendille & Gabra', in Gisli Palsson (ed.), *From Water to World Making.* Uppsala: SIAS.

Oba, G. 1985. 'Perception of Environment Among Kenyan Pastoralists: Implications for Development'. *Nomadic Peoples* 19: 3–57.

Oba, G., Stenseth, N.C. and Lusigi, W. 2000. 'New Perspectives on Sustainable Grazing Management in Arid Zones of sub-Saharan Africa', *Bioscience* 50: 35–51.

Oboler, R. 1996. 'Whose Cows are they Anyway? Ideology and behaviour in Nandi cattle ownership. *Human Ecology* 24: 255–272.

O'Leary, M. 1990. 'Drought and Change among Northern Kenya Pastoralists', in G. Palsson (ed.). *From Water to World-making.* Uppsala: Scandinavian Institute of African Studies.

Osbahr, H. and Allan, C. 2003. 'Indigenous Knowledge of Soil Fertility Management in Southwest Niger', *Geoderma* 111 (3): 457–79.

Ostergaard, L. 1992. *Gender and Development*, London: Routledge.

Ostrom, E., Burger, J., Field, C., Norgaard, R. and Policansky, D. 1999. 'Revisiting the Commons: Local Lessons, Global Challenges', *Science* 284, 278–82.

Oxby, C. 1999. 'Mirages of Pastoralist Futures: A review of aid donor policy in Sahelian pastoral zones', *Review of African Political Economy*, 80: 227–37.

Pacey, A. and Payne, P. 1985. *Agricultural Development and Nutrition*. London: Hutchinson with FAO and UNICEF.

Pankhurst, R. and Johnson, D. 1988. 'The Great Drought and Famine of 1888–1892 in North East Africa', in D. Johnson and D. Anderson (eds), *The Ecology of Survival*. London: Lester Crook.

Pantuliano, S. 2002. *Sustaining Livelihoods Across the Rural–urban Divide: Changes and challenges facing the Beja pastoralists of north eastern Sudan*, Pastoral Land Tenure Series no 14, London: IIED.

Parmesan, C. and Yohe, G. 2003. 'A Globally Coherent Fingerprint of Climate Change Impacts Across Natural Systems', *Nature* 421: 37–42.

Pearce, F. 1991. 'A Sea Change in the Sahel', *New Scientist* 129 (1754): 31–2.

Pearce, D. and Moran. D. 1994. *The Economic Value of Biodiversity*. London: Earthscan.

Pedersen, J. 1995. 'Drought, Migration and Population Growth in the Sahel: The case of the Malian Gourma 1900–1991', *Population Studies* 49 (1):111–26.

Peires, J.B. 1989. *The Dead Will Arise*. Johannesburg: Ravan Press.

Pelletier, D. 1994. 'The Potentiating Effects of Malnutrition on Child Mortality: Epidemiological Evidence and Policy Implications', *Nutrition Reviews* 52(12):409–15.

Pelletier, D.L., Frongillo, E.A., Schroeder D.G., and Habicht J.P. 1995. 'The Effects of Malnutrition on Child Mortality in Developing Countries', *Bulletin of the World Health Organization* 73(4):443–8.

Pelletier, D.L., Kraak, V., McCullum, C., Uusitalo, U. and Rich, R. 2000. 'Values, Public Policy and Community Food Security', *Agriculture and Human Values* 17(1): 75–93.

Pellew, R. 1983. 'The Impacts of Elephant, Giraffe and Fire upon the *Acacia tortilis* Woodlands of the Serengeti', *African Journal of Ecology* 21: 41–74.

Peluso, N. 1993. 'Coercing Conservation? The politics of State resource control', *Global Environmental Change* 3: 199–217.

Penning de Vries, F.W.T. and Djiteye, M.A. 1982. 'La Productivité des pâturages saheliens'. Wageningen: Center for Agr. Publishing and Documentation, summarised as *Productivity of Sahelian Rangelands, A summary report*, Pastoral Network Paper 15b. London: Overseas Development Institute.

Pennington, R. and Harpending, H. 1993. *The Structure of an African Pastoralist Community. Demography, History and Ecology of the Ngamiland Herero*. Research Monographs on Human Population Biology, No. 11. Oxford Science Publications, Oxford: Clarendon Press.

Perlov, C. 1984. 'Exploiting the Forest: Patterns and perceptions in highland Samburu', in C. Barnes, J. Ensminger and P. O'Keefe, *Wood Energy and Households: Perspectives on Rural Kenya*. Uppsala: Beijer Institute and Scandinavian Institute of African Studies.

Perry. B., Randolph, T., McDermott, J., Sones, K. and Thornton, P. 2002, *Investing in Animal Health Research to Alleviate Poverty*, Nairobi: International Livestock Research Institute.

Peters, P. 2004. 'Inequality and Social Conflict over Land in Africa', *Journal of Agrarian Change* 4 (3): 269–314.

Petit-Maire, N. 1991. 'Recent Quaternary Change and Man in the Sahara'. *J African Earth Sciences* 12: 125–32.

Phillipson, D.W. 1977. *The Later Prehistory of Eastern and Southern Africa*. ch.III & IV. London: Heinemann.

Phillipson, D. 1985. *African Archaeology*. Cambridge: Cambridge University Press

Pilkington, J. 2006. 'Dying Trade of the Sahara Camel Train'. *From our Own Correspondent*, BBC News, Mali. 21 October http://news.bbc.co.uk/2/hi/programmes/from_our_own_ correspondent/6070400.stm

Platteau, J-P. 2000. 'Does Africa Need Land Reform?' in C. Toulmin and J, Quan (eds), *Evolving Land Rights, Policy and Tenure in Africa*, London: DFID/IIED/NRI.

Poland, M. and Hammond-Tooke, D. 2004. *The Abundant Herds. A celebration of the cattle of the Zulu people*. Simonstown, South Africa: Fernwood Press.

POLEYC 2002. *Integrated Assessment Results to Support Policy Decisions in Ngorongoro Conservation Area, Tanzania*. POLEYC project. Denver, CO: Natural Resource Ecology Laboratory,

Colorado State University, and Nairobi: ILRI.

Potkanski, T. 1994. *Property Concepts, Herding Patterns and Management of Natural Resources Among the Ngorongoro and Salei Maasai of Tanzania.* London: IIED.

Potkanski, T. 1999. 'Mutual Assistance Among the Ngorongoro Maasai', in D. Anderson and V. Broch-Due, *The Poor Are Not Us.* Oxford: James Currey.

Pratt, D. and Gwynne, M. (eds) 1977. *Rangeland Management and Ecology in East Africa*, London: Hodder and Stoughton.

Prentice, I. and Jolly, D. 2000. 'Mid-Holocene and Glacial-maximum Vegetation Geography of the Northern Continents and Africa'. *J Biogeogr.* 27 (3): 507–19.

Prior, J. 1994. *Pastoral Development Planning.* Development Guidelines no.9. Oxford: OXFAM.

Quarles van Ufford, P. 1999. *Trade and Traders. The making of the cattle market in Benin.* Amsterdam: Thela.

Raikes, P. 1981. *Livestock Development and Policy in East Africa.* Uppsala: Scandinavian Institute of African Studies, Publication of Centre for Development Research, Copenhagen.

Raikes, P. 1988. *Modernising Hunger.* London: James Currey, Portsmouth, NH: Heinemann, in association with CIIR.

Ramisch, J. 1999 *In the Balance? Evaluating soil nutrient budgets for an agro-pastoralist village of southen Mali. Managing Africa's soils* 9. Drylands programme, London: IIED.

Randall, S.C. 1984. 'The Demography of Three Sahelian Populations'. PhD thesis (unpublished) University of London.

Randall, S. 1985. 'Issues in the Demography of Sahelian Pastoralists and Agropastoralists', in A. Hill (ed.) *Population, Health and Nutrition in the Sahel.* London: Routledge and Kegan Paul.

Randall, S. 1988. *The Displaced Population in Douentza. (La Population Deplacée de Douentza)* PIA/Feru Occasional Report. Bamako, Mali: Save the Children Fund (UK).

Randall, S. 1989. *Une Enquête Socio-Sanitaire du Gourma.* Bamako, Mali. INRSP, BP 1771.

Randall, S. 1991. 'Multi Method Perspectives of Tamasheq Illness. Care, Action and Outcome', in J. Cleland and A. Hill, *The Health Transition: Methods and Measures.* Health Transition Series no.3. Canberra: Australian National University.

Randall, S. 1994. 'Are Pastoralists Demographically Different from Sedentary Populations?' in B. Zaba and J. Clarke (eds), *Environment and Population Change.* Liège: ORDINA.

Randall, Sara 1996. 'Whose Reality?' Local perceptions of fertility versus demographic analysis'. *Population Studies* 50(2): 221–34.

Randall, S. 2001. 'Who are the Populations of the Northern Sahel?', in B. Zaba and J. Blacker (eds), *Brass Tacks: A tribute to the memory of Professor William Brass*, London and New York: The Athlone Press.

Randall, S. 2004. *Fertility of Malian Tamasheq Repatriated Refugees: The Impact of Forced Migration* Roundtable on the Demography of Forced Migration, Committee on Population, National Research Council. Washington, DC: National Academies Press.

Randall, S. 2005. 'Demographic Consequences of Conflict, Forced Migration and Repatriation: A case study of Malian Kel Tamasheq', *European Journal of Population*, 21 (2–3): 291–320.

Randall, S. and Fulton, D. 1988. 'Households, Women's Role and Prestige as Factors Determining Nuptiality and Fertility Differentials in Mali', in Caldwell, Hill and Hull (eds), *Microapproaches to Demographic Research.* London: Kegan Paul International.

Randall, S. and Giuffrida, A. 2006. 'Forced Migration, Sedentarisation and Social Change: Malian Kel Tamasheq', in Dawn Chatty (ed.), *Handbook on Nomads in the 21st Century*, Leiden: Brill.

Randall, S. and Hampshire, K. 2005. 'High Fertility in the Sahel: Challenging conventional understanding', in K. Homewood (ed.), *Rural Resources and Local Livelihoods in Africa.* Oxford: James Currey.

Randall, S. and Hill, A. 1984. 'Différences géographiques et sociales dans la mortalité infantile et juvenile au Mali', *Population* 6.

Randall, S.C. and Winter, M.M. 1985. 'The Reluctant Spouse and the Illegitimate Slave', in A.G. Hill (ed.), *Population Health and Nutrition in The Sahel.* London: Kegan Paul International.

Rasmusson, E. 1987. 'Global Climate Change and Variability: Effects on Drought and Desertification in Africa', in M. Glantz (ed.), *Drought and Hunger in Africa,* Cambridge: Cambridge University Press.

Raynault, C. 1997. *Societies and Nature in the Sahel.* London: Routledge.

Reid, R. and Ellis, J. 1995. 'Impacts of Pastoralists on Woodlands in South Turkana, Kenya.

Livestock-mediated tree recruitment'. *Ecological Applications* 5: 978–92.

Reij, C., Scoones, I. and Toulmin, C. (eds) 1996. *Sustaining the Soil. Indigenous Soil and Water Conservation in Africa.* London: Earthscan.

Republic of Kenya Ministry of Planning and National Development. 2003. *2003/4–2007/8 Strategic Plan for National Statistical System,* Nairobi: MPND.

Reynolds, J. E. and Stafford-Smith, M. (eds) 2002. *Global Desertification: Do Humans Cause Deserts?* Berlin: Dahlem University Press.

Richards, P. 1985. *Indigenous Agricultural Revolution,* London: Hutchinson,

Riesman, P. 1977. *Freedom in Fulani Social Life.* Chicago: University of Chicago Press.

Rirash, M.A. 1988. 'Camel Herding and its Effect on Somali Literature', in A. Hjort (ed.), *Camels in Development: Sustainable production in African drylands.* Uppsala: Scandinavian Institute of African Studies.

Robertshaw, P. (ed,) 1990, *Early Pastoralists of South west Kenya.* Nairobi: British Institute in East Africa.

Robertshaw, P. and Collett, D. 1983a. 'The Identification of Pastoral Peoples in the Archaeological Record'. *World Archaeology.* 15:67–78.

Robertshaw, P. and Collett, D. 1983b. 'A New Framework for the Study of Early Pastoralist Communities in East Africa', *J. Afr. Hist.* 24:289–301.

Robertshaw, P. and Marshall, F. 1990. 'Ngamuriak', in P. Robertshaw (ed.), *Early pastoralists of south west Kenya.* Nairobi: British Institute in East Africa.

Rodgers, W. and Homewood, K. 1986. 'Cattle dynamics in a pastoralist community in Ngorongoro, Tanzania during the 1982–83 Drought', *Agricultural Systems* 22:33–51.

Rogers, D. 2000. 'Satellites, Space, Time and the African Trypanosomiases', in S. Hay, S. Randolph and D. Rogers (eds), *Remote Sensing and Geographical Information Systems in Epidemiology. Advances in Parasitology.* 47: 133–74.

Rogers, D., Hay, S. and Packer, M. 1996. 'Predicting the Distribution of Tsetse Flies in West Africa Using Temporal Fourier-processed Meteorological Satellite Data'. *Ann. Trop. Med. and Parasitol* 90: 225–41.

Rogers, P.J., Brockington, D., Kiwasila, H. and Homewood, K. 1999. 'Environmental Awareness and Conflict Genesis: People versus Parks in Mkomazi Game Reserve', in T. Granfelt (ed.), *Managing the Globalised Environment.* London: Intermediate Technology Publications.

Rosenzweig, C. and Parry, M., 1994. 'Potential Impact of Climate Change on World Food Supply'. *Nature* 367: 133–8.

Roset, J-P. 1987. 'Palaeoclimatic and Cultural Conditions of Neolithic Development in the Holocene of Northern Nigeria (Aïr and Ténéré)', in A. Close (ed.), *Prehistory of Arid North Africa,* Dallas, TX: Southern Methodist Press.

Rossiter, P.B., Jessett, D.M., and Karstad, L. 1983. 'Role of Wildebeest Fetal Membranes and Fluids in the Transmission of Malignant Catarrhal Fever Virus', *The Veterinary Record* 113: 150–2.

Roth, E.A. 1985. 'A Note on the Demographic Concomitants of Sedentism'. *Am. Anthrop.* 87: 380–2.

Roth, E.A. 1990. 'Modelling Rendille Household Herd Composition'. *H. Ecol.* 18(4):441–56.

Roth, E.A. 1993. 'A Re-examination of Rendille Population Regulation'. *American Anthropologist* 95 (3): 597–611.

Roth, E.A., 1994. 'Demographic Systems: two east African Examples', in E. Fratkin, K. Galvin, and E.A. Roth (eds), *African Pastoral Systems: An integrated approach.* Boulder, CO: Lynne Rienner.

Roth, E.A. 2004. *Culture, Biology and Anthropological Demography.* Cambridge: Cambridge University Press.

Rubel, P. 1969. 'Herd Composition and Social Structure: On Building Models of Nomadic Pastoral Societies'. *Man* 4:268–73.

Russell, N., Martin, L. and Buitenhuise, H. 2005. 'Cattle Domestication at Çatalhöyük Revisited', *Current Anthropology* 46(5):S101–S108.

Ruttan, L. and Borgerhoff-Mulder, M. 1999. 'Are East African Pastoralists Truly Conservationists?' *Current Anthropology* 40:621–52.

Rutten, M. 1992. *Selling Wealth to Buy Poverty. The Process of the Individualization of Land Ownership among the Maasai pastoralists of Kajiado District, Kenya, 1890–1990.* Saarbrücken: Verlag für Entwicklungspolitik.

Sachedina, H. (forthcoming). 'Tanzanite and Tourism: Impacts on Poverty, Land Use Change and Conservation in Simanjiro District Tanzania', in Homewood et al. (eds), *Staying Maasai:*

Livelihood, Conservation and Development in East African Rangelands. New York: Springer.

Sadr, K. 1991. *The Development of Nomadism in Ancient Northeast Africa.* Philadelphia: University of Pennsylvania Press.

Salih, M. 1985. *Pastoralists in Town: Some Recent Trends in Pastoralism in the North West of Omdurman District.* Pastoral Development Network 20b. London: Overseas Development Institute.

Salih, M. 1990. 'Agropastoralists' Response to Agricultural Policies: the Predicament of the Baggara, Western Sudan', in M. Bovin and L. Manger (eds), *Adaptive Strategies in African Arid Lands.* Uppsala: Scandinavian Institute of African Studies.

Salih, M. 1993. 'Pastoralists and the War in Southern Sudan: the Ngok Dinka/Humr conflict in South Kordofan', in J. Markakis (ed.), *Conflict and the Decline of Pastoralism in the Horn.* Basingstoke: Macmillan.

Salih, M. 1994. 'The Ideology of the Dinka and the Sudanese People's Liberation Movement', in K. Fukui and J. Markakis (eds), *Ethnicity and Conflict in the Horn of Africa.* Oxford: James Currey/Athens, OH: Ohio University Press.

Sandford, S. 1982. 'Pastoral Strategies and Desertification: Opportunism and Conservatism in Dry Lands', in B. Spooner and H. Mann (eds), *Desertification and Development: Dryland ecology in social perspective.* London: Academic Press.

Sandford, S. 1983. *Management of Pastoral Development in the Third World.* Chichester and New York: John Wiley and Sons with the Overseas Development Institute, London.

Sandford, S. 1995. 'Improving the Efficiency of Opportunism: New directions for pastoralist development', in I. Scoones (ed.), *Living with Uncertainty: New directions in pastoralist development in Africa.* London: ITP/IIED.

Sandford, S. 2006. 'Foreword', in J. McPeak and P. Little (eds), *Pastoral Livestock Marketing in Eastern Africa. Research and Policy Challenges.* London: Intermediate Technology Publications.

Sandford, S. 2006. *Too Many People, Too Few Livestock: The crisis affecting pastoralists in the Greater Horn of Africa.* www.future-agricultures.org/ pdf%20files/Sandford_thesis.pdf

Santoir, C. 1994. 'L'archipel peul'. *Cahiers d'Études africaines,* XXXIV-1-3: 133–5.

Sarbo, G. 1977. 'Nomads on the Scheme: A Study of Irrigation Agriculture and Pastoralism in Eastern Sudan', in P. O'Keefe and B. Wisner (eds), *Land Use and Development.* London: International African Institute.

Schelling, E. 2002. 'Human and Animal Health in Nomadic Pastoralist Communities of Chad: zoonoses, morbidity and health services'. Unpublished PhD thesis, University of Basel.

Schillhorn van Veen, T.W. 1996. 'Sense or Nonsense? Traditional methods of animal disease prevention and control in the African savannah', in C.W. McCorkle, E. Mathias and T.W. Schillhorn van Veen (eds), *Ethnoveterinary Research and Development,* London: Intermediate Technology Publications.

Schneider, H. 1979. *Livestock and Equality in East Africa.* Bloomington, IN, Indiana University Press.

Schoenbrun, D.L. 1998. *A Green Place, a Good Place: Agrarian change, gender, and social identity in the Great Lakes Region.* Kampala: Fountain Publishers; Nairobi: EAEP; and Oxford: James Currey.

Scholte, P. 1992. 'Leaf Litter and Acacia Pods as Feed for Livestock During the Dry Season in Acacia – Commiphora Bushland, Kenya'. *J. Arid Envt.* 22:271–76.

Schreckenberg, K. 1996. 'Forests Fields and Markets: a Study of Indigenous Tree Products in the Woody Savannas of the Bassila Region, Benin'. Unpublished PhD thesis, School of Oriental and African Studies, University of London.

Scoones, I. 1991. 'Wetlands in Drylands'. *Ambio* 20(8): 366–71.

Scoones, I 1993. 'Exploiting Heterogeneity: Habitat use by cattle in dryland Zimbabwe', *J Arid Environments* 29: 221–37.

Scoones, I. (ed.) 1995. *Living with Uncertainty: New directions in pastoralist development in Africa.* London: ITP/IIED.

Scoones, I. 1995b. 'New Directions in Pastoralist Development in Africa', in I. Scoones (ed.), *Living with Uncertainty: New directions in pastoralist development in Africa.* London: ITP/IIED.

Scoones, I. 1999. 'Ecological Dynamics and Grazing Resource Tenure: A case study from Zimbabwe', in M. Niamir-Fuller (ed.), *Managing Mobility in African Rangelands: The legitimization of transhumance.* London: IT Publications, and Rome: FAO.

Scoones, I. and Toulmin, C. 1999. *Policies for Soil Fertility Management in Africa.* DFID with IDS, IIED. Nottingham: Russell Press.

Scoones, I, and Wolmer, W. (eds) 2002. *Pathways of Change. Crops, Livestock and Livelihoods in*

Africa. Lessons from Ethiopia, Mali and Zimbabwe. Oxford: James Currey.

Scoones, I. and Wolmer, W. 2006. *Livestock Disease, Trade and Markets: Policy choices for the livestock sector in Africa.* IDS Working Paper 269, Brighton: Institute for Development Studies, University of Sussex.

Scoones I., Toulmin, C. and Lane, C. 1993. 'Land tenure for pastoral communities', in M. Young and O. Solbrig (eds), *The World's Savannas: Economic driving forces, ecological constraints and political options for sustainable use.* Man and Biosphere vol. 12. Paris: UNESCO.

Scott, G.R. 1985. 'Rinderpest in the 1980s'. *Prog.Vet. Microbiol. Immun.*, 1:145–74.

Scrimshaw, N. and Murray, E. B. 1988. 'The Acceptability of Milk and Milk Products in Populations with a High Prevalence of Lactose Intolerance'. *Am. J. Clinical Nutrition* (suppl) 48: 1079–159.

Seaman, J. and Holt, J. 1980. 'Markets and Famines in the Third World. *Disasters* 4:283–97.

Sellen, D. 2003. 'Nutritional Consequences of Wealth Differentials in East African Pastoralists: the Case of the Datoga of Northern Tanzania', *Human Ecology* 31 (4):529–70.

Sen, A. 1981. *Poverty and Famines: An essay on entitlements and deprivation.* Oxford: Clarendon Press.

Shankar, A. 2000. 'Nutritional Modulation of Malaria Morbidity and Mortality', *Journal of Infectious Diseases* 18 (Suppl 1): S37–53.

Shaw, T. 1985. 'The Prehistory of West Africa', in A. Ajayi and M. Crowder (eds), *The History of West Africa.* Harlow and Ibadan: Longman.

Sheik-Mohamed, Abdikarim and Velema, Johan P. 1999. 'Where Health Care has No Access: The nomadic populations of sub-saharan Africa', *Tropical Medicine and International Health*, 4 (10): 695–707.

Shell-Duncan, B. 1994. 'Child Fostering Among Nomadic Turkana Pastoralists: Demographic and Health Consequences', in E. Fratkin, K. Galvin and E.A. Roth (eds), *African Pastoral Systems: an integrated approach.* Boulder, CO: Lynne Rienner.

Shell-Duncan, Bettina, J., Shelley, K., and Leslie, P.W. 1999. 'Health and Morbidity: Ethnomedical and Epidemiological Perspectives', in M. Little and P. Leslie (eds), *Turkana Herders of the Dry Savanna. Ecology and biobehavioural response of nomads to an uncertain environment.* Oxford: Oxford University Press.

Shivji, I. 1998. *Not Yet Democracy: Reforming Land Tenure in Tanzania.* London: IIED and Dar es Salaam: Hakiardhi.

Shivji, I. and Kapinga, W. 1998. *Maasai Rights in Ngorongoro, Tanzania.* London: IIED and Dar es Salaam: Hakiardhi.

Shoup, J. 1990. 'Middle Eastern Sheep Pastoralism and the Hima System', in J. Galaty and D. Johnson (eds), *The World of Pastoralism.* New York: Guilford Press.

Sieff, D. 1997. 'Herding Strategies of the Datoga Pastoralists of Tanzania: is household labour a limiting factor?' *Human Ecology* 25: 519–44.

Sieff, D. 1999. 'The Effects of Wealth on Livestock Dynamics Among the Datoga Pastoralists of Tanzania'. *Agricultural Systems* 59: 1–25.

Sikana, P. and Kerven, C. 1991. *The Impact of Commercialisation on the Role of Labour in African Pastoral Societies.* Pastoral Development Network 31c. London: Overseas Development Institute.

Sikana, P., Kerven, C. and Behnke, R. 1993. *From Subsistence to Specialised Commodity Production: Commercialisation and Pastoral Dairying in Africa*, Pastoral Development Network 34: 1–46. London: Overseas Development Institute.

Simpson, J. and Evangelou, P. (eds), 1984. *Livestock Development in Sub-Saharan Africa. Constraints, prospects and policy.* Boulder, CO: Westview Press.

Sincell, M. 1999. 'A Wobbly Start for the Sahara', *Science* 285:325.

Sinclair, A. 1975. 'The Resource Limitation of Trophic Levels in Tropical Grassland Ecosystems', *Journal of Animal Ecology* 44: 497–520.

Sinclair, A. 1977. *The African Buffalo.* Chicago: University of Chicago Press.

Sinclair, A. 1979. 'Dynamics of the Serengeti Ecosystem', in A. Sinclair and M Norton-Griffiths, (eds), *Serengeti: Dynamics of an ecosystem.* Chicago: University of Chicago Press.

Sinclair, A. 1983a. 'The Function of Distance Movements in Vertebrates', in I. Swingland and P.J. Greenwood (eds), *The Ecology of Animal Movement*, Oxford: Clarendon Press.

Sinclair, A. 1983b. 'Management of African Conservation Areas as Ecological Baseline Controls', in R. Owen-Smith (ed.), *Management of Large Mammals in African Conservation Areas.* Pretoria: HAUM Educational Publishers.

Sinclair, A. 1985. 'Does Interspecific Competition or Predation Shape the African Wildlife Community?' *Journal of Animal Ecology* 54: 899–918.

Sinclair, A. and Arcese, P. (eds) 1995. *Serengeti II. Dynamics, management and conservation of an ecosystem.* Chicago: University of Chicago Press.

Sinclair, A. and Fryxell, J. 1985. 'The Sahel of Africa: Ecology of a disaster'. *Canadian Journal of Zoology,* 63: 987–94.

Sinclair. A. and Norton-Griffiths, M. (eds) 1979. *Serengeti: Dynamics of an ecosystem.* Chicago: Chicago University Press.

Sinclair. A. and Norton-Griffiths, M. 1982. 'Does Competition or Facilitation Regulate Migrant Ungulate Populations in the Serengeti? A test of hypotheses'. *Oecologia* 53: 364–69.

Sinclair, A., Dublin, H. and Borner, M. 1985. 'Population Regulation of Serengeti Wildebeest: A test of the food hypothesis'. *Oecologia* 65: 266–8.

Sinclair, A.R.E., Simon, A.R., Mduma, J., Grant, C., Hopcraft, J., Fryxell, M., Hilborn, R. and Thirgood, S. 2007. 'Long-Term Ecosystem Dynamics in the Serengeti': Lessons for Conservation', *Conservation Biology* 21(3): 580–90.

Sindiga, I. 1987. 'Fertility Control and Population Growth Among the Maasai'. *Human Ecology.* 15(1):53–66.

Smith, A. 1990. 'On Becoming Herders: Khoikhoi and San Ethnicity in southern Africa'. *African Studies* 49: 51–73.

Smith, A. 1992. *Pastoralism in Africa: Origins and Development Ecology.* London: Hurst; Johannesburg: Witwatersrand University Press.

Smith, A. 1992. 'Origins and spread of pastoralism in Africa'. *Annual Review of Anthropology* 21: 125–41.

Smith, A. 2000. 'The Origins of Domesticated Animals of Southern Africa', in R. Blench and K. MacDonald (eds), *The Origins and Development of African Livestock.* London: UCL Press.

Sobania, N. 1993. 'Defeat and Dispersal: the Laikipiak and their neighbours at the end of the nineteenth century', in T. Spear and R. Waller (eds) *Being Maasai.* London: James Currey.

Sobania, N. 1988. 'Fishermen Herders: Subsistence, Survival and Cultural Change in Northern Kenya'. *J. Afr. History* 29:41–56.

Sobania, N. 1991. 'Feasts, Famines and Friends: Nineteenth Century Exchange and Ethnicity in the Eastern Lake Turkana Region', in J.G. Galaty and P. Bonte (eds) *Herders, Warriors and Traders. Pastoralism in Africa.* Boulder, CO: Westview Press.

Sollod, A.E. 1990. 'Rainfall Variability and Tuareg Perceptions of Climate Impacts in Niger'. *Human Ecology* 18(3): 267.

Sollod, A. and Stern, C. 1991. 'Appropriate Animal Health Information Systems for Nomadic and Transhumant Livestock Populations in Africa'. *Revue Scientifique de l'Office Internationale des Epizooties* 10(1): 89–101.

SOS Sahel 2002. *Moving with the Times.* Video documentary. London

Southgate, C. and D. Hulme. 2000. 'Uncommon Property: the Scramble for Wetland in Southern Kenya', in P. Woodhouse, H. Bernstein and D. Hulme (eds), *African Enclosures? Social Dynamics of Land and Water.* Oxford: James Currey.

Spear, T. 1993a. 'Introduction', in T. Spear and R. Waller (eds), *Being Maasai.* London: James Currey; Dar es Salaam: Mkuki na Nyota; Nairobi: EAEP.

Spear, T. 1993b. 'Being Maasai, but not "People of Cattle": Arusha agricultural Maasai in the nineteenth century', in T. Spear and R. Waller (eds), *Being Maasai.* London, James Currey; Dar es Salaam: Mkuki na Nyota; Nairobi: EAEP.

Spear, T. 1997 *Mountain Farmers.* Oxford: James Currey; Berkeley, CA: University of California Press; Dar es Salaam: Mkuki wa Nyota.

Spear, T. and Waller R. (eds) 1993. *Being Maasai.* London: James Currey; Dar es Salaam: Mkuki na Nyota; Nairobi: EAEP.

Spencer, P. 1973. *Nomads in Alliance.* Oxford: Oxford University Press.

Spencer, P. 1988. *The Maasai of Matapato: Rituals of Rebellion.* Manchester: Manchester University Press.

Sperling, L. 1987. 'Food Acquisition during the African Drought of 1988–89: A Study of Kenya Herders' *Disasters* 11(4):263–72.

SSE, 1992. *Rapport d'Etape Plantes Sauvages:* Annexes 12, 13, 14, 15. Programme Sahel-Soudan-Ethiopie (SSE) Mali-Norvége Centre Nationale de Recherche Scientifique et Technologique, Mali and Oslo University, Lysaker.

Stanley, D. and Warne, A. 1993. 'Sea Level and Initiation of Pre-dynastic Culture in the Nile

Delta' *Nature* 363: 435–38.

Starr, M. 1987. 'Risk, Environmental Variability and impoverishment', *Africa*. 57(1):29–56.

Stelfox, J.B. 1988. 'Effects of Livestock Enclosures and the Vegetation of the Athi Plains', *African J. Ecology* 24: 41–5.

Stenning, D. 1957. 'Transhumance, Migration and Migratory Drift', *Journal of the Royal Anthrop. Institute* 87:57–73.

Stenning, D. 1958. 'Household Viability Among the Pastoral Fulani', in J. Goody (ed.), *The Developmental Cycle of Domestic Groups*. Cambridge: Cambridge University Press

Stenning, D. 1959. *Savannah Nomads*. Oxford: Oxford University Press for IAI.

Stewart, F. 2002. 'Root Causes of Violent Conflict in Developing Countries', *British Medical Journal* 324: 342–45.

Stinson, S. 1992. 'Nutritional Adaptation'. *Ann. Rev. Anthr.* 21: 143–70.

Stone, G.D. 1996. *Settlement Ecology: The Social and Spatial Organization of Kofyar Agriculture*. Tucson, AR: University of Arizona Press.

Stott, P. 1997. 'Dynamic Tropical Forestry in an Unstable World'. *Commonwealth Forestry Review* 76 (3): 207–9.

Stott, P. and Sullivan, S. 2000. 'Introduction', in P. Stott, and S. Sullivan (eds), *Political Ecology: Science, myth and power*. London: Edward Arnold.

Straight, B. 2000. 'Development Ideologies and Local Knowledge Among Samburu Women in Northern Kenya', in D. Hodgson (ed.), *Rethinking Pastoralism in Africa: Gender, culture and the myth of the patriarchal pastoralist*. Oxford: James Currey.

Sullivan, S. 1996. 'Guest Editorial: Towards a non-equilibrium ecology: perspectives from an arid land'. *Journal of Biogeography*, 23: 1–5.

Sullivan, S. 1996. *The 'Communalization' of Former Commercial Farmland: Perspectives from Damaraland and implications for land reform*. Research Report 25, Social Sciences Division of the Multidisciplinary Research Centre, University of Namibia.

Sullivan, S. 1999a. 'Folk and Formal, Local and National: Damara cultural knowledge and community-based conservation in southern Kunene, Namibia'. *Cimbebasia*. 15: 1–28.

Sullivan, S. 1999b. 'The Impacts of People and Livestock on Topographically Diverse Open Wood and Shrub-lands in Arid North-west Namibia'. *Global Ecology and Biogeography* (Special Issue on Degradation of Open Woodlands). 8: 257–77.

Sullivan, S. 1999c. 'Rural Planning in Namibia: State-led initiatives and some rural realities'. Appendix 3, in B. Dalal-Clayton, *DfID-funded IIED Overview of Rural Planning*. London: IIED.

Sullivan, S. 2000a. 'Gender, Ethnographic Myths and Community-based Conservation in a Former Namibian 'Homeland', in D. Hodgson (ed.), *Rethinking Pastoralism in Africa: Gender, culture and the myth of the patriarchal pastoralist*. Oxford: James Currey.

Sullivan, S. 2000b. 'Getting the Science Right, or Introducing Science in the First Place? Local "facts", global discourse – 'desertification' in north-west Namibia', in P. Stott and S. Sullivan, (eds), *Political Ecology: Science, myth and power*. London: Edward Arnold.

Sullivan, S. 2001. 'Difference, Identity and Access to Official Discourse: Haiǀǀom, "Bushmen", and a recent Namibian ethnography'. *Anthropos* 96: 179–92.

Sullivan, S. 2005. 'Detail and Dogma, Data and Discourse: Food Gathering by Damara Herders and Conservation in Arid North-West Namibia', in K. Homewood (ed.) *Rural Resources and Local Livelihoods in Africa*. Oxford: James Currey and New York: Palgrave.

Sullivan, S. and Konstant, T.L. 1997. 'Human Impacts on Woody Vegetation, and Multivariate Analysis: a case study based on data from Khowarib settlement, Kunene Region', *Dinteria*. 25: 87–120.

Sullivan, S. and Rohde, R.F. 2002. 'Guest Editorial. On nonequilibrium in arid and semi-arid grazing systems: a critical comment on A. Illius and T.G. O'Connor (1999), On the relevance of nonequilibrium concepts to arid and semiarid grazing systems'. *Ecological Applications*. 9: 798-813. *Journal of Biogeography* 29: 1–26.

Sullivan, S., Konstant, T.L. and Cunningham, A.B. 1995. 'The Impact of the Utilization of Palm Products on the Population Structure of the Vegetable Ivory Palm' (*Hyphaene petersiana*, Arecaceae) in north-central Namibia'. *Economic Botany* 49(4): 357–70.

Sunseri, T. 2005. 'Something Else to Burn: Forest Squatters, Conservationists, and the State in Modern Tanzania'. *J. Modern African Studies* 43 (4): 609–40.

Sutherland, R.A., Bryan, R.B. and Wijendes, O.D. 1991, 'Analysis of the Monthly and Annual Rainfall Climate in a Semi-arid Environment, Kenya', *Journal of Arid Environments* 20: 257–75.

Sutherst, R.W. 1987. 'Ectoparasites and Herbivore Nutrition', in J.B. Hacker and J.H. Ternouth (eds), *The Nutrition of Herbivores*. Sydney: Academic Press.

Sutter, J. 1987. 'Cattle and Inequality'. *Africa*. 57(2):196–218.

Sutter, J.W. 1982. 'Commercial Strategies, Droughts and Monetary Pressure: Wo'Daa'Be Nomads of Tanout Arrondissement, Niger'. *Nomadic Peoples* 11:26–60.

Sutton, J. 1993. 'Becoming Maasailand', in T. Spear and R. Waller (ed.) (1993). *Being Maasai*. London: James Currey; Dar es Salaam: Mkuki wa Nyota; Nairobi: EAEP; Athens, OH: Ohio University Press.

Sutton, J. 1968 (reprinted 1974). 'The Settlement of East Africa', in B.A. Ogot (ed.), *Zamani: A survey of East African history*. Nairobi: Longman.

Swift J. 1976. 'The Economics of Traditional Nomadic Pastoralism: The Tuareg of the Adrar N. Ifora (Mali)'. Unpublished PhD thesis.

Swift, J. 1977. 'Sahelian Pastoralists: Underdevelopment, Desertification and Famine'. *Annual Review of Anthropology* 6: 457–78.

Swift, J. 1979. 'The Development of Livestock Trading in a Nomad Pastoral Economy: the Somali Case', in Equipe Ecologie et Anthropologie des Sociétés pastorales (ed.), *Pastoral Production and Society*. Cambridge: Cambridge University Press and Paris: Maison des Sciences de l'homme

Swift, J. 1983. 'The Start of the Rains'. Research memo, Institute of Development Studies, University of Sussex.

Swift, J. (ed.) 1984. *Pastoral Development in Central Niger: Report of the Niger range and livestock development programme*. Niamey: USAID.

Swift, J. 1986. 'The Economics of Production and Exchange', in M. Adamu and A. Kirk-Greene (eds), *Pastoralists of the West African Savanna*. Manchester: Manchester University Press.

Swift, J. 1996. 'Desertification: Narratives, Winners and Losers', in M. Leach and R. Mearns (eds), *The Lie of the Land*, Oxford: James Currey.

Talle, A. 1988. *Women at a Loss. Changes in Maasai Pastoralism and their Effects on Gender Relations*. Stockholm Studies in Social Anthropology No.19, Stockholm University.

Talle, A. 1990. 'Ways of Milk and Meat Among the Maasai', in G. Palsson (ed.), *From Water to World Making. African Models and Arid Lands*. Uppsala: Scandinavian Institute of African Studies.

Talle, A. 1999. 'Pastoralists at the Border: Maasai Poverty and the Development Discourse in Tanzania', in D. Anderson and V. Broch-Due (eds), *The Poor Are Not Us*. Oxford: James Currey.

Talle, A. and Abdullahi, A. 1993. 'Labour Resources in Pastoral Production: Some implications of increasing trading', in M. Baumann, J. Janzen, and H. Schwartz (eds), *Pastoral Production in Central Somalia*. Berlin: Deutsche Gesellschaft für Technische Zusammenarbeit (GTZ).

Tanzania Natural Resources Forum. 2006. *Dodoma Policy Brief. More voices for better choices*. www.tnrf.org

Thébaud, B. 1995a. 'Land Tenure, Environmental Degradation and Desertification in Africa: Some thoughts based on the sahelian example', Drylands Issue paper no. 57. London: IIED.

Thébaud, B. 1995b. 'Pastoralisme et dégradation du milieu natural au Sahel: Mythe ou réalité? L'experience de ferlo sénégalais'. Sahel-Sudan Environment Research Initiative (SEREIN) Occasional Paper No. 1, A. Reenberg & Secher Marcussen (eds). Copenhagen: Institute of Geography, Copenhagen University.

Thompson, D.M. 2002. 'Livestock, cultivation and tourism: Livelihood choices and conservation in Maasai Mara Buffer Zones'. Unpublished PhD thesis. Anthropology Dept, University College, University of London.

Thompson, M. and Homewood, K. 2002. 'Elites, Entrepreneurs and Exclusion in Maasailand'. *Human Ecology* 30 (1):107–38.

Thompson, M., Serneels, S. and Lambin, E.F. 2002. 'Land-use strategies in the Mara Ecosystem (Kenya): A spatial analysis linking social-economic data with landscape variables', in S.J. Walsh and K.A. Crews-Meyer (eds), *Remote Sensing and GIS Applications for Linking People, Place and Policy*. Amsterdam: Kluwer Academic Publishers.

Thornton, P., Burnsilver, S., Boone, R., and Galvin, K., 2005. 'Modelling the Impacts of Group Ranch Subdivision on Agro-pastoral Households in Kajiado, Kenya'. *Agricultural Systems* 87: 331–56.

Tiffen, M., Mortimore, M., and Gichuki, F. 1994. *More People, Less Erosion: Environmental Recovery in Kenya*. Chichester and New York: John Wiley.

Tiffen, M. 2006. 'Urbanisation: Impacts on the Evolution of 'Mixed Farming' Systems in sub-Saharan Africa'. *Experimental Agriculture*, 42/3.

Timaeus, I., Zaba, B. and Ali Mohamed 2001. 'Estimation of Adult Mortality from Data on Adult Siblings', in B. Zaba and John Blacker (eds) *Brass Tacks: A tribute to the memory of Professor William Brass*. London and New York: The Athlone Press.

Tolsma, D., Ernst, W., and Verwey. R. 1987. 'Nutrients in Soils and Vegetation around Two Artificial Waterpoints in Eastern Botswana', *Journal of Applied Ecology* 24: 991–1000.

Tomkins, A. 1993. 'Environment, Season and Infection', in S. Ulijaszek and S. Strickland (eds), *Seasonality and Human Ecology*. Society for the Study of Human Biology Symposium 35. Cambridge: Cambridge University Press.

Tothill, J.C. and Mott, J.J. (eds) 1988. *Management of the World's Savannas*. Canberra: Australian Academy of Sciences.

Toulmin, C. 1983. *Economic Behaviour Among Livestock-keeping Peoples*. Development Studies Occasional Paper, No.25. Norwich: University of East Anglia.

Toulmin, C. 1983. *Herders and Farmers or Farmer-herders and Herder-farmers?* Pastoral Network Paper. 15d:1–22. London: Overseas Development Institute.

Toulmin, C. 1992. *Cattle, Women and Wells: Managing Household Survival in the Sahel*. Oxford: Oxford University Press.

Toulmin, C. and Quan. J. 2000. *Evolving Land Rights, Policy and Tenure in Africa*. London: DFID/IIED/NRI.

Toulmin, C., Delville, P. and Traoré, S. (eds) 2002. *The Dynamics of Resource Tenure in West Africa*. London: IIED; Oxford: James Currey; Portsmouth, NH: Heinemann.

Toupet, C. 1975. 'Desertification South of the Sahara'. *African Environment*. 1(2):6–10.

Traoré, Sadio. 1984. *La Sédentarisation et la Migration en Mauritanie, de 1965 à 1976: mesure et interpretation*. Memoire à la faculté des études supérieures, University of Montreal.

Troy, C., MacHugh, D., Balley, J., Magee, D., Loftus, R., Cunningham, P., Chamberlain, A., Sykes, B. and Bradley, D. 2001. 'Genetic Evidence for Near Eastern Origins of European Cattle'. *Nature* 410: 1088–91.

Tubiana, M. and Tubiana, J. 1977. *The Zaghawa from an Ecological Perspective*. Rotterdam: Balkema.

Turner, M. 1992. *Life on the Margin: Fulbe Herding Practices and the Relationship between Economy and Ecology in the Inland Delta Region of Mali*. PhD Dissertation. Berkeley: University of California.

Turner, M. 1998a. 'Long Term Effects of Daily Grazing Orbits on Nutrient Availability in Sahelian West Africa I'. *J.Biogeog.* 25: 669–82.

Turner, M. 1998b. 'Long Term Effects of Daily Grazing Orbits on Nutrient Availability in Sahelian West Africa II', *J.Biogeog.* 25: 683–94.

Turner, M. 1999. 'The Role of Social Networks, Indefinite Boundaries and Political Bargaining in Maintaining the Ecological and Economic Resilience of the Transhumance Systems of Sudano-Sahelian West Africa', in M. Niamir-Fuller. (ed.), *Managing Mobility in African Rangelands: the legitimization of transhumance*. London: IT Publications, and Rome: FAO.

Turner, M. 1999b. 'Spatial and Temporal Scaling of Grazing Impact on the Species Composition and Productivity of Sahelian Annual Grasslands'. *J Arid Environments* 41: 277–97.

Turner, S. and Ntshona, Z. 1999. In T. Hoffmann (coordinator), *National Review of Land degradation in South Africa*. SANBI www.sanbi.org/landdeg

Turton, D. 1988. 'Looking for a Cool Place: The Mursi 1890–1980', in D. Johnson and D. Anderson (eds), *The Ecology of Survival. Case studies from northeast African history*. London: Lester Crook.

Turton, D. 1996. 'Migrants and Refugees: A Mursi case study', in T. Allen (ed.), *In Search of Cool Ground: War, flight and homecoming in North East Africa*. Oxford: James Currey and Lawrenceville, NJ: Africa World Press in association with UNRISD.

Ulijaszek, S. 1990. 'Nutritional Status and Susceptibility to Disease', in G. Harrison and J. Waterlow (eds), *Diet and Disease in Traditional and Developing Societies*. Society for the Study of Human Biology Symposium 30. Cambridge: Cambridge University Press.

UN. 1983. *Indirect Techniques for Demographic Estimation* ST/ESA/SER.A/81. New York: United Nations.

United Republic of Tanzania. 1997. *Livestock and Agriculture Policy*. Section 3: Soil conservation and land use planning. Section 4: range management. Policy statements. Dar es Salaam: URT.

UNOCHA PCI. 2007. 'The Future of Pastoralism in Ethiopia', paper presented at Ethiopia Policy Seminar, IDS, University of Sussex and UNOCHA PCI, Addis Ababa.

Unruh, J. 1990. 'Integration of Transhumant Pastoralism and Irrigated Agriculture in Semi Arid East Africa'. *H.Ecol.* 18(3):223–46.

van den Eerenbeemt, M.I. 1985, 'A Demographic profile of the Fulani of Central Mali with Special Emphasis on Infant and Child Mortality', in A. Hill (ed.), *Population, Health and Nutrition in th Sahel*. London: Routledge & Kegan Paul.

Vansina, J. 1990. *Paths in the Rainforests. Towards a history of political tradition in Equatorial Africa*. London: James Currey, and Madison, WI: University of Wisconsin Press.

Vedeld, T. 2003. *State Law Versus Village Law: Law as an Exclusion Principle Under Customary Tenure Regimes*. Ås: NORAGRIC, Centre for International Environment and Development Studies, Agricultural University of Norway.

Vereecke, C. 1989. *Nigeria's Experiment With a National Programme for Nomadic Education*. Pastoral Development Network 28d. London: Overseas Development Institute.

Vetter, S. 2005. 'Rangelands at Equilibrium and Non-equilibrium: Recent Developments in the Debate'. *J Arid Environments* 62: 321–41.

Wagenaar, K., Diallo, A. and R. Sayers. 1986. *Productivity of Transhumant Fulani Cattle in the Inner Niger Delta of Mali*. ILCA Research Report, No.13. Nairobi: ILCA.

Wagenaar-Brouwer, M. 1985. 'Preliminary findings on the diet and nutritional status of some Tamasheq and Fulani groups in the Niger Delta of Central Mali', in A. Hill, (ed.), *Population, Health and Nutrition in the Sahel*. London: Routledge & Kegan Paul.

Waller, R. 1976. 'The Maasai and the British 1895–1905', *Journal of African History* 17: 529–53.

Waller, R.D. 1979. 'The Lords of East Africa: the Maasai in the mid-nineteenth century (c. 1840-1880)'. Unpublished PhD Thesis, Cambridge University.

Waller, R.D. 1985. 'Ecology, Migration and Expansion in East Africa'. *African Affairs* 84: 347–70.

Waller, R.D. 1988. 'Emutai: crisis and response in Maasailand 1883–1902', in D. Johnson and D. Anderson (eds), *The Ecology of Survival: Case studies from Northeast African History*. London: Lester Crook Academic Publishing/Boulder, CO: Westview Press.

Waller, R. 1990. 'Tsetse Fly in Western Narok, Kenya.' *J.Afr. Hist.* 31:81–101.

Waller, R. 1993. 'Acceptees and Aliens: Kikuyu Settlement in Maasailand', in T. Spear and R. Waller (eds), *Being Maasai: Ethnicity and Identity in East Africa*. Oxford: James Currey; Dar es Salaam: Mkuki wa Nyota, Nairobi: EAEP.

Waller, R. 1999. 'Pastoral Poverty in Historical Perspective', in D. Anderson and V. Broch-Due *The Poor Are Not Us*. Oxford: James Currey.

Waller, R. and Homewood, K. 1996. 'Elders and Experts: Contesting veterinary knowledge in a pastoral community', in A. Cunningham and B. Andrews (eds), *Contested Knowledge: Reactions to Western Medicine in the Modern Period*. Manchester: Manchester University Press.

Waller, R. and Sobania, N. 1994. 'Pastoralism in Historical Perspective', in E. Fratkin, K. Galvin and E.A. Roth (eds), *African Pastoral Systems: An integrated approach*. Boulder, CO: Lynne Rienner.

Waters-Bayer, A. 1985. *Dairying by Settled Fulani Women in Central Nigeria and Some Implications for Dairy Development*. Pastoral Development Network 20c. London: Overseas Development Institute.

Waters-Bayer, A. and Bayer, W. 1994. 'Coming to Terms. Interaction between immigrant Fulani cattlekeepers and indigenous farmers in Nigeria's subhumid zone'. *Cahiers d'études Africaines* XXXIV, 133-5: 213–29.

Webb, J. 1996. 'Risky Business'. *New Scientist* 149 (no. 2018): 32–5.

Wendorf, F. and Schild, R. 1998. 'Nabta Playa and its Role in Northeastern African Prehistory'. *J Anthropol Archaeol* 17: 97–123.

Wendorf, F. and Schild, R. (eds) 2001. *Holocene Settlement of the Egyptian Sahara. Volume 1: The Archaeology of Nabta Playa*. New York: Kluwer Academic/Plenum Publishers.

Wendorf, F., Schild, R. and Close, A. 1984. *Cattle Keepers of the Eastern Sahara: the Neolithic of Bir Kiseiba*. Dallas, TX: Southern Methodist University.

Wendorf, F., Schild, R. and Close, A. 1987. 'Early Domesticated Cattle in the Eastern Sahara'. *The Palaeoecology of Africa and the Surrounding Islands*. 18: 441–8.

Wendorf, F., Schild, R. and Close, A. 1992. 'Saharan Exploitation of Plants 8000 yrs BP'. *Nature* 359: 721–4.

West, P., Igoe, J. and Brockington, D. 2006. 'Parks and Peoples: The social impact of protected areas'. *Annual Review of Anthropology* 35 (14): 1–14.

Western, D. and Dunne, T. 1978. 'Environmental Aspects of Settlement Site Decisions Among Pastoral Maasai'. *Human Ecology*. 7:75–98.

Western, D. 1975. 'Water Availability and its Influence on the Structure and Dynamics of a Savanna Large Mammal Community'. *East African Wildlife Journal* 13: 265–86.

Western, D. 1993. *Ecosystem Conservation and Rural Development: the Amboseli case study*. New York: Liz Claiborne/Art Ortenberg Foundation.

Whelan, R. 1995. *The Ecology of Fire*. Cambridge: Cambridge University Press

White, C. 1986. 'Food Shortages and Seasonality in WoDaaBe Communities in Niger', *IDS Bulletin*, 17(3): 19–25.

White, C. 1991. 'Increased Vulnerability to Food Shortages Among Fulani Nomads in Niger', in R. Downs, D. Kerner & S. Reyna (eds), *The Political Economy of African Famine*. London: Gordon & Breach.

Whitehead, E.E., Hutchinson, C.G., Timmerman, B.N. and R.G. Varady (eds). 1987. *Arid Lands: Today and Tomorrow*. Proceedings of an International Research and Development Conference, Tucson, Arizona, 1985. Boulder, CO: Westview Press.

Williams, A. 2006. 'People Cascades, Land and Livelihoods: Farmer and herder land-use relations in the Idodi rangelands.' Unpublished PhD thesis, Department of Anthropology, University College London.

Williamson, G. and Payne, W.J. 1984. *An Introduction to Animal Husbandry in the Tropics (Tropical Agriculture Series)*. Harlow: English Language Book Society and Longman Scientific and Technical.

Wilmsen, E. N. 1989. *Land Filled with Flies*. Chicago and London: University of Chicago Press.

Wilmsen, E. 1991. 'Pastoro-foragers to "Bushmen"', in J.G. Galaty and P. Bonte (eds), *Herders, Warriors and Traders. Pastoralism in Africa*. Boulder, CO: Westview Press.

Wilson, C. 2001. 'On the Scale of Global Demographic Convergence 1950–2000. *Population and Demographic Review* 27(1): 155–71.

Wilson, K. 1990. 'Ecological Dynamics and Human Welfare: A case study of population, health and nutrition in Zimbabwe'. Unpublished PhD thesis, Department of Anthropology, University College London.

Winter, M. 1983. 'Pastoral Production Systems: The Tuareg', in J. Swift (ed)., *Pastoral Development in Central Niger: Final Report of the Niger Tuareg Range and Livestock Project*. Govt. of Niger/USAID.

Wolmer, W., Chaumba, B. and Scoones, I. 2003. *Wildlife Management and Land Reform in Southern Zimbabwe: A compatible pairing or a contradiction in terms?* Sustainable Livelihoods in southern Africa 1. Brighton: Institute of Development Studies, University of Sussex.

Wolmer, W., Sithole, B. and Mukamuri, B. 2002. 'Crops, Livestock and Livelihoods in Zimbabwe', in I. Scoones and W. Wolmer (eds). *Pathways of Change in Africa*. Oxford: James Currey.

Woodhouse, P., Bernstein, H. and Hulme, D. (eds). 2000. *African Enclosures: The Social Dynamics of Wetlands in Drylands*. Oxford: James Currey.

Wyckoff, J. 1985. 'Planning Arid Land Development Projects', *Nomadic Peoples* 19: 59–69.

Zaal, F. 1998. *Pastoralism in a Global Age*. Amsterdam: Thela Press.

Zaal, F. and Dietz, T. 1999. 'Of markets, meat, maize and milk: pastoral commoditisation in Kenya', in D. Anderson and V. Broch-Due, *The Poor Are Not Us*. Oxford: James Currey.

Zaal, F., Ole Siloma, M., Andiema, R., and Kotomei, A. 2006. 'The Geography of Integration: Cross Border Livestock Trade in East Africa', in J. McPeak and P. Little (eds), *Pastoral Livestock Marketing in Eastern Africa. Research and policy challenges*. London: Intermediate Technology Publications.

Zeder, M. and Hesse, B. 2000. 'Initial Domestication of Goats in the Zagros Mountains 10,000 years ago'. *Science* 287: 2254–7.

Zeder, M., Emshwiller, E., Smith B., and Bradley, D. 2006. 'Documenting Domestication: the Intersection of Genetics and Archaeology'. *Trends in Genetics* 22: 139–55.

Zinsstag, J M., Ould Taleb, P. and Craig P.S. 2006. 'Health of Nomadic Pastoralists: New Approaches Towards Equity Effectiveness'. *Tropical Medicine & International Health* 11 (5): 565–8.

Zinsstag, J. and Weiss, M. 2001. 'Livestock Diseases and Human Health'. *Science* 1294: 477.

Index

access, to resources 2, 3, 5-8,
72-6 *passim*, 82, 85, 86, 90,
92, 108, 110, 113, 119-21
passim, 123, 126, 133, 135,
136, 145-52, 177-8, 236,
239, 248-9, 252, 253
Adamawa Plateau 24, 51, 73,
91, 104-7, 146, *see also fig 2.1*
Ader 95, 97, 98, 100, 233, *see
also fig 2.2*
adjustment, structural 7, 81,
161, 228, 232, 242, 243
Afar 31, 32, 81
Afroasiatic/Afrasan people 12-
15 *passim*, 19, 29, 36
age: division of labour, 143,
144; demography, 199-225;
herd structure 159, 161-2
ageset systems 35, 38, 74, 86,
126, 133, 141, 143-4, 149,
154, 156, 157, 208, 212
agribusiness 125, 152
agriculture 74, 199, 222-4
passim see also cultivation;
farming
agropastoralism 1, 2, 11-16
passim, 29, 30, 32, 35, 36, 39,
40, 43-7 *passim*, 69, 79, 82,
83, 87-90, 100, 101, 116,
124, 126, 130, 137, 139, 156,
158, 161, 183, 186, 188, 192,
206, 222, 224, 236, 246, 252
agro-pastoro-foragers 49
Ahaggar 26, 95-7 *passim; see also
figs 2.1, 2.2*
aid 33, 151, 193, 222, 235, 243;
food 184, 243
Aïr 20, 26-8, 95-8 *passim; see
also figs 2.1, 2.2*
Akou 104, 106, 107
Algeria 25, 29, 78, 95, 97, 98,
100, 147, 232
Almohads 25
Almoravids 25, 147
Al Yaq'ubi 25
Amboseli 61, 120, 124, 126
Anderson, D. 38-9, 51, 65, 79-
80, 86, 120, 124, 229, 240,
243, 249
anthropology, social 4, 35, 43,

138, 200
Anuak 35, 121
Aquatic people 18, 19
Arabs 7, 20, 22, 25-32 *passim*,
35, 75, 107, 111-14, 121;
Baggara 30, 35, 99, 111, 121,
136, 181, 202, 204, 206, 208,
209, 213, 230, 248; Hillalian
20, 25; Kababish 95, 111
archaeology 10-12, 18, 20, 37,
43, 47, 63
Arhem, K. 175, 181
Ariaal 39, 124, 202, 212, 216
aridity 19, 53-7
Arssi 129-30
Australia 83
Awlad Hamid 112, 181, 182
Azawagh valley 95-8 *passim; see
also fig 2.2*

Bakgalagadi 45, 48, 149, 154
Bambara 22, 23, 88-91, 100,
206
Bantu 13, 16, 19, 36, 38, 40,
41, 44, 47, 124
Barabaig 136, 149, 156, 191,
193
Baringo 61, 84, 92, 120, 150,
193, 243
Barre, Siad 33, 116, 234
BaSarwa 86, 149, 154, 236
Bassi, M. 90, 79, 128
Baxter, P. 84, 128-130, 139,
147, 227, 240
beef 91, 102, 234, 236
Behnke, R. 32, 33, 45, 64-6
passim, 69, 74, 91, 92, 115,
130, 131, 139, 151, 195,
231-4 *passim*, 237, 238, 244
Beja 15, 30-2, 91, 111-14
passim, 118, 132, 148, 231,
241, 244
Bella 97, 100, 140, 154, 181,
188-9, 203, 211, 216, 220
Beni Amr 112
Bénin 22, 24, 107, 132, 143,
148, 192, 231, 247
Berbers 13, 15, 16, 22, 25, 26,
29, 100, 141, 147, 232, 249
Bernus, E. 12, 26-8 *passim*, 33,

52, 60, 61, 85, 86, 95-8
passim, 100, 132, 140, 146,
147, 149, 154
Berti 30, 112
Bideiyat 30
biology of herd 8, 158-70;
human biology: 177-225
BMI (Body Mass Index) values
183
Bonfiglioli, A.M. 29, 78, 134,
153, 162, 163, 167, 222, 233,
238
Boni 32
Bonte, P. 6, 29, 42, 75-6, 149,
193, 227
Bophutatswana 80, 130, 174
Boran 8, 33, 37, 78, 79, 128-30,
139, 147, 161, 181, 183, 186,
191, 215, 245
Borgerhoff-Mulder, M. 136,
205, 209, 217
Botswana 43-5 *passim*, 47, 48,
91, 92, 130, 149, 150, 152,
154, 231, 236-8 *passim*
boundaries 3, 5, 39, 72, 76, 85,
124, 131, 149, 175, 221
Boutrais, J. 24, 25, 56, 62, 69,
73, 84, 86, 102, 104, 106,
107, 137, 143, 169, 230
boys 142-4 *passim*, 187, 249
Brainard, J. 126, 178, 217, 222
bridewealth 74, 153, 211
British 29, 33, 39, 233 *see also*
colonialism
Broch-Due, V.40, 156, 159,
161-2, 192, 240, 243, 249
Brockington D.6, 39-40, 56,
60, 76-7, 79-81, 124-5, 131,
133, 149, 152-3, 163-5, 193,
244-6, 249
Brown, L. 63, 80, 178, 189-90
Bryceson, D 7, 132, 228, 238,
242, 244
Buhl, S. 84, 89, 100-2, 135,
139, 141-3, 145, 155-6, 180,
192, 196-8, 230, 246
Burkina Faso 84, 95, 101-2,
132, 136, 144-5, 151, 152,
155, 192, 197, 206, 208,
223-4, 231-2, 241, 249;

Gestion de Terroirs 152
Burnham, P. 25, 106, 146, 153-4, 197, 227
Burundi 40, 42, 154

camels 12, 19-20, 25, 28, 29, 31, 83, 84, 95, 97-9, 110-19 *passim*, 127, 128, 130, 154, 159, 168, 202, 225, 230, 234
Cameroon 19, 22, 24, 51, 103, 104, 197
capital 16, 153-4, 156-7, 159 *passim*
CAR 22, 24, 51, 62, 103-4, 106-7, 137, 143, 230
caravan trade 28-9, 31, 33, 100, 112, 132, 154
carrying capacity 4, 64, 66-9 *passim*
Cassanelli, L. 31-3 *passim*, 72, 115, 117, 118, 120, 147, 148, 241
caste 133, 140-1, 149, 154
cattle 14-16, 18, 22, 29, 36, 37, 41-8, 51, 63, 84, 88, 98-100, 104, 110, 115, 119-22 *passim*, 127, 130, 153-5, 159-63 *passim*, 234, 236
CBPP (Contagious Bovine Pleuro-pneumonia)123, 166, 171-3 *passim*
Chad 16, 22, 29, 78, 95, 106, 107
Chagga 90, 124
Chambers, R. 140, 185
Charney, J. 56, 63, 66
Chatty, D. 76, 78, 81
chiefs 13, 29, 149
childlessness *see* infertility
children 155, 211, 212, 214, 215-18, 249, 250; see also fostering
clans 12, 13, 118-19, 157
Coast, E. 135, 143, 145, 200, 206-8 *passim*, 211, 215, 243, 249
colonialism 5, 24, 29, 33, 35, 39, 48, 62, 73, 80, 81, 85, 105, 111, 121, 124, 133, 142, 149, 154, 168, 172, 200, 221, 224, 233, 235, 247; pre- 221, 251
commercialisation 9, 91-2 153, 193, 197, 198, 227-37, 248
common property 5, 8, 72, 80, 85, 93, 145-7, 152
competition 8, 72, 75-6, 78, 104, 230-1, 233
conflict 2, 6-8 *passim*, 29, 33, 48, 72-9 *passim*, 83, 98, 103-5, 110, 117, 119, 121-2, 249, 252
conservation 78, 81, 125, 152, 193
contraception 203, 205, 206
Coppock, D. 61, 68, 84, 126, 129-130, 159
CPR 5, 145-52 *passim*, 178,

231, 240, *see also common property*
culling 80, 173
cultivation 14-19 *passim*, 37, 51, 85, 87, 88, 102, 103, 108, 112, 119, 124, 135
Cushites 7-8, 13, 15, 16, 18, 29-32 *passim*, 36, 38, 40, 41, 111, 112

Dahl, G. 36, 72, 75, 86, 111-14 *passim*, 118, 128, 130, 134, 139, 141, 143, 147, 148, 153, 155, 158, 159, 162-5 *passim*, 231, 245
dairying 31, 142, 143, 197, 198, 229-31, 248
Dallol Bosso 96, 134 *see also fig 2.2*
Damara 48, 49, 130, 143, 148, 179, 192
Damergou 28, 29, 86, 95, 233 *see also fig 2.2*
Darfur 7, 27, 36, 95, 99, 112, 121, 192
Darod 32
Dassanetch 124
Datoga 38, 124, 191, 205, 209, 217
De Bruijn, M. 100, 143
decision-making 4, 8, 134-8, 164
degradation, environmental 4, 5, 63-72 *passim*, 79, 80, 103
demography 8-9, 199-226
destocking 63, 117
devaluation 89, 102, 232, 234
development 9, 227-52 *passim*; agencies 225, 237
De Waal, A. 30, 34, 77-9 *passim*, 111, 112, 115, 116, 121-3 *passim*, 148, 182, 192, 193, 234, 235, 240
diet 8, 86, 125, 128, 130, 148, 178-98
Dietz, T. 78, 87-8, 107, 124, 191, 236
Digil 32
Dina code 23, 69, 108
Dinka 18, 34-6, 121-3 *passim*, 83, 186
Dir 32
disequilibrium 4, 65-72 *passim*, 79
dipping 170, 175
disease 2, 4, 5, 8, 9, 18, 19, 22, 36, 41, 43, 59, 61-3, 65, 82-4 *passim*, 87, 99, 103, 105, 106, 109, 125, 126, 129, 139-40, 163, 164, 166-76, 185, 193, 203, 215, 216, 238, 251 *see also individual entries*
displacement 7, 20, 34, 36, 76-8 *passim*, 81, 92, 97, 116, 121, 177, 184, 189, 193, 198, 244
dispossession 45, 92, 130, 149, 151, 152, 236, 237, 248

diversification 3, 5, 7, 9, 31, 40, 86, 106, 126, 132, 136, 157, 224, 227, 238-52
divorce 213, 214
Djafun 86, 104, 107
Djibouti 33, 78, 115
donkeys 15, 18, 110, 119, 127, 130, 174
Doornbos, M. 32, 33, 76, 227
draft power 87-90 *passim*, 100
drought 4, 8, 56-7, 63, 66, 87, 98, 112, 115, 117, 126-9 *passim*, 140, 165, 167, 192, 193, 222, 224, 232-3, 238
Dupire M. 86, 101, 154, 233
Dyson-Hudson R., 208, 224

East Africa 3, 8, 12, 18, 20, 34, 36-40, 51-6, 69, 81, 124-8, 142, 147, 152, 154-6, 161, 163, 169-72, 184, 191, 211, 215, 219, 231, 235-6
ECF (East Coast Fever) 18, 62, 63, 129, 166, 169-71, 173, 176, 229, 237
economy 132-57
education 6, 7, 76, 115, 121, 206, 211, 223, 224, 234, 237, 248-51
Egypt 18, 20, 27, 29, 51, 53
Ehret C., 10, 12-15, 18-9, 22, 25, 40, 88
elders 5, 35, 74, 144, 154, 187, 88
elites 6, 7, 42, 44, 45, 73, 81
Ellis F. 6, 130, 156, 226-8, 238, 240, 242-3
Ellis J. 65, 68-70, 120, 128
El Nino 56, 57, 170
employment 7, 157, 241-3
energy expenditure 180, 184-5, 195
entitlements 3, 6, 157, 189, 247
environment 3, 4, 8, 50-62, 135-7, 203, 206, 216; social/political 72-80
equilibrium theory 4, 64-72, 79
erosion 58, 63, 67, 116, 129
Ethiopia 12, 13, 15, 16, 18, 31, 33, 39, 78, 79, 87, 88, 115, 116, 128-30, 151
ethnicity 4, 29, 35, 76-7, 101, 103, 108, 121
EU 173, 230, 231
Evans-Pritchard, E.E. 34-5, 121, 154
eviction 6, 7, 64, 76, 77, 80, 125, 163, 164, 193
exchange 30, 74, 86, 87, 123, 153, 156, 195-7, 235, 251
exports 34, 115-17 *passim*, 126, 173, 174, 176, 234, 236
expropriation 130, see also dis-possession

family planning 203, 206
famine 8, 35, 63, 75, 121, 123,

126, 177, 192-3
FAO 51, 177
Farah, A. 31, 32, 81, 129
farming/farmers 7, 8, 24, 28,
40, 51, 57, 64, 74, 75, 79,
86-8 *passim*, 93, 100, 101,
119, 125, 126, 132, 139, 140,
146, 200, 215, 245
fencing 150, 151, 234, 247
fertility 9, 66, 128, 159, 163-5
passim, 200, 202-14
fire 4, 59, 60, 70, 71, 110
fishing 8, 10, 14, 16, 18, 19, 22,
23, 36, 122, 123, 132, 146,
192, 243
FMD (Foot and Mouth Disease)
166, 173, 174, 237
food systems 2, 8, 177-98;
security/insecurity 138, 177,
189-91, 198, 229, 247
forage 2, 68, 82, 84, 90, 163,
251
Ford, J. 19, 39, 42, 62, 71, 167,
168, 171
forest 51, 70, 79, 124
Fratkin, E., 2, 39, 112, 175,
181, 184, 187, 199, 216, 240,
245, 246
fostering 139, 196
French 23, 27, 28, 46, 98, 105,
134, 233-4
Fukui K. 20, 75
Fulani 7, 20-25, 27, 39, 51, 58,
61, 83, 84, 86, 88, 90-5, 99-
111, 133-45, 149-56 *passim*,
164, 180-8 *passim*, 192, 194,
196, 197, 202, 204, 206, 208,
211-21 *passim*, 230, 232-4,
241, 246-9 *passim*; Bororo
24, 104-7; Diallo 22, 23;
Djelgobe 101-2, 206, 214,
224, 249; Gaobe 101, 214,
224, 249; Liptaako 101, 214,
221, 224, 249; Peul 20, 91,
132; Uda'en 87;Wodaabe 24,
51, 99, 104, 106, 107, 133,
134, 136, 155, 182, 183, 186,
223
Fulbe 24, 62, 91, 104-7 *passim*,
153, 167, 197, 210, 217
Fur 30, 112, 136

Gabbra 205, 215, 218, 221
Galaty, J. 6, 29, 39, 52, 75-7,
125, 146, 148-9, 151-2, 193,
227, 238, 249
Galvin, K. 86, 178-183, 185-6,
190-1, 196
gender issues 135, 141-2, 154,
245-9
Germans 39, 48
Ghana 22, 25, 27
Gifford-Gonzalez, D. 18, 36,
43, 59, 63, 175
gifts, livestock 41, 155
girls 144, 185, 187, 208, 249
gold 22, 25, 27, 44, 47, 90, 102

Gourma 97, 100, 189, 192, 219,
224
grazing 45, 64, 70, 72, 75, 81,
84, 85, 90, 92, 99, 122, 125,
126, 147-9 *passim*, 229, 237
Great Lakes 36, 40-3, 88, 154,
156, 160, 171
growth (of children) 178, 185-8
Gulf states 33, 34, 115, 234
Guinean zone 83, 88, 94, 103-
11 *passim*

Hadendowa 30, 31
Hamar 30, 112
Hampshire, K. 84, 86, 100-102,
135-6, 139-140, 144-5, 197,
199, 203-4, 206, 208, 210,
212-4, 217, 220-1, 224, 241,
249
Hanotte, O. 160
Hardin, G. 5, 63, 73
Harpending, H. 49, 130, 200,
203, 207, 214, 215, 219
haud 115, 117
Hausa 22, 23, 30, 88, 142, 233
Hawazma 30, 112
Hawiya 32
Heald, S. 86, 150
healing 143, 247
health, animal 176, 227-8;
CAHWs 176
health care 203, 215, 216, 224,
249
Heffernan, C. 7, 140, 143, 156,
160, 167, 243, 245, 248, 250
Henin, R.A. 202, 205-8 *passim*
herd composition 158-67, 231;
breeds 160-1; species 159-60
herders/herding 1, 19, 37, 45,
57, 74, 87, 122, 124, 127,
138-43 *passim*, 146, 150, 219,
221, 237, 240, 243, 244,
250-1
herd owners 1, 7, 92-3, 109,
110, 152, 243, 245, 250
Herero 44, 47, 48, 130, 203,
205-7 *passim*, 209, 211-14
passim, 217, 219
Hill, A. 108, 111, 140, 179,
181, 185, 193, 204, 216
Hima 40-2 *passim*
Himba 130
HIV/AIDS 210-11
Hjört, A. 31, 63, 86, 111-14
passim, 118, 134, 148, 153,
155, 158, 159, 162-5 *passim*,
231
Hodgson, D. 1, 38, 73, 133,
141-4 *passim*, 151, 154, 172,
198, 247
Hogg, R. 31, 33, 75, 115, 117,
128, 129, 227, 240
Hopen, C. 86, 91, 153, 197
Horn of Africa 3, 8, 15, 19, 29-
34 *passim*, 51, 52, 69, 75, 78,
112, 114-20, 129
Horowitz, M. 64

household
composition/formation 8,
133, 136-57 *passim*
Huduk 36
Hulme D., 43, 56, 120, 238
Hungarob 47, 60, 61
hunter-gatherers 10, 13, 19, 36,
37, 43, 45, 86, 200
hunting 36, 132, 192
Hutchinson, S. 35, 36, 78, 121,
154, 162
Hutu 42, 154

Ibn Hawqual 25
Ibn Khaldun, A. 25, 74
Igoe J. 39, 60, 76, 78, 80, 125,
152, 244, 249, 252
IIED (International Institute for
Environment and
Development) 69, 73, 80
Il Chamus 84, 86, 92, 124, 136,
150, 156
Illius, A., 69
immunisation 173, 176, 215,
216
infanticide 215
infertility 9, 207-10
inflation 89
infrastructure 6, 76, 121, 157
inheritance 23, 142, 154, 156
inoculations 173
insecticides 51, 105, 229
intensification 228, 244-5
investment 8, 64, 73, 136-7,
163, 244
IPCC 56, 70, 177
irrigation 126, 147, 186, 244
Isaq 32
Islam 20, 25, 27, 29, 30, 32-3,
141-3, 154, 156, 249
ITCZ (Inter-Tropical
Convergence Zone) 52-3,
111, 117, 120
ITM (Infect-and-Treat Method)
170-1
ivory 44, 45, 48, 90, 123, 234
Ivory Coast 22, 103, 208

Jahnke, A.E. 2, 51, 52, 54, 177
Jie 39
Johnson, D. 7, 30, 35-6, 52, 61,
72, 75, 77-8, 112, 121, 123-
4, 132, 154, 180, 192-3
Kaarta 23
Kalahari 44, 45, 47-8, 86, 148,
236, *see also fig 2.1*
Kalenjin speakers 38, 124
Kawahla 30, 112, 202, 206, 208,
209, 213
Kenya 18, 19, 30, 32-6, 51-3
passim, 62, 74, 76, 79, 91,
115, 117, 124, 126, 128, 160,
169, 170, 172, 181, 188, 196,
197, 201, 206, 210-11, 215,
219, 224, 230, 231, 235-8
passim, 243, 248, 252
Kerven C. 86, 91, 155, 229-

236, 248
Khami 48
Khoi/Khoisan 8, 13, 14, 19, 36, 40, 43-8 *passim*
Kibreab, G. 113, 147-8
Kikuyu 76, 90, 124
Kinahan J. 11-13, 20, 37, 43, 47-8, 60-61, 148
kinship 4, 32, 33, 118-20, 141, 149, 155
kingship 41, 42
Kipsigis 38, 76
Kjekshus H., 31, 42, 71, 168, 171
knowledge, indigenous 6, 18, 61-3, 79, 82, 137, 172-6, 229, 245, 250
Kofyar 88, 90
Krätli, S. 249
Kuper, A. 44, 87, 154, 162, 237
Kuria 40, 88, 156
Kurimoto, E. 35-6, 38-9, 74-5, 121, 123, 143, 193

labour 6, 8, 24, 31, 45-7 *passim*, 64, 68, 85-7 *passim*, 90, 92, 100, 102, 103, 113, 116, 130, 132, 138-45, 196, 197, 200, 202-3, 223-4, 234, 236, 240-8, 248; division of 90, 122, 133, 141-3
lactose intolerance 194-5
Lamphear, J. 35, 38, 74, 126, 156
Lamprey, H. 63, 66, 79
Lane, C. 72-3, 76-8, 80, 124, 149, 193
land 6-8 *passim*, 73, 82, 83, 135, 145-52, 157, 244, 251; alienation/expropriation of 76, 85, 130, 235; communal 66, 68-9, 74, 85, 88, 130, 146, 148, 152; reform 150, 227; tenure 3, 6, 8, 9, 63, 64, 80, 82, 85, 92, 93, 105-6, 112-16, 129, 133, 145, 148-52, 176, 228, 231, 234, 235; use 2, 4, 6, 8, 39, 59, 63, 66, 69, 71, 79, 82-6, 93, 108, 112, 115, 120, 124-6, 130, 149-52, 175, 176, 245, 250, 251
Laris, P. 59, 68, 84, 175
law, land 73, 80, 133, 149, 152
Le Houérou, H. 53, 55, 63, 94, 96, 99-100, 111-12
Leslie P. 86, 101, 126, 136, 153, 165, 178-81, 185-7, 194, 204, 206, 212, 214, 217, 243
Lesotho 87, 156
Lewis, I. 31, 34, 112, 115, 117-19, 227, 234-5
Libya 92, 99, 225, 231, 232, 234, 237
linguistics 12, 15, 20, 47
Little M. 86, 101, 126, 148, 165, 178-181, 183, 185-7, 190-1, 194, 212, 243, 245

Little P. 32-4, 63, 79, 86-7, 92, 115-17, 119-20, 139-40, 142, 150, 197, 227-31, 233-6, 242, 244, 248
livelihoods 6-7, 9, 132-57, 238-45 *passim*
livestock management 62-3, 82-7, 94-131; acquiring 155-6, 159, 164-5; as capital 6, 153-4; domestication 11-16 *passim*, 18, 19; as wealth store 88, 89, 100, 103, 133, 154, 157
loan(s) 92, 107, 139, 148, 156, 240
Lobbo, Ahmed 23

Maa speakers 38, 39, 76, 124
Maasai/Maasailand 8, 20, 38-40 *passim*, 51, 58, 61, 62, 74, 77, 82, 83, 86, 124-6, 135, 136, 137, 139, 142-9 *passim*, 156, 157, 161, 162, 170-6, 180-8 *passim*, 191, 195, 204-21 *passim*, 230-1, 235-6, 238, 244-9 *passim*
MacDonald, D. 11, 14-16
Mace, R. 136, 138, 145, 159, 160, 164, 195, 209, 219
Machakos 56
Macina, (Maasina) 22-3, 27, 140, 149
Maghreb 20, 22, 23, 25, 28, 29, 82, 95, 147
malaria 185, 194
Mali 22-3, 27, 29, 78, 88, 89, 95, 96, 98, 99, 101, 107, 132, 181, 201, 206-8 *passim*, 212, 216, 223-5 *passim*, 230, 249, 252; *Code Pastoral* 252
Malignant Catarrhal Fever (MCF)18, 62
Mambila Plateau 24, 103, 104
manure/manuring 58, 87-90 *passim*, 100, 119
Mapungubwe 27, 44, 48, 236
Marakwet 38
marginalisation 5, 33, 39, 51, 73, 76, 149, 193, 203, 207, 216, 225, 227, 238
Markakis, J. 20, 35, 39, 75, 76, 78, 79, 227, 252
markets 5, 27, 82, 84, 87, 92, 99, 100, 102, 103, 153, 229, 230-7 *passim*
marriage 9, 74, 123, 154, 174, 208, 211-14, 225-6
Marshall F., 11, 12, 14, 16, 36-7, 160
Mauritania 20, 201, 223, 224
McCabe, T. 71-2, 74-5, 77-8, 83-4, 101, 126-8, 146, 154, 156, 159, 165, 181, 183, 187-8, 190, 193
McPeak J., 33, 87, 231, 234-6, 243
meat 2, 51, 64, 82, 87, 91, 92,

115, 139, 141-2, 158, 163, 173, 178, 182, 197, 198, 229, 232, 234
Meru 88, 90
migration/migrants 9, 20, 29, 32-4, 45-7 *passim*, 93, 102, 103, 118, 130, 135, 136, 144-5, 198, 200, 202, 208, 216, 220-6, 230, 232, 236, 241, 248
milk 2, 51, 64, 82, 86, 87, 90, 92, 105-11 *passim*, 123, 125, 131, 142, 143, 158, 163, 178, 182-9, 192-8 *passim*, 215-16, 229-31, 234, 248
minerals 5, 6, 58, 82-5 *passim*, 97, 147
Mkomazi 53, 56, 60, 81, 124, 143
mobility 2-3, 5, 6, 8, 9, 52, 58, 63, 69, 73, 74, 78, 79, 82-6, 103, 122, 135, 145, 146, 152, 176, 199, 207, 220-5, 252
modelling 134-8, 145, 164; Savanna-PHEWS 137-8
Moors 95, 99, 108, 110
Morocco 23, 25, 27, 147-8, 150
mortality 9, 65-7 *passim*, 128, 159, 163, 165, 171, 172, 200, 203, 210-11, 215-20, 249
Mortimore M., 58, 72, 79, 88, 100, 177, 227, 244-5
Mozambique 151
Mursi 154
Mutapa 41, 46
Mzilikazi 46

Nama/Namaqualand 48, 130
Namibia 20, 43, 47-9 *passim*, 51, 130, 143, 148, 152, 192, 247; Namib desert 52, 60
Nandi 38, 124
nationalisation, land 151
Ndagala D., 126, 156, 193, 198, 244, 247
Ndebele 44, 46
negotiation 74, 119, 126, 149
networks, social 74, 188, 193, 196-8, 207-10 *passim*, 246
Ngamiland 48
Ngamuriak 37
NGOs 116, 119, 225, 243
Ngoni 46
Ngorongoro 61, 83, 84, 124, 125, 170-1, 180
Niamir-Fuller, M. 5, 72-4, 83, 86, 104, 120, 136, 149-150, 152, 175
Nicholson S., 53, 56-7, 65-7, 95
Niger 16, 20, 29, 78, 95-9 *passim*, 132, 134, 182, 183, 231, 233
Niger-Congo peoples 13, 16, 19, 20, 22, 36
Niger Delta 21-4 *passim*, 61, 73, 83, 84, 95, 99, 100, 107-11,

140, 146, 149, 164, 188, 216, 217 *see also* Macina
Nigeria 22, 24, 88, 103, 142, 143, 150, 167, 171, 230-3, 248-50 *passim*, 252
Nilotic people 8, 18, 19, 30, 34-7 *passim*, 40, 121, 156; Nilo-Saharans 13, 14
nomads 19-22, 25, 96, 224
North Africa 13, 14, 16, 20, 25, 27, 30
North-east Africa 7, 13, 29-31, 111
Nuba 30, 112
Nuer 18, 34-6 *passim*, 83, 121, 122, 154, 186, 192
nutrition 2, 8, 178, 182-4, 193-5, 248
Nyamwezi 88

Oba, G. 71
Ogaden 116, 129
oil 7, 75, 122, 232-4
Orma 148, 156
Oromo speakers 32, 79, 112, 128-30
overgrazing 63, 64, 66-8 *passim*, 175
overstocking 5, 63, 67, 69
ownership, livestock 2, 5, 8, 24, 63, 74, 147, 148, 154-6, 222, 246, 247, 251
oxen 89, 90; ploughing 89, 100, 103, 119, 161

Parakuyo 81, 143, 149
Pare 36, 88, 90, 124
pastoralism, definitions, 1-7 *passim*, 199
pastoro-fishing 11, 86
pastoro-foraging 11, 44, 45, 47, 86, 130, 148, 234
pasture 5, 6, 22, 52, 83, 95, 104, 106, 110, 122
patronage 133, 156, 232, 237
Pennington, R. 49, 130, 200, 203, 207, 214, 215, 219
Pokot 38, 124
politics 24, 27, 72, 79-80, 145, 242, 247, 252
polygamy 213, 214
population density 4, 51, 65, 67, 69, 127, 146, 161, 200, 201, 228, 242; growth 177, 200, 212, 226, 228, 251
Portugal/Portuguese 23, 46
Potkanski T., 40, 62, 72, 84, 124, 147, 149, 170, 175
poverty 6, 103, 136, 238, 240-1, 243, 246, 249
prehistory 10-16
privatisation 5, 6, 73, 80, 82, 85, 93, 105-6, 115, 120, 125, 138, 147, 150, 151, 228, 247, 251
production systems 51, 53-6, 86-167 *passim*, 198, 228-37

passim
products, pastoral 86-7, 92, 125, 128, 130, 162, 177, 236 *see also individual entries*
protected areas 80, 81
Puntland 34, 116

quarantine 173-6 *passim*, 231, 234, 235, 237
Quarles van Ufford P., 102, 229, 231-3

Rahanweyn 32
raiding 2, 5, 30, 31, 35, 40, 42, 48, 72, 74-5, 83, 105, 112, 123, 126, 128, 130, 156, 193, 203, 219, 235-6, 238
Raikes P. 52, 170, 174, 177, 228, 229-31, 235, 237
rainfall 4, 51-7 *passim*, 68, 70, 82, 84, 94-6 *passim*, 99, 108, 117, 120, 124, 125, 127, 129, 150-2 *passim*, 184, 235
ranching 45, 52, 93, 105, 130, 150, 158, 159, 162, 163, 165, 167, 198, 227, 229, 236, 238
Randall, S. 86, 99, 101, 135-6, 139-140, 143, 184, 192, **199-226**, 241, 245, 249
rangelands 2, 5, 39, 49, 52, 54, 58, 63, 70, 79, 82, 115, 117, 135, 148, 238, 251
Raynault C. 52, 94, 100
refugees 7, 29, 34, 36, 45, 78, 97, 116, 118, 126, 177, 189, 219
religion 12, 13, 15, 19, 25, 28, 141
remittances 46, 47, 68, 130, 242
Rendille 32, 38, 39, 124, 141, 181, 184, 186-7, 202, 204, 206, 212-17 *passim*, 247
repatriation 223, 225
reproduction, herd 164-5
reserves 147, 240
resettlement 105
Rift Valley 36-8 *passim*, 53, 58, 76, 124-6 *passim*
rights 72, 77, 113, 120; human 76, 77, 81; property 72, 105-6, 145-52 *passim*, 154; women's 141-2, 247
Rimaibe 23, 101, 140, 188
rinderpest 19, 39, 42, 48, 105, 123, 166, 171, 229, 237
risk 7, 133, 134, 238
rock art 11, 13, 16, 20, 25
Roth E.A., 141, 199, 204-5, 212-15, 217, 245-6
Rutten M. 39, 150-1
Rwanda 40, 42, 79, 154

Sahara 11-16 *passim*, 19, 25, 27, 29, 51-3 *passim*, 87, 90, 94-5, 146; Saharo-Sahelian zone 14-16 *passim*, 18, 19, 95-9
Sahel 3, 28, 29, 41, 52, 56, 57,

60, 62, 66, 67, 69, 83, 88, 94-6, 99-103, 161, 163, 177, 183; Sahelo-Sudanian zone 95-9, 103, 177
salt 22, 25, 29, 48, 84, 90, 95, 98, 100, 105, 129
Samburu 37-9 *passim*, 124, 148, 156, 161, 167, 231, 235-7, 243
San 6, 20, 45, 48, 86, 236
Sanasita 112
Sandford, S. 2, 52, 64, 69-70, 91, 92, 153, 159, 163, 164, 229, 243, 251
Sanhaja 25
Saudi Arabia 33, 116, 234
Scoones I., 58, 61, 63, 65, 68, 84, 86, 88, 90, 100, 120, 124, 149, 152, 163, 172, 174, 176, 228-9, 237, 243, 245, 250, 251-2
seasonality 52-3, 80
Sebei 38, 124
sedentarisation 6, 63, 73, 80, 88, 130, 146, 178, 198, 199, 216, 222-3, 226, 244-6 *passim*
seere system 230
Sellen D. 136, 178-9, 188, 190-1
Senegal 16, 22, 24, 29, 147, 182, 186, 200
Senusi 28
Serengeti 53, 54, 124, 126, 171
shea butter making 107, 132, 143, 148, 192, 247
sheep and goats 15, 16, 18, 33, 36, 37, 511, 84, 87, 88, 110, 115, 119, 127, 130, 159, 160, 164, 234
Shell-Duncan, Bettina 139, 143, 186, 193, 194, 215
Shilluk 35, 121, 122
Shona 44, 88
Sikana P. 141, 195-7, 229-31, 248
Sinclair A. 55-6, 63, 66, 171
Simonse, S. 35, 38, 39, 74, 75, 143, 193
Sirikwa 38
slaughtering 172
slavery 22, 46, 97, 120, 140, 216
Smith, A. 11, 16, 20, 43, 47
smuggling 2, 236
social services 76, 121, 242
soils 58-61, 70, 88, 124-5, 129
Sokoto Caliphate 23, 24, 134
Somalia 30-4, 72, 78, 79, 91, 92, 112, 114-20, 128, 129, 132, 142, 147, 148, 150, 151, 153, 197, 201, 230, 234-5, 237, 241, 248
Somono 22, 23
Songhai 22, 23, 95, 100
South Africa 43, 46, 54, 64, 66, 68-9, 74, 85, 88, 130, 146, 151, 152, 236

Southern Africa 3, 8, 11-13 passim, 18, 43-7, 130-1, 170
South-East Africa 8, 51, 81
South-West Africa 11-12, 37, 43, 47-9
Spear T. 20, 36-8, 51, 88, 124-5, 149, 235, 240, 244
Spencer P. 141, 144, 202, 212, 247
Sobania N., 20, 39, 192
Stenning D., 101, 133-4, 155, 197, 202
sterility 208-10 see also infertility
STDs (sexually transmitted diseases) 200, 207
Sudan 7, 16, 19, 27, 29, 30, 34-6, 51, 53, 75, 78, 83, 112, 113, 121, 132, 147, 230
Sudanic people/zone 14, 16, 18, 19, 36, 41, 83, 87, 88, 94, 103-11
Sudd 8, 18, 34-6, 61, 84, 120-4
Sukuma 62, 88
Sullivan, S. 49, 58, 68, 70, 79, 131, 143, 148, 188, 192, 245, 247, 248
Swift J. 32-3, 65, 69-70, 87, 91, 100-1, 107, 115-6, 139-140, 151, 153, 181, 185, 202, 233-4

Talle A. 6, 128, 141-2, 151, 193, 198, 245-7
Tamasheq 132, 143, 184, 188, 192, 211, 212, 219, 247 see also Tuareg
Tamesna 95-7 passim, 100 see also fig 2.1, 2.2
Tanzania 19, 40, 46, 51, 76, 79, 80, 87, 124, 151, 152, 164, 170, 181, 188, 201, 206, 231, 236, 240, 243, 245, 248, 249
taxation 28, 155, 201, 231, 233, 235, 245
Teda 30, 95, 96
tenure, resource 2, 3, 5, 6, 72-5, 80, 85, 92, 110, 120, 121, 146, 154-5, 177-8, 238, 247, 251, 252
Thébaud B., 72, 146-8, 152
Thornton P. 137-8
Timbuktu 27, 28
topography 52-3, 61, 70, 125
Toposa 205, 213, 214
Toucouleur 22, 23
Toubou 141
Toulmin C., 5, 29, 58, 72-4, 87-9, 100, 105, 150, 152, 199
tourism 40, 49, 81, 126, 152, 240-1
Toutswemogala 24, 44
trade 7, 8, 12, 22, 23, 25, 27,

28, 30-4, 43-8 passim, 51, 74, 90-3, 98, 102, 105-7, 115, 123, 125, 126, 129, 142, 153, 155, 171, 229-36, 241-6, 251
transhumance 8, 23, 58, 61, 78, 82-6, 90, 95-9, 101-10 passim, 113, 119, 122, 125, 135, 135, 144-5, 197, 221, 235, 245, 252
trees 146, 147, 151
Tripolitania 25, 26, 28
trypanosomiasis 16, 18, 39, 42, 51, 61-3, 104-6 passim, 123, 129, 160, 161, 166-9, 171, 173, 175, 229
Tswana 8, 44-6, 154, 156, 236
Tuareg 7, 23, 25-9, 39, 60, 61, 82, 83, 85, 86, 90, 91, 94-9 passim, 103, 108, 110, 132, 134, 140, 141, 146, 147, 149, 150, 154, 155, 189, 203-8, 210-25 passim, 233, 249; Igdalen and Iberkoreyen 26; Kel Adrar139, 183; Kel Denneg 52, 96-8; Kel Gress 97, 100; Kel Owey 29, 86, 96, 98, 100; Ouillimeden 27 see also Tamasheq
Tugen 38, 88, 156
Turkana 8, 38-40, 53, 61, 72, 74, 75, 83, 85, 86, 126-8, 136, 146, 148, 154, 156, 161, 179, 181-6 passim, 191, 194, 202-17 passim, 224, 245, 250; Ngisonyoka 86, 126-8, 179-86 passim
Turkana, Lake/District 11, 18, 19, 34, 36, 53, 74, 126-7; STEP 126-8
Turner M., 5, 58, 70, 72-4, 83-5, 108, 113, 128, 146, 149, 151
Turton D. 75, 78, 120, 124, 154
Tuutsi 41, 42, 154

Uganda 19, 30, 40, 75, 78
UK 173, 174, 236
USA 173, 230
Uthman dan Fodio 23, 24

vaccination 170-1, 173, 176, 229, 233, 237
vegetation 59-61, 63, 66-8, 70, 71, 96, 124, 125, 127, 129, 168
veterinary care 158, 161, 167, 173, 174, 228, 233, 244, 251
Vetter S. 64, 71
Victoria, Lake 37, 40, 53, 120, 124

Waller, R. 20, 38, 39, 51, 62,

74, 124, 125, 149, 167, 169, 171-3 passim, 175, 193, 235-7 passim, 240
warfare 2, 23, 28, 33, 35, 38, 75-8, 116-17, 123, 129, 130, 193; civil 29, 33, 35, 76, 98, 121, 123, 230, 235
warriors 5, 86, 144, 156, 179, 180, 187
water 2, 5, 6, 22, 29, 52, 54, 60, 61, 64, 72, 75, 81-5 passim, 90, 92, 95, 96, 99, 115, 117, 145-51 passim, 163, 167, 228, 237, 251; developments 63, 115, 158, 234
watering 97, 118, 130, 139, 142, 143
Waters Bayer, A. 104, 141-3, 197, 248
wells 89, 96, 113, 117, 129-30, 142, 147, 150
Wendorf F. 11, 14, 31
West Africa 3, 12, 13, 16, 19-25, 27, 28, 39, 54, 60, 69, 85, 94, 95, 152, 154, 155, 183, 184, 186, 203, 212, 215, 219, 223, 224, 231-4
wetlands 61, 84, 107-11, 120-4, 146
WFH (weight-for-height) 187-8
White C. 92, 140, 165, 203, 223, 233, 238
wild products 132, 143, 151, 178, 179, 192, 234, 236, 242, 247
wildlife 7, 40, 49, 62, 80, 122, 125, 126, 135, 152, 171, 175
Wilmsen E. 11, 13, 20, 43-5, 47-8, 75, 86, 148-9, 154, 236-7
women 6, 34, 42, 73, 86, 91, 105-7, 113, 115, 117, 119, 140-4, 151, 156, 189, 192, 197, 198, 202-3, 205-21 passim, 230, 231, 240, 245-7, 249
Woodhouse P. 61, 84, 120

Xhosa 8, 38, 46, 13

Zaal F. 87, 102, 107, 191, 231, 236
Zaghawa 30, 88, 95, 111, 112, 136, 182
Zeder M. 11, 12, 15
Zeyadiya 136
Zimbabwe 87, 88, 152, 175; Great 27, 44, 46, 48, 168, 236
Zinsstag J. 174
Zulu 8, 38, 46-7, 74, 130, 154